More praise for *The Point of Departure*

'Great fun to read. It has the authentic touch of both the great and the trivial issues that dominate the daily life and the grind of ministers in any government' *Guardian*

'Cook does not accuse Blair of deliberate deception. Cook's restraint makes an even more damning case. He guides the reader towards a devastating guilty verdict on the Prime Minister without making too many sweeping judgments himself. While narrating a tragic and humiliating failure in foreign policy, Cook also manages to be very funny' *Independent on Sunday*, Political Books of the Year

'On Iraq, Cook's diary builds up a devastating critique . . . Robin's clarion offers a summons to advance for progressives everywhere' *Independent*

'As clear and eloquent as its author . . . It contains a sharp critique of New Labour and Blairism and above all of the road to war in Iraq . . . A well-thought-through and comprehensive criticism of New Labour and Tony Blair' Clare Short, *Independent on Sunday*

'His arguments on the Iraq war are incisively, indeed corrosively, phrased' Gerald Kaufman, *Sunday Telegraph*

'Interesting and extraordinarily well written . . . the stories he has to tell of the build-up to the Iraq war, reform of the House of Lords, and modernisation of the House of Commons are valuable history . . . It is also refrshingly peppered with Robin's humour . . . He gives a crucial ringside seat with all the authority of the ex-foreign secretary . . . a riveting account' Sir David Steel

Robin Cook first entered Parliament as MP for Edinburgh Central in 1974. He held a number of senior positions in Opposition – Shadow Foreign Secretary, Shadow Trade and Industry Secretary, Shadow Health and Social Services Secretary – before becoming Foreign Secretary in 1997. In 2001 he was appointed Leader of the House of Commons, a position from which he resigned in March 2003 in protest at the imminent war in Iraq.

THE
POINT OF DEPARTURE
Diaries from the Front Bench

ROBIN
COOK

POCKET
BOOKS

LONDON • SYDNEY • NEW YORK • TORONTO

First published in Great Britain by Simon & Schuster UK Ltd, 2003
First published by Pocket Books, 2004
An imprint of Simon & Schuster UK Ltd
A Viacom Company

1 3 5 7 9 10 8 6 4 2

Simon & Schuster UK Ltd
Africa House
64–78 Kingsway
London WC2B 6AH

www.simonsays.co.uk

Simon & Schuster Australia
Sydney

A CIP catalogue record for this book
is available from the British Library

ISBN 0-7434-8377-4

Typeset by M Rules
Printed and bound in Great Britain by
Cox & Wyman Ltd, Reading, Berks

To
Iain Jordan
1930–2001
A WEA tutor-organiser
and an incorrigible teacher

CONTENTS

THE
POINT OF DEPARTURE

PROLOGUE

In my resignation speech in March 2003 I said that Tony Blair is the most successful Labour leader in my lifetime. I hope that the following pages fairly present some of the strengths and successes which make him such a dominant political figure, as well as the reasons why ultimately I could not continue to serve in his Cabinet. He deserves every credit for establishing Labour as the party of economic competence, for reversing a generation of neglect in the public services and for achieving more than any previous Prime Minister in promoting Britain's place in Europe, until the hurricane over his support for the war on Iraq blew him off course. I also find it admirable, indeed astonishing, that he remains a normal human being after seven years at Number 10 under pressures that no one who has not seen them at first hand can imagine. I want him to continue as our leader, and I certainly want him to be successful in recovering the support of those electors who have left Labour.

It is easy to exaggerate the current electorate difficulties of his government. The remarkable truth remains that on its seventh anniversary in office Labour retained a lead in most opinion polls that no previous government had enjoyed in its mid-term period. The problem is not that people are unwilling to vote Labour, but that their enthusiasm for it has drained away. Labour has lost the political momentum of the historic landslide that propelled it into government and is now becalmed in a second term marked by caution rather than radicalism. Labour's current doldrums is the product of New Labour's strategy of stripping the party bare of any value that may prove a negative, but failing to fill the gap.

Political movements that leave their mark on history do so because they shape the political culture of society to their values. By that test New Labour is in danger of leaving no mark behind despite a combination of Labour's record length in office with Labour's record majority in office.

The crisis for myself and many other Labour supporters arose from the commitment of Britain as junior partner in the US invasion of Iraq. But Tony Blair's alliance with George Bush is symptomatic of a wider problem from New Labour's lack of ideological anchor. Tony approached relations with the incoming US Administration as a question of power politics. He never comprehended the perplexity he would cause his supporters at home by becoming the trusty partner of the most reactionary US Administration in modern times. It was always inevitable that such an unlikely alliance would put him at odds with many in the coalition that had elected Labour to office.

In my own case it resulted in my leaving the Labour front bench on which I had served for over twenty years. Journalists sometimes asked if I regret resigning. I am sorry that I could not continue in a post that I relished, managing the proceedings of Parliament and listening to the House in its many moods. There is some justice in the charge of a Cabinet colleague that I am more of a parliamentarian than a politician. But being sorry that I could not stay is not the same as regretting my decision to go. I left because I could not support a war based on a false prospectus and waged without any international authority. Not a week has gone by since that has not left me even more relieved that I am not obliged to appear before my colleagues in Parliament to defend the insupportable.

This book therefore was not written in bitterness. Those who hoped it would contain venomous personal attacks will be disappointed. However they will find that it provides them with colour on the life of a Cabinet minister and insight into how parliamentary democracy functions today. And also some of the humour and fun of ministerial life. It is, after all, the memoir of a man who was happy in his work and who still regards his colleagues with warm regard. I have, though, been frank about the events that led up to the war on Iraq. I believe the public cannot reach an informed judgement on whether that war was justified without an understanding of how the decision was reached, and the government cannot learn essential lessons without openness about how they became committed to their most divisive international decision.

Most of the following text consists of my account of the two years from June 2001 to March 2003. But no professional politician can be satisfied with only observing events. We are driven by a compulsion to comment on them, to interpret them and to shape them to our political perspective. A third of the text, therefore, is commentary and analysis of the events I observed at first hand, particularly the political developments that came to trouble me and most especially the commitment of Britain to Bush's war on Iraq. The narrative charts a personal journey in which my early enthusiasm over my role in modernising the Commons and reforming the Lords became overshadowed by growing concern and eventual dismay at our complicity in George Bush's intentions on Iraq. Although the culmination may have been Bush's war, the prelude records my deepening disaffection with elements of the domestic agenda. It is the story of how I found myself losing touch with a leadership which often appeared to have instincts that were at odds with values that had brought me into the Labour Party and had sustained me through long barren years of Opposition.

It is a journey which will be familiar to many who elected this government into office, but who now feel it does not belong to them, and whose voice is too often suppressed within the party for whom they voted. New Labour has been phenomenally successful in silencing the dissent among its own supporters. It has replaced old Labour's culture of dissent with New Labour's culture of discipline. The irony is that this central control has solved the old problem of splits and divisions at the expense of contributing to a new problem of trust. The longer I have served in politics, the more respect I have for the basic good sense of the British public. They are not taken in by politicians whom they suspect of reciting the party line. They want a more mature style of politics that values sincerity and independence of mind at least as much as conformity and adherence to party discipline.

Labour will only regain the trust of the electorate if we are honest about where we have gone wrong. This book is my honest attempt to explain how I arrived at the point of departure.

1

'This is the job for you.'

8 JUNE–24 JULY 2001

Friday 8 June 2001

My first warning that something was wrong was the way Anji Hunter treated me when I arrived at Number 10. Anji is a prime exponent of the touchy-feely school of expression and this morning she was keeping to her own private space. If there was no embrace from Anji there would be no good news from Tony. This was a surprising turn, as only last Tuesday I had been sent a message that I would be carrying on.

Tony was so exhausted from lack of sleep on election night that throughout our interview I found myself feeling sorry for him rather than angry with him. The security agencies in some of the more repressive countries that I have visited around the world reckon on thirty to forty hours sleep deprivation being the point at which the will of the interviewee cracks. In Britain this is the point at which prime ministers decide who will be the key figures in the Cabinet for the next four years. Perhaps because of exhaustion he wasted no time in getting down to business. 'I want you to move. I know this is not fair. You have not done anything wrong, but I do need to make changes.'

I did not argue. There was no point. Foreign Secretary and Prime Minister work so closely together and I had stood in for him so often at international gatherings that I knew it was impossible to do the job with authority if I did not have Tony's backing. The only question was whether I went on the back benches or took another post in the Cabinet. He offered me the job of Leader of the House. I said I would think about it, but I couldn't give him an answer straight away. On the way out I found Anji had recovered her touchy-feely mode. She stroked my arm and said in a soft voice, 'I am sorry'. I took this to be a statement of general sympathy for my feelings rather than a signal of her disagreement with my removal.

Before the end of the afternoon I had picked up on the grapevine that the Cabinet reshuffle had been settled on the afternoon of polling day in Sedgefield between Tony and his travelling entourage of Anji and Alastair Campbell. It was a very tight little cabal in which to decide on the major offices of state. Even Jonathan Powell, the Number 10 Chief of Staff, did not seem to have been present when the key decisions were taken. I had heard it said that Anji had lobbied for a vacancy at the Foreign Office which would enable Number 10 to lever Gordon out of the Treasury. However, I had always got on well with Alastair and was disappointed he had not spoken up for me. But maybe he had.

I rang Gaynor to break the news to her. She was every bit as astonished as myself, and said I must do what I thought was right. There is no post which puts you more at the heart of Parliament than Leader of the House. It provided a prominent platform which Michael Foot used to support a Labour government and John Biffen used to undermine the Thatcher government. No one was going to give me any sympathy because I had turned down such an opportunity out of pique. I took the job and knew as soon as I had agreed that I had done the right thing. After I had rung Tony there was nothing more for me to do in my old room. I wandered through the front office thanking the team for their support and bidding my farewells. Then I got the lift for the last time down to the discreet side door through which ministers and ambassadors come and go to the Foreign Office.

In the evening Jack Straw rang me up for a supportive conversation. If I was surprised to be moved from my job he sounded even more surprised to get it. I had already heard from my protection team that his Special Branch officers had moved in to the Department of Transport, Local Government and the Regions (DTLR). They were so confident that their boss would be joining them that they had set up their radio operation. The first call they got over the radio was to tell them that their boss was actually walking in the direction of the Foreign Office. Jack himself was so sure that he was going to the DTLR that when he went in to see Tony he had a strategy for the railways in his back pocket. I am glad it is Jack who is replacing me. We have been close colleagues for twenty years and I know he will give the Foreign Office his best.

Monday 11 June

Late in the morning Tony rang up to ask whom I wanted as my junior minister. Tony volunteered, 'Really sorry about the press coverage. I thought with everything going on they would accept you were moving to another office of high status. I accept it was too sudden, and I'm to blame for that. I should have handled it differently.' At this point, as it frequently does, the Number 10 switchboard disconnected us. It was five minutes before we were reconnected, by which time both of us had had the time to reflect. He said, 'Look, we must get together so we can talk about this.'

One happy consequence of my move is that there appears to be a collective guilt complex at Number 10 and an eagerness to mollify me. They meekly submitted to my request for Stephen Twigg as a junior minister. I am pleased about securing him as he is a bright, popular member of the 1997 intake and his appointment will send out all the right signals on my commitment to modernisation of the Commons.

In the afternoon I walked over to the Cabinet Office for my first meeting with Gareth Williams, leader of the House of Lords, to discuss the state of the legislative programme. On the way over Horse Guards Parade I noticed that the mood of my protection officer did not match the bright June sunshine. When I asked what troubled him he responded, 'This Lord Williams we are going to visit. He got off a lad who broke my jaw on a charge of GBH.' I promised to rebuke Gareth for this lack of solidarity and indeed Gareth winced when I teased him for falling short on New Labour's commitment to be tough on crime.

The legislative programme itself looks as if it has a bad case of broken jaw. Work has not even started on sixteen bills, including all the flagship bills which we have been talking up as the political centrepieces of the session. I am taken aback on opening the cupboard door that I find the shelves so bare. There is no alternative to putting a brave face on the short-run emergency, but I vow that we start now preparations to avoid being in the same empty boat again in the next session.

Wednesday 13 June

I attended the first PLP meeting to respond to the proposals for the Queen's Speech. A vast meeting – I haven't seen such a large meeting since the first meeting after the last General Election. I used my speech to unfurl the standard for modernising the House. I get loud growls of approval when I say that we want a House of Commons with hours and working methods that belong to the twenty-first century, not the nineteenth century, and rapturous applause when I say that if we are to retain our majority sitting members must be able to get back to their constituencies. Afterwards my long-standing special adviser, David Mathieson, told me that his neighbour turned to him halfway through the speech and said, 'it must be gratifying for Robin at last to be able to speak to an audience to whom English is their first language'.

Before the election of the Speaker we were summoned to get the Queen's consent in the House of Lords. The front bench trooped along leaving the rest of the House behind. I found myself walking behind Ann Widdecombe. There was a large group of Labour MPs standing between the bar and the door who parted to let us through. As Ann goes past they all roar 'Go for it, Ann – we're right behind you. You let them know, Ann.' I rather doubt that it provided the encouragement she may have been seeking to run for leader of the Tory Party.

Later I had a whisky with Stephen Byers, who is equally surprised to be moved out of the DTI. He says the first hint he got of it was at 10.30 on election night, when he rang from his count to Tony's entourage and sensed that something had happened that afternoon. We were both struck that whether intended or not the effect of the reshuffle has been to weaken the line-up on the euro. He and I had been the most outspoken champions of the euro and now I had been moved out of the Foreign Office and he had been moved away from the Trade portfolio which had given us legitimate platforms from which to argue for British membership. If Tony really intends to have a referendum this Parliament he is preparing for it in a very odd way.

I shared with Steve my frustration that I have no big bills to put before Parliament. Like many of the true modernisers he is conscious of the growing impatience within the party at the lack of radicalism of the Blair administration. We both agreed on the urgent need in the second term to restore to Labour some radical spirit.

Thursday 14 June

First meeting of the Cabinet of the new Parliament. The main business was to approve the legislative programme on which the Queen's Speech is based. I explained that my big problem with managing the business is that none of the flagship bills on health, education, crime or enterprise are ready yet, and indeed instructions have yet to go to the draftsmen on any of them. I express added amazement that I find the business is organised on the tidal wave principle, and what we really must do over the next year is start to prepare now for the start of the next session so that we replace the tidal wave with a pipeline. A number of colleagues cheerfully proceed to add to the tidal wave, and I am robust in fending them off.

At the end of Cabinet, Gordon asked for a word and we went next door to his room at Number 11. He was anxious that I should be aware that he had not known anything in advance of my dismissal, and I assured him that I was quite clear that nobody outside Sedgefield had known. I added that maybe we had not seen enough of each other in the past four years, and we should do more now. I kept reading that we had fallen out, but I could never quite remember when this had happened, at which he laughed.

Wednesday 20 June

The day of the Queen's Speech. I made one small blow for modernisation by flatly refusing to turn up in tails and pinstripe trousers. I saw off the protests by pointing out that the last two Leaders of the House were women and that I bet neither Ann Taylor nor Margaret Beckett had turned up in tails and pinstripe trousers. So long as I do not revive the tradition everyone else will have forgotten it. As a result I am the only one in the procession who does not look dressed like a playing card.

The one advantage of my place in the procession is that I am guaranteed a ringside spot at the foot of the steps to the throne. For the first time in three decades I do not have to jostle with six hundred other MPs for a space behind the bar at the far end of the Chamber. The speech itself is commendably on message. The first third is taken up promising bills on the New Labour trinity of education, health and crime. I console myself that I am the only person in the Chamber who knows that pen has not yet been put to paper on any of these bills. Afterwards Derry Irvine and I escorted the Queen back to her robing room and waited outside it to bid her farewell. I had been assured that the Queen normally pauses for five minutes for conversation before leaving, but today she was already running late for Royal Ascot and I subsequently heard that the coach cut four minutes off the standard return time to Buckingham Palace.

In the afternoon William Hague gave a swansong appearance as Leader of the Tory Party. It was a witty and self-deprecating speech. Hague's personal tragedy is that his undoubted ability to command the House does not translate itself into an ability to impress the world beyond the political activists. He had a powerful final passage in which he warned that the lowest turnout for a century showed that 'people increasingly see politics and parliament as remote from their lives'. He pleaded for urgent reform to make Parliament strong and relevant. There is clear evidence on both sides of the Chamber of momentum for modernisation. The trick will be to capture it to secure changes before it fades.

Thursday 21 June

My first appearance at the weekly ritual of Business Questions. In theory I announce the business of the next week or two and then take questions on it. In practice everybody ignores the business and takes out their own hobbyhorse for a canter around the Chamber. For backbenchers it is a valuable noticeboard on which they can pin messages to their local press and constituents, and for the government it is a useful opportunity to put right the record on the controversy of the week. The problem, of course, for the Leader of the House is that it is quite impossible to know the answer to everything that you are going to be asked, even if I do clock in early to cram for my oral exam and surreptitiously spend most of the Cabinet meeting studying my brief.

Unusually this week there are legitimate questions relating to business because there are a number of procedural issues that need to be resolved at the start of every Parliament. One of these is the establishment of the select committees. I have a real conundrum over the select committees. There are two schools of thought, both of which lobby me today. The first sees it as a test of the government's commitment to parliamentary scrutiny whether it sets up the select committees as quickly as possible. The second school of thought wants the rules to be changed so that MPs, not the party whips, control who is appointed to the select committees. There is also a third school which wants both, but that is impossible. As I explained today to Nick Winterton, if we want the committees set up quickly we have to do it under the rules that we have got. I go for broke and rashly promise Andrew Bennett that I will get the select committees set up before the summer recess. That only gives me another four weeks, heaven help me.

Monday 2 July

Off for lunch with Niall Fitzgerald at Unilever. We have a very frank exchange about where the government is (or is not) on the euro. I am very disloyal in recommending to Niall that at their meeting with Tony on Thursday they must lay it firmly on the line that they need not only a private assurance but a public demonstration of his commitment to the euro. Niall is commendably blunt that if they do not get such an assurance, then Unilever and others will be unable to plan with confidence that Britain will join the euro, and will have to plan on the worst case scenario that Britain will not be joining the euro. He also predicts that Britain in Europe as a campaign will collapse.

Niall stresses it is well known that Nissan and others have been given private assurances that Britain will be joining the euro. If those assurances are not fulfilled then the government's credibility across the board will be undermined. I suggest – which obviously comes as a bit of a surprise to him – that he and those around him should reach out to Anji Hunter as the person most likely to encourage Tony to take a gamble, but if not brought on side she is the one who will reinforce all his cautious instincts which make him shrink from the risk.

Tuesday 3 July

I had a meeting with Tony to which I had been summoned. It soon becomes apparent that this meeting is motivated partly by a genuine interest in what I'm up to, and just a little by a wish to humour me in case what I'm getting up to is mischief. He begins by asking about modernisation of the House, and I talk through some of the urgent priorities. I stress to him that the House of Commons has lagged behind our modernisation of the constitution of other parts of British political life, and that we need to bring the House of Commons up to speed with the rest of the modernisation of Britain. I also hint at the broad alienation of our backbenchers. If we want less difficulty on policy it is important that we give them a clearer opportunity to scrutinise policy and gain ownership of it.

We move on to reform of the House of Lords. I put it to him that reform of the House of Lords will be his historic monument. He is playing for his place in history. He is wasting an opportunity if he simply puts up a model that will not last a single Parliament before crumbling away. The present proposals have no friends. They stem from the Report of the Royal Commission chaired by John Wakeham, which reached agreement among its membership by listing three options, none of which commanded consensus outside its membership. I vividly remember the moment in the Cabinet sub-committee in April when I asked everybody in the room who thought the proposals of Wakeham would work. Nobody did, but most of the sub-committee thought we had to carry them out because we were committed to them. This is a project that will end in tears. He asks me for a paper on what we might do instead that might be more credible and more capable of a consensus.

Later he dismisses the officials in order that we can speak together. He asks me how I am enjoying the job. I say, truthfully, that it's very congenial – that I like being back in the House of Commons where I have addressed bigger audiences in four weeks than I ever did in the previous four years. He volunteers that he had heard I'd done well in the Commons last Wednesday, winding up the debate on the Queen's Speech, and goes on to say, 'This is the job for you. You're going to thank me for having put you in it.' I said, 'Fine – there's a real job to be done here. I just ask to be given time to finish it.' He said, 'Oh, I don't think you've got anything to worry about on that.' I reminded him, 'That's what you said the last time.' He laughed and said, 'This time I really mean it.'

I raised the euro with him and warned him that the businessmen he would be seeing on Thursday would want a very clear assurance that he would speak out publicly on this. The response was reassuring, but formulaic. He was in favour of us going into the euro, and he believed we could win a referendum on it. There was also a new line. We had to be very careful that we did not worry the markets and start a run on the pound. I left worried. If we always have to tiptoe around market reaction, we will forever put off taking the plunge. This is an issue which he does not see as pressing and is handling by postponing it. Unless some external shock pushes it up his agenda, I would be prepared to put money on us not holding a referendum in this Parliament.

Wednesday 4 July

In the course of Prime Minister's Questions, Tony gets some difficult passages over the proposals on incapacity benefit. In the morning Alistair Darling had made a speech to the Institute for Public Policy Research in which he announced that there would be a three-year review of all claimants of incapacity benefit, and it was heavily spun to the morning press as New Labour getting tough on 'welfare reform'.

The problem for Tony at Question Time was not so much what our backbenchers did, but what they did not do. Throughout Hague's attack on him on this point, our backbenchers remained truculently silent. It was not a roasting by our backbenchers so much as a work to rule on applause. I cannot remember Tony ever getting such a silent reception from his own backbenchers, and he was frequently mocked by the Opposition benches with the pantomime cry of 'Look behind you'.

Afterwards we had the meeting of the Parliamentary Committee which brings together Tony with those elected by the backbenchers in the PLP. Tony responds robustly to the criticism of the proposed restriction on incapacity benefit. The worrying feature about his line of response is that it was all about money. He said that every penny saved on incapacity benefit was money for schools and hospitals. Tony adds that he and Alistair were taken aback by the scale of the press coverage because they had both been saying these things for some weeks. This may well be true, but the extent of press coverage varies immensely depending on the news context. The news context since the Queen's Speech is Tony in difficulty with Labour backbenchers. A repetition of the line on incapacity benefit suddenly put roller skates on the story. As a result, what was intended to get good press coverage in the right-wing press now gets us bad coverage in everybody's press because of Labour's split. It was a favourite trick, which New Labour exploited mercilessly in Opposition, to get praise in the press for standing up to your own party. It is long overdue that they learn that in office all this produces is stories of government in difficulty.

Thursday 5 July

The day begins with a phone call from Alistair Darling. He is anxious that I should get the line right on incapacity benefit before Business Questions. Believe me, so am I.

He tells me that it would be very helpful if I was to make it clear that the new rules on three-yearly reviews are to apply only to new claimants following the forthcoming legislation, and not to any of the two million existing claimants. I enthusiastically assure him that I am only too pleased to make that clear, and I repeat it twice to him so there can be no doubt that he is telling me that existing claimants will be exempt.

Over to the House, where one of the very first questions is indeed on incapacity benefit. Angela Browning, my opposite number, bowls a lumbering ball asking how can she reassure her constituents who are concerned about what this means for their benefit. I am positively delighted to assure her that she can tell all of them that they needn't worry at all as the new rules will apply only to new claimants. The announcement goes down spectacularly well on our own benches. Dennis Skinner likes it so much that he turns round to others behind him, and I could hear him urging them to 'ask it again so he has to repeat it'. Which, of course, they did.

We go straight from Business Questions to the debate on MPs' Pay and Rations. It is a full House. Chris Mullin has tabled an amendment, demanding that we should only get rises in line with the Pay Review Body recommendations for nurses and teachers. I take pleasure in pointing out to him that over the past five years this would actually have given us an extra £2000 a year on our salary, and warn him that if he presses amendments they would result in MPs receiving a bigger salary.

Immediately after the debate on Pay and Rations, I moved the motion to set up the new departmental select committees. By the end of the day I had been on the bench solidly from 12.30 until 7 p.m. but I enjoyed it. I'm at home in the House, and find it much more congenial than spending the same number of hours in an ancient VC10.

Gaynor and I end the evening visiting John and Jenny McCririck at home for dinner. They have done even more work on their rear patio. In such a tiny space they have replicated a wonderful junglescape with an eating area in a clearing. They have just added a gas heater on a stand, and John is keen that I should officially inaugurate it by turning it on for the first time. I manage to produce a satisfying flare of flame, but only just in time before a thunderstorm reaches us. Much ribbing that I turned on the flame and produced lightning.

Friday 6 July

Saunter round the corner to my office to find Greg Power, my new special adviser, much exercised over a report prominent in the *Daily Mirror* about my speech to the Progress conference on Saturday. The *Mirror* have got a quote from person unknown saying that 'Robin Cook will be controversial. He will be outspoken. He is a bitter man.' There could not be a less helpful trailer for my speech, as anything remotely disloyal, or even original, will now be assessed as a bid to lead a leftist faction.

Greg Power reports the telephone has been jumping off the receiver all morning with journalists wanting to know what I'm going to say. I ask him how he replied, and he said, 'Well, I tell them we've not yet written the speech.' Actually this is absolutely correct, but may not

have given the impression of calm, orderly organisation that I could
have hoped for. I spend the day preparing my speech, and Greg spends
the day fending off journalists. And Millbank. And Number 10. All of
them in varying degrees of anticipation and anxiety about what might
be said the next day.

Saturday 7 July

Before my speech to the conference there is a video from Gordon,
who is attending the G8 Finance Ministers meeting. He is displayed
on a very large cinemascope screen immediately behind the platform.
As he launches into his first statistic I suddenly realise that I am sitting
immediately beneath him and scamper to the side of the stage,
ostensibly so that I can study him more carefully, but in reality to
avoid the appalling press photograph of Gordon peering over my
shoulder.

I show lots of loyalty, but I did include two strong messages. First,
on welfare I said 'we should provide benefit levels for those who can't
work that help them out of poverty rather than keep them trapped in
poverty'. The second was aimed at the current talk of reform through
greater private sector involvement in public services: 'One of the
principles of good private sector management is that change is more
likely to come if the people who work in an organisation understand
the change will protect their future, not threaten their future. We need
to find a way of talking about change that embraces the workforce in
the public services as partners in change, not as the objects of change.'
Both passages provoked applause from an audience which was skilled
in the language of coded positioning.

Monday 9 July

In the course of our routine Start the Week meeting Hilary Armstrong,
the Chief Whip, sounds me out on the membership of the select
committees which we have to table this week if we are to get them
approved by the Commons before it rises next week. To be fair to
Hilary the timetable is putting a lot of pressure on her and her team

to complete the nightmare jigsaw puzzle of matching almost two hundred committee places with the preferences of over two hundred Labour backbenchers.

I am taken aback when she says she is under pressure to leave Gwyneth Dunwoody and Donald Anderson off the two select committees which they have been chairing in the past Parliament. I am brisk in responding that if the members of those committees want to change their Chairs that's fine, but it would look like the worst kind of government authoritarianism for the whips to deprive them of their Chairs by the dubious device of leaving them off their committees.

Wednesday 11 July

I stood in at Prime Minister's Questions for Tony who is engrossed in talks to rescue the Northern Ireland peace process. I spent the morning, and much of yesterday, in Number 10 debating with officials and colleagues how I am going to talk my way out of the tricky questions. Ironically, the Prime Minister's room is so small that only half a dozen people can comfortably get in it and for much of the time we had to gather round the more expansive Cabinet Room table. The big story of the week is the shambles of the Tory leadership vote. The bottom two candidates have both tied which means that they have no candidate whom they can drop from the ballot paper. Given their crushing defeats in the last two General Elections it is ironic that the Tories cannot identify a loser. Both the House and the media will expect me to have something to say about the biggest political event of the moment, but strictly speaking the Tory leadership contest is not government business and the Speaker would bring me up short if I laboured the point. I think it was Meg Russell, my special adviser, who first had the idea that we could make a joke of it by comparing it with *Big Brother*, which is attracting much more interest among the public than the Tory leadership election.

I got off to a sticky start with a hard ball from Gerry Steinberg who complained of his experience with the public finance initiative hospital in his constituency. I had some sympathy with his criticism but if I betrayed that, the next half hour would have disintegrated into a rout.

Then Kevin Brennan obligingly tossed me a straight ball on the importance of encouraging women candidates, which I took as an opening to express the hope that Ann Widdecombe could come to the aid of her party to help them out of their leadership impasse. I then added, 'I see the press have been comparing the Tory leadership elections to *Big Brother*. That, I think, is unfair – to *Big Brother*. At least when they have a vote in *Big Brother* someone gets kicked out.' Thereafter I had the House on my side.

In politics, disaster lurks behind every triumph. I had no sooner left the Chamber than Lorna Fitzsimons, my PPS, took me aside to tell me she had been concealing from me what had happened at the PLP until I had got through my combat in the Chamber. Despite what I had said on Monday, Hilary Armstrong had put to the PLP membership of the select committees without the names of Gwyneth Dunwoody and Donald Anderson. All hell had broken loose at the PLP, who had nearly rioted when they were told that the standing orders did not allow them to amend the lists, but only to swallow them whole or not at all. In the end the party had agreed to swallow them rather than see the whole timetable for the select committees wrecked, but this only meant that their mood of rebellion would roll forward to the debate which I was opening next week, in which the standing orders of the House do allow them to amend the lists. I had just emerged unscathed from half an hour of the worst that the Tories could throw at me, only to find out I had been badly injured by friendly fire within my own party.

Thursday 12 July

Gwyneth Dunwoody has been transformed by the press into a paradigm of parliamentary virtue shamelessly silenced by a ruthless government machine embarrassed by her fearless scrutiny. Infuriatingly, this is the very day when I have arranged to make my agenda-setting speech on modernisation of the Commons before the Hansard Society, but I am not going to be taken seriously promising more effective scrutiny by Parliament in the wake of this display of the naked power of government over Parliament. Just to complete my discomfiture, I was already booked to appear on the *Today* programme to discuss my speech on modernisation but instead spend much of my time discussing the martyrdom of Saint Gwyneth.

By the time I get to my weekly meeting with the lobby the word had got round that I don't much like what I have been asked to move in the House next week. I am caught off guard by a question about how I will vote on Monday. Clearly I cannot say I'll vote for a motion which is intended to show the government's control over select committees and retain any credibility for the many commitments to reform I have been making. On the other hand I can hardly announce that I am going to vote against the motion which I myself am doomed to move on Monday. I therefore opt for a Third Way solution, that as it is important to the House to resolve this matter for itself it would be wrong for me to influence the outcome by expressing a preference. I shall therefore abstain.

Monday 16 July

The day begins with more newspaper editorials inciting Labour backbenchers to riot. This follows quite a bit of the same from the Sunday newspapers.

My weekly Monday morning tête-à-tête with Hilary is fraught. I am pretty blunt that I am hacked off. After four weeks in which I had worked to position the government as being on the side of reform and modernisation in the House of Commons, the controversy over Gwyneth has put us all squarely in the box marked 'control freaks'. She in turn complained with feeling that my decision to abstain in the vote had put her in a false position.

I spent the rest of the morning preparing my speech for the debate. Our collective judgement is that the only way out of the hole is to come on strong with the case for reform of the procedure. In the event this strategy worked well. My commitment that I would make reform of the process of appointing the select committees the first priority for the Modernisation Committee was welcomed. Jean Corston intervened as arranged so that I could commit the government also to reforming the internal process within the PLP.

Sixty-nine Labour MPs voted with the other parties against the proposed membership of the DTLR Select Committee, and a score more on the Foreign Affairs Select Committee. As a result we were defeated by margins of over a hundred. I could see which way the vote was likely to go in the course of the debate. The only question that was left was how did I respond in a way that would immediately close it down as a controversy.

I left the Despatch Box and went across to where the officials were sitting in what's known as the box, but in reality is a bench out of which they can't climb into the Chamber. Not that I've ever met a civil servant who has shown the least inclination to climb into the Chamber. I wanted the advice of Eve Samson, the Commons clerk seconded to my team, about what I might get away with procedurally in terms of a business statement immediately after the divisions. It was all a bit awkward since I didn't want to climb the steps so far that I'd be too visible to the Opposition, which meant I had to stand on tiptoe from the lowest step. Eve herself is quite small and had to peer over the wooden parapet of the bench. It would have looked really crazy if anybody had caught us on television. The upshot was that we agreed that the rational thing to do was to make a statement giving effect to my commitment to Andrew Bennett to bring back a revised membership before the summer recess. I sent Eve scurrying away to draft it in a procedural and businesslike manner before the divisions trapped her in the box and unable to leave.

I then convinced Hilary that if I did not make a statement immediately after the division we would have monumental problems with the media next day, as every broadcaster this side of the Arctic Circle tried to 'take the story on' by speculating on what the government would do next. We needed to close that down before the speculation could even begin. Eventually she accepted, and after the division I got up and announced that we would bring a revised membership before the House on Thursday. The statement was welcomed in all parts of the House, and pre-empted demands on us for action which we would have looked churlish to resist.

Tuesday 17 July

I have a meeting with Alan Milburn about the forthcoming Health Bill. But the most interesting moment is when the officials leave us and he stays behind for a private chat. He has had a rough two or three weeks because of the publicity for private sector involvement in the Health Service. I express the view that the real problem has been that we appear to have spun this as a big story, when in truth we only had some modest proposals, all of which are eminently defensible, even within the party. He does not disagree. At the end I am left puzzling. If even Alan Milburn disapproves of the Number 10 strategy of positioning ourselves in relation to the right-wing press, who actually is there left in the Cabinet who believes that recent briefings have been a sensible way of proceeding?

I settled down afterwards for a session to catch up on the paperwork that had backed up during the controversy over the select committees. I am startled to discover in my correspondence a P45 from the Foreign Office, confirming my dismissal. I suppose it is entirely logical that I should get a P45. Somehow I never quite imagined anybody in the Personnel Department settling down to send a P45 to the former Secretary of State.

I put a call through to Jack Straw to seek his support at the Cabinet Sub-Committee on House of Lords Reform. He assured me that he had played no part in the debacle of Monday night, and had thought it mad to try and take Donald Anderson off.

—⁊⁊⁊—

I could not have hoped for a clearer illustration of the case for modernising the proceedings of Parliament than the debacle into which we tumbled over membership of the select committees. It was a classic example of the tussle between Parliament's right to scrutiny and the Executive's power of control. Hilary is unfairly blamed for the imbroglio. I subsequently learnt that she had got her instructions from Number 10 – but that only sharpened the question why the government should decide who it was that sat in scrutiny of them. If Parliament cannot control the membership of its own committees, what real power is left to it?

The most pressing case for modernisation, though, is not the balance between Parliament and government but the growing gulf between Parliament and public. Crisis is a word worn out from overuse by headline writers. It also does not easily lend itself to a problem that has been decades in brewing. But we need an equally dramatic term to capture the widening disconnection between Parliament and people. In the thirty-odd years in which I have contested General Elections, I have seen the proportion of electors willing to turn out slip by virtually 20 per cent. By the last General Election less than 60 per cent exercised their vote and a full 40 per cent saw no point in doing so. A smaller percentage of electors turned up at the polls than at any point in the century since women won the right to have their votes counted. But within the headline figure there is an even more alarming set of statistics, which suggests that without a significant cultural shift we will see turnout continue to decline. Among young voters the proportions of participation are precisely reversed. In their age group only 40 per cent voted and 60 per cent passed up the opportunity to select the government of the nation. If this cohort retains the same participation rate as they grow older we will have a true crisis of parliamentary democracy.

There is no glib solution to this trend. It is in part a product of other deep-seated developments in modern society. The growth of an individualist culture makes it more challenging to sell the relevance of participation in a mass ballot, which is the mother of all collectivist decision-making. In an era in which the extended family has largely vanished, union solidarity has decreased and community groups often struggle to find activists, it would be naïve to expect participation in official elections to be bucking the decline in social capital. And the inevitable tendency of decision-making in the modern world to recede to European and even global forums makes political power appear even more remote to individual electors and even further beyond the practical influence of their votes.

But we need not accept steady erosion in support for parliamentary democracy as an inexorable process before which we are helpless. Other countries, including most comparable European nations, do much better than Britain in sustaining turnout at a respectable figure. Shamingly, Britain now languishes fifty-fifth in the international league of election turnouts. Nor should we blame low turnout on apathy. The many surveys that have been undertaken of young people who did not vote have found that non-voters may be alienated from Parliament but are often not apathetic about issues. Thousands of young people who did not walk down the street to vote in June 2001 subsequently crossed Europe to protest against globalisation at Genoa. Bob Worcester, the legendary Chairman of MORI, points out that the number of people in the 2001 election claiming to be 'very interested in politics' was the same as twenty years before. The problem is not that the British people have no opinion on the issues of the day but that more and more of them no longer feel ownership of their parliamentary democracy or believe that its political culture can solve the problems in their lives.

The Commons does not help itself to bridge this widening gulf when it lovingly preserves the image and the working methods of a bygone age (do not even start me on how the House of Lords appears to anyone under seventy). Our constituents live in a world of rapid changes in working practices and dramatic advances in technology. To them veneration for hallowed procedures does not express an admirable respect for tradition but a stubborn refusal to move with the times. Parliament is not going to reconnect with the electorate of tomorrow unless it addresses the perception of the young voters of today who see it as stuffy, formal and out of date.

I admit it with a heavy heart as it is the craft by which I have earned my bread for most of my adult life, but in the age of the world wide web there is something curiously old-fashioned about communicating by making a speech to a room of people – or more often in the case of the Commons to an empty room. In modern business meetings or community gatherings the qualities which are prized are brevity and informality, qualities not normally associated with parliamentary debate. The most frequent complaint of those who refuse to vote is that there is no point as 'You are all the same'. By this they do not really mean that we have the same views or political priorities. What they are articulating is that we all sound the same, talk in the same secret, coded language and rarely lapse into the colloquial English of our constituents. For good measure we also look much the same – white, middle-class, middle-aged men, belonging to about the last profession in which every male turns up every day in a lounge suit. If the Commons really wants to connect with the voters it needs to look more as if it represents the immense, rich diversity of modern Britain and to conduct its proceedings nearer to the businesslike, informal style of the rest of the country.

Perplexingly, the same non-voter who complains that MPs are all the same, in the next breath will criticise them for squabbling over everything. The Commons has always been a bear pit of raucous debate. Two hundred years ago Byron complained that MPs were more formidable as an audience than they were as speakers. But now we are on television. Or, more precisely, our most vituperative, bad-tempered exchanges make it on to television. Broadcasting loves the party political mud-wrestling of contests such as Prime Minister's Questions because for entertainment value it rivals any theatre. However, the kind of drama that gets the Commons air time with the broadcasters also gets it a bad name with the public.

The country beyond Westminster is today much less tribal in its political loyalties. When I first went canvassing as a teenager I knew, on discovering a Labour voter, that in all probability everyone in the family was Labour. Even more comfortingly, when I went back next time, four years later, I knew they would all still be Labour. Nowadays voters have a healthy tendency to change their minds between elections and very few buy into the complete programme of even their party of choice. Voter identification with parties is weak and getting weaker. Yet when they switch on their television sets they see a Chamber of MPs behaving with as much partisanship as if they were at a football match. Too often we give the impression that the really important consideration about an idea is not whether it is any good but whether our party thought of it first.

The adversarial method is going out of fashion elsewhere as the means of establishing the truth, but it remains the animating principle of the Commons. In part it is the fault of Henry VIII who gave us a redundant chapel in which to meet first, which has doomed us for ever more to confront each other across two sides of a rectangle. In part it is because our parties have been spared the foreign experience of coalition building, which obliges parties to discover on what they can agree. Enoch Powell caught the character of the Commons well when he described it as the forum of a continuous General Election. But for an era when the public seriously dislike the campaigns that go with General Elections, this may not provide the best recipe for restoring the respect of the public. The Commons must demonstrate to its wider audience that the pursuit of the nation's interests is more important to its members than the struggle for party advantage.

It pains me to say these things. I am a tribal politician of the old school. I will go to my grave clutching my party card. And I know how hard some of these truths will be for many of my colleagues. I understand the Commons because I love it. Some of my happiest hours at the Despatch Box have been spent grappling with a full Chamber growling and snapping back at me. But it is because I love Parliament that I never want to see it sink into an irrelevance, a top draw on the tourist circuit but no longer the crucible of our nation's politics. Its authority rests on public confidence, and if it is to restore that confidence it must change. It is those of us who most love Parliament who therefore most want to see it modernised.

Wednesday 18 July

Began the day with the first meeting of the Modernisation Committee. We had expected the Tories to oppose my taking the Chair on the grounds that a Cabinet minister should not chair a select committee, which should be the prerogative of backbenchers. In the event, Nick Winterton jumped in first and nominated me. Lots of bubbling enthusiasm from the members of the committee on the agenda we should examine, from the parliamentary calendar to electronic voting. Everyone present recognised that Monday's defeats had created a momentum for reform. The important thing now for us is to surf it.

Afterwards I went to preside over my second Privy Council meeting at Buckingham Palace. This one has as its centrepiece the historic act of introducing a new Great Seal for the Lord Chancellor – the first new Great Seal since one was cast fifty years ago at the time of the Queen's coronation. To mark the occasion the ceremony is to be recorded by television.

The ceremony, hilariously, should consist of the Queen smashing the old Seal with a hammer. I find this hangover from the days of the warrior kings highly amusing, and can tell from the dark glances of Alex Galloway, Clerk to the Privy Council, that he regards me as being inappropriately frivolous. He rebukes me by explaining that all that is required of the Queen is a ceremonial tap on the Seal in order that it can be considered ritually defaced. There then follows much theatrical business in which both Alex and a palace official produce rival hammers for the ritual defacement. Both have fetching silver finishes to the hammer head. Bizarrely, though, Alex's has that pattern of indented diamond heads which you find on kitchen hammers used to tenderise meat. Ruefully, he himself has to admit that it looks a bit like it came out of a butcher's shop. The palace official wins. There then follows further business with the Lord Chancellor on the presentation of the old and the new Seal. Strictly speaking, Derry should hand them over one after the other to Her Majesty. The problem is each of them weighs a stone. There is much hefting of Great Seals by Alex and palace officials which rapidly leads to the conclusion that we cannot expect Her Majesty to hold either of them. A perfect protocol compromise is worked out by which Derry will graciously wave to indicate the old Seal, and then, after it has been ritually defaced, wave excitedly to indicate the pleasing new Seal.

A bell buzzes and closes what has been the most entertaining twenty minutes I've had all week. The ceremony of the Seals is kept to the end of the meeting. The Queen carries out the ritual defacing with aplomb by taking the approved silver hammer and striking the silver mould. The net result is a rather pleasing tinkle, but not much evidence of defacement. I suspect the Plantagenets did not stop at purely ritual defacement.

I scramble back for Prime Minister's Questions. It passes off well, if a bit flat. Tony gets in a good final parting shot with his line, 'As the Two Ronnies would say, it's goodnight now from Mr Boom [indicating William Hague] and from Mr Bust [indicating Michael Portillo].' It was a neat out-line for the end of the parliamentary term, but only a few of us know just how much it meant to Alastair Campbell that he managed to make boom and bust the last words heard at the final Prime Minister's Questions before the summer recess.

Afterwards, Pat Hewitt comes round for a discussion about progress on her bills this session. She's a bit late, and arrives as a refugee from the Royal Garden Party at Buckingham Palace. She is immensely entertained by the experience. She had asked for two cups of tea and was handed a small teacup for herself accompanied by the question whether the other cup was for a man. On indicating that it was for her male Private Secretary, she was dumbfounded to be handed a second cup twice the size of the one that was appropriate for her as a lady. As a result, Labour's Minister for Women found herself meekly accepting two fine china cups neatly encapsulating the Establishment's distinction between men and women.

Thursday 19 July

Before Cabinet I put the finishing touches to my paper for next week's Cabinet Sub-Committee on House of Lords Reform. It has now been through two or three complete redrafts in the past seven days since Meg alerted me to the impending meeting. All the reworking has been well worth it as it has helped to clarify for me the big problem – the sheer unpopularity of our proposals. This is a much bigger picture than all the footling details about what Wakeham may or may not have said two years ago.

At the end of the Cabinet meeting I buttonhole Derry. No, that's not quite right – no one buttonholes Derry. I place my body between him and the exit so that he is obliged to notice me. I mention to him that I have done a note on House of Lords reform for the meeting next week and intend to circulate it to all members. With unruffled assurance he cheerfully tells me that of course he recognises my right to put in writing what I want, but his job is to tell Tony what is the view of the majority of the Cabinet committee. One of Derry's redeeming features is that he is so self-assured he is incapable of being ruffled by those who are not convinced he is right.

Later in the afternoon I return to the Chamber for the resumed debate on the membership of the DTLR and Foreign Affairs Select Committees, a much more docile affair, reflecting the fact that we had fully accepted the will of the House. The main significance of the debate is that as the last item on the last substantive day of business I had delivered on my commitment that we would get all the select committees up and running before the summer recess. We managed it within the target four weeks, which is the quickest time that select committees have ever been set up in any Parliament. But it was touch and go. One more day's delay and it would have had to wait until October.

Friday 20 July

Robert Hill comes round. We have a useful first canter over the course on House of Lords reform. He is studiedly careful, but appears concerned at the compelling evidence I offer on the unpopularity of our present scheme. He gently warns me that this is all very well but that there are people urging Tony to proceed with Wakeham on the basis that we will never get agreement to anything else.

Sunday 22 July

Start the day with an appearance on *Breakfast with Frost*, which is more than Frost does as he has very sensibly gone off on holiday. Before going on set we leaf through the Sunday papers. I am immensely flattered to discover one of Jeffrey Archer's mistresses has told a Sunday paper that he found me 'loathsome'. In all the circumstances it's a real compliment to be reviled by Jeffrey Archer. It is the ones that he flattered who are feeling embarrassed in the week he has been sent to prison.

I finish the day making dinner. I have just put the lamb in the oven and am trying to get the roast potatoes on when the telephone rings.

It is a nice lady at Number 10 switchboard telling me she has Lord Levy on the phone. I stop what I'm doing and she puts through Michael, who says, 'Hi, Jack, is that you?', and is a bit surprised when all that greets him is me bursting into laughter and saying, 'Michael, you must have asked for the Foreign Secretary and they had completely forgotten it was no longer me.' I must have come a long way, now that I only see the funny side of it.

Monday 23 July

Paul Tyler drops by for a friendly and frank exchange of views. He tells me that Liberal Democrats have had a strategy session on whether to continue with the Joint Consultative Committee (JCC) with the government. The conclusion in all the circumstances seems very mature. They have decided not to pull out with a big fanfare, smashing the furniture as they go. Instead they simply won't activate the JCC and will say to Tony that it is up to the government to come up with a persuasive example of something they could usefully discuss. This has the neat result of not putting on them the blame for the JCC being broken up and the onus on us to make it work.

Afterwards I leave for my first meeting of PSX, the Cabinet sub-committee which controls public spending. We have a fascinating presentation by two senior managers from the BBC who have been studying the management of change in the Civil Service, and have broadly come to the conclusion that it is not managed at all. The key problem they identify is there is no culture of leadership in the sense of accepting responsibility for delivery. The Civil Service is all process and no outcome. They give a wonderfully revealing response from a civil servant who was asked to state what he was responsible for, and after thought replied, 'I am accountable for the validity of the reporting system.'

Tuesday 24 July

The climax of my day is the meeting of CRP (HL), the Cabinet Sub-Committee on House of Lords Reform. It is held in Derry Irvine's room in the Lords. For reasons that are obscure, they are festooned with prominent paintings of equally obscure naval battles. An appropriate backdrop for this meeting.

Derry invites me to talk through my paper and then makes it impossible by constantly interrupting me. Derry's approach to meetings is not to chair them but to cross-examine the other members as witnesses. This is profoundly irritating and makes it very difficult to maintain the thread of an argument, but he does it with courtesy. It is at least preferable to the approach of Charlie Falconer, who makes an aggressive speech in which he treats the rest of the meeting as a jury on which he is calling for my conviction. By the time he finished I would not have been surprised if he had demanded the death penalty. I get robust support from Gus Macdonald, who describes Wakeham as 'all nonsense', and more restrained support from John Prescott and Jeff Rooker. Charles Clarke helpfully states that in principle he would prefer a 90 per cent directly elected House of Lords. Even Derry admits that when the debate commences it will be more about the merits of the proposal rather than the authority of Wakeham.

Like the men-of-war in the paintings around me, I take a bit of damage but nevertheless make some progress. There is consensus that I have a fair point when I argue that 11 per cent is a derisory proportion for the democratic element, and an agreement that we should raise it to the marginally less derisory 20 per cent. There is absolutely zilch support among those around the table for indirectly elected peers, which is an idea whose time has not yet come.

More significantly, I win the argument that there really can be no question of legislation in this first session. Rather than the commitment to a White Paper followed by legislation fulfilling Wakeham, with which Derry had hoped to end the meeting, we end up with an agreement to a consultation document. I have bought time for something better. We all limp away from the meeting to our respective harbours to reflect and regroup.

—⁂—

In truth, I left the meeting quite optimistic about the prospects for a democratic outcome. Perhaps it was the bright, sunny weather that greeted me in the Palace courtyard when I emerged from the Victorian, panelled gloom of the Lord Chancellor's office. Perhaps I was overconfident in my faith that in a free society political authority belongs only to those who secure the consent through election of those over whom they exercise power.

At least we all agreed that the present half-reformed state of the Lords was unsupportable. Britain now shares with Lesotho the unenviable distinction of being the only two countries in which hereditary chieftains still retain the right to pass laws for the rest of the nation. As Foreign Secretary I had spoken in support of open government at a Europe–Africa Summit. I was rebuked by the President of an African country, which might generously be described as a guided democracy, who objected that he could not be blamed for failing to introduce full democracy after only fifty years of independence, when Britain had failed to get rid of the hereditary principle after five hundred years of Parliament.

The very building which provides the habitat of the Lords underlines its detachment from the modern world. During the war the Luftwaffe took out the Commons with accidental precision. As a result, the Commons end of the building is a period piece of post-war utility architecture – stark, spare and severely purposeful. By contrast, the Lords remains a Victorian extravaganza, an exuberant riot of richly carved and gilded ornament. Their Chamber is in its own way a good metaphor for the House of Lords. It is impressively strong on tradition but hopelessly inappropriate to its function in a modern democracy.

As befits the ambience it remains an incorrigibly conservative institution. Despite two landslide Labour victories, the Conservatives are still the largest single party in the House of Lords. It is fashionable these days to praise the House of Lords for its courage in resisting measures which government has to put before it. Commentators tend to overlook the fact that the House of Lords only discovers this bold spirit of independence under Labour governments. In the first year after the last General Election, the House of Lords defeated the Labour government more often than it did the last Conservative government in its entire eighteen years in office. The Lords meekly swallowed even the poll tax, although that was when Britain could have benefited from a genuinely independent second chamber.

Nor is the conservative character of the House of Lords entirely down to its unrepresentative party colouring. The *average* age of peers is almost seventy, nearly double the average age of the population for whom they legislate. Many peers are admirable individuals but it is hard to see how the institution as a collective can help Parliament restore a sense of relevance to a generation of young electors, most of whom have given up on voting.

I was excited that the post of Leader of the House came with a role in Lords reform. In the run-up to the 1997 General Election Tony Blair had asked me to act as Co-Convenor with Bob Maclennan of a Joint Committee of Labour and Liberal Democrat Parties to agree on a common programme of constitutional reform which both our parties could support in the subsequent Parliament. The democratic reform of the House of Lords was a conspicuous item of unfinished business among its proposals and was the clear candidate for modernisation in the second Blair term.

At the first Cabinet sub-committee on the subject I felt I had made a good start in nudging the government's position towards a more democratic outcome. I did not worry that at this meeting the sub-committee had camped on an elected element of only 20 per cent, as I knew it would be buried in derision the moment we went public. I was not to know that this would also be the last meeting of the Cabinet sub-committee, and that throughout two years of intense debate on the direction of Lords reform I was to be denied another opportunity to argue it out collectively with the ministers most involved.

—◊◊◊—

2

The Siege of Derry

9 AUGUST 2001–22 JANUARY 2002

Thursday 9 August

A nightmare drive to Edinburgh. We appear to have chosen the wettest day of the year, if not the century. Everywhere flooded. It took us over two hours to get as far as Brent Cross. Gaynor very sensibly suggested we should turn back and try again tomorrow. Like a fool, I stubbornly refused. The first thing that greets us when we make it to the M1 is an overhead sign telling us that it is closed further up the line. We are forced off the motorway and around the byways of Nottinghamshire. A great place to be if we had set out intending to explore D. H. Lawrence country, but deeply frustrating when your objective is to get to the city of Walter Scott and Irvine Welsh.

To keep our minds in gear as we sit in long tailbacks with the car in neutral, we fall to discussing the complexity of Tony's character and the psychological ease with which he picks up political theories, only to drop them when they have outlived their novelty. Whatever happened to the Third Way, which only Anthony Giddens now writes about? How can he have so readily turned off the tap on the euro, when during the election it sounded as if this was one thing on which he had serious conviction? Personally, I can understand that in a media-driven political era Tony is successful precisely because, rather like Clinton, he has grasped that novelty of ideas makes a bigger impact than consistency. The problem is that in the long run it is a strategy that leaves us appearing rootless and lacking direction.

Tuesday 14 August

At my surgery there is a single mum with two children who was placed in work under the New Deal but left the job a few months later when she discovered that she was worse off after child care costs than she was on benefit. In the meantime, housing benefit had been withdrawn from her rent and she had accumulated massive arrears. She has just received her eviction notice. The press with their vast middle-class bias perpetually write about students leaving university in debt. If they had the same interest in the proportion of the public who lived on the breadline they might find it just as convincing to write about those whose spell in work leaves them saddled with debt. But nobody writes about such people now.

Wednesday 15 August

I called for morning coffee on Roy Hattersley who is up for the Book Festival. Roy was deeply impressed that his article complaining about the betrayal of Labour values by the government has sparked such a resonance among fellow old Labourites. He does shrewdly make the point that I will survive if I make the price of sacking me too high, and the best way to do that is to make myself a champion of the Commons.

There was, as we both acknowledged, great irony in Roy from the old right and myself from the old left meeting to swap anecdotes and share complaints about the new leadership. Roy insists that he has stood where he always was. It is the leadership that has moved to the right of him. I think the real truth is that both Roy and I are tribal Labour politicians. Tony himself is not, which is the secret of his mass popularity, but at the same time is a potential source of trouble because it leaves him insensitive to what motivates the thousand people who wrote to Roy after his article.

Roy is a fund of revealing anecdotes. In part these reflect the fact that although out of office he is still better connected than most Cabinet ministers. He tells me of an exchange with a journalist who interviewed Tony Blair. He had asked Tony Blair why he had courted the political difficulty of sending Euan to The Oratory, when with his home background Euan was likely to have succeeded at any secondary school and still secured a university place. Tony had responded saying that the school environment was every bit as important as the home environment. Then surprisingly he added, 'Look at Harold Wilson's children.' The journalist, not unreasonably, demurred and said that one son had become a headmaster and the other a professor at the Open University. To which Tony responded, startlingly, that he certainly hoped that his children did better than that.

To Roy and me it is difficult to think of two posts which would better demonstrate both a degree of success and also a valuable contribution to society. It was a striking revelation of the extent to which Tony himself did not share our value system that he should regard such posts as comparative failures.

Saturday 18 August

In the evening we attend the premiere of *Enigma*, the film of the book by Robert Harris. Robert is still exercised by the dismissal of Peter Mandelson, who is a close friend. He said that with such a thumping majority, both in Parliament and in the opinion polls, Tony could have afforded to protect Peter.

He was scathing of the Tories' inability to take account of the centre ground. We both agreed that this was supremely illustrated by the current leadership contest in which it is Iain Duncan Smith who is the favourite of the membership. I made the point that I could understand why the Tory members are attracted to Duncan Smith. He holds all the Tory prejudices, and has achieved his party popularity by pandering to those prejudices. If the Tory Party should have learnt anything from the success of New Labour it was that Tony Blair was popular precisely because he was not a tribal politician. That is why the Tory Party should go for Kenneth Clarke, who is the one candidate surviving who could reach beyond the Tory tribe.

Monday 20 August

I went to the Book Festival to listen to the conversation between Naomi Klein, author of *No Logo*, and Will Hutton, author of many books. The conversation began only five minutes late, which must be a new Will Hutton personal best. Naomi Klein is very good in pointing up the hypocrisy and double standards of the approach of the US to globalisation. They preach free trade but they themselves opt out of globalisation whenever it suits their domestic audience – witness their rejection of the Kyoto Protocol. Will Hutton was particularly strong on the importance of developing the European Union as a balance to the United States and the euro as an alternative to the dollar.

Interestingly, Naomi Klein was plainly uncomfortable with this approach as it implied an acceptance of increased multinationalism between the European states.

I spoke to Will after the event and expressed my enthusiasm for what he'd said about the strategic importance of developing a European Union. We had that warm exchange which is only possible between two people expressing strong agreement with each other's views, and it ended as it usually does with an enthusiastic undertaking that we'd meet soon to do it all over again.

As I left I was intercepted by a man of a similar age to myself but with a rather grander beard. I was psychologically prepared for him to debate with me the merits of global capitalism. I was not prepared for him reminding me that I owed him two and sixpence for the outstanding electricity bill on a flat we shared as students in 1969. We reached an amicable agreement that he got more out of the debt as an asset for dinner table conversation than he would gain from my now restoring to him the original debt of 12½p.

Thursday 23 August

The Tory leadership contest has distinct echoes of the closing scenes of *Medea*, with Margaret Thatcher, who has never forgiven Clarke for knifing her a decade ago, predicting that his election would lead to 'disaster'. John Major, who has never forgiven Duncan Smith for almost knifing him over Maastricht, has denounced the Duncan Smith supporters as 'electoral poison'. For good measure, he has also punctured Duncan Smith's claims to have turned down a ministerial job by revealing that he was never offered one. To the outsider what is fascinating is that this is a party living totally in the past.

Friday 24 August

It's that time again when the predictions start to pour in that the forthcoming TUC conference will be a difficult one for Labour. Today the peg is a statement by John Monks that unions 'have got the feeling that public services delivered by the private sector might be the way

Tony Blair prefers'. I do not see how we can readily dispel the view, since it plainly is accurate.

Saturday 1 September

A culturally challenging weekend in Italy with our sister party at their annual Festival of Unity. I have seen nothing like it in Britain for a long time. They have taken over an entire airfield in Emilia Romagna which has become a tent city with tens of thousands of supporters wandering between concerts, entertainment and catering marquees. In the middle of all this there is a large canvas amphitheatre in which, as dusk falls, I find myself addressing five hundred intimidatingly serious party members on the future of Europe. One of the joys of consecutive translation is that you get a break every couple of minutes in which to collect your thoughts for the next spurt. Afterwards I am taken for dinner in what must be the largest tent I have ever been inside with the senior figures of the Italian left, all of us sitting at the same long trestle table.

Unwisely I mention that Gaynor regards parmesan cheese as a staple of life, and since I am in its home region I am immediately showered with immense blocks of the real thing. I grow disheartened at the prospect of eating pasta until Christmas to use it up. But I left encouraged by the vivid impression of a lively political culture in which party politics is still interwoven with people's lifestyle, culture and leisure. There were hundreds of youths and teenagers wandering between concerts at the festival, whose counterparts in Britain would regard it as deeply uncool to be seen anywhere near a party political rally.

Tuesday 11 September

I had promised my mother that we would take her back to Appin where she had spent much of her childhood with her grandmother. I fear this may be her last visit as she has been fading over this past year. By a stroke of good fortune I had discovered that Ardsheal House, where her aunt had been housekeeper, is now a country house hotel and still in the ownership of the family who had been lairds when her aunt was there. My mother is satisfyingly thrilled to be returning there, but sent me back to the phone to ask if she can have her old room overlooking the rose garden. I got a perplexed but very sympathetic response from the current generation of the family that the rose gardens disappeared some time after the end of the Second World War. Nevertheless, the house has been treated with love and respect. It still felt very much the genuine home of a Victorian laird, right down to the bevy of pets scattered around the front porch. My mother immediately lost eight decades and chatted with all the enthusiasm of the young child she was when last here.

We took a turn along the shore of Loch Linnhe to spy on the old cottages of her relations and then, while she and Gaynor got ready for dinner, I took a malt whisky into the drawing room. And there I saw the appalling TV footage from Manhattan of the destruction of the Twin Towers. Gaynor and I had once spent a happy afternoon on the top floor of one of the Twin Towers absorbed in the distant bustle around Manhattan's shoreline. We complained at the time how long it took to get up and down by lift and had some sense of how hopeless would be the chance of survival of those on the top floors when that central nervous system was severed. The most sickening moment came with the shots of people throwing themselves from the windows to embrace a quick death by falling rather than an agonising and slower death from the fire.

Tony had been about to address the TUC when he had seen the same pictures. With a courage that few other politicians could have shown he had abandoned his proposed speech to the TUC and instead made a moving and extempore response to the tragedy which everyone had seen.

Fortunately, my mother was not really capable of internalising this event which came the best part of a century after the period she was psychologically inhabiting, which put a good discipline on Gaynor and me to sustain her cheerful enjoyment of dinner.

Wednesday 12 September

Unfortunately mother fell during the night and it was some hours before I discovered her in the morning. The owners were wonderfully kind and promptly produced a local GP who was straight from the pages of *Dr Finlay's Casebook*. On hearing that my mother was almost ninety he gave us the astounding news that he was only the third GP to hold his practice in those same ninety years. With a speed of which many more urban health services would have been proud, he produced an ambulance and two paramedics to take my mother into Fort William hospital.

While we were following the ambulance into town I had to pull over by the lochside to take a call from Jonathan Powell about the parliamentary response to yesterday's atrocity. It was clear that Parliament had to be recalled and only questions about the precise arrangements remained. There was some suggestion that I might open the debate but I explained that given my current preoccupation with my mother's condition that would be impossible. In any event it was better that the debate was in the hands of the departments who would most have to provide the response to this tragedy – either Jack Straw and Geoff Hoon because of international action that would be necessary, or David Blunkett because of the implications for domestic security.

Friday 14 September

The House was full and in sombre mood. Tony spoke with visible emotion but did not waste much time on reaction to the tragedy. Instead, his statement was notable for the firm resolve which it showed to take the necessary action in response to it. He was commendably strong on the message that terrorism is the enemy of both the West and the Muslim world, and in response to Khalid Mahmood he quoted the denunciation which had been put out by British Muslims. Tony has always been very strong on interfaith dialogue and that is an important asset at this time.

Duncan Smith made his first appearance at the Despatch Box as the Leader of the Conservative Party. He made a decent and humane statement about the atrocity, but he must be conscious that he is in the uncomfortable position for a new Leader of the Opposition of having to spend the rest of the year expressing total support for the government on what is already the biggest political issue not just in Britain but globally.

The recall debate kept to Friday hours and stopped at 2.30 p.m. Afterwards I went to Grosvenor Square to pay my respects for the tragedy that has befallen America. The US Embassy had set up a special area within the central gardens and were processing with efficiency but dignity the thousands who were coming to express their feelings. I spoke briefly to the new ambassador, but in truth the magnitude of this disaster is such that too many words diminish the emotional response, which for once is best expressed by empathetic silence.

Tuesday 25 September

A full morning at the first Legislative Committee meeting since the start of the recess. The state of the legislative programme has not improved over the recess. It is an infuriating irony that the very bills that are slipping down the parliamentary timetable are the ones we wish to push forward in terms of their public profile.

Stephen Byers does offer a silver lining by confirming that we are now ready to legislate to remove the legal bar against all-women shortlists. I warmly welcome this breakthrough which, unusually in present circumstances, gives us a bill the principle of which will be popular with the party. Too much of the legislative programme is managerial and too little of it offers political meat for our own backbenchers and the party in the country. It is a sharp contrast with Thatcher's second term in which the political ideology came to the fore much more strongly than in her first term. Looking at the legislative programme, it is hard to spot the more radical second term which Tony promised.

In the margins of the meeting Robert Hill and Charles Clarke beard me on how we handle the proposed recall of Parliament. There is now an acceptance that there will have to be a further parliamentary debate.

I float the delicate question of whether or not we hold the debate on Adjournment, or, as I prefer, on a substantive motion. This is a key distinction between whether Parliament is being recalled for deliberation only, or being recalled in order to be part of the decision-making process. My advice would be that we approach the Tory and Liberal leadership to see if they would back an agreed motion which would provide a display of Parliamentary unity and would give Tony the authority of the backing of 90 per cent of the Commons.

I round off the day with dinner with David Blunkett at Gran Paradiso in Victoria. David is obviously well known there, and the patron brings him his favourite bottle of red wine without being asked. It is a convivial and confiding occasion.

David recalls being at the disastrous launch of the General Election campaign at the girls' school when Tony got panned for giving highly party political advice to a gathering of schoolgirls. The fault, of course, was not in Tony's speech. What other kind of speech can a party leader give on the first day of an election campaign than a party political one? The fault lay in the selection of the audience. David remembers being stunned when he went into the hall and sat down to discover he was sitting next to an eleven-year-old. Conversation was made more problematic by the immediate proximity of a *Sun* photographer, but he did whisper to her a question about whether the rest of the hall were from the school, to which she sweetly replied, 'Oh yes, the hall's full of the school because we were told to leave our classes and come here.' David was struck that after the event Tony was absolutely silent in the way that we all are when we know something has gone badly wrong.

Thursday 4 October

This is the day of the second recall of Parliament. The first recall had been not so much a debate as an opportunity for the House to pay its respects for the loss of life in New York. Today, though, had a harder sense of purpose. Everyone knew that we were being recalled to discuss a military assault on the Taliban to close down the use of Afghanistan as a base for world terror. It had not been possible to get agreement to a motion providing specific authorisation for military action and the debate took place on a procedural motion that the House adjourn. However, there are many ways of judging the sense of the House and there was no doubt today that its mood was one of overwhelming resolve to take the necessary action against al-Qa'ida. The front benches on both sides went out of their way to express the merit of Parliament sending out a strong signal of unity. The very members who would normally have reservations about military action are also those who are most respectful of international cooperation. Today they found it impossible flatly to resist military action given the impressive global coalition that has been assembled against the Taliban and the clear mandate of the United Nations.

It was the first sitting of the House to be attended by my new opposite number, Eric Forth, who I understand had been stranded on the other side of the Atlantic by the disruption to air travel and unable to get back for the last recall. His appointment as Shadow Leader of the House was both surprising and alarming. In the last Parliament Eric Forth had been on the Tory back benches from where he had waged a single-handed guerrilla campaign in which he had repeatedly ambushed the government from behind every obscure procedure that he could turn to advantage. However, when we met up in my room he began by volunteering that he knew the difference between being on the back benches and on the front benches, and he understood the obligations on him now to behave responsibly. Personally I am quite glad to have him as an opposite number, as he is a good Commons performer and we should do well against each other at Thursday Business Questions. Parliamentary debates are like tennis, at least in the sense that you can only perform your best if you have a good opponent.

Thursday 11 October

We had set aside the morning for a long discussion on strategy with my officials. I had insisted on my PPSs, Lorna Fitzsimons and Ken Purchase, being asked along too, as we have not got a strong enough sense of political direction to the work of the office. I am deeply frustrated that so much time is taken up attending weekly meetings to resolve routine business. The reason for calling this session was to try and get a better sense of political priorities and a diary that matches them.

Lorna and Stephen Twigg, who both served on the Modernisation Committee in the last Parliament, have been pressing on the need for a change in tactics towards modernisation. Although a lot of good work was done in the last Parliament, it was done piecemeal with the result that eventually it ran out of steam. Greg Power, my special adviser, came up with the strategy that I should stake out the territory by publishing a comprehensive programme of modernisation with a view to getting early progress on it as a package. Certainly this would give us the initiative. It would also help solve a tactical problem of which

I am becoming acutely aware. There are two very different constituencies for modernisation. The first is the large number of members who want an improvement in working conditions and more sane hours. The second is a smaller but more vocal group of MPs who want Parliament to be more effective and are less fussed about how long they sit to do it. I am not going to muster a majority on modernisation unless I can get both groups behind the same proposals and producing a package that touches base with both of them may be my only hope. We resolved that the sensible way to prepare the ground would be for me to write my own Memorandum on modernisation and publish it with the authority of the Modernisation Committee for consultation.

Afterwards I fly to Athens to bring a message of solidarity from the Party of European Socialists to the PASOK conference. The national political cultures of our European neighbours continue to spring their surprises. On this occasion I got to the hotel at 11 p.m. and was positively kidnapped (I think that is a fair expression) and bundled off to the discotheque of the youth section. My protests that it was too late were wilfully misconstrued and I was told not to worry as the dancing didn't start until midnight.

In Britain the normal relations between the generations on the left have been inverted. It is the old Labour figures, such as Roy Hattersley and myself, who find ourselves on the left. The younger members often seem to be ultra-Blairite. In Greece, reassuringly, the old correspondences still apply, and the youth section is the leftist wing. They gave a hero's welcome to their favourite champion among the leadership, Akis Tsohatzopoulos. I was propelled next to him for the cameras and only allowed to escape after there had been enough photographs taken to provide evidence of my presence.

Friday 12 October

Today was more humbling. The conference was immense with about three times as many delegates as come to Labour Party conferences, in itself a striking testimony to the level of political activity in a country a sixth the size of Britain. To seat them all, the conference was held in a football stadium. Just to compound the distance between myself and the audience, my microphone was in silent mode and what was broadcast over the PA system was a simultaneous translation of my speech, which must have given my audience a sensation similar to watching a badly dubbed film, as my lips were plainly not moving in unison with what they were hearing. Very sensibly they responded to this dilemma by chattering volubly among themselves, but my dignity was soothed to discover they did this to all the speakers, including those who addressed them in Greek.

Before I left I had a private meeting with Costas Simitis, who has shown great courage in getting his party to face up to the need to modernise. Unwisely, I once asked him if he had read *Captain Corelli's Mandolin*. When he asked me what it was about I replied that it was about Greece during the Second World War, and was put down with the rejoinder, 'I do not need to read about Greece during the Second World War. I was there.' However, I was glad I had said it because it released a fascinating series of reminiscences of what life had been like as a child in a partisan family.

Saturday 20 and Sunday 21 October

On the Friday we had driven down late to Lyndhurst in the New Forest in order that we could have a full day on Saturday tramping the woods and observing the fallow deer rut. It is an almost primeval experience to wander the ancient woodland and hear the bellow of the bucks which has haunted this area for the millennium since it was designated hunting ground. We were lucky in our dawn walk to get close to a magnificent buck too busy restlessly pacing and challenging to notice we were within fifty yards of him.

On Sunday we had to cut short the respite and travel back to London where I was due to do an extended *Panorama* with Richard Perle, who in his own way is also a magnificent buck too obsessed with what he is saying himself to hear what others might have to say for themselves. This was the BBC's attempt to stage a global debate on the war. The theory was that Richard Perle would be my ally and that together we would have dialogue with an Islamic panel in Pakistan. The participants from Pakistan made points that were expressed in a civilised manner and were reasonable from their cultural and regional perspective. Given the long complicity between Pakistan and the Taliban, the panel would have been very unrepresentative if they had not reflected the doubts in their national public opinion on the war.

Conscious that the BBC was transmitting the debate worldwide, I set out a reasoned response that there was no need for division between the West and Islam in halting a violent terrorism that was a threat to us both. The frail, tentative bridge I had constructed to our Muslim audience was then demolished by carpet bombing from Richard Perle, who bluntly told the panel in Islamabad that they had to accept the reality of US power and policy. Not surprisingly this raised rather than lowered the heat in the Pakistan studio, but when the BBC next cut to the camera in North America it beamed round the world a photograph of an empty chair, Richard Perle having flung down his earpiece in disgust at the opinions it was feeding him and stomped out of the studio. For the remainder of the programme I had to keep up the case for military intervention with no support from my supposed US ally, although in truth I was glad to be spared further risk of my moderation becoming a casualty of his friendly fire.

It was Alastair Campbell who had suggested that I should be a member of the War Cabinet during the Afghan conflict. Modern warfare involves as much hand to hand combat in the television studio as on the battlefield and Alastair recruited me as an auxiliary.

This brush with Richard Perle was an instructive lesson to me in how much of a liability the new breed of Neo-Cons could be as allies. At the time we did not know it, but while we were fighting in Afghanistan, they were already focused on Iraq. Occupying Iraq had been a long-standing objective of the Neo-Cons and to be fair to them they had never made any bones about it. They shared the normative human reactions to the attack on the Twin Towers of horror and outrage, but they also saw in it a catalyst for securing their goals for American foreign policy. Condoleezza Rice admitted in an interview 'that she had called together senior staff people of the National Security Council and asked them to think seriously about "how do you capitalize on these opportunities" to fundamentally change American doctrine, and the shape of the world in the wake of September 11th'. With astonishing insensitivity to local feeling this observation was volunteered to, of all publications, *The New Yorker*. There was, though, no shortage of Neo-Cons willing to overlook the lapse in taste and get on with capitalising on the opportunities. Three years before Bush was even elected Perle, Paul Wolfowitz and *five* others who were to be appointed to the Bush Administration had signed an open letter arguing it was time to move on from the strategy of containment of Iraq. By the Camp David strategy meeting on the weekend after 9/11, Paul Wolfowitz was already urging Bush not to focus on Afghanistan but to go straight for Iraq.

As unilateralists by conviction, the Neo-Cons were the last people to be deterred by worries that an attack on Iraq would be opposed by the public of just about every country in the world except Israel. The support of Likud, though, was important in confirming their belief that their strategy was the right one. It is a paradox of the Neo-Cons that they combine in equal measure uncritical admiration of the robust military culture of modern Israel with contempt for the long and honourable liberal tradition of Jewish-American intellectuals and the Israeli Labour Party.

Osama bin Laden's evil intention in attacking the Twin Towers had been to precipitate violent confrontation between the West and the world of Islam. Even he cannot have imagined that there were already in the Bush Administration so many people who were only too happy to reciprocate his feelings and to seize on 9/11 as the pretext to fulfil their ambitions for a US attack on Iraq. In so doing they were to deliver the very divide between the West and the Islamic countries that Osama bin Laden had desired.

—⁂—

Friday 26 October

A day in the constituency. The only tricky bit of the day was the visit to my local mosque. You are always left at a psychological disadvantage on these visits. First they take your shoes away, which leaves those of us from another culture feeling vulnerable. Then you have to remain standing because there is not a chair in sight across the wide expanse of the mosque carpet. Finally, you are entirely surrounded by a circle of the community elders, each of whom can count on total solidarity from everyone else encircling you.

As always, there was good humour in the discussion, and one or two of them had touching stories of their customers expressing solidarity with them in their shops, and wanting to know if they had faced any threats. For all that, they were unanimously against the military action in Afghanistan. The fundamental problem is that it is not perceived as a targeted campaign against terrorists or the Taliban, but a war against the people of Afghanistan.

I know them well and they are all solid citizens. I left disturbed at the unanimity with which they expressed sympathy with Afghanistan and no sympathy for our action against bin Laden. I have a deep fear that the conflict will have as big an impact on community relations at home as it is having on international relations abroad.

Sunday 28 October

The Sunday papers are again full of questions on the campaign. I understand Alastair Campbell's impatience with the media. With impressive manoeuvrability they have switched from constant criticism of the government over its handling of domestic affairs into constant criticism of the government for its handling of the war campaign. Alastair said during the week, 'If we had had today's press in 1940 we'd be having this conversation in German.'

Wednesday 7 November

The big day for the White Paper on Lords reform.

Number 10 have convened a meeting of myself and Gareth Williams under Andrew Adonis to satisfy themselves that we have both learnt our answers to difficult questions. They are fretting nervously that we may give different answers. Mischievously I turn the tables by asking Andrew how he will answer the question why we are producing this package when Tony Blair said in 1995, 'We want a properly directly elected second chamber', or, in 1996, 'We have always favoured a wholly elected House of Lords.' My sense of mischief is satisfyingly rewarded when Andrew looked even more nervous and said he hadn't known Tony had ever said that. I gently suggested he should warn Tony that he might be reminded of the quotes at Prime Minister's Questions. I suspect he did because Tony rather surprised Charles Kennedy by having a well-prepared and convincing three-point rejoinder to the idea of a wholly elected second chamber.

The statement itself was almost an anticlimax. I had not appreciated quite how hamstrung the Conservative Party is by their failure to reach agreement on their own plans for reform. As a result, their attempts to appear more democratic than ourselves keep falling flat when they are asked to explain just how many elected members they want. Lorna and Ken had done a great job among the backbenchers who were mostly quite kind to my efforts to secure democratic reform before putting the boot in to the minimalist approach to democracy in the proposals. Afterwards the two of them took me to the tearoom for a celebratory beverage. Since the last election it serves cappuccino. How very New Labour.

Thursday 8 November

The papers are pretty bloody about the House of Lords reform proposals. This really must be the end of the road for the argument that we will get by as long as we are seen to be implementing Wakeham. Not a single paper compliments us on translating Wakeham into action, and most don't remember Wakeham. Even members of the Wakeham Commission in both Houses (Douglas Hurd in the Lords and Gerald Kaufman in the Commons) have criticised us.

Tuesday 13 November

I had a late dinner in the Strangers' Cafeteria with Charles Clarke. I was pleasantly surprised when Charles, with no prompting from me, launched into an attack on the package for Lords reform: 'They should have listened to you and me and John Prescott when we warned them at the committee meeting that the package needed to be more democratic.' He shrewdly made the point that the whole rationale of the committee's approach had been exploded when Wakeham himself came out against our package.

I asked him if Tony knew the true scale of the panning the proposals had got in the press. Charles's response was blunt: 'He has been told that in uncompromising terms by myself, by Hilary, and by his own private office. I said to him that reform of the House of Lords needs a champion. This package has no champion. Nobody in the Cabinet backs it except Derry, and Derry simply does no work to sell it to the public. I was appalled that Derry did not square Wakeham in advance of publication, which was an elementary step.' I said that I had an appointment with Tony next week but needed to use it to talk about modernisation in the Commons. Charles responded briskly, 'Don't worry about modernisation. Tony will agree to anything that you and Hilary can agree between you. The political priority is to rescue a credible position on reform of the House of Lords.' We were interrupted by the ten o'clock division bell. But I had already heard enough to remind me that often a critical moment in politics can come in a chance encounter in the cafeteria.

Wednesday 14 November

At Question Time Iain Duncan Smith plonks again. Today he brings his assault on our record on manufacturing jobs to the excruciatingly embarrassing conclusion: 'Give British manufacturing a break.' I watch the Press Gallery during exchanges and find them convulsed with laughter. A woman journalist catches my eye and giggles. This is bad news for the Tories. A politician can survive anything but the expectation that his appearances in the Chamber will be a joke.

Tony Blair is rare among the leaders I have known in that his speeches have got better, not worse, with the cares of office. On the way from the Chamber to the Parliamentary Committee he says to me, 'Thank you for all those interviews you've done during the war. They have been just . . .' in that characteristic manner of his, accompanied by a gesture of his right hand with thumb and forefinger closed as if to suggest that words alone were not sufficient to express how good they were. The net effect of this understatement is far more effective than Duncan Smith's climaxes at full throttle.

After Questions, Tony made a statement on the dramatic collapse of Taliban resistance in Afghanistan. There is no getting away from it that he does put these things well. A lesser man might have been inclined to gloat at the victory, or at least indulge in a jibe at those who told us that the Taliban were tough fighters who'd never be dislodged by air power alone. Not a bit of it. He is understated about the remarkable success of liberating most of Afghanistan within less than a week. John Simpson could usefully have taken his cue from Tony before his early morning broadcast in which he announced that he had been one of the first 'to liberate Kabul'. The nearest point he gets in the statement to passion is his description of what we must now do to rebuild Afghanistan. I turn to Hilary to whisper, 'He is going to call it New Afghanistan any minute now', but before I can get the words out he announces our commitment to New Afghanistan.

At the Parliamentary Committee, Tony shares a startling insight into the cultural gulf with the Afghan Northern Alliance. Its principal commanders were asked what weapons or equipment they would find most useful in the struggle against the Taliban. 'One of them came back and said that what they most needed were leather saddles, because their backsides were getting sore riding long distances on the wooden ones.' Presumably there's a war band roaming the Afghan plains today with surplus Household Cavalry saddles.

At the end of the meeting I lobby Jean Corston about a discussion in the PLP on House of Lords reform. To my dismay it has been put to her that she should ask Gareth Williams to address the PLP on the subject. I insist that if the meeting is to be useful we must get Derry Irvine there in order that he can feel the strong view of the PLP on the proposed package. Jean is very quick on the uptake and readily recognises that the point of any such meeting should not be for the PLP to hear from Gareth, but for Derry to hear from the PLP.

Thursday 15 November

Matthew Taylor of the IPPR and Neal Lawson come round for a chat. Matthew is in good form and warms to his latest theme that we need a leadership that can translate politics for a modern consciousness. 'We are still operating our democracy for a society that has vanished. We need a politics for a non-deferential society . . . A political style that neither expects deference from electors, nor replaces deference with cynicism. Our constitution needs the same kind of openness which we are applying in the public service – more participation, decentralisation and devolution, and a greater capacity to be responsive.'

He is particularly scathing about the reduction of democracy to a vote in the ballot box every four years. 'Would you choose the same supermarket for four years? Nobody would tell an elector that they could not go to Sainsbury's because they made a four-year contract with Tesco.'

I'm not sure that I'm entirely comfortable with a consumerist model of democracy, but although we are both too polite to point it out, he has put his finger on the problem with our reform package for the House of Lords. It requires a deferential public to accept that Derry, and for that matter Tony, knows the right kind of people with the expertise to fill up the second chamber. The non-deferential society we've got regards that as a piece of insufferable arrogance and understandably wants to choose the members of the second chamber for themselves. They may not be reliable turning up to vote, but they most certainly don't want to entrust anyone else to take the decision for them.

Saturday 17 November

A fragilous, glorious day at the races. We travelled down to Cheltenham for the Thomas Pink Gold Cup. All the way there on the train I pore single-mindedly over the form. Gaynor gazes out of the window all the way. The result was entirely predictable to a seasoned racegoer. I do not get a single winner for my two and a half hours of work and Gaynor picks two by instinct.

Peter Scudamore was in the press stand and recalled the extraordinary ride of Fred Winter when he went round in the Grand National after the bit in his reins had snapped. I said that they were really brave in those days. Peter, in his very down-to-earth way, denied it. 'Oh no, Fred was not being brave. He had no alternative as he had no way of stopping the horse.'

Wednesday 21 November

I go for my weekly briefing to the Islamic press in my role as a member of the War Cabinet. It takes me back to the rooms at Number 12 Downing Street, from which Hilary and her team have just been evicted to make room for the expanding media operation of the Prime Minister's office. The large room overlooking the park in which Hilary held receptions is now entirely taken over with rows of earnest young beavers with a phone to one ear and both eyes on a computer screen. I am led past them and into a side room where Alastair Campbell is ensconced as the presiding genius.

There is no longer any drama to these occasions. The Taliban are now penned in to a few remaining corners from where they are vowing to fight to the death, but are no more likely to do so this time than on any of the previous surrenders they have made all across Afghanistan. The only thing that could now go wrong for us would be in the shape of friendly fire if President Bush succumbs to pressure from the far right to do it all over again in Iraq, or Yemen, or Sudan, or Somalia. Any of the above would make it impossible to get a fair hearing in the Islamic press.

Thursday 22 November

After the Cabinet Tony took me through to his room to talk about the modernisation package. He is very friendly and his response is supportive. He strongly welcomes the idea of bringing Prime Minister's Questions forward to noon. But parliamentary reform does not excite him. He has always been much more interested in politics in terms of outcome rather than process. What interests him is not the democratic principles of parliamentary reform, but the practical effect it will have. Moreover what has made him such a powerful and successful politician has been his understanding that in a mass democracy, command of the media is as important as dominating Parliament.

In the evening I did *Question Time*. It is so much easier now I am not Foreign Secretary and I do not have to spend my entire day catching up on what's been happening in Britain while I have been going round the world. Oliver Letwin was the Tory representative.

During the programme he was studiously amiable and skilfully avoided any party point-scoring. As a result we had some rather civilised discussions.

After the programme David Dimbleby was in despair with him. 'How on earth am I supposed to put together an interesting programme if the Tories are going to start agreeing with you?' he said to me. However, I can't help feeling that the message has sunk home to some at least on the Tory front bench that the public want to believe that the politicians are reasonable people, not fanatical fundamentalists. As John Bercow said just before the election, 'I have learned that we must not appear to be foaming at the mouth.'

Despite David Dimbleby's worries, the producer of *Question Time* later told me that this evening's broadcast prompted one of their largest crops of positive e-mails from their audience welcoming its serious, non-confrontational tone. His letter betrayed his own surprise at this result, but it confirmed my own suspicion that the adversarial mode which is now all the rage among broadcasters is part of the reason for the growing alienation of the public from political debate. From breakfast with John Humphrys to bedtime with Jeremy Paxman, they are served up interviews on political issues that often appear designed more to produce studio drama than to inform their audience. This has two malign consequences. First, most political choices involve a trade-off between positive and negative consequences, but reducing every political interview to a one-dimensional confrontation suppresses any chance of an honest and balanced discussion of the real dilemma. Secondly, the presumption behind the badgering is that all politicians set out to evade the truth and deceive the public, which feeds cynicism with the political process.

It is tough for any politician to write about the nexus between politics and the media because we have become so locked in an adversarial relationship that any comment on either side is discounted as self-serving. Yet both of us are at fault and we both need to change. Between us we have created a style of political discourse which is aggressive and overpersonalised and which has become a barrier between us and our joint public.

To demonstrate my impartiality, let me begin with politicians. We are in danger of seriously boring our voters. The first cardinal principle of modern campaigning is constantly to repeat the same single-line message. I remember Neil Kinnock in the old days complaining that the Labour front bench was full of people who wanted to be poets and could not lower themselves to repetition. Neil himself was the greatest poet *manqué* among us and one of his endearing traits as leader was that he would have mutinied rather than endlessly repeat the same one-liner. But leaders today bang away at the same phrase that they are told works best on focus groups. That is why Labour constantly identified Conservative governments with 'boom and bust' and Iain Duncan Smith finished every paragraph by asserting 'Nobody believes Tony Blair any more.' It is a depressing feature of single-line politics that the hardest hitting message is more likely to be negative about the threat of your opponent than positive about the promise of your own policies.

The second rule of modern campaigning is that nobody in the party must say anything original. New Labour goes to elaborate lengths to ensure that everyone knows the message and runs with it. This is deeply baffling behaviour to our electors who live in a defiantly individualist society which respects honesty, self-expression and originality. They simply cannot comprehend why politicians repeat the central line rather than speak their own minds.

The reason why politicians stick to their hymn sheet is that they are dealing with a media which is no longer capable of handling an original idea but knows how to report a personality conflict. In my years in the Cabinet I became resigned to the knowledge that if I moved a comma in the hallowed mantra on the euro I would be reported the next day as having committed 'a gaffe'. On day two the papers would run round colleagues until they found one who was outraged that I had the nerve to move the comma, at which point the media would report 'a row'. With a bit of luck and heavy-duty fanning, by day three they may be able to announce 'a split' over the comma. The irony is that the press constantly complain that politicians are boring, but they are not going to dare to be interesting unless the media starts to reward rather than punish originality.

The BBC's own opinion research threw up the arresting insight that the public would like their MPs to be more 'like Bob Geldof'. I shared this result in an airport lounge with Bob Geldof, who growled, 'Tell them they are wrong.' But I can understand what the public are trying to tell us. They want more MPs with whom they can feel some psychological empathy – MPs who have thrown away their pagers, speak what they think and demonstrate real passion for a cause. In truth, I believe most of my colleagues would be happy to rise to that challenge if they felt it was safe to come out of the bunker. In my experience the majority of MPs on both sides of the Chamber went into politics because they really believed in the values of their party and are as fed up as everyone else with a media environment that obliges them to practise safe sentiment. New Labour can fairly be criticised for focusing too much on spin and not enough on substance. But any democracy is only as healthy as its press and there are three aspects of our modern media culture that are corrosive of democracy.

The first is the single-minded pursuit of the negative story. Today's headline writers want drama, and drama requires conflict and exposure, not progress and solutions. The ratio of negative to positive media stories has increased from three to one in 1974 to a daunting eighteen to one in 2001. Objectively this makes no sense. I was in Parliament in 1974. There was a lot to be negative about in the year of the three-day week. By comparison, economy, lifestyle and living standards are all much more cheerful today. Only the press is more gloomy. The BBC's own research into public disillusion with politics solemnly reported the criticism of their focus groups that 'There's never any good news' without apparently drawing any conclusions for their own bulletins. The danger is that if we constantly present the political process as resulting in unremitting failure we will stifle any faith that democracy can produce solutions.

The second problem with the modern media is its remorseless demand for novelty to spice up the next bulletin or the next edition, a demand that has become insatiable in the era of 24/7 news. Any profound political achievement requires long-term application and does not lend itself to novelty quick fixes. I vividly remember before the last General Election briefing the political editor of a major broadsheet that the big objectives of the next Parliament would be full employment and fewer children in poverty. He put down his pen and asked, 'What's new about this?' The overhyped daily initiatives for which government has been much criticised were born of that demand for novelty rather than substance.

The awkward truth is that serious politics does not throw up a novelty every day for next morning's edition. As a result the search for novelty often ends in treasuring trivia. I have known the news lobby spend a whole session demanding 'background' on the Prime Minister's new spectacles and whether they were deliberately chosen to copy those of Sven-Göran Eriksson. By contrast, the most profound changes to society happen gradually over a long period of time and therefore never pass the novelty test for front-page treatment. One of the most dramatic changes for the better under Labour is the virtual abolition of long-term youth unemployment, a remarkable contrast with the Thatcher era and much more important to delivering the cut in crime than any of the panoply of repressive measures that have flooded out of the Home Office. Yet this extraordinary change in our society has never qualified as news, because its gradual achievement lacked the immediacy demanded of a dramatic story.

I have left to last the most damaging development in the modern media. Political reporting is now obsessed with personalities and therefore with process rather than outcome. Politicians find themselves conscripted to parts in a soap opera, in which the plot line is solely about who is on the way up, who is on the way down and who is on the way out. The damaging consequence of this school of celebrity politics is that it reinforces the growing perception that politics is something that top people do within that curiously introverted and gossipy Westminster village. The elector is reduced to being a spectator rather than the owner of the process. Both Parliament and media are trapped in a culture that is too introverted, too much about what goes on in the lives of celebrity journalists, spin doctors and MPs, and not enough about what is going on in the lives of anonymous readers and electors. It is not even as if the readers and electors share the media obsession with personalities. One survey of young voters found a clear majority were critical of media coverage of politics because it was more concerned with personalities than issues.

If we are lucky the worst result will be a steady decline in the number of electors who bother to turn up and vote for a parliamentary institution that appears irrelevant to the problems in their lives. If we are unlucky the even worse result will be a vacuum which will be occupied by extremist political movements with simple destructive solutions. Neither politicians nor press can break out on their own from the sterile relationship into which they are now locked. But I find it difficult to be optimistic about the future of parliamentary democracy unless we recognise that our present political culture is destroying trust not just in government but in our democratic process.

—∽—

Tuesday 27 November

This is Gordon's day. It is the day when his pre-Budget report dominates the parliamentary scene.

In the morning he gives a read-out to the Cabinet of what he will say to the Chamber. It is an impressive presentation. Unemployment is now lower than in any other country in the G7. Our National Debt as a proportion of GDP is lower than at any time in the century since the First World War drove it up. Despite difficulties in the international economy he is still able to increase public spending because we have cut debt repayments by £8 billion a year. The lesson of the political disaster over the 75p increase to pensioners has been well absorbed. Gordon now gives pride of place to his commitments to pensioners, including a new commitment that no pensioner will be living on less than £100 a week by 2003, and thereafter every pensioner will be guaranteed a minimum increase of £100 a year.

Curiously, the presentation to the Chamber was not such a triumph. All went well until Gordon disappeared into an extended cadenza on the funding of the NHS. He presented at length the new report by Derek Wanless which helpfully concluded that a public health service funded by general taxation was the most efficient form of health provision. This is a thoroughly sound conclusion, but the House was bemused at the Chancellor of the Exchequer metamorphosing into the Health Secretary. Any other Chancellor would have referred to the report briefly and announced that his Right Honourable Friend the Health Secretary would be making a statement on it tomorrow. If Gordon would only be satisfied with being our best Chancellor for half a century he would have fewer problems and a lot more personal satisfaction.

Wednesday 28 November

I got to the House in good time to take my seat beside Tony for Prime Minister's Questions. Charles Kennedy bowled him a fast one by asking whether the discussion yesterday on proper funding of the NHS meant that he stood by his commitment to increase NHS funding to the European average by 2005. You can tell when Tony has prepared an answer because he has already composed his face with a demeanour appropriate to the tone of the rejoinder – contempt, humour or sympathy. This time I could see from the blank expression on his face that he had not anticipated this question. He plumped for 'yes'. What else could he have said? But the Tory benches immediately erupted, pointing with glee at Gordon's face which revealed his full discomfiture at the principles he had enunciated yesterday being reduced so quickly to arithmetic today.

The Parliamentary Committee that evening was chiefly notable for the vast array of whisky bottles awaiting Tony's signature. The season of Christmas parties is approaching and every MP wants a bottle signed by Tony for a raffle. As he answers questions from the committee members, I sit next to him and pass him a steady supply of bottles for him to sign while speaking. I suppose it is entirely appropriate that I should be official Master of the Bottles, as they are all bottled in my constituency at the Broxburn plant. We build up a good, steady rhythm for over twenty minutes, in the course of which Tony signs enough bottles to stock a good-sized bar while, without pausing, he handles questions on Afghanistan, the Health Service and education.

Thursday 29 November

Cabinet was a disaster. And for the most prosaic of reasons – my Memorandum on modernisation had not got round private offices early enough for most Cabinet ministers to see it. I began with a cheerful, upbeat introduction to the paper stressing that it set out a comprehensive programme for modernising Parliament. At this point I was totally oblivious that only a few people in the room had got the paper and most did not know what I was talking about. I sat back in smug anticipation of broad agreement only to drown in a tidal wave of resentment from colleagues who had not got the paper and who obviously held me to blame, with just a touch of suspicion among some that I might deliberately be pulling a fast one. After a bad-tempered and fractious exchange I agreed that we would return to the subject next week when colleagues had had a fair chance to study the paper.

Privately, though, I was seething. As a result of a cock-up in the post room I have now lost a whole week in the schedule for publication of my Memorandum and provoked suspicion on the part of my colleagues for which there will be a price to be paid on what I can now get through Cabinet. What made it all the more unfair is that I am about the only Cabinet minister ever to have put a paper round for collective discussion. Part of the problem was this Cabinet hardly ever gets a written document for discussion and colleagues did not wish to miss out on this unique opportunity of being asked for their views. It was a relief to go across to the Commons and vent my spleen in tart rejoinders to the Opposition at Business Questions.

Tuesday 4 December

Began the day with a visit to Jack Straw at the Foreign Office to make my peace. The Secretary of State's room has reverted to tradition. My examples of the best of British design have gone from the bookcase which has once again gone back to sleep with a collection of leather-bound early Hansards which no one will ever disturb.

I began by getting my apology in first. 'Look, I'm sorry that I snapped at you at the Cabinet. But what's important to me now is that we quit the argument as to who saw the document first and who got the document too late, and get on with agreeing on a package for modernisation.' Jack was generous in accepting the apology. 'I have now had a chance to read the paper and it does have a lot of good ideas. I'll make a point of writing in to support the revised version.'

I rounded off the day with a private meeting with Anne Campbell, Tony Wright and Margaret Moran, who each chair different groups on Parliamentary reform, and I wanted to make sure I'd got them on side. I went through the content of the package and stressed, 'I am already running into enough resistance from the traditionalists, and they will seize on any evidence that the modernisers themselves are dissatisfied with it. I know some of you will want the package to go a bit further, but criticism of the present package for not going far enough will simply play into the hands of those who do not want modernisation to go anywhere.'

Encouragingly, they fully understood the tactics. Tony Wright said, 'If we get half of this through you have done a good job in getting this place at least moving towards the twenty-first century.' It was a good note on which to end the day.

Wednesday 5 December

The discussion on my Memorandum with the Modernisation Committee goes very well. There is near universal agreement to getting earlier the big statements of the day to set the media agenda. Support for shorter debates was strengthened fortuitously by the knowledge that the previous day's second reading on the Education Bill had to be prolonged artificially to last until 10 p.m. by whips going round the building finding people to speak.

Afterwards I went straight along the corridor to the PLP. It meets in the largest of the rooms on the committee corridor – an enormous barn of a place with long windows on to the Thames down one side and an enormous painting of Oliver Cromwell and his four fellow parliamentarians escaping on to the Thames by boat from the attempt by Charles I to arrest them in the Commons Chamber. An encouraging backdrop to stimulate us to revive the rights of Parliament.

Lorna and Ken had done a magnificent job in mobilising support for the package at the meeting. Nineteen MPs spoke in the discussion that followed my speech, and eighteen of them spoke unequivocally in support of the package. Rosemary McKenna was magnificently condescending to those colleagues who said they did not know what to do with themselves if the House finished at 7 p.m. 'For Heaven's sake, you can always watch *EastEnders*. Go home and watch TV like the people who elected you.' But most of those who contributed buttressed my theme that the object of modernisation was not to make life easier for MPs but to enable them to do their job better. After the meeting Lorna and David Mathieson met me in the corridor, elated by how well it had gone. I thanked them, but also warned them, 'That was a home crowd I was playing to today. The traditionalists simply stayed away from the match.'

Jean Corston at the Parliamentary Committee did a good number of reporting in front of Tony how well the meeting had gone, and how popular my proposals were. Tony was in good humour and turned to me in a tone of mock confrontation: 'You're accused of being popular with your colleagues. What have you got to say in your defence?' I replied, 'In mitigation I would enter the plea that it will soon fade when we get down to implementing the proposals.'

Saturday 8 and Sunday 9 December

A weekend trip to visit our two Scottish terriers who are undergoing a month of re-education to make them behave with a bit more of the discipline that should be expected of New Labour dogs. Peter, my son, will keep referring to them as having been sent off to borstal, but in truth it is a very jolly training camp deep in Welsh Wales. Pure Merlin country. The London couple who run it tell us that in their first week a dog escaped and when they reported it missing to the police they were advised to take some of its hair to an old woman living in a cottage by the sea. She spread the hair on a map of the area and swung a pendulum over it but sadly announced she was getting no message from it. This came as a surprise to the police who said that she had found several missing persons for them.

Thankfully, neither of ours have escaped and show no inclination to do so. They have a whole estate in which to explore and an obstacle course over which to play. The energetic trainer keeps them hungry, bullies them rotten and exercises them until they are exhausted, and the truly sickening thing is that they utterly adore him for it. Gaynor travelled back rather quiet and ruminative about the ingratitude of dogs to those who pet them and their pathetic affection to those who order them around.

Monday 10 December

I was invited to the annual Christmas outing of the Strangers' Bar regulars. To say it is organised by Dennis Turner would be to do him an injustice. He is the moving spirit, presiding genius and financial officer for the occasion. It was held, as ever, in the top room of the Albert in Victoria Street. The interior is every bit as Victorian as the name, and is a fitting venue for the spirit of Christmas. Dennis insists that everybody has to sing a song, either solo or in chorus. Some of my colleagues were a revelation. Margaret Beckett impressively sang solo an urban folksong. John Battle, surprisingly, turns out to be an expert on the mandolin, but has forgotten to bring it with him. However, he did a number with a borrowed guitar and it was clear that he did have a talent for stringed instruments. All that, however, was capped by the revelation that Jean Corston is an enthusiast at tap-dancing and is giving a performance on behalf of charity in January. All in all it was a tremendously fun outing. One of the drawbacks in being in the top rank of politics is that you just don't have the time to discover the many sides to colleagues with whom you otherwise put in a sixty-hour working week.

We all had to adjourn early for the ten o'clock division. The rest went down to the Strangers' Bar to continue, but I returned to the office where I found Catherine Nalty, one of my Private Secretaries, much exercised that I was being left to hang in the wind over the proposed parliamentary facilities for the Sinn Fein Four. The Prime Minister, who had got us into the controversy, is now distancing himself from the debate by refusing to let his name be added to the motion. And the Northern Ireland Office has spent all day prevaricating on whether John Reid would participate in the public announcement by giving a simultaneous written statement. I insisted on speaking there and then to John Reid in Belfast and made it clear that while I was willing to take the motion through I needed him as a partner. To be fair to John, he readily agreed to make a statement. It was a classic example of two Cabinet ministers being able to resolve in a frank ten-minute exchange a problem on which their officials had been stalemated for a whole day.

Tuesday 11 December

To the Palace around lunchtime for the monthly meeting of the Privy Council. Immediately before us the new Bosnian ambassador has been presenting her credentials. This is a ceremony frozen in time from the nineteenth century, underlining the rule that dress codes and rituals become ossified at the point when real power passes from an institution.

A good friend from my Foreign Office days is senior diplomat in attendance. He is dressed up in the court dress of the British Diplomatic Service, which is a bit of a cross between a head wine waiter and an officer of the Hussars. The dress sword tips the balance in favour of the officer of the Hussars. He is comically apologetic for his appearance: 'I promise this will be the very last time.'

It was a long agenda today, but somehow that only confirmed its inconsequential character. For instance, we conferred on a citizen of Jersey the privileges of the office of jurat for life. My explanatory notes advised me that this means that she will have a free parking space for life.

Alex Galloway has, though, introduced a topical note to the proceedings. We appoint one of the administrators at the Privy Council to be the third clerk of the Council. The background note explains that this is a precaution against a terrorist attack taking out central London. As this particular administrator only works part-time, there is a fifty-fifty chance she would survive and enable the Privy Council to function. Personally I work full-time in London and am unlikely to survive such an historic event, and cannot claim that my last thoughts will be 'I wonder how the Privy Council will get on without us all.'

Wednesday 12 December

The rest of the day was taken up with stroking the press in the hope of a fair coverage for my Memorandum on modernisation. I gave commentators and leader writers a sandwich lunch in my room. Afterwards I climbed up to brief the lobby in the barren little attic where they hold their regular meetings. It is a curious room, the sort of Commons equivalent to the crow's nest. You take the lift as high up as it will go, and then climb some more up a spiral staircase to the room at the top of a turret looking out in two directions at the Thames. It is probably the most Spartan room left in the building, with wooden benches against the walls and no carpet on the floor. I doubt if anything behind that door has changed since the 1930s. It is all the more curious since the journalists who go there twice a day come from a communications industry which has seen as fast a change in technology as any other.

On the whole the discussions go well. I had been caught unprepared by a question from the commentators on whether this package will benefit the Opposition, but I am fluent and practised by the time I get to the lobby. And in truth there is a lot in it for the Opposition. They also can turn to their advantage the opportunity for earlier publicity, and they will benefit more than us from the greater powers of scrutiny of the select committees and over legislation. As I said to the lobby, 'If my objective was to make life easier for the government I would have produced a very different package from this one.'

Thursday 13 December

The press are accurate and fair in reporting the modernisation package. The *Guardian* opens by noting that I've a painting of John Pym, the great parliamentarian and contemporary of Cromwell, over my desk. Actually it is Cobden and Bright over my desk. Pym, a little awkwardly for a Puritan, is over the door to the booze cupboard. The common note of reserve is that my package should go further, but that is encouragement I am happy to receive.

At the Business Statement I find half the Tory Party psyched up by the news of the motion on Sinn Fein facilities. When I announce the motion for debate on Tuesday I am interrupted by cries of 'Shame' which mingle genuine indignation with what must be fake surprise. Eric Forth sets the tone for a repeated theme of Tory questioning, which is about the threat to themselves, their staff and the antiquities of Westminster if we admit such known terrorists. As I point out, all four of the Sinn Fein MPs at Westminster have been regularly attending for three years the Northern Ireland Assembly without a single problem of security. It is an unattractive double standard to say that it is all right for the population of Northern Ireland to be exposed to such a risk but wholly unacceptable for it to happen in Britain. I came out of the hour's grilling alive, but alert to the real challenge that I face on Tuesday.

I dash straight from the Chamber to Eurostar where I just have time for a large brandy to revive myself after the rigours of the combat, then on to the relative tranquillity and studied courtesy of European diplomacy at the European Summit at Laeken. The PES dinner was held in the imposing Grand Room of the Town Hall. In one sense it is quite fitting for the representatives of Labour as the walls were covered in representations of the craftsmen of the medieval guilds. As a result, our debate had an audience of joiners, masons and bakers. In another respect it was a real handicap as the Brussels fire brigade forbids any hot meals for fear that the cooking of it will bring down the priceless historic building.

This time I was pleased that Tony had agreed to come to the subsequent private meeting even if he would be too late for the dinner, and I suggested that he go straight to the private room where we would be meeting. Unfortunately, Belgian protocol would not hear of ushering the Prime Minister into an empty room and insisted on marching him into the Grand Chamber where dinner was just breaking up. This was mildly embarrassing as it revealed to everybody else present that Tony was coming to the private meeting with Prime Ministers but not to dinner with other party leaders. But they took it fairly philosophically.

There was really only one controversy to be resolved in the subsequent private meeting – who would chair the new Convention to prepare ideas on the Future of Europe for the next inter-governmental conference. Antonio Gutteres opened the discussion bluntly with 'The only question is, are we a real political party? If we are a real political party then we have the capacity to get the post for one of our family, but only if we all agree.' But everyone round the small table knew that Schröder had privately agreed with Chirac to back his candidate, Giscard d'Estaing. The outcome was that I would ring Wim Kok and urge him to put his hat in the ring and that Tony Blair would speak to Schröder and try and talk him into backing out of his deal with Chirac.

Saturday 15 December

In the afternoon Antonio rang me from Laeken to lament, 'We are not a political party. We cannot even agree to support one of our own family.' He was full of praise for Tony Blair for having done his best, but disappointed with Schröder for standing shoulder to shoulder with Chirac and contemptuous of other Social Democrat politicians who stayed silent. The net result is that we now have a right-wing President of the Convention approved by a meeting at which the largest single political force present was of the left.

Monday 17 December

The day begins with a call by Dennis Stevenson, a successful banker, but for the purposes of this meeting a rather less successful Chairman of the Appointments Commission to the House of Lords. He is engagingly philosophical about the press treatment of his first batch of appointments which were panned for not living up to their title of 'the people's peers'. He recalls the experience resignedly as, 'I took a bath over it.'

Denis Stevenson has one very revealing insight into the background to our present controversies. 'I asked Wakeham once what he actually meant by suggesting that the Appointments Commission should be responsible for nominating the party political representatives . . . I said, "Look, I can't think of anything more inconsistent than a Commission that's independent appointing members who are party political." He told me, "I never meant the Appointments Commission to make all the political nominations . . . All I had in mind was that if there was somebody who could have brought a really independent perspective to the Lords but had fallen out with the party leadership, then the Appointments Commission could put him on. For instance, Ken Livingstone will never be appointed by Blair, but he could make a really useful contribution to the House of Lords." ' I refrain from pointing out if the structure was all about getting Ken Livingstone into the House of Lords it was unlikely to make Tony warm to the idea.

Much of the afternoon is spent wrestling with the challenge of producing a speech for tomorrow's debate that makes handing a quarter of a million pounds of allowances over to the political allies of Britain's only home-grown terrorist organisation sound entirely reasonable. My rhetorical problem is that the only reason for doing this is that it was part of the price of persuading the IRA to commence decommissioning in October. However, I am barred from letting that particular cat out of the bag. Nor, in any case, would it assist my attempt to keep the whole debate low-key and procedural.

In the ten o'clock vote I am buttonholed by Clare Short, who is full of her latest struggle to prevent the licence for the sale of an air defence radar to Tanzania. It is a long-running saga which goes back to my own days at the Foreign Office. Personally, I always thought she had a point, as it was never clear why we should be encouraging the sale of expensive long-range military radar to a country which with another hat on we had judged to be so poor and so indebted that it needed special measures to keep its economy afloat. Clare is very upset that with my departure from the Foreign Office she is now outnumbered on arms sales.

Tuesday 18 December

The debate on the Sinn Fein Four was always going to be an uphill one. The Tory Party turned out formed up in mass ranks in a mood in which their surface indignation vied for the upper hand over an all too evident hope that they could skewer me. I played my strongest card early, by pointing out that during the nine years in which Gerry Adams was an MP and the Conservative government was in office, they never acted to prevent him having access to the facilities of the Commons. Indeed, for every month of those nine years, Gerry Adams was mailed his allocation of tickets for the Public Gallery and occasionally used them.

Fortunately for me, this came as news to the Tory Party. Their Northern Ireland spokesman, Quentin Davies, looked so bewildered when I explained this that I challenged him to get up and say whether he had been aware of it. Perhaps wisely he did not, but he never really recovered from having to ditch a large part of his prepared speech in the light of his new knowledge. I began to enjoy myself as it became clear I'd caught the Tory Party off guard. Confidence is two-thirds of the battle in a crowded and heated debate. Quentin Davies had lost his confidence and made a poor speech which got worse as it got longer. I never heard such a weak cheer from crowded Tory benches as when he sat down. By now I knew we had won.

In his wind-up speech John Reid was given an appalling barracking by a Tory Party which had plainly not enjoyed a dinner in the cafeteria washed down with a cup of tea. It was one of those occasions when the only possible strategy is to stand your ground and defiantly plough through your text, which John did with great courage. There were half a dozen votes but we won them all comfortably. The verdict had not been in doubt since the opening speeches. In the last division I stood in front of the clerks who record the names of members voting and thanked all our colleagues for staying and wished them a merry Christmas in return. It is an irony on such occasions that you are genuinely more thankful to your colleagues for their loyalty in supporting you when you have a weak argument.

Wednesday 19 December

Screaming front-page headline in the *Guardian* on the 'Cabinet Row' over the Tanzania deal. The opening sentence talks of 'an embarrassed government', 'forced to delay the decision'. Allegedly Tony Blair has 'thrown his weight' behind the deal after strong lobbying by British Aerospace. The last bit sounds only too plausible. In my time I came to learn that the Chairman of British Aerospace appeared to have the key to the garden door to Number 10. Certainly I never once knew Number 10 come up with any decision that would be incommoding to British Aerospace, even when they came bitterly to regret the public consequences, as they did in overruling me on the supply of Hawk spares to Zimbabwe.

My first meeting is with Tony, who has asked me to call for reasons unknown. I pause to polish my shoes – one of the public school traits which he retains is compulsive shoe-polishing. However, when I arrive I am intercepted by Jonathan Powell who explains that the Master is still in his flat. I find Tony sitting with his feet up on the sofa in a tracksuit and barefoot. I try to soften the inappropriate glare from my reflective footwear behind the fabric on the easy chair. He comes to the point. He will be out of the country from 2 to 8 January and so will John Prescott. Would I take over the shop and be the duty Cabinet minister for the period. I respond, 'Happy to oblige. I'll be in London over the period and am only a walk away across the park.' I cannot resist teasing him a little bit by adding, 'It may be necessary to resolve one or two points of policy. For instance I could take the opportunity to confirm that the next General Election will be held on proportional representation.'

What is interesting is not that I've been asked but those who have not been asked. The logical person to ask would be Gordon Brown, and it is a weakness of this government that the Prime Minister would not dream of inviting his Chancellor to stand in and wonder what policy announcement might be made in his absence.

He is very exercised with Clare Short briefing the *Guardian* over the Tanzania deal. I point out that Clare is a formidable operator because she is so well briefed. I say, 'Hats off to Clare, she reads all the telegrams and knows what is happening.' He responds, 'Thanks, but I'll keep my hat on all the same.'

The rest of the day is mostly taken up with flying up to Livingston and back for an emergency meeting on the NEC closure. West Lothian Council has an excellent local economics team but their figures are so depressing today that I rather wish they were not quite so on the ball. Startlingly, we have lost 40 per cent of our manufacturing jobs within a single year. Not so surprising when you recognise that Motorola and NEC, who have both closed down completely, were the second and the third largest private-sector employers in the district.

The meeting was a striking example of how industrial politics have moved on in the past decade. Back in the eighties the meeting would have been all about what protest or action we could take to compel the company to change its mind. Today nobody even asked if there was any prospect that the company would change its mind. Instead we had a businesslike discussion on what we can do to offset the blow to the local economy, such as getting a local connection to broadband. Of course this is the right and mature response, but it does underline the decline of participatory democracy. Challenging factory closures was the stuff of mass-movement politics. But who goes on a demonstration to demand the broadband connection?

I fly home encouraged by the rational knowledge that I'd been to a useful meeting, and depressed by the emotional truth that I'm getting too old to feel comfortable with the spirit of the times.

Thursday 20 December

Much hilarity in the Private Office at an e-mail from the top floor. It advises them that 'The Queen's Christmas card has arrived.' We are cordially invited to visit the mantelpiece to admire it. Ah well, I suppose such an event should be big news in the Privy Council.

In the late afternoon Tammy and Tasker came back from their training camp in Wales. Strictly speaking their registered names are Tamdhu and Talisker, but it is a bit embarrassing standing in the park calling for a couple of Scotch whiskies. Gaynor was immensely excited to see them and, flatly refusing to stay aloof when they came out of the van, swooped down and hugged them contrary to guidelines on conduct appropriate to a pack leader. We all went for a celebratory walk in the park, and there's no doubt that they are much improved. Not exactly quite on message, but definitely responding to the noise of the pager.

Monday 24–Wednesday 26 December

Chris, my older son, came round on Christmas Eve and flung open the door with characteristic exuberance and a cry of 'Blessings on this House'. He was in champagnoise form, bubbly, breezy, effervescent and incapable of being recorked. Chris is as happy as a sandboy getting paid to follow horse racing. Ours is an example of influence in reverse. Instead of my son acquiring his passion from his father's hobby, it is the father who has acquired his notorious enthusiasm for horse racing in order to keep abreast of his child's fixation. Since he was about eight he has inveigled me into accompanying him to racecourses all over Britain. Indeed, I recall that when it slipped out that I took Chris to the races, Roy Hattersley's Yorkshire Methodism was affronted. 'You mean you take a child with you to a racecourse?' On the contrary – it was the other way round.

I have always felt it deeply unpatriotic to go to a warm climate for Christmas. It's not a real Christmas unless your breath hangs in the cold air and the sun sets in time for afternoon tea. Last year I got into the bad books of Sir Richard Wilson by offering the advice, 'Never trust a man who goes abroad for Christmas' when he was just about to fly out of the country.

On Christmas Day all three of us took Tammy and Tasker for a walk in a crisp, clear and largely deserted St James's Park. It is a delight at this time of year when you can actually find a spot of solitude in central London. For most of the year it is more a thoroughfare of busy commuters and bored tourists. Tammy and Tasker are now as obedient as it is within the character of a Scottish terrier to be. Estelle Morris would be proud of the expansion in their literacy. They now know the meaning of 'Stay', and if you catch them in a good mood will admit they know the meaning of 'Fetch'.

On Boxing Day we all went down to Kempton. Gaynor had a very happy day without stirring from the Directors' Room, chatting most of the time with Jenny McCririck. I suspect they were the only two people in the whole of Kempton who talked about dogs more than horses in the course of the day. Chris and I ran from paddock to grandstand and back again to the bookies' ring. Chris picked up a long-priced winner in an early race. I had a valuable exacta by predicting the first and second in the big race, the King George VI Chase. We were, though, humbled by Gaynor who, without stirring from her table, picked three winners out of six, including the winner of the last race who had been spotted by so few others that it came in at 14–1. She even beat into second my choice, Oliver Cromwell, which made her almost guilty of a breach of parliamentary privilege.

Monday 7 January 2002

The interview with Jackie Ashley in the *Guardian* comes with an editorial taking me to task for using the word 'Dickensian' to describe Parliament's procedures and style. The *Guardian* comes out resoundingly on the side of Dickens, recalling his own strong support for reform.

My Sunday interview on *Frost* and the interview of Andrew Smith, the Chief Secretary, on *The World This Weekend* are written up as expressing 'diametrically opposed perspectives on the euro'. This is hilarious as Andrew tells me he listened carefully to my interview and made sure he used the same phrases in order to prevent such mischief. The truth is all the press know that in reality Gordon does take a different position from the rest of the Cabinet and therefore whatever anyone from the Treasury may actually say, they are doomed to find it written up as expressing a division.

Tuesday 8 January

Long morning meeting mulling over what bills we put forward for the second session. There is no shortage of candidates. There never is. But there is a distinct absence of any political logic to the higgledy-piggledy pile assembled by the Cabinet Secretariat. It was a telling illustration of the extent to which we are dwindling into a government running an administration, rather than a political movement trying to change society. Charles Clarke brings a healthy political eye to the discussion: 'What we need to do is first of all establish what is the political narrative for the second session, and then identify the bills which fit that narrative. We cannot produce a programme for the second session which simply consists of those bills which are conveniently ready.'

Wednesday 9 January

Quite the most entertaining meeting of the PLP I have attended in thirty years. Derry came down – I think that is how he would express it – to address us on House of Lords reform. This was a wicked idea by Meg who suggested he should be exposed to opinion in the Commons by being asked to speak at the PLP. It worked beyond our wildest dreams. The masterstroke was holding it on the first Wednesday back after a break when there's a large attendance of colleagues wanting to get back in touch with each other.

I have never actually heard a Cabinet minister heckled before in the PLP and it is a chilling expression of displeasure. Derry brought it on himself by self-importantly lecturing them that they could not have more than 120 elected members of the second chamber because there were already too many peers who were there for life. This message did not gain ready acceptance with MPs who are up for compulsory career review every four years.

Twenty MPs spoke in the subsequent discussion, and only one had a good word to say for Derry's proposals. Wyn Griffiths was loudly cheered when he told Derry that the proposals were unacceptable. Some of those who spoke were among the loyalist members of the PLP. Even good-natured Joyce Quinn told him, 'It is difficult to be proud of these proposals.' But the awkward squad were also in strong voice, relishing the fact that for once they had the PLP behind them and the Cabinet in front of them. One of them was jocularly candid that his preferred solution was, 'One Lord, one Lamp-post.'

Derry did not help himself at the end by failing to show the slightest understanding of the strength of feeling in the audience in front of him. Instead, he chose to hector them with the threat that if they would not agree they would not get anything. 'The alternative to doing something is to do nothing.' We might have started the revolution at this point if Gareth Williams had not intervened with what was one of the finest and most carefully judged rescue operations I have seen at a political meeting. Unlike Derry he had the wit to realise that he had to modulate the government approach. He did so by very neatly shifting the White Paper from being presented as the last word on the subject. 'These plans are not the ultimate prize. They are a part of the journey.' Remarkably, when he sat down he got as good a round of applause as any of the critics of the White Paper.

Thursday 10 January

I spent the afternoon in the Chamber attending the debate on our House of Lords White Paper. By the end of the debate the White Paper was firmly skewered to the floor with the printer's ink fading from every page. There is simply nobody left who can believe that a bill based on this White Paper will get through the House. It is as dead as *Monty Python*'s famous parrot.

Friday 11 January

I went back to the constituency to find refuge. Photoshoot of the day is of me launching a campaign for a high-fibre diet in the Colorectal Unit at St John's. The nurses have saved a month's supply of gifts of chocolates and biscuits from grateful patients. I am photographed rejecting this mouth-watering chocolate mountain and receiving, with eyes that light up in gratitude, a basket of fruit from the ward sister. This asceticism is so out of character that it has Gaynor in stitches of derisive laughter when I describe it afterwards. I am one of nature's unsaveable chocoholics.

John Duncan, my constituency assistant, produces an oleaginous letter from the *Mail on Sunday You Magazine*. For over two years they have been sending such letters to Gaynor begging her for an interview. Gaynor has stuck to a firm rule, ever since the first dark days, that she does not speak to the press. At first I thought she was mistaken, but now I regard it as immense wisdom on her part. She has preserved her dignity and her privacy throughout all these turbulent years, and has not provided a single sentence on which the press could rest a word of criticism.

In the evening we took my Member for the Scottish Parliament, Bristow Muldoon, and his wife, Cathy for dinner. It was a very pleasant occasion, and as it was at Livingston's largest Chinese restaurant, it should be all over town by Sunday that we were there together. I constantly thank my luck and my constituency party that I have such a sane, steady colleague in Bristow.

Sunday 13 January

I addressed my constituency party. There was a querulous edge to some of the discussion that followed. One of the central paradoxes of Labour activists is that they hold it to be a truth that is self-evident that the press are liars, but that does not stop them believing the press when it tells them that their government is failing them.

Moreover, they never hear Tony talking to them in terms of how we have dramatically reduced child poverty, and greatly widened job opportunities. The danger for Tony is that the sole reason he has retained the affection and support of the party is because he has delivered phenomenal popularity for the party. The risk is that if he ever loses that popularity, there will be no other reason left for the party to give him their support.

Monday 14 January

Hilary came round for our regular Start the Week exchange. I asked her, 'Where do you think we are on Lords reform after last week's debates?' 'No one thinks we can get the present package through. We'll have to look at what changes will get us more support.' 'Yes,' I responded, 'but we're going to have to make real changes to get that support. We will not get the centre of gravity support for reform unless we propose at least half of the new second chamber are elected.' To my surprise Hilary responded vigorously: 'Oh, there's no way you'll get that through the PLP. The majority would be opposed to such a large number of elected members in the Lords.' I found this implausible. Almost half the backbenchers have signed the Early Day Motion calling for a Lords that is 'wholly or substantially elected'. Nearly every speaker at the PLP and during the Commons debate had demanded such a package. Indeed, my problem was in trying to make headway with the argument that the reformed Chamber should not be wholly elected.

In the evening I addressed the South East Group of Labour MPs as part of my programme of consultation on modernisation. The schedule has me starting with the MPs for the South who are broadly sympathetic, and working up to the more difficult colleagues in the

Northern groups. Martin Salter is in the Chair and I cannot resist beginning by recalling the week after the reshuffle when I was sitting in the tearoom in what I described as 'a state of ambivalence', when Martin breezed in and said to me, 'I read somewhere that you wanted on your tombstone that you were Labour's longest serving Foreign Secretary. I thought what crap to have on your tombstone. Now you have the chance of a tombstone that says, "He brought Parliament into the twenty-first century." Now that would be something really worth having on a tombstone.'

Tuesday 15 January

In the evening I took Gareth Williams for dinner at Wilton's. They gave us the booth at the far end of the restaurant where only a couple of tables can even see us and nobody can overhear us. A perfect environment for a frank and confiding exchange of views. I had planned to spend the first course bonding, and only later in the meal work up to the difficult question of Lords reform. Helpfully, Gareth got straight down to brass tacks before we'd even ordered.

'I believe I can do a deal with Shirley Williams if I'm allowed to talk to her. If we think Derry's figure of a hundred and twenty elected members is the magic number, then we can preserve it by electing a hundred and twenty at each of three successive General Elections, which would give a majority of elected members in the new Chamber of six hundred.'

Gareth then said, 'There is the problem of what we do with the Bishops and the Law Lords.' Before he could go further I interrupted him by saying, 'Oh, come on, Gareth – the Bishops and the Law Lords have no place in any modern second chamber.' In reply he smiled and said, 'How about a proposal that we should replace the Law Lords with a Supreme Court, a modern, purpose-built building entirely separate from the House of Lords. Politicians have no place appointing judges. We are very superior when President Mugabe takes emergency powers to do it in Zimbabwe, but we do it all the time in Britain.'

I was taken aback by the degree of radicalism which Gareth displayed, and rather suspect that the Prime Minister would have been even more. He was enthusiastic about Anthony Lester's bill to provide a legal status for stable but unmarried partners, both gay and mixed sex. 'Most young people today are not marrying. If we want to connect with young people today we've got to show that we understand how they live. They are the people who will most support us in our referendum on the euro because they think nothing of travelling through Europe and are not afraid of it. But they won't vote for us if they think we don't understand them.'

I left Wilton's feeling I'd found a new common spirit. Better still, one with whom I can make cause upon a common project.

Wednesday 16 January

Tony spoke to a packed meeting of the PLP this morning. He has an attractive, well-pitched style for them. He does not address them as a public rally, but is discursive and gives the appearance of taking them into his confidence. He also understands the importance of giving them a bit of a lift and ends – the first time I've heard him say it – 'Now is the time to set the goal of winning an historic third time.' This, of course, is exactly what his audience wants to hear. He sits down to thunderous applause. For all that, he has not actually said anything new. The four mantras of Blairism remain the structure of his speech – stable economy; tough on individual responsibility; investment plus reform in public services; strong on defence and engaged in the world. This is all good stuff for keeping our eyes fixed on the snow-capped mountains in the distance. He didn't actually have much to say about the immediate problems beneath our feet. The PLP did.

Dennis Skinner and Peter Pike may both be from very different political wings of the party, but they share the same roots and backgrounds in the party grass roots. Dennis tells him, 'Out there in the country we are not recruiting hardly at all. If you find you are facing a crisis you will find that there is not a party behind you.' Peter Pike, more soberly, adds, 'I have never known membership so low, or so few members doing anything on the streets.' In his case it is particularly serious because of the real threat of the BNP in Burnley. Nick Palmer, who sometimes is too thoughtful to appear streetwise, can nevertheless come up with a penetrating insight. This afternoon he puts his finger on the reason for seepage in party activity: 'People do not join parties or love governments because they are inspired by managerial change.'

Tony, as he often does, gives a better reply to the discussion than the initial presentation. I thought he was at his weakest in responding to the criticism of the image of the al-Qa'ida prisoners in Guantanamo Bay manacled, held in cages and open to the elements. Everybody in the audience would have understood why he could not criticise the United States in public, but left perplexed that he was not more understanding in private of their concerns. Even Labour MPs fail to understand that Tony's support for the United States is not a calculation of *realpolitik*, but a deeply held conviction.

In the afternoon Andrew Adonis comes to see me about where we go on House of Lords reform. For all that he is a special adviser he is too much the perfect civil servant openly to encourage me to persist in my strategy of undermining the official position. Nevertheless, he is very helpful in mapping out the pitfalls ahead and suggesting how I get round them. I explain that I am writing to Tony with my thoughts. 'I am stressing that we must have a clear vision of the state where we want to end up. If we can offer the public a credible and popular vision of a reformed second chamber we will get their understanding and tolerance of the transition steps that are necessary to get there.' Carefully he responds, 'If this is your thinking you really must spell it out clearly to Tony. His conclusion from the objections to the White Paper is that we should focus on approaching reform in stages and make the next step abolishing the remaining hereditary peers.' I was stunned. 'That is simply not to understand the depth of our problem. Replacing the House of Lords with a House of Cronies will be seen as no more popular than what went before.'

Thursday 17 January

At Cabinet some heart-searching about where we are in public perception. Pat Hewitt observed that part of our problem with the Health Service is that we were so successful in Opposition in convincing the public that any reform of the NHS must be part of a secret plot to privatise it. At which point Tony good-naturedly said, 'So it's all the fault of Robin.'

Immediately after Business Statement I rushed along to the far end to address the PLP group in the House of Lords. It was a cunning plan to give me the opportunity to meet them, but to keep the discussion safe on the basis of me informing them of our plans to modernise the Commons rather than our lack of plans to modernise the Lords. It worked a treat, but partly because they are such very, very *nice* people. It is terribly tempting to be patronising, coming from the rough end of Parliament where we still practise the hard school of political scrummage, but I suspect that their courteous and thoughtful style is more attractive to the public than our blood-and-thunder debates.

Saturday 19 January

A fun evening when John and Jenny McCririck came for dinner. John blew through the door even larger than life than usual. He got Tammy and Tasker so excited that they were beside themselves at such a fun pack leader. John and Jenny had just come up from Kempton where they had been attending the Lanzarote meeting. John and I remembered that it was this meeting fifteen years ago which launched Christopher on his career of horse tipping. I had done ten minutes straight discussion with John on the politics of racing and he ended it by turning to Christopher and asking him for his racing tip. Chris had responded by nominating Atlaal, which stood at 14–1 for the Lanzarote Hurdle. To my consternation the odds immediately shortened to 10–1 as Labour supporters around Britain piled on to a politically sound tip. And it did win. I have never been so excited at any race finish before or since. It is the only time I actually threw my hat away. For months afterwards taxi drivers would slow down after picking me up and say, 'I made a nice touch out of that Atlaal.'

Monday 21 January

George Cubie and Alan Sandall, the two clerks to the Modernisation Committee, come round for a long chat about my latest text on select committee reform. The report balances additional resources, specialist staff and administrative support for the select committee with the discipline of a new statement of core tasks. Taken in the round, the report adds up to the most comprehensive overhaul of the select committee system since it was created just over twenty years ago. About time they had an MOT. Select committees have proved a far better way of bringing ministers under scrutiny than the Chamber. It is almost always possible to evade difficult questions in the brief sprints at the Despatch Box in oral questions. It is much more difficult to get away with such devices when you're stuck in front of a sub-committee for an hour and a half facing repeated questions. As a result they have produced some revealing and troubling reports.

Tuesday 22 January

The morning is taken up with interviews for my assistant on House of Lords reform. One of the applicants worked for the Stevenson Commission when they were preparing the list of so-called 'People's Peers'. 'But the PR disaster was not their fault,' I threw out, hoping it would lead somewhere interesting. 'No,' she replied, 'but they could have been much more courageous. There were a lot of very suitable candidates with an excellent record of a lifetime in ordinary professions, such as a very popular woman GP. But they played safe. They went for exactly the great and the good who would have got appointed under the old system.' In the end, I appoint a young and engagingly idiosyncratic candidate who was mercifully free of the Civil Service standard responses.

In the evening Derry offers me his return match on our dinner exchanges. He has chosen Maison Novelli in Smithfield, the heart of the London Dickens knew. When I arrive I discover it was also in a state which Dickens would have recognised as a power cut has plunged the entire street into pre-electricity darkness. As a result I find Derry sitting in a restaurant lit entirely by candlelight. The effect is to make our rendezvous appear even more conspiratorial than we had planned it.

He was not the self-confident, buoyant Derry whom the world knows and, up to a point, loves. Despite our sinking two bottles of wine together and a whisky apiece, he remained subdued. He was obviously personally wounded at the tidal wave of criticism which the White Paper provoked, and hurt by his reception by the PLP. The real puzzle is what kind of reaction he ever expected to his White Paper. God knows, I tried to warn him. The danger for the government, though, is that Derry's reaction to the criticism is not to improve the package to blunt the force of criticism, but to retreat in petulance into his shell. In brief, his attitude was that he had tried to come up with a solution, the nation didn't like it, well the nation will jolly well not get anything. 'Of course, doing nothing must be an option available to us,' he claims. 'But we will be drowned under an even bigger tidal wave of criticism if you do nothing,' I retort. 'Can you imagine what the press will say the first time we appoint more political peers without any prospect of reform?' 'It'll be a one-day wonder and then blow over.' I fear the office of Lord Chancellor, the oldest in government, is something of a time machine hurtling its occupant back through the centuries. Derry tonight sounds straight out of the Establishment before the 1832 Reform Act. He seriously asks me, 'But are there enough people of calibre out there to fill an elected House of Lords?'

In compensation for his bruising encounters with the press, Derry is keen to impress on me his close ties to Tony and the many visits by Tony and Cherie to his house in Argyll. 'Tony never wanted any elected members of the House of Lords. Wakeham let us all down. He was put in to find a formula by which every member of the House of Lords would continue to be appointed. It was Wakeham who let the genie out of the bottle.'

D erry is normally apportioned most of the blame for the failure of the government to bring the House of Lords into the democratic era, because he is credited with a Svengali-like hold over his former pupil at Number 10. I fear this is unjust to Derry and too generous to Tony Blair. It is true that both of them encouraged the perception that Derry was the dominant figure by hamming up their respective past roles. Derry frequently referred to the Prime Minister as 'young Blair' and Tony Blair would describe the Lord Chancellor as 'my old pupil master'. But this was strictly for the entertainment of bystanders. In the power relationship between them it was always the Prime Minister who had the upper hand. In the epic struggle between Derry and David Blunkett over the tilt in the rules of evidence to ensure conviction, the Prime Minister consistently came down against his old pupil master in his attempts to sustain the rights of the accused. It is an awkward truth for modernisers to face, but the reason we are to be lumbered with an all-appointed House of Lords is because that is what Tony Blair has always wanted. Derry was never the real obstacle to an elected second chamber, but was only trying to deliver the Prime Minister's preferred option of an appointed one.

Unfortunately, my resignation opened the way for Number 10 to abandon any search for a democratic version of reform and to commit the government to a wholly appointed House of Lords 'in a stable state for the medium term'. Modernisation is to be limited to moving from the fifteenth-century principle of heredity to the eighteenth-century principle of patronage. In effect, the three party leaders will become responsible for selecting three quarters of the members of the new second chamber. Ironically, this expansion of party patronage comes at the very time when the wider public is increasingly alienated by political parties and their culture of discipline and patronage. More patronage will in turn strengthen the new political culture of discipline as it enhances the power of the party chiefs to reward and encourage good conduct. Those selected for appointment will not be the independent spirits who would make the second chamber a creative, exciting parliamentary institution. Appointment is more likely to put a premium on that colourless bane of modern party politics, the safe pair of hands. The harsh reality is that a second chamber will be taken seriously only if it has to be taken seriously, and no Prime Minister need take too seriously a body to which he makes the biggest number of appointments.

Nor can the damage of greater party patronage be undone by a token number of independent appointees. The fiasco of the so-called People's Peers exposed the impossibility of reconciling an elite and unaccountable system of appointment with a representative and popular outcome. The term People's Peers had raised expectations which were never going to be fulfilled. Its invention is often laid at the door of Alastair Campbell but this is not entirely fair. The reality is that he had been asked by a mischievous journalist whether the forthcoming nominations could be described as the People's Peers and, as has happened occasionally to all of us in public life, he just was not fast enough in shouting 'No' before the phrase was hung round his neck. Unfortunately for all of us, there could be nothing less plebeian than the safe, conventional sample of the establishment that was subsequently served up by the Appointments Commission. A typical example was the selection of Elspeth Howe, who was already titled as a result of marriage to a knight and again as a result of his subsequent promotion to a peer, prompting the observation that she was once, twice, three times a lady.

The net result was such a public relations disaster that through-out the two years I was in the loop, ministers were relieved the Appointments Commission did not to come up with any more names. There is an odd contrast between the conviction of Number 10 that appointment is the best entry route to the second chamber and their terror of making any appointments because they are so unpopular. This unpopularity is not the fault of the members of the Appointments Commission. They are all estimable people, whose main fault is a predictable tendency to pick people like themselves and, famously in one case, to choose someone who selected themselves. The problem is deeply embedded in a system in which the great and the good choose others from their number to rule over us. Unless the public have their say in the process, no system of picking lawmakers will command public confidence.

We come back to the question of trust, which now is such a major problem for the government. Trust is a two-way process. You cannot secure trust simply by asserting that you are trustworthy. You can only win trust by showing that you are willing to work in a spirit of mutual respect with those whose trust you seek. Politicians who make it plain that they do not trust the public to elect the right people to rule over them have no prospect of securing the trust of that same public. Nor do they deserve it.

—·ɯɯ·—

3

A Bridge Too Far

23 JANUARY–14 MAY 2002

Wednesday 23 January

In the afternoon Lorna brought round to see me a group of the key MPs campaigning for a more democratic solution to the House of Lords, led by Chris Bryant and Fiona Mactaggart. They are an impressive bunch and represent the future of the party in the way that those opposing a democratic solution represent its past. They have carried out an instructive poll of the members of the PLP. It shows that the proportion favoured for election by Labour MPs is all over the place, but with three quarters of the total in favour of a majority-elected House.

Before I leave the office a letter is put in front of me about Lord Lester's bill, which comes up in the Lords on Friday. It proposes a register for unmarried couples in order to provide a basis for regularising their legal rights. The draft of the letter in front of me proposes in formulaic terms that Gareth Williams should oppose the measure on Friday on the standard basis that it is not government policy. Moreover, giving unmarried partners legal rights might cost us something in Social Security benefits. I put a line through the draft and dictate my own, recommending that on Friday we take a position of 'studied neutrality'. This is precisely the type of issue which should be left to backbenchers. It reflects a new and growing social reality which needs to be addressed, but which is difficult for government to address because it raises sensitive moral questions on which there are strong passions. It is in direct line with reforming private members' legislation of the 60s and 70s on divorce, homosexuality and capital punishment.

Friday 25 January

A flying visit to the constituency. We go out to Addiewell to unveil a memorial to those from the community killed in both wars and in mining accidents. Addiewell is one of those many communities in isolated spots across Britain which retain the culture and solidarity of a mining community decades after they have lost the mines. It is inconceivable to Addiewell that they could put up a memorial to those killed fighting Hitler without also putting up a memorial to those killed winning coal and shale oil.

It's a strange and indefinable thing, community spirit. Every politician agrees we need more of it but none of us can artificially conjure it up. Addiewell has few practical assets going for it. It is planted in a bleak, high moor, where no one would have put a settlement if they could not make money out of the geology below it. It has no architectural feature other than council housing of pre-war and post-war years. And it now has little local industry. Those in the village who do manage to stay in work mostly find their work a long journey from home.

Yet despite all that it has a stronger, fiercer sense of community, pride and solidarity than you'll find in Windsor or Maidenhead. The memorial, for instance, has a statement not just of their respect for their past but an assertion of their pride in their present community and identity. So here we are now, in a snowstorm, over six hundred feet above sea level, posing by the new stone cairn in the hope that my presence will persuade the local paper to carry a photograph, which they failed to do at the official opening.

Sunday 27 January

My red box contains the press cuttings and reports on Derry's appearance before the Public Administration Committee. He appears to have been at his most defiant, Olympian worst. There was a calculated put-down of me when he was asked about what had been said by Robin Cook and replied, 'Robin who?' There was a flat refusal to face reality that most MPs want a majority-elected House. Indeed, the lack of contact with reality is so great that John Lyons, a Scottish member of the committee, interjected, 'I have a feeling you'd bet on Bolton Wanderers to win the Premiership.' At this rate we are certainly not going to be winning a consensus on reform of the Lords.

Monday 28 January

Meg, who had attended the Public Administration Committee for me, drops by to give me her read-out. I ask her if it was as entertaining as the papers made out, and she replies, 'I know this may make me a rather sad person, but I can't remember when I last had so much fun.'

When Gareth comes round for our weekly chat I put to him Derry's assertion that Tony does not want a single elected member in the Lords. Gareth looks unconvinced. 'That may have been true once upon a time, but it isn't true now.' Gareth himself believes he can get through the Lords a package which would provide for 50 per cent of the new membership to be elected. I know that he has discussed his plan with Tony and that he believes he was encouraged to go away and explore this option with the Liberals and others, but I also know Tony's immense capacity to leave the last person who spoke to him with the impression of his total agreement.

Mercifully, I could forget it all for the evening as Gaynor and I, special advisers and Stephen Twigg, were booked into the Camden Jazz Café to hear Georgie Fame. It is a testimony to the pressures of political life that this is actually the Christmas office outing for which there was no space at the right time. When we are all gathered David Mathieson lifts his wineglass and toasts, 'Merry Christmas'.

Tuesday 29 January

In the afternoon I had a heated meeting with Hilary to whom I have sent a copy of the draft report on select committees. She arrives with a large posse in which she has pressed into service half of Number 10. She is particularly worked up over the proposal for a Commons Committee of Nominations. This she sees as an affront to the new system we have agreed in the PLP to decide on the Labour nominations. 'What we want is a system that puts the party nominations before the Commons and does not make any changes.' Not unreasonably I point out that there is no way I can draft a standing order that stipulates the Committee of Nominations shall not make any change to nominations. Even the old Committee of Selection in theory could have done that. The real problem, of course, is that the old Committee of Selection was controlled by the whips and this new committee will not be.

In the end I offer a deal. I will go through the text and remove any prejudicial reference to whips, or political parties, but I cannot tamper with the recommendations which are not mine but the committee's. Most of the rest of those present stayed quiet and kept their heads down, as children do when the two leading members of the family are shouting at each other and throwing the plates around.

All engagements have been scrubbed for the afternoon so I can do the redraft of the text in an attempt to defuse the confrontation with Hilary. In the late evening Lorna rounds up as many of the Labour members of the Modernisation Committee as she can find and I take them into my confidence about the degree of our problem with the whips. They are all remarkably sweet and reasonable. Martin Salter even welcomes the fact that if we can get the whips on board with these changes it is a price worth paying. Nobody wants to pick a fight so long as we can retain all the policy recommendations.

Wednesday 30 January

I began the Modernisation Committee by cheering them up with the fact that we had an agreement with the Speaker and the Deputy Speaker on the Committee of Nominations. Before the general grunts of satisfaction had ebbed I then plunged in and explained that we had a problem with the whips on both sides. There followed a prolonged and delicate discussion. I had two things going for me. The first is that I have built up a lot of goodwill with the opposition parties by the trouble I have taken to build consensus within the committee. The second is that most of the committee are realistic and practical, who want to get things done rather than produce a sensational report that is going nowhere.

Our dilemma was bluntly but perfectly expressed by John Taylor: 'If we want we can, of course, write a report that pleases us and rejects the changes. We will all feel good about it. But there will be a price. And if that price is resistance to our recommendation then I don't think we should pay it.' It helped, of course, that there were to be no changes to the conclusions and recommendations. On that basis I was able to secure an agreement to delete all references in the narrative text that would offend the sensibilities of the whips.

Later I was given the privilege of addressing the Women's Group on my modernisation plans. They were all enthusiastic supporters of modernisation. But what struck me most about the meeting was the absence of gesture politics or playing to the gallery. The discussion was mature and non-combative. Once again I was struck that one of the most important catalysts for cultural change in the Commons would be a proper gender balance with a couple of hundred more women.

In the evening Gaynor and I go for dinner to L'Oranger with Swraj and Aruna Paul. Swraj has been one of the most successful steel magnates on the globe and the only one to be given honorary membership of the steelworkers' unions. He is straight, honest and deeply committed to social values. A couple of years ago when he got wind that Tony Blair was going to attend the Hindujas' Diwali he asked me to warn Tony against going. I did so with vigour and remember telling him, 'Don't go. If necessary break a leg to find the excuse but don't go.' He listened politely but he still went. The result is that any time the Hinduja scandal is back in the news we have the photograph yet again of Tony and Cherie at the Diwali side by side with the Hinduja sponsors.

Thursday 31 January

My cuttings include the latest MORI poll in *The Times*. This shows Labour on 51 per cent and the Conservatives on a miserable 27 per cent, figures which would give us an even larger majority than we obtained on polling day. Bizarrely, *The Times* report this crushing support for Labour with the headline 'Gloss Comes Off Blair'. If politicians ever attempted to spin as brazenly as press sub-editors we would be rightly pilloried.

Perhaps because of this helpful encouragement the mood at Cabinet was very good-humoured. When Clare mentioned that Mugabe had gone to Malaysia to visit a top hospital there, Alan Milburn jocularly made a pretence of noting that Malaysia has top hospitals that will take foreigners. Tony, before he went out to catch the new leader of Afghanistan, said, 'And if you believe you have problems in your Department, just listen to the problems that he has.' Steve Byers then brought the roof down by asking, 'What kind of railway system does he have?'

Hamid Karzai himself I found seriously impressive. He is sophisticated, urbane and has fluent command of idiomatic English. He was sober about the challenges he faces, but not crushed by them. He was candid about the extent to which the Taliban had systematically looted Afghanistan: 'When we went to the banks there were no notes left.' He then added dryly, in a rather Western touch of national self-deprecation, 'They even took the Afghan notes which they had printed in trillions.'

Friday 1 February

As it was a Friday we had taken advantage of the absence of duties in the House to fix a seminar arranged by my old friend Ivor Gaber on political disengagement. The discussion was much more thoughtful and certainly better informed than most I hear in the House. It was also desperately depressing for a professional politician.

First, there was pessimism about the prospects for reviving election turnout. We live in a marketised and therefore individualised society. People are accustomed to taking individual decisions and actions that demonstrate control over what happens to themselves and immediate family and home. They are no longer accustomed to taking part in collectivist decisions that have a bearing on the health of their community.

Secondly, there was gloom about the widening gap between political parties and the voters. Society is now much less tribal than before. As one participant put it, 'Party politics were once part of the web of people's lives. Today people don't talk politics in the home and not much in the workplace.' As a result of the decline in identity with political parties, the politicians whom the public most admire are those who talk from the heart, not from a party line. They are not into the pager politics of New Labour.

Finally, there was depression about alienation of the public from democratic process. There is now a perception that politics is a matter for politicians. It is something that is done to people, not something in which the people themselves have any control. Hence a growing tendency in election behaviour to use the ballot box to give politicians a good kicking. This trend is enhanced by the growth in celebrity-driven politics, which is necessarily top-down and the opposite of mass democratic politics.

The problem with academics is that they can be ruthlessly frank. If a professional politician was half as honest he would not be praised for talking from the heart, but accused of committing a 'gaffe'. Nor are they under any obligation, like politicians, to pretend that the problem has a solution. Indeed, to the academic the growth in political disengagement is a social phenomenon, not a problem. The discussion therefore was not, as they would say in Downing Street, solution-orientated. There were pointers to things that would help, but they appeared modest against the awesome tide of social revolution around us. For starters, Parliament needed to come across much less as a ritual from a bygone era. As one ruthlessly frank academic put it, 'The Scottish Parliament and Welsh Assembly are not inspiring, but at least they look normal. Parliament does not look normal.'

I left feeling both intellectually stimulated at the quality of the discussion, and politically depressed by its conclusions.

Tuesday 5 February

A day's outing to Wales. I got my fill of foreign travel in my last post, and all the jet-setting got in the way of what I really love, which is pottering about Britain. Journalists and MPs are privileged in at least one respect: we both have endless reason to explore Britain and Britain's wide variety of economic and cultural activities.

My contribution to the Ogmore by-election campaign takes me to an economic activity totally new to me – the mass production of toilet rolls. The boardroom proudly displays the finished product in alternate rows of Sainsbury's, Tesco and Safeway branding. All from the same production line, by the same process and by the same workforce. The candidate, Huw Irranca-Davies, and I wander through the immense cathedral-like vaults of the processing line trying to sound intelligent and to look interested in the competition challenges to the toilet-roll industry. Mercifully not much globalisation here as the stuff is too bulky to transport. Most of the time, though, our brains are racing trying to avoid the caption traps being dug for us by the accompanying posse of photographers. A party worker swiftly and firmly intervenes to veto the proposal that we are photographed sitting on a gigantic toilet roll waiting to be shredded into a hundred thousand versions of a domestic size.

I got back in time for an evening drink with Steve Byers. He has had a rough time over faults with Railtrack which were none of his making. Just as Alan Milburn, perfectly understandably, blames the Treasury for having boxed him in to private finance initiatives and then walked away to leave him to face the music, Steve Byers blames the Treasury for refusing to put extra money into transport in our first two years, which could now be producing results. I told Steve not to let the press coverage get him down. 'Every contact I have with the public convinces me that your decision to take Railtrack out of private ownership is the most popular thing we have done since the election.'

Wednesday 6 February

At the Modernisation Committee we finally completed agreement on our report on select committees. John Taylor made a characteristically offbeat and entertaining speech in which he complained that the Labour Whips' Office had got too worked up. 'In the Tory Party the Whips' Office is regarded as the officers' mess of a cavalry regiment. They are the elite, and the people from whom future leaders will emerge. In the Labour Party you still regard them at best as the NCOs who will not be going any further. That is why they get so easily rattled when they should be taking a more detached view.'

In the evening Yevgeny Primakov, the former Russian Foreign Minister and Prime Minister, had asked me round for dinner. He was warm in recalling the time we worked through the night in Geneva to get common agreement among the Security Council permanent members to condemn the Indian and Pakistan nuclear tests. I refrained from reminding him of his consternation in Paris when Yeltsin without warning announced that from that day no Russian missiles would be targeted on NATO. Sitting next to me Primakov muttered that the translator had misunderstood what his President had said.

He was in good form, and Russians are more relaxed now than ever before in accepting a place in Europe. The conversation also skirted round the growing problems for both our nations from the increasingly aggressive unilateralism of the Bush Administration. Curiously, his view was that it is a bigger problem for Britain. Nobody now expects the Russia of the post-Cold War era to be able to stop the Americans. Everybody imagines that Tony Blair with his hot line to President Bush will be able to restrain him, and as a result Britain also gets the blame when the world discovers that he cannot.

Friday 8 February

A day in the constituency. Or perhaps a day in the middle of Japan. The morning was entirely taken up with visits to Japanese factories. The NEC plant has started the process of descent towards full closure in two months' time. It is a surprisingly caring, considerate closure. The operation to help employees find new openings is on a grand scale and takes over the whole of the foyer entrance and neighbouring rooms. This is one of the most successful and skilled hi-tech engineering workforces in Britain, but I was struck, looking down the jobs to which they were going, how few had found openings in manufacturing. The plant director was philosophical about this. 'If they want to carry on being engineers in hi-tech they'll have to leave Britain. That is where the openings are today.' And, indeed, companies from Düsseldorf and Singapore and France are coming to next week's Job Fair.

Saturday 9 February and Sunday 10 February

In my weekend box there's a copy of a letter from Number 10 to Steve Byers' office. Steve had written in response to my trawl for subjects for debate suggesting that we should hold a debate on reform of local government finance. The letter from Number 10 very sharply rapped him over the knuckles for his impertinence. 'On this issue, the Prime Minister doubts that it would be useful to facilitate further parliamentary debate before the government has decided on its preferred approach.' This is a revealing letter. It confines parliamentary debate to those issues on which the Government has already closed its mind. There is not the least glimmer anywhere in this letter of the recognition that the function of government is to respond to the parliamentary view, or even that an exchange of views in Parliament could be helpful to government in defining sensible options.

There is an intriguing report in the *Independent on Sunday* that quotes John Prescott as rejecting any elected element in the House of Lords other than the White Paper's figure of 20 per cent. He has a palpable dig at me in a quote: 'Some are saying that they're looking for a new centre of gravity which talks about a substantial proportion being elected. My centre of gravity is a choice between 100 per cent and zero, and I would like to reassert the option of zero.' What is going on?

Monday 11 February

The press are awash with reports that 'friends of Michael Martin' are convinced that he is the victim of class snobbery. There is actually a lot of truth to this. Personally, I think it is an illustration of the health of democracy that a metalworker from the Gorbals can become the Speaker of the House of Commons. And I believe he is proving a great Speaker. But many in the right-wing press simply find it impossible to take seriously somebody who sounds from the Gorbals. If you want to be taken seriously by them you've got to work like Roy Jenkins at developing an accent that did not locate him anywhere remotely near his origins in South Wales.

In the afternoon I call at Downing Street to brief the Prime Minister on progress on the legislative programme for the second session. Tony is commendably robust about the long fat bills struggling to get down the pipeline. With a few leading questions I guide him into the instructions that we want to hear, and get a mandate for shorter, more focused bills.

I have to leave early to dash back to the House for 3.30 to make a Business Statement. When I get back to my office I ring Clare Sumner, the private secretary in Tony's office who handles parliamentary relations, to find out what happened after I left. Clare has lost her earlier fear of me, and winds me up perfectly by sombrely replying, 'Well, after you left we all agreed that the programme was rubbish and you had a lot more work to do on it.' Maybe it was because every Cabinet minister suspects that is how they talk about him behind his back at Number 10, but for ten seconds I did not realise she was having me on.

Tuesday 12 February

The day begins with the launch of the Modernisation Committee report on select committees. To ensure that it is seen as non-partisan I have asked Paul Tyler for the Liberal Democrats and Nick Winterton for the Tories to join me. Both do a splendid job of presenting the report as a common work.

The proposal for extra pay for Chairs of select committees is the sensitive part of the report, as is entertainingly demonstrated by the man from the Bristol evening paper who asks the first question on whether the Human Rights Committee would qualify for the extra payment, and when told 'Yes' immediately leaves the room to file a headline about Jean Corston, MP for Bristol East, getting more pay. Otherwise those who come treat the matter seriously, even respectfully.

After oral questions Ken Purchase, who has been my PPS since Opposition days, takes me aside in the 'Aye' lobby to share with me a serious piece of intelligence. Apparently the previous night there was a covert meeting of colleagues secretly sworn to resist elections to a reformed House of Lords. Twenty turned up and pledged to defend Commons supremacy over the House of Lords. What made it truly remarkable is that the guest of honour was the author of the White Paper himself, Derry Irvine, who apparently spoke strongly against any elected element, even the 20 per cent in his White Paper. It is truly perverse of Derry to respond to the criticisms of his White Paper for not allowing enough elections by deciding to remove even what elections it had permitted.

Wednesday 13 February

The press is fair to the Modernisation report and the question of paying the Chairs of committees is kept in proportion. The Times is generous, thanks to the very positive reaction of Peter Riddell who has written a laudatory editorial. There is a cartoon of myself with hammer and chisel chipping away at the power base of Tony Blair. As far as the press goes this is the highest flattery they can pay me, but it doesn't actually help me carry my corner in the Cabinet.

Jaime Gama, the Portuguese Foreign Minister, asked me round for breakfast while he was in town. Jaime is now the longest serving Foreign Minister in the European Union. But it is evident from his tone that he does not expect to be so for much longer, as our socialist colleagues in Portugal will be hard pressed to survive next month's election. As a result he is in a confiding mood. 'First, we were relieved that the United Kingdom could exercise restraint on the wilder instincts of the United States. Secondly, when the fighting began in Afghanistan we respected what Britain could do because it has a capacity for such intervention that the rest of us do not. Thirdly, there is now some amusement among the rest of us that Britain gets no reward from the United States for all it has done. President Bush listens no more to the views of Britain than he listens to the views of any of the rest of us.' If these are the conclusions which Portugal has come to, then there is a much bigger problem with other countries who do not have the same tradition of affection for Britain. I leave with a deepening apprehension as to whether Tony can really get away much longer without making a choice on which side of the Atlantic he sees Britain spending the rest of the century.

It is a fixed pole of Tony Blair's view of Britain's place in the world that we must be the No. 1 ally of the US. While Bill Clinton was President this worked well. The two of them shared broadly similar values in their domestic politics and had the same goals in their international strategy. It was not just a matter of the personal chemistry between them, although that was important; there was also real common ground to their politics.

Relationships between Britain and the US were at a low ebb when we took office. The Conservative Party likes to pose as a party that puts the transatlantic relationship above European integration, but in the latter years of the Conservative government relations with the US had gone as sour as with Europe. The White House under Clinton had never forgiven John Major for overtly backing Bush Senior in the election campaign and the State Department had been frustrated by the infuriating caution of the Conservatives on Bosnia and their reluctance to get tough with Milosevic. At our first meeting Madeleine Albright very tentatively asked, 'Can I be frank about your Conservative predecessors?' When I responded that she could be as rude as she liked about them, she turned to her advisers and said, 'This is going to be fun.'

There were real world benefits from the close partnership between the Blair and Clinton teams. The turning point in the Balkans came with the defeat of Milosevic in Kosovo, which was more feasible because the strong axis between Washington and London gave the alliance a spine. Every evening throughout the conflict Madeleine and I would hold a five-way conference call with our opposite numbers in Germany, France and Italy. These were focused exchanges in which we would agree on a united front to the diplomatic and media challenges of the next twenty-four hours, but other priorities sometimes broke in. On one occasion Madeleine was interrupted in mid-flow by a howl that sounded as if someone had stood on the tail of their cat. When she asked what had happened, Joschka Fischer owned up and informed us that Bayern Munich had just hit the bar again in their match with Manchester United, which he was watching while listening to her.

We knew Milosevic's ambassadors kept promising him that NATO's resolve would crack under the strains within the alliance, although we were never sure whether they really believed it or just knew that was what he wanted to hear. But in truth the alliance might not have stayed the course if there had not been such a solid bond between the US and British governments. Or if Tony Blair had not had the warmth of relationship with Bill Clinton that enabled him during a wobbly moment in the NATO Summit to sit up into the small hours with the President, and both their wives, to ensure they agreed that their countries had to do whatever was required to win. It was a time when Britain did indeed prove its value as a bridge between the US and Europe.

It is worth recalling those years of close collaboration with the Clinton Administration to underline that I am not anti-American. It is possible to believe that the foreign policy of President Bush is profoundly mistaken and dangerous for all of us, including the US, without any loss of affection for the American people. Indeed, it is a logical absurdity to argue that to demonstrate a lack of enthusiasm for President Bush is to be anti-American, as most Americans so lacked enthusiasm for him that they did not vote for him.

Sometimes old friends in the Democratic Party ask me in puzzled tones why Tony gets on so well with Bush. They remember how good was the relationship with Clinton and cannot understand how it is possible to achieve the same kind of rapport with someone like Bush who has such flatly opposite politics. It is not quite the same as it was with Bill, although Tony does talk with genuine warmth of his new friend. They have religion in common and, as President Bush famously revealed, they share the same brand of toothpaste. But the real mortar in the relationship is power. It would never occur to Tony Blair that there might be more respect for a Prime Minister who had the courage to say no to someone as powerful as the President of the US. He is programmed to respect power not to rebel against it. Psychologically, Tony Blair is ill-equipped to repeat Harold Wilson's refusal of US demands for British troops in Vietnam. I do not doubt that Tony Blair genuinely believed the world would be better without Saddam. I am certain that the real reason he went to war was that he found it easier to resist the public opinion of Britain than the request of the US President.

When Bush Junior won the election Tony Blair repeatedly expressed his worry to me that the Conservative strategy would be to claim that Labour could not work with a Republican in the White House. And indeed at one point we did have to deploy our Washington Embassy to impress on Rumsfeld that he could not receive Iain Duncan Smith, who was then the Opposition Defence spokesman, before he met Geoff Hoon, who was his official opposite number. In the event, George Bush was to prove so unpopular with the British public that close association with him has turned out to be a major liability to Tony. In retrospect letting IDS be photographed first with Rumsfeld might have been the smart move.

In my last months as Foreign Secretary I played my part in bonding with the new Administration by making my number with Colin Powell who had replaced Madeleine Albright at the State Department. It was not difficult as Colin Powell is a decent, honourable man with an enthusiasm for finding a future for kids from deprived communities, like the one in the Bronx where he himself started. If the rest of the Bush Administration were people more like Colin Powell, we could have avoided most of the transatlantic tensions of recent years.

Unfortunately they are not. Management of the transition to government was entrusted to Dick Cheney, the hard-line Vice President, a politician so far to the ideological right that while a Congressman he opposed the release of Nelson Mandela. He seized the opportunity to stack the Administration with Neo-Cons like himself. I met Dick Cheney when I visited Washington in the first week of the new Administration to welcome it. Welcome might not be an appropriate description of Cheney's reception of me, as his long silences were eloquent of his distaste for a European leftie. I have no problem with Dick Cheney not wishing to spend time with me, but it did not augur well for a British strategy centred on bridge-building.

The problem is that the Blair strategy of keeping Britain the No. 1 ally of the US only works when there is an Administration in the US that sets store on having allies. For the first time since America entered the Second World War we are dealing with a US Administration many of whom regard allies as potential liabilities rather than sources of strength. They are opposed to America joining worldwide agreements such as the Kyoto Protocol on global warming not just because the Bush Administration is dripping in former oil executives and because its election campaign was bankrolled by US oil companies, but because they have an ideological objection to US national policy being constrained in any way by international obligations.

The Bush Administration is firmly committed as a matter of principle to US supremacy without any need to count on allies. Their response to the collapse of the Cold War is not to welcome the opening for a new multilateral order, but to insist on the unilateral supremacy of the US, not just through superiority in Full Spectrum Dominance of military capacity, but in the industrial and diplomatic fields as well. The classic text of their global strategy was the Defense Planning Guidance written in 1992 to help the Bush Senior Administration shape the new world order. This set out a strategy of determined unilateralism, 'convincing potential competitors they need not aspire to a greater role or pursue a more aggressive posture to protect their legitimate interests . . . to discourage advanced industrial nations from challenging our leadership and maintain the mechanisms for deterring political competitors'. What is striking about the text is that it plainly is not only, nor mainly, about rogue states or other enemies. It contains no perspective in which other sovereign countries, including European allies, can be viewed other than as potential rivals. It was written by Paul Wolfowitz and Lewis Libby, who now occupy even more senior posts in the Bush Administration, the latter as Chief of Staff for Vice-President Cheney.

When Donald Rumsfeld mused on the eve of war that the US could always go it alone without Britain, he was widely perceived as having committed another of his entertaining gaffes. But to Rumsfeld it was nothing more than a statement of the Neo-Con creed that the US should be capable of acting unilaterally at all times and in all circumstances. It was indeed embarrassing to the UK government, but only because it threw into sharp relief the extent to which they had yoked themselves to an Administration that had difficulty in seeing the point of allies.

It is hard not to feel some sympathy with Tony Blair. No British Prime Minister has ever shown more courage in taking on his domestic public opinion to deliver military support for the foreign policy of the US government of the day. Yet what has he got to show for it in return, other than a Congressional medal which he dare not pick up for fear of the outrage at home? In terms of hard economics there has been a sharp shift of new US investment from Britain and, with exquisite political irony, to France.

It was rewarding being a close ally to a Clinton Administration committed to multilateralism and to the recognition of the interests of other states. It is tough being the same ally to a Bush Administration with an ideological commitment to unilateralism and little appreciation that allies also can have political pressures of their own.

—⁓—

Thursday 14 February

Valentine's Day. The internet printout provided by my staff informs me that as well as Valentine's Day it is also National Impotence Day. I summon them in to find out if they're having me on. But apparently not. Who on earth chose 14 February for National Impotence Day?

What worries me in terms of likely Tory attack for Business Questions is the story splashed across the *Mirror* and the *Express* that Jo Moore had again suggested that we bury some bad news on Friday while the press was focused on Princess Margaret's funeral. It seems to me improbable that Jo would have done this, since she has enough sense to know that there will not be that much media fixation with Princess Margaret's funeral. But the press carry a blown-up version of an e-mail from the Head of Press at the DTLR, Martin Sixsmith, apparently rebuking Jo Moore for suggesting that they can bury any more bad news along with Princess Margaret.

By convention none of us enters the Cabinet Room until Tony is ready to receive us. He is always at least five minutes late, sometimes longer, but far from being a matter of regret it creates an opportunity for valuable milling time. Today I spot Derry and cannot resist teasing him about his address to the backbench group opposed to elections to the Lords. I open rather archly with, 'I hear you've been down to my end of the building to speak.' To my delight he misunderstands me and volunteers the unexpected gossip, 'Oh yes, John Prescott wined and dined me very agreeably.' The plot thickens.

After Cabinet I hang around with Godric Smith, the Prime Minister's Official Spokesman, to catch Steve Byers and make sure we both give the same story to the lobby and to the House. Steve is being good-natured and confident about the whole thing. He has had inquiries made in the Department, and assures us that the whole business is an invention. There is no such e-mail. There was no such suggestion from Jo. Godric and I both agree to describe it as a fiction.

Back at Westminster, Stephen Hillcoat, the Private Secretary who arms me for Business Questions, has extracted from the clerk at the DTI a form of words that commits them to making a statement as soon as policy conclusions are agreed in response to the PIU Energy Review. I read this into the record at the earliest possible opportunity and keep referring back to it. It just about sees me through several sticky encounters. I am on more comfortable ground on the publication this morning of the report by the Public Administration Committee on House of Lords reform, which unanimously recommends that 60 per cent should be elected. Without impaling myself on the figure I seize on the very fact of a figure as evidence that it is possible for those committed to reform to reach agreement on a specific format for reform.

Eric Forth asks about the issue of the e-mail to Jo Moore in the opening joust when he expresses ironic hope that I can give a clear denial that such an episode ever happened. He looks discomfited when I give him the denial he requested, and describe the e-mail, as agreed, as a fiction. I go straight from the Chamber to the car, to the airport and to Granada for the PES dialogue on Europe and the Muslim world. There is one disturbing bump along the way. While we are waiting for a plane in the Executive Lounge I get a call from Stephen. Unbelievably, the DTLR have discovered that there is such an e-mail, and that it was not a fabrication after all. It looks an even better day to get out of the country for a week than I had thought when we planned the trip to Spain.

Friday 15 February

Over a coffee at the end of the PES dialogue, José Luis Rodríguez Zapatero, the Spanish socialist leader, raised with me the familiar complaint that the only capital he had not been able to visit in two years since taking over was London because he cannot get an appointment to see Tony Blair. The truth is that Tony does not have the tribal instinct to want to see other socialist leaders unless they are in government.

Prime Ministers are another matter. Several times in the course of the morning I am tackled by socialist colleagues on what Tony is doing in Italy signing agreements with Berlusconi. The more mature among them understand that Tony has to have a partnership with Aznar who may be the enemy in Spain, but when all's said and done he is the Prime Minister of Spain with whom other governments have to deal. None of them would deny that Aznar is a legitimate politician. Berlusconi is not. No gain from a tactical alliance in the European Council chamber can compensate for the degradation of doing deals with him. Yet I wonder whether Tony even glimpses the cost he pays across the left parties in Europe for associating with the most reactionary government in Europe.

I get back to the *parador* in time for lunch with Gaynor. We had two beers and I felt relaxed. It was the end of work and the start of our holiday. Unfortunately, David Mathieson chose just that moment to ring with the news that the front page of the *Mirror* has taken its revenge on my claim that the Martin Sixsmith e-mail was a fabrication. Apparently it has a screaming headline, 'Liar', along with my photograph. It thoroughly punctured our happy mood.

Saturday 16 February–Sunday 24 February

There followed a magical week in Seville. Everything was perfect and I will never hear a word against Seville. It even has five socialist MPs. The only awkward moment came when we visited the ancient bullring made famous by *Carmen*. The high point of the guide's tour was the hospital room in which toreadors, great heroes of Spain, had been laid out after being gored to death. Gaynor wanted to know what happened to the bull after he had turned the tables on the toreador, and was told, 'The bull is always killed by the next toreador.' Before I could stop her, Gaynor protested that this was unfair because the bull had 'won' and should be allowed to go free. For a moment I thought we were going to be unceremoniously flung to the next bull.

Monday 25 February

Anthony Zacharzewski, the civil servant who I appointed to liaise with Derry's office, comes in for his weekly report on House of Lords reform. He has managed to secure the job of analysing the responses to consultation, and they are proving pretty damning to Derry's plans. Three-quarters of those responding want a substantially elected House. Nearly everyone wants a smaller second chamber, and a sizeable number want no Bishops or Law Lords. With Civil Service understatement he adds, 'This is a tricky one, as the government will in effect have to publish a document demonstrating that the public rejects government policy.'

Tuesday 26 February

Newspaper coverage on poor Steve Byers has boosted out of orbit and is heading off to a different galaxy with no remote connection to Planet Earth. The big front-page issue now is whether Steve Byers behaved improperly by suggesting that Martin Sixsmith should not be offered a job elsewhere in the Civil Service. Of course he should not. Anyway, what other Cabinet minister would let him over the door of their Department after his behaviour towards Steve?

On my way over to the House, Steve Byers rings me in the car. He wants my agreement to come to the House and make a statement this afternoon. I enthusiastically agree. 'It is far better, Steve, that you come to the Despatch Box on your own terms, voluntarily, than have the Tories put it about that you had to be dragged there.' Generously, Steve starts to apologise for having got me into the row over the last Business Statement, but I cut him off short. It is something I can handle and he has enough to worry about for himself.

In the event his statement turned out to be wise. It was detailed, comprehensive and convincing. By contrast his opposite number, Teresa May, was awful. She addressed the House of Commons in headlines strung together. But the bludgeon only works as a weapon in Commons debate when you're addressing some grand affair of state. Minutiae over the dismissal of an employee calls for the stiletto. It was one of those rare defining occasions when the mood of the House perceptibly shifts. Halfway through the exchanges it became clear that there was nothing of substance to the complaints and that the Tories had simply run out of fresh lines of attack. Conversely, our backbenchers provided a magnificent display of solidarity and support. A succession of independent MPs, Peter Kilfoyle, Gerald Kaufman and Mike O'Brien, got up to express full support for Steve, and, in Gerald's case, a masterly contempt for the Conservatives.

Wednesday 27 February

A fascinating session in the Modernisation Committee. We took the first hearing of evidence in our study on improving the relevance of the Chamber to political and press life outside Westminster.

The most interesting response was from Andrew Marr when he was asked why so much media coverage now was about personality rather than content. 'Some years ago, probably during the disintegration towards the end of Mrs Thatcher's period, the press got into a culture that the real stories were gaffes and splits. In understandable reaction to this culture politicians stopped talking in human. We then reacted by looking through the quotes for even smaller nuances of difference. And it is easier for us because there are more speeches than ever before and therefore more opportunities to produce a split story. The net effect is that we have got into a downward spiral of ever more sensational headlines over ever smaller areas of difference.'

Afterwards I scrambled to catch the Eurostar to a meeting of the PES Praesidium and steamed into two growing storm clouds for Britain over the Channel.

The first arises from the Blair–Berlusconi Summit in Rome, which has provoked uproar in the Italian left and among their close sympathisers in the Mediterranean countries. It doesn't help that Berlusconi hailed this as a new 'Anglo-Italian axis'. As far as the Mediterranean socialists are concerned, he might as well be including it in George Bush's 'axis of evil'. Berlusconi belongs more inside the Château d'If than in government. It is preposterous to sign a joint declaration celebrating liberalisation of the economy with a man who has just hobbled the courts in case they imagine that liberalisation and the rule of law applies to his companies. People will eventually forget about the Berlusconi photo-op. Unfortunately, the other problem rests in deep anxiety about what George Bush intends to do around the world, and that problem will increase as he gets on with it. There is particular concern tonight about the possibility that he will take military action against Iraq. I share the deep concerns about how quickly the United States has moved from building a global coalition against terror, to reverting to a unilateralist foreign policy. When I rehearse some of my own anxieties, Jan Marinus Wiersma responds, 'How refreshing to hear these worries from somebody from Britain.' I provoke laughter when I check, in comic anxiety, 'This meeting is private, isn't it?'

Thursday 28 February

I walk across Green Park to the Cabinet troubled by my discussion in Brussels on Iraq. Before I can raise it, David Blunkett asks if we can have a discussion at an early meeting on Iraq. I come in to back him up by explaining that military action against Iraq will not be supported in Europe. Nor throughout the Arab world. 'In present circumstances Arab governments would not comprehend such obsession with Iraq. They see Sharon, not Saddam, as the problem for the Middle East.' Somewhat to my surprise this line provokes a round of Hear Hears from colleagues which is the nearest I've heard to a mutiny in the Cabinet. Afterwards David Blunkett thanks me for not leaving him isolated, and we agree to compare notes before any discussion.

At Business Statement I put up both hands and say sorry, that in all good faith I misled the House over the notorious Sixsmith e-mail. There are few things that the House likes better than an apology, and it is greeted by a ferocious growling of approval. Harold Macmillan allegedly once claimed that you can knock down your grandmother and get away with it, just as long as you make a full statement of apology the next day in the House. In any event, my apology was quickly overshadowed by my announcement that in two weeks' time we will have yet another vote on hunting.

After the Business Statement I throw a small birthday drinks party for my regular attenders. The Speaker very kindly came round and, characteristically, was courteous to Gaynor. When she told him that her father had been a draughtsman his eyes lit up. 'When I worked on the shop floor, my ambition was one day to be a draughtsman. You see, a draughtsman got a tea break in the afternoon, which those of us on the shop floor were never allowed. Many a day I was gasping with thirst and envying those draughtsmen.'

To celebrate my birthday Gaynor and I went to the Pizza Express Jazz Club to hear Lynne Arriale, who provides a marvellous blend of traditional melody and inventive arrangement. It was a great evening. So great that we forgot to pay on leaving and I had to ring up in consternation as soon as we got home. Peter, the manager, was very relaxed about it, as well he might be. Cabinet ministers are a safe commercial proposition. If they fail to pay, you always know that you can make more money by selling the story to the newspapers.

Sunday 3 March

I do a couple of interviews for Sky and BBC Radio, mostly about the latest twists to the saga of Stephen Byers and his ghastly, faction-ridden Department. However, today there is a real sense of the story petering out.

Afterwards I walked back from Millbank through St James's Park. It was the first day of spring and it brought out both the sun and the tourists. Maybe it was because I had just celebrated a birthday, but as I walked over the grass I thought life was good and I had much for which to be grateful.

Monday 4 March

Mounting speculation in the press that we will all be off to war soon to sort out Saddam Hussein. To a large extent this is generated by the newspapers themselves, who are each terrified that they will be the last to get in on the storyline. On the other hand, it is true that, whenever he gets the opportunity, Tony fails to kill the mounting speculation.

Wednesday 6 March

An entertaining meeting of the Modernisation Committee. We had asked Charles Moore, editor of the *Daily Telegraph*, and Simon Kellner, editor of the *Independent*, to come and give us their views on how we could improve coverage of Parliament.

Charles put in a class performance, which came as a bit of a shock to some on my side on the committee who had never previously met such a high-church Conservative. Martin Salter looked stunned at this self-confident new creature, exactly like Tammy when confronted in the park by a Newfoundland. In his heart I suspect Charles believes that modernising anything is a mistake, and his ability to help us improve the scrutiny of legislation was handicapped by his candid view that 'It would be a bad idea if Parliament was too efficient. We would get too many laws.' But he had one insight on which there is no argument. 'The issue is not when you meet, but what you do when you're meeting.'

Simon Kellner was more down-to-earth and practical. Helpfully, he offered the view, 'Getting the House to sit earlier is a "no-brainer".' What came across very strongly from both of them was the sense that the Commons today is less newsworthy because it is more predictable. There is no sense of drama about the ten o'clock vote because there is never any sense of surprise that the government won. More and more I believe that the biggest single problem for us is that mega-majorities have become the norm. I always warned that the problem with the first past the post system was precisely what was claimed as its greatest asset, namely that it produced strong government. The danger now is that the strong majorities in Parliament which it produces are proving a profound threat to Parliament as an institution. And yet still there are too few backers for electoral reform.

I round off the day with a small piece of history. I address the Liberal Democrat Parliamentary Party, which makes me the first Labour Cabinet minister ever to address them. I go through with them my proposals on modernisation, which go down well. The Liberal Democrats neither have the hang-ups of the Labour leadership in wanting to keep Parliament in check, nor even the hang-up of the Conservatives over not wanting to create too much trouble for themselves when they get into office. They are natural supporters for change, and I am quite explicit. 'I never want to be in the position of coming to the House with a proposal that is backed only by the Labour Party. Modernisation of the Commons cannot become the property of just one party.'

Thursday 7 March

A momentous event. A real discussion at Cabinet. Tony permitted us to have the debate on Iraq which David Blunkett and I had asked for last Thursday. For the first time I can recall in five years, Tony was out on a limb.

David Blunkett was first over the top. Being now Home Secretary he cunningly camped on the need for a proper legal authority for any action. 'What has changed that suddenly gives us the legal right to take military action that we didn't have a few months ago? Has anybody asked the legal opinion of the Attorney General, and what is he saying?' They are good questions, but in the context of Cabinet they are what might be termed rhetorical questions. In other words, nobody seriously expects an answer to them.

I went next. I began by establishing my bona fides by rehearsing my contempt for Saddam. 'He is almost certainly the only psychopath actually in government, who according to legend shot his first man at ten.' But I then went on to raise the serious, profound questions about whether it is right to take military action. 'We should not take part in a military campaign unless we first meet two conditions.

'First, we must make sure Britain is not isolated in Europe. At the end of the day our national interests are in Europe, and we cannot afford to be the only European government supporting an American military venture. Second, we must make sure that it is Saddam who is isolated by resolving the conflict between Israel and the Palestinians.' The last point drew a murmur of Hear Hears from around the table.

Pat Hewitt lamented that we were expected to listen to US worries about Iraq when we could not get them to listen to us before slapping higher tariffs on our steel exports. 'We are in danger of being seen as close to President Bush, but without any influence over President Bush.'

I am told, not that I have witnessed it, that in the old days Prime Ministers would sum up the balance of view in the discussion. This would be simple in the present case as all contributions pointed in one direction. However, Tony does not regard the Cabinet as a place for decisions. Normally he avoids having discussions in Cabinet until decisions are taken and announced to it. Tony appeared totally unfazed that on this occasion the balance of discussion pointed strongly in the reverse direction of his intentions. Rather than attempt to sum up the discussion of this supreme body of collective government, he responded as if he was replying to a question and answer session from a party branch. He was very patient with us, as is his inimitable style with those who ask difficult questions, but he was very firm with us about where he saw that Britain's national interests lay. 'I tell you that we must steer close to America. If we don't we will lose our influence to shape what they do. That is understood in Europe. I have spoken to both Jospin and Schröder, and they both understand that we cannot oppose the Americans.'

I suspect the latter point is true. The problem is that this insight on their part will remain a private one. There is a severe risk of ending up publicly isolated if he is the only European leader to take part in an operation.

At Business Statement I am asked about Iraq. I reply in the approved formula of the Prime Minister: 'No decision has been taken.' But I am emboldened, by the discussion in Cabinet, to stick my neck out by adding, 'And no decision may ever be taken.'

———~m~———

This was the last meeting of the Cabinet at which a large number of ministers spoke up against the war. I have little sympathy with the criticism of Tony that he sidelined the Cabinet over Iraq. On the contrary, over the next six months we were to discuss Iraq more than any other topic, but only Clare Short and I ever expressed frank doubts about the trajectory in which we were being driven. Perhaps it was because I had followed policy on Iraq for so long that I was sceptical of the sudden discovery of an urgent necessity to invade it. Certainly I was inoculated against Washington's sanctimony about the evil of Saddam by my exposure to the complicity of the West in strengthening Saddam, and in conniving with him as an ally right up to the day he invaded Kuwait.

The trial of the Matrix Churchill executives collapsed only a month after I took over as the Labour Shadow on Trade and Industry, and before I had caught up on the issue. When David Hill, then Labour's senior press officer, rang to pass on a bid for a radio interview on the collapse of Matrix Churchill, I had to ask him what Matrix Churchill actually was, and got the perplexed response that he thought it was an engineering firm that had gone bust. It was another couple of hours before I discovered that we had been talking about a political scandal that was to absorb half my waking hours for much of the next three years. By that evening, I was picking up the thousand pages of documents which the government had tried to suppress, and my assistant, Tom Franklin, sat up all night sorting them down to a dozen pages of evidence that acquitted the Matrix Churchill executives but condemned the Conservative government.

The real scandal was not the original decision of Conservative ministers to relax the rules on exports to Saddam, reprehensible though that had been, but the subsequent attempt to cover it up, even to the extent of risking the conviction of innocent men by claiming immunity for evidence of ministerial complicity. At the end of the Scott inquiry ministers compounded their image as a government with something to hide by the risible access they allowed me to read five volumes in three hours. To dramatise the restrictions for the benefit of the cameras, I went through a ceremony of formally handing over to Andrew Hood of my staff my mobile phone, which I was prohibited from taking in with me. In fact, when I was ushered into the DTI, I discovered that they had laid out the Scott report in a basement which had no reception for mobiles, just in case I had smuggled one in!

What the Scott report exposed was that the then British government secretly relaxed the guidelines on defence sales to Saddam, and then refused to admit it to Parliament or the criminal courts. As a result Matrix Churchill were tolerated when they supplied the specialised machine tools that Saddam needed for his munitions factories. For good measure, the government insured defence sales to Iraq through the Export Credit Guarantee Department (ECGD), with the consequence that after the Gulf War the UK had to pay almost a billion pounds on contracts on which Saddam had reneged. The UK not only equipped Saddam's weapons factories, but also helped pay for them.

Evidence of our connivance in underwriting Saddam's military ambitions kept resurfacing in the efforts to convince us Saddam was a menace. The September Dossier on Iraq's Weapons of Mass Destruction identified the chlorine plant at Falluja as one of the chemical warfare plants which Saddam had rebuilt. The original Falluja plant was constructed by a British-based company with the approval of Paul Channon, then Secretary of State at the DTI, despite a warning that it could provide the feedstock for mustard gas. Once again, the ECGD insured the project, with the predictable result that the UK ended up paying for the final instalment on the very plant about which last year we expressed such alarm.

Then there is the case of the two trucks which were paraded with much publicity after the war as examples of mobile chemical weapons laboratories. Rather less publicity has been given to the subsequent conclusion that they were most probably trucks to produce hydrogen for meteorological balloons used by artillery to measure wind speed. Even less publicity has been given to the awkward discovery that they were built to a design sold to Iraq by Britain.

There have been many citations in recent months of the gassing of thousands of Kurdish villagers at Halabja in 1988 as evidence of Saddam's willingness to employ chemical weapons. It was a truly appalling atrocity, made all the more of an offence to the laws of war in that few men of fighting age were in the village and the victims overwhelmingly were women, old men and children. However, far from being revolted at the time, it was only months after Halabja that the British government decided to relax the rules on defence exports to Iraq and the completion of the chlorine plant at Falluja continued regardless.

Tony Blair is wholly innocent of responsibility, either individually or collectively, for these decisions. They were taken by a Conservative government and taken in secret. No such defence is available to the Republican Party. The US under Reagan was just as active in equipping Saddam, and it was US companies that supplied the growth mediums for Saddam's biological laboratories and even his early stocks of anthrax. A Senate inquiry after the Gulf War discovered that in the five years up to the invasion of Kuwait the Reagan/Bush Administrations had approved almost eight hundred export licences to Iraq, including the supply of biological agents, chemical warhead-filling equipment and missile-guidance equipment. The provision of this arsenal of prohibited weaponry was the result of President Reagan's personal order to his Administration to do 'whatever was necessary' to help Iraq win its war with Iran. Some of the prominent personalities of the recent confrontation knew exactly who helped Saddam develop his original chemical and biological weapons capacity. In 1983 Donald Rumsfeld visited Baghdad and met Saddam as President Reagan's special envoy. According to the State Department telegram Rumsfeld 'conveyed the President's greetings and expressed his pleasure at being in Baghdad'. This was at a time when the State Department assessed that Saddam was engaging in 'almost daily use of chemical weapons', frequently from helicopters supplied by the US for 'crop spraying'.

Forgive me, therefore, if I reacted with cynicism to the sudden alarm in Washington at Saddam's military capacity as a pretext for invasion. This might have carried more credibility if both the US and the then British governments had not been together in it up to their armpits in creating that capacity in the first place.

Their motive in doing so was one of cynical calculation. At the time, Saddam was their ally against the Islamic Revolution in Iran, and Iraq was their front line. I do not suppose they ever expected, or even wanted, Saddam to win the war he had started, but it suited them to keep Iran preoccupied with the security threat posed by its well-armed neighbour. Western support for Iraq helped keep going a brutal and bloody war in which unknown hundreds of thousands of young men died, many of them victims of the chemical weapons of our ally Saddam. Nor did our help end with the war. In 1989 a Ministry of Defence report concluded that British support had made 'a very significant enhancement to the ability of Iraq to manufacture its own arms, thus to resume the war with Iran'. What makes this assertion so stunning in its cynicism is that it was written when Iraq and Iran were at peace, following a ceasefire arranged by the UN.

Yes, Saddam did once have chemical and biological weapons. The US and the UK should know because both countries helped build his military machine and turned a blind eye to his arsenal of prohibited weapons so long as they were for use against Iran.

—⁂—

Friday 8 March

Somebody has been briefing on yesterday's Cabinet discussions. Nearly every paper uses the same expression, describing me as 'a dove'. Unusually the *Financial Times* is more sensational than its rivals and hints that a Cabinet minister will resign if there is an attack on Iraq. The lack of colour and the absence of any quotes makes me suspect that the source was somebody who was not even in the room. I travel down to the Chequers away-day in the gloomy knowledge that the first rule of leaks is that the guy with his name in the story gets the blame.

At the start of the meeting John Prescott gives a firm warning to us all to keep discussions secret, and adds, 'Anyone who goes out there telling the press that they're a dove or a hawk isn't helping us, but is only helping those in the press who want us to have a fight.'

I am increasingly impressed by Alan Milburn, who made a striking contribution. He is often accused of being a complete Blairite, but today spoke from a perspective more radical than Blair. 'Our enemy is not our opponents but cynicism. We ought always to remember that we are not managers. We are politicians. We will only defeat cynicism if we get back to value-based politics. That means we need to be more bold and more confident.'

For myself I focused on the risk of us being perceived as an elite. 'Every time Gordon has to address a conference of businessmen, overweight and in suits, or Tony has to attend an international summit in some five-star luxury resort, we convey the visual image of ourselves as part of an elite, not part of the people.'

I then apologised in advance in case what I was about to say would offend Gordon, who looked suitably glowering and ready for a fight. 'The truth is Gordon is outstandingly and clearly the most redistributionist Labour Chancellor in history. He has taken millions of children and pensioners out of poverty. Yet the paradox is that when I talk proudly of what we've done for the poor, inside I feel vaguely uneasy as if I've somehow gone off message.' When I was finished Gordon gave a beaming smile and said, 'Thank you very much.' Part of Gordon's tragedy is that he is an old believer in redistribution, but stuck within a Blairite ideology which only allows him to do it by stealth. The result must be a constant frustration of not getting credit for the enormous amount he has achieved.

Tony's response stressed the importance of sticking with our successful strategy, and showed no sign of a fresh direction. 'We must keep the coalition that we won with twice. We will only get a third term if we keep the coalition between our core vote and the aspirational new voters.' Of course, nobody in their right mind would seriously break up that coalition. But Tony seems incapable of recognising that right now the wing of the coalition that is crumbling is among the core voters, not the aspirational voters. I fear, as Gordon warned in the discussion, there is a real danger that we go in to the next election still fighting it as we did our first victory.

Sunday 10 March

Plainly somebody has sent out the word to their trusty retainers to duff me up over Iraq. Several papers tag me as 'an appeaser'. The *Sunday Telegraph* quotes 'one Minister close to the negotiations' telling their columnist that 'Saddam's best friends on the planet right now are Clare Short and Robin Cook'. The *Sunday Times* speculates that I might quit the Labour Party and set up a leftist challenge to it, a curious charge as I regard myself as the party loyalist and the war party as the people who are at odds with Labour.

On Sunday I addressed my constituency party. I found my party members perplexed rather than disaffected. It is not easy for them to come to the dawning realisation that the leader of the Labour Party does not share many of the values that brought most of them into the Labour Party. Even his formidable success in mobilising vast majorities of electoral support puzzles them as they do not themselves quite see why other people get so positive about him. On the other hand, they understand that he is successful, and that our party that has just won two crushing election victories and appears to be in no immediate threat of a forthcoming election defeat. The tone of criticism therefore was one of regret, not of anger. We will only lose that mood in the party if Tony appears to have lost his one strength, as a leader who delivers votes.

Monday 11 March

In the afternoon I met Charles Clarke to follow up our conversation on Lords reform. Charles has been a great success as Chair of the party. The formula for his success is that he has maintained his reputation for a vigorous, independent mind, while at the same time commanding respect for his close relationship with Tony Blair. Charles shared the rather surprising news that Tony was becoming convinced of the logic of a second Chamber that was all elected or all appointed. My response was that Tony would need to understand that the House, if it was given that choice, would reject a zero-elected Lords and go for a fully elected Lords. Charles did not disagree, but then he is himself committed intellectually to a fully elected Lords.

Wednesday 13 March

I addressed the PLP on priorities for legislation next session. To be more precise, they addressed me on their priorities for the next session and I collected twenty separate bids. It was not a bad insight into the concerns of Labour MPs who are in touch with people on the ground. Their suggestions for legislation reflect the way our policies affect individuals, such as the need for an amendment to minimum wage legislation to exclude tips in the catering industry, or to amend the working family tax credit to better protect the interests of shiftworkers. Others reflected the constituency issues that are brought to any diligent constituency MP, such as the need to control high hedges or abandoned cars. It is the strength of our constituency system in Britain that such issues get fed into the pipeline of representative democracy, but it will be hard to mould them into strategic priorities for a coherent legislative programme.

At Prime Minister's Question Time, Iain Duncan Smith challenged Tony on crime figures, which cannot have come as a surprise to Tony as it is the day of the Police Lobby on their pay. IDS used up most of his allocation of time coming back repeatedly on his first question on crime, but the only effect was to rub in the weakness of the Conservative position. It is not just that in the past they had a record of cutting police numbers, it is also that in the future their commitment to cutting public spending cannot be squared with matching our expansion in police numbers. Tony is superb at deflecting the Opposition attacks at PMQs, and the job gets even harder for them the longer he stays in office and grows in stature.

It would be wrong to say that the Parliamentary Committee provides a more testing exchange as the tone is always civil and conversational, but on the other hand it does provide for a more honest and serious exchange than is possible in the baying pit of a packed Chamber. Today there was no mistaking a general sense of unease among the elected representatives of the backbenchers. Chris Mullin made the intelligent observation, 'There is a danger of fighting on too many fronts at once.' He ended by asking what had happened in the last few weeks suddenly to propel Saddam forward as an urgent menace. Tony's response on Iraq was frank and unsettling: 'I cannot offer the comfort that no military action will be taken.'

Afterwards Robert Hill caught me in the corridor and asked how I interpreted the temper of the PLP. My advice was very similar to that of Chris Mullin. Any one of the issues is manageable. The problem is that a lot of issues are coming up on which Labour MPs did not feel the Prime Minister shared their own instincts. He could not simultaneously take them on in public service finance, war on Iraq and blocking their wish for legislation on hunting.

Thursday 14 March

Immediately after Business Statement I hitched a lift with Jack Straw in his RAF plane to the Barcelona Summit. The premises for the PES pre-Summit dinner were superb as we were hosted in one of Gaudí's characteristically ebullient, stylish buildings. The meeting itself, though, was dire and degenerated into a succession of set-piece speeches. Tony had the wisdom to make his excuses and leave early to find somewhere where he could carry out real political business.

I went on to the hotel that had been booked for me and was further depressed to find myself in a room which had all the charm and detail of an outsize shoebox. I switched on the television in hope of some mood change, but found my gloom confirmed by a bleak recreation of a fight between Cro-Magnon man and Neanderthal man over a fish. I cannot remember when I felt so depressed. I swore that we must change the format of PES meetings.

Monday 18 March

Gareth Williams drops by for our Start the Week conversation. We are both much perplexed to know how to take forward reform of the House of Lords, given that Derry is now showing no interest in any alternative to his much derided White Paper.

But there is something more immediate weighing on Gareth's mind. Lord Stevenson has been lobbying Number 10 for permission to appoint more of his independent peers. Derry refuses to express any view on the matter, and although a submission has gone up to him he has announced he will leave it to 'young Blair' to decide what to do. As always none of us knows what he is privately urging on young Blair. Gareth regards the proposal with consternation. 'If the big problem in reform is getting down the numbers of life peers, why make it worse by appointing more of them?' I fully agree, and undertake to write to Tony to say so. The notion that we should now appoint more life peers only to buy them out again in a year or two's time with a pension package is so loopy that we would all deserve to end up in front of the National Audit Office trying to explain ourselves.

The House of Lords came up again in the afternoon at my briefing meeting for tomorrow's oral questions. The first question asks me about the responses to our consultation document. To everyone but me the responses are deeply embarrassing as they show massive public support for a substantially elected Chamber. To me the only problem is whether I can come out and say so. I resolve to conscript piety to my cause. I fix the civil servants from Derry's department with a look of deeply troubled sincerity. 'I must be mindful of the Ministerial Code of Conduct which obliges me to be as candid and as full as it is possible to be. If asked, I cannot dodge a question about the responses.' Afterwards I suggest to Lorna that she makes sure that I do get a question I cannot dodge.

I spend the evening very cheerfully at the annual dinner of Chris Smith's Islington party. Their dinners have become a Labour Party institution. They are held in Frederick's restaurant just beyond the Angel in the heart of gentrified Islington. Very sophisticated. Very New Labour. And very moneyed. The audience includes such luminaries as David Puttnam, Anthony Sher and Simon Fanshawe. With only 150 people in the room, they manage to raise over £20,000. I remember reading about an American general whose career began as an officer with the cavalry and finished as commander of the US Air Force. I feel my fundraising career has spanned a similar transformation from the jumble sale to the chic dinner set in one generation.

Tuesday 19 March

Simon Buckby of Britain in Europe came round to give me a presentation on their focus groups on the euro. It was all surprisingly positive. The 'Yes' case was consistently identified by the sample as the positive case with the future on its side. Conversely, 'No' can neither escape its inevitable negative quality nor being pigeonholed in the past. The threat of isolation if we were left outside the euro was powerfully resonant, and there was also a healthy scepticism about the media bias against it.

The one weakness was the extent to which the public, because of their own uncertainty, look to government as people whom they can trust for advice on a complex decision. This could be a potential asset in a campaign, but its value will quickly degrade if the public lose their trust in us. None of the pollsters could answer my question, 'Could a government which was itself unpopular win a referendum which requires it to make the euro more popular than its own poll ratings?'

Later, Lorna gives me a political interpretation of last night's large majority for a ban on fox-hunting. 'I know several colleagues who really don't care about fox-hunting, but went through the lobby for a ban because they're fed up with Tony Blair refusing to listen to them.

They believe that with such a large majority for a ban now he will have to listen to them.' I suspect he will have to.

Lorna did a good job in getting people to bowl me soft balls at Question Time on Lords reform. With every appearance of reluctance I allowed myself to be forced into the admission, 'I would deceive the House if I did not admit that the great majority of responses to consultation supported a substantially elected second chamber.' It may turn out to be a slow-burning fuse, but it is another piece of evidence smuggled into the public domain which will increase the pressure on Derry to come to terms with reality.

Wednesday 20 March

I address the PLP morning meeting on our proposals to strengthen select committees. There were really two storylines to the discussion that followed my presentation. The first was the general support from the great majority of those taking part, led by Alun Williams, Chair of the Liaison Committee, who began the discussion by repeating their endorsement of the package.

The second storyline was a darker and more troubling theme. A few MPs, whose contribution did not always show a close acquaintance with the actual report, expressed a political anxiety that the new arrangements for independent nomination to the select committees would override our own recent agreement to democratise how Labour nominees were approved. One or two of these voices came from the far end of the hall where members of the whips' team sat in a mutinous muttering to the colleagues who got up to express worries. Afterwards, when I saw Hilary in my room I voiced my perception that there had been prompting of those who had voiced criticism, at which she smiled and replied, 'Robin, you're getting paranoid.'

Thursday 21 March

At Cabinet there was a wide-ranging discussion on where we are at on our own agenda. It was tinged with some thoughtfulness following the contraction of our poll lead. Steve Byers observed that what the public and press need is a route map for our strategy and a sense of direction, not a daily initiative. Gordon put it rather more bluntly. 'Government by announcement does not work.' David Blunkett gave alarming figures on how the increase in the prison population is outstripping the substantial increase in prison places, and offered the observation, 'Prison does not work.' Tony pulled a face at this.

Monday 25 March

The press is full of claims of growing dissent to any military adventure against Iraq. Some of it suffers from the overheating that journalists find necessary to give a story to get it on to the front page. There is simply going to be no challenge to Tony as leader of the party, and anyone who tried would be subjected to a military assault as great as anything coming Saddam's way. But for all that Tony ought to worry about the coalition opposed to military action on Iraq. Unlike trade union rights this is an issue which transcends the divide between our members and the *Daily Mail*-reading classes.

Among my old contacts in the Foreign Office I cannot find any who can convincingly demonstrate that something dramatic has changed in Iraq in recent months which would produce a justification for military action that was not there a year ago. Indeed, among the Arabists there is palpable anxiety. The project which I set in hand to sharpen the focus of sanctions to frustrate the military programmes of Iraq is now coming to fruition. But at the very moment when there has been more progress and more unity than for a decade in the Security Council, the US looks like dashing off on its own exotic unilaterist military adventure.

Geoff Hoon, who does not appear as sensitive to these complexities as Jack Straw, was on television yesterday giving soothing assurances that any military action would be 'proportionate'. The dilemma is that it will take gloriously Technicolor disproportionate military action to topple Saddam.

I spent much of the rest of the afternoon in the Chamber where we had two tough statements. Patricia Hewitt had the unenviable task of explaining to the House why the Royal Mail were laying off fifteen thousand jobs. Not even Bill Clinton could have presented this retrenchment as a rhetorical triumph. However, I was surprised that there was absolutely nothing in the statement to indicate a positive government strategy to the crisis in the Post Office.

The whole experience was made even more gruesome because the Tories have got their tails up and are going through the familiar but unedifying process of thoroughly enjoying themselves as the government hits the rocks. They jeered with redoubled fervour when poor Steve Byers came before them again to explain that he is after all going to put taxpayers' money into bailing out the shareholders of Railtrack. Steve stonewalled with commendable dignity and courage.

Tuesday 26 March

Andrew Adonis came in to talk to me about where we were on Lords reform. The bad news was that the Prime Minister is still to engage intellectually with the issue. However the good news was that he had asked for briefings from Andrew in his recess papers.

Andrew repeated the same puzzling point as Charles. Tony appears persuaded that in terms of election of the House of Lords it should be all or nothing. He tends to refer to a mixed membership as hybridity and is set against it. This could be a problem in the endgame if we ever get to it, as a purely elected or purely appointed House is not likely to offer the room for compromises that could be necessary to build any kind of consensus.

Afterwards we had a meeting with Hilary and officials from Number 10 to talk about the current state of play on the modernisation proposals. Robert Hill stayed behind at the end for a one-to-one about the politics of Iraq. He stressed to me that Tony understands the degree of hostility in the party over military action, and that there may be a way forward through getting the UN inspectors back in. When I stressed that the Arab world would view it with incomprehension if we started another war with an Arab country without first solving the war between Sharon and the Palestinians, Robert responded that Tony had warned Bush that there must be parallel progress in the Middle East as well as with Iraq.

Easter Recess

On Wednesday we packed the car and escaped to Edinburgh where we had planned to spend the rest of the recess recuperating and nursing the constituency. Then came the news of the death of the Queen Mother over Easter weekend. I had met with her on a number of occasions both as Foreign Secretary and as horse racing enthusiast. I had always been impressed by the clarity of her mind and the vigour of her views in someone of her age.

At one of the state banquets at Buckingham Palace I was tapped on the arm over the aperitifs by her Lady-in-Waiting, the formidable Lady Grimethorpe. 'Her Majesty the Queen Mother wishes to speak with you over coffee.' I was charmed by the invitation and foolishly spent the dinner happily looking forward to a conversation on the prospects for the jumps season. When the time came it turned out that the Queen Mother had other ideas on how we were going to spend the time. Charlie Whelan had just done a classic background operation with the *Sunday Times* which, the previous weekend, had run a prominent story that Gordon was not going to put up any longer with the waste and extravagance of the Foreign Office, and was going to oblige our ambassadors to downsize their residencies into something more modern and New Labour. The *Sunday Times* faithfully reported Charlie's briefing that Gordon was particularly appalled by the luxury of our embassy in Paris.

The Queen Mother was not up for any of this. She had known the wives of ambassadors to Paris and did not want them dispossessed. 'Now, promise me you will not let the Treasury roll all over you,' she said, tapping me with her fan. What could a subject do but agree? When I got back I wrote to Number 10 to state that we could not possibly sell the embassy in Paris as it would cause great distress to Her Majesty the Queen Mother.

We were recalled for Wednesday 3 April. I travelled down the previous night, both so that I could avoid any risk of planes going wrong in the morning and in order to be on College Green for the breakfast round of broadcasters covering the Recall. As Leader of the House I took my seat first on the front bench. Tony came in a few minutes before he had to address the House and sat down beside me. He was about to fly over to the States to see Bush at his private ranch. I took the opportunity to say to him, 'I hope you're going to avoid getting boxed in to any commitments to action on Iraq at Crawford.' He looked a bit taken aback and asked me to come and see him after the proceedings.

We went along to his room in the corridor behind the Speaker's Chair where he asked me bluntly, 'How serious is it?' I replied, 'It could be terminal for you if it goes wrong.' He looked more than a bit taken aback at that and he asked me to go on. I went through a number of the foreign policy problems that it could bring about our ears and ended up with Europe. 'Britain's strategic interests lie in its relations with the rest of Europe, and your own greatest contribution to Britain's standing in the world has been to transform those relations for the better. If Bush is going to carry out a military intervention in Iraq he will do it at the turn of the year and that means we will be fighting and mopping up into the spring. I just don't see how we can make Iraq the big foreign policy issue for Britain in the first half of next year and then hope to persuade the public in the second half of the year that they should join the euro when we've just been out of step with most of Europe.' Tony looked thoughtful, and he's obviously troubled in his own mind. He ended the conversation by saying, 'We ought to make sure you are able to take a full part in our strategic discussions.'

Tony Blair is arguably the most pro-European Prime Minister in modern times, certainly since Edward Heath. It is an irony of history, and a personal tragedy for him, that his commitment to support President Bush in war on Iraq should have torpedoed his strategic objective of restoring Britain as a respected major player in Europe, and, as an integral part of that project, taking Britain into the euro.

When Labour took office six years ago, we set ourselves the target of establishing Britain as a player in Europe of influence equal to Germany and France. In our first week I undertook the first of many eccentric schedules as Foreign Secretary, when on the same day I had lunch in Paris and dinner in Bonn. Gastronomy, unfortunately, is inextricably linked to diplomacy, and since leaving the Foreign Office I have lost over a stone. But on that occasion, gourmandising for Britain was worth it. The immediate product was to sign up both France and Germany to a joint communiqué endorsing our manifesto commitment to ban landmines. The more fundamental achievement was to signal that the new British government sought a culture of cooperation in place of the dynamics of confrontation.

We had a lot of ground to make up to prove this claim was credible after the Major years in which Britain had persistently been the odd one out, heckling every proposal from the bottom of the table. On one celebrated occasion, their minister tried to halt a directive governing traffic on cross-border canals, although it is a geographical impossibility for Britain to share a cross-border canal.

One unintended consequence of the obstructionism of the Major government was to make it easier for other governments to parade their communitaire credentials by speaking publicly in support of measures that they privately expected Britain to block. I still remember the consternation at an early council meeting when I refused to play the part scripted for Britain by staying silent, until other members realised that they would have to say what they really thought if they were not to be lumbered with a frankly loopy outcome.

It is to Tony Blair's credit that in his first term in office he transformed Britain's relations with Europe. This was very much his personal achievement, and I saw how he came to command attention in the European Council, where his intervention was often pivotal in determining which view would come out on top. For the first time since Britain joined the European Council, it had a government that was taking the initiative in Europe, rather than responding to the agendas of others. The Lisbon Process of economic reform was a product of Tony Blair's advocacy of knowledge-based economy and established full employment as a goal of the European Union for the first time. During his first term, Tony Blair delivered on his objective of making Britain an equal partner of Germany and France.

Iraq has demolished that achievement. We are back to the familiar geometry of a Franco-German axis with Britain the odd one out. Nor can this fairly be put down to unprovoked aggression from the other side of the Channel. We in Britain had our Rumsfeld moments of disdain for our nearest neighbours.

The dispute in the Security Council unleashed a wave of xenophobia towards France of an intensity that must have made Margaret Thatcher envious. Passing through Number 10 at a late stage in the crisis, I was surprised to find Jonathan Powell optimistic about the prospects of isolating France on the Security Council. When I asked about Germany, he replied, 'Germany does not matter, as it does not have a veto.' It was an exchange which left me worried that Number 10 was losing any grasp of the scale of opposition to war. In diplomatic reality, there is no sentence that can begin, 'Germany does not matter.'

The political consequence is that Tony Blair is now further away than ever from his objective of persuading the British people to feel at ease with their place in Europe. Britain's core problem with Europe is that we are the only member state who associate the development of Europe with a weakening of our own status. For Germany and France, the European Community provided a national rebound from post-war devastation. For Spain, Portugal and Greece, joining the Community was a guarantee of their democracy as they shook themselves free of fascism. For Austria, Sweden and Finland, it was confirmation that they had emerged from the shadow of the Cold War. Only for Britain was European entry not accompanied by a sense of national regeneration, but, on the contrary, angst over our declining international power. In that context, the adventure in Iraq was an immense historic anachronism. It encouraged the delusion that Britain had recaptured a global role, albeit as auxiliary to the American legions, and obscured the present reality that Britain's destiny is in Europe.

It was therefore entirely predictable that hard on the heels of victory in Baghdad should have come retreat on the euro. The government is not credible in urging the British electorate to vote for deeper integration with Europe, when the Prime Minister himself is marching out of step with the two major European powers on the biggest issue of the day. The dynamism of retreat creates a momentum that is difficult to reverse.

There are, of course, other voices within Europe that were more sympathetic to the invasion of Iraq, mostly from countries in Central or Eastern Europe, which Donald Rumsfeld is pleased to describe as New Europe. But it would be a strategic error to imagine that they represent a pro-American bloc, awaiting Tony Blair's leadership. The entire population of all the candidate countries barely approximates to that of Germany, and none of them is looking for a fight with their dominant neighbour. Even after Enlargement, it will be hard to make progress on any issue without either Germany or France on board. The folly of our diplomatic positioning on Iraq is that we forced Germany and France into a common alliance with ourselves as their opponent.

Our weakened position in Europe stemmed from the aversion to making hard choices that is a defining characteristic of New Labour. Tony Blair's favourite image of Britain's relationship with the US is that we are its bridge to Europe. The concept of a bridge is perfectly tailored for New Labour, as a bridge cannot make choices, but by definition is in the middle. Lord knows, I used it often enough myself when I was at the Foreign Office, but at least in the Clinton years it had some contact with reality. There were people in Washington in those years who wanted a bridge to communicate with allies. The Neo-Cons around Bush often sound as if the only bridge they would welcome would be a drawbridge, although, of course, one with the latest satellite controls. In their one-dimensional world view, you can be on their side, but if you choose to be on the other side, do not expect them to do any bridge building.

The problem for Tony Blair was that there was no Third Way on a decision whether to go to war. He refused to make a conscious choice between being a leader in Europe, or a follower of Bush, and found too late that unconsciously he had chosen Bush. It was the wrong choice for Britain.

Tuesday 9 April

Funeral of the Queen Mother at Westminster Abbey. The entire Cabinet is on parade seated in the Canons' Stalls in the choir. The ceremony was conducted with minimum pomp and maximum dignity.

The medieval acoustics of Westminster Abbey trump any state-of-the-art concert hall. The meticulous punctuality of the whole ceremony was stunning, especially as it was carried out at a week's notice. Stephen Byers was sitting next to me on the pew and got mercilessly ribbed on why Britain could run a royal funeral with such punctuality but could not get its trains to run on time. Would it not be better to take Railtrack out of administration and hand it over now to the Household Cavalry?

In the hopeless melee outside the Abbey afterwards it was impossible to find our cars. I walked down Victoria Street to the flower stall where I bought a bouquet of white lilies for Gaynor as it is our wedding anniversary. The quickest way back was past Buckingham Palace and up The Mall. For half a mile up The Mall the verge was carpeted with flowers laid outside Clarence House by well-wishers of the Queen Mother. It was only when I was coming to the end of this field of commemoration that it dawned on me I was getting suspicious looks from members of the public who were clearly concerned that I'd helped myself to one of her bouquets of flowers.

Wednesday 10 April

At Prime Minister's Questions there are a number of challenging points on Iraq made from our own side which have an uncustomary hard edge to them. Nor do they come from the usual suspects, who are expected to be difficult and therefore are tolerated almost as if they have a licence to be difficult.

Yet the PLP meeting which Tony addressed demonstrated the ambivalence of attitudes to the leader. The warmth of the ovation when Tony stopped speaking was as great as I have heard for any Labour leader. And many of those who were critical in the discussion over Iraq joined in the thunderous applause. The reality is that Tony is given admiration within the party even by those who cannot give him affection. They may be perplexed or appalled by individual decisions he takes, but that does not yet translate into a general rejection of his leadership.

In the evening I went to a jolly party at Number 10 to celebrate Jim Callaghan's ninetieth birthday. Jim was in good form and reminisced happily about his days in Number 10. The party was well attended by the giants of the Labour Party from the time when I first became a Labour MP. Stan Orme, Denis Healey, Roy Hattersley and Jack Jones were all there. Barbara Castle conspicuously was not present. I asked Michael Foot about her and he replied vigorously, 'She would not come. She never forgave him for sacking her, you know. Some people said that I should resign too because she'd been sacked, but what good would that have done?' Curiously, the event was not well attended by the present Cabinet. Other than Tony, the only Cabinet colleague I saw was Gordon Brown. Before leaving I joked to him, 'I've never seen such a gathering of old Labour figures in Number 10 in the five years since we won.'

In my box there is a pained note from Jon, my diary secretary. Number 10 had asked him to cancel my meeting on Thursday to discuss House of Lords reform as the Prime Minister 'is not ready to see you yet'. This is symptomatic of an established pattern of procrastination on House of Lords reform, but this particular reason is deeply unpersuasive to me. I want to see Tony before he is ready to discuss reform plans, and not after he has already made up his mind.

Thursday 11 April

At Cabinet, Tony reported in full on his visit across the Atlantic to spend the weekend with President Bush. The core of his message was captured in his statement of personal credo: 'I do believe in this country's relations with the US.'

Pat Hewitt spoke up bravely when he was finished on the importance of UN cover for any military action on Iraq. 'There will be a lot of tension among the Muslim communities in Britain if an attack on Iraq is seen as a unilateralist action. They would find it much easier to understand and we would find it much easier to sell if there was a specific agreement at the UN on the need for military action.'

Tony characteristically refused to be boxed in by an explicit commitment to a possible roadblock. He regards the UN process as important, but 'we should not tie ourselves down to doing nothing unless the UN authorised it'. Rather more alarmingly he said, 'The time to debate the legal base for our action should be when we take that action.' This suggests a worryingly low priority for respect to international law when we come to a decision on whether to take action.

I was prompted to speak by this response. 'It may not be wise to give a commitment in advance that we will seek a UN resolution for any action we take. But the political reality is that both Labour MPs and the British public will want to know that what we do has the support of the international community, and the UN is the proxy for the international community which most people accept. If France or Russia are opposed to what we do, and Kofi Annan is denouncing it, we will not convince the public that we are acting on behalf of the international community.'

After Cabinet I stormed Tony's Private Office to demand a date on Lords reform. The Cabinet Room is very much an ante-room to the Prime Minister's private room. When we were elected the Prime Minister's office was at the gable end of the rear wing. Tony has now moved into a room sandwiched between the Cabinet Room and the Private Secretaries. It is mildly more spacious, but is by far the smallest office of any head of government I have visited in five years. It is also probably the smallest of any Cabinet minister, and a tenth the size of the wide open prairie which passes for the Foreign Secretary's office. Basically, it has room only for two sofas facing each other over a coffee table with the Prime Minister's writing desk diagonally placed across a corner. There is too much history, mystique and elegance to Number 10 Downing Street for the Prime Minister of Britain ever to contemplate an alternative working environment, but modern Britain has to be forged within the structural limitations of what remains an eighteenth-century town house.

I press him: 'We need to talk. It is six months since the White Paper and there are only two more months left to go in which we must decide our policy if we are going to have a bill in the next session. We cannot let this drift any longer.' Tony readily agreed, although I got the impression that for him the main attraction of the meeting was that he could put me right on Iraq rather than allow me to put him right on the House of Lords.

Monday 15 April

The highlight of the day was in the evening when I took Madeleine Albright out for dinner. I took her to Le Pont de la Tour, which was the same restaurant that Tony had famously taken Clinton to, along with half the photographers of London. Fortunately, we did not have any attending press entourage and were able to talk frankly as old friends.

Madeleine was as blunt as ever. 'Europe and the US have not achieved a mature relationship of equals. When you express a concern there is still a touch of the student calling Mom on collect.' She was also characteristically perceptive. 'There's a big political difference in style between Bush and Clinton. Bush will say on any issue "It is simple". Clinton used to say "It is difficult".' She characterised the Bush foreign policy as ABC – Anything But Clinton. At the end of dinner she generously signed a cartoon I had brought of the two of us at the height of the Kosovo crisis, and we went away regretting that we were no longer in business together.

Wednesday 17 April

I had a long drive out to Windsor for this month's meeting of the Privy Council. Apparently the Royal Household always spends April in Windsor, an arrangement which no doubt dates back to Tudor times when it was essential for the Royal Family to move on when the local supply of livestock had been wholly exhausted. It docs, though, lack the advantage of convenience for the ministerial members in attendance who have to come out from central London, and on this occasion have to dash back to be in time for the Budget.

I got back to the Chamber just in time to hear Gordon's statement. It demonstrates all of Gordon's immense strengths. It demonstrates his complete mastery of the subject. It takes forward his strategic objectives on social justice. And it contains a typical gesture to the gallery when he promises cheaper beer from small breweries in time for the World Cup.

Thursday 18 April

Cabinet was preoccupied with the aftermath of the Budget, which Tony described as 'a brilliant budget, brilliantly delivered'. The press are full of speculation about the tension between Tony and Gordon. Undoubtedly the tension is there, and Tony has reluctantly come to grasp Gordon's undimmed ambition to replace him. But it would be a big mistake to regard their relationship as only one of tension. Tony's admiration of Gordon's political skills is genuine, and there's a strong bond between them which in any other circumstances would border on a mutual psychological dependency.

Tony identifies the top priorities of this Parliament 'apart from the euro' as delivery on the Health Service and the fight against crime. The 'apart from' is, of course, a fascinating parenthesis and it remains to be seen whether it will get the same priority as the other two.

Monday 22 April

The newspapers are full of reports from France of citizens lamenting stitching themselves up because they had voted for romantic fringe left candidates in the expectation that they could switch to Jospin in the second ballot. Now they have discovered that their self-indulgence has left them with the option of switching only to Chirac or Le Pen. The double voting round is a positive incitement to a protest vote on the first round. The French, curiously, have become victims of a particularly savage illustration of the dangers of first past the post. Why they do not use an alternative vote system among so many candidates I cannot imagine.

I rang Alastair Campbell to offer advice on press handling. He reads me a statement they've prepared from Tony in response to Le Pen's vote which includes the disclaimer, 'It is for the people of France to decide for whom they are going to vote.' I tell him to drop it. 'We don't have to be diffident about telling the French people not to vote for a Fascist, and, anyway, all the rest of Europe will be shouting the same message at them.'

High spot of the day is my long-promised meeting on the House of Lords with the Prime Minister. Encouragingly he has none of his officials in to take notes, which is always a good sign that he wants to open up. He has a surprise in store for me. 'Can't we put to Parliament different options for the composition of the House of Lords? I'll be frank with you. I just don't see how I can get an agreed position around the Cabinet table. John Prescott won't agree to substantial elections and you won't agree to minority elections. But if we let Parliament decide we do not have to fix an agreed Cabinet line.'

He was curiously tentative as he spoke, uncharacteristically looking at the coffee table rather than fixing me with his eyes as he usually does. He seemed relieved, even surprised, when I responded, 'I could make that work. It is what we've just done with the options on hunting. I think it would do a power of good to your own image to be seen to be consulting Parliament.' It was a characteristically original Blair way out of the dilemma, and I wanted to grab it and run before he had second thoughts.

He, though, was keen to talk about Iraq. I had rather suspected I was going to get a lecture to convince me of the need for military action, but it never came. On the contrary, he seemed genuinely interested in why I was worried.

'My big concern is that by sticking too close to Bush, we are putting at risk our strategy of establishing leadership in Europe. I am all for us keeping a foot in both camps, but if we have to choose there is no contest. Our national interests lie heavily inside Europe. And if we are going to win a euro referendum next year we've got to convince the public that is true. If we have a euro referendum next spring we will only just be finished fighting a war against Iraq with a lot of criticism from the European neighbours whom we are trying to persuade our public to join.'

When Tony is confident that he's right and you're wrong, he will robustly argue his case. This time he did not, but looked reflective. My impression was that he was genuinely perplexed how to square his strategic ambition to stay on the inside track with Washington with the difficult strategy that is coming out of Washington.

When I got back to my office I realised I still did not really know which of the options for the House of Lords Tony would prefer. As it happened, I found myself on the phone on other matters to Tony Wright. He had been PPS to Derry in the first year after the 1997 election, which he has described as 'an awful torrid year'. I put to him Derry's claim that Tony had never wanted anybody elected to the House of Lords. 'In that Derry tells the truth. In his own conversations with the other parties in the Lords the common talk was that about two-thirds of a reformed Chamber would be elected, but Tony would have none of it. Wakeham was appointed to come forward with a wholly appointed second chamber. Unfortunately for Tony, instead of closing down the options Wakeham opened them up.'

In the evening I hosted a dinner on behalf of the Foreign Office for Zoran Djindjic, now Prime Minister of a democratic Serbia, a transformation from the brave but persecuted opposition leader I had met before the Kosovo war. He is just as brave now that he is in office, and has made dramatic progress in stabilising the economy, handing over Milosevic and regularising relations with his neighbours. When I look back to my time at the Foreign Office, supporting the military action which ended in the defeat of Milosevic and now his prosecution, produced the single biggest change in the diplomatic shape of the Continent.

It was a jolly evening which had an element of both reunion and celebration to it. When they'd all left I stripped the flower display of the centrepiece and took it upstairs to Gaynor as an apology for a long and late day.

Tuesday 23 April

I spend the morning with Greg putting together an article on how we should respond to the rise of the far right. Of course, we must expose racism for the poisonous, destructive political force that it is. But racism is a symptom, not the cause, of the problem. It is only seductive to people who already feel insecure, threatened and alienated. But unfortunately this is now the condition of much of the lower income groups of Europe, who have seen globalisation transfer their jobs to countries with even poorer labour, or effectively depress their wages in order to keep their jobs in their own country.

The phenomenon has caught out a number of our continental sister parties who have not had Blair's skill in turning crime into a strength rather than a weakness for the left, or Brown's ruthless determination in pursuing a social agenda to help the poor.

Wednesday 24 April

I go to the House just in time for Prime Minister's Questions, where I was startled to hear Tony announce that crime in London will be under control by September. For the master of the maxim 'Always underpromise and then overperform', this does seem rather a bold claim. One of the reasons why PMQs is a necessity for me is that it enables me to spot what I'll be asked tomorrow at Business Questions. This will be one of them.

In the late afternoon Andrew Adonis calls to take forward my conversation with Tony on Lords reform. I am impressed that my conversation with Tony has been followed up at unusual speed, and we get down to business. The big problem is Tony's notion that we can announce that there will be two stages to the reform. I explain that this is supposed to be the second stage, and we will not be taken seriously if we announce that there is actually going to be a third stage. 'But couldn't you have a bill setting out the arrangements for a reformed Chamber? And later on bring in another bill on how it is to be made up?' I am appalled at the notion of stealing through the Commons a bill based on a promise that when it's all over we'll tell the Commons how the new Chamber will be made up. He advises me that I had better have it out with Tony and I undertake to do a note for his weekend box.

Thursday 25 April

For Business Questions I have armed myself with the explanation of what Tony meant when he said we'd bring London crime under control by September. He was referring back to his commitment when we first announced in February that we would 'halt the rise and then reverse' street crime in London. It is just as well I am armed with it because it quickly becomes evident that the Tories have come to the Chamber with everything they can throw at me over what is seen as yesterday's hyperbole. They retreat baffled and perplexed when I appear so confidently low-key about its meaning.

Later Tony himself rings me with another surprise. Last December during a discussion of my Memorandum on modernisation I had pressed him to agree to give evidence to the Liaison Committee. At the time he was reluctant to commit himself, but Clare Sumner has kept assuring me that they are not letting up on trying to get him to agree. Today's call is the fruit of those efforts. 'I meant to tell you this morning that you will want to know that I've decided to appear twice a year before the Liaison Committee.' I give a cry of delight and a short jig of joy. 'Yes, I thought you'd be pleased with that.'

Yes, I am. It fits in nicely with the package we are bringing forward to strengthen select committees, and it kills the story that Tony does not take parliamentary accountability seriously. I also cannot help noting that it is exquisitely timed to provide new positive interest to all the pieces on five-year retrospectives that are being prepared for the weekend.

Friday 26 April

The story about Tony appearing before the Liaison Committee comes out in the middle of the morning and I follow it up with an interview on *The World at One*. The big picture is still epic. It is the first time a Prime Minister has agreed that he'll answer questions on any policy for two hours before a select committee.

Yesterday I had seen Derry and Andrew Adonis slope into Tony's study prior to Cabinet. I couldn't resist ringing Andrew up and asking how it had gone. Andrew was obligingly frank and encouraging. 'Derry could see the case for a way of proceeding that did not require him to give up his own views. He does seem convinced, though, that when the question is put to MPs they will come to their senses and not vote for a largely elected element in the second chamber.'

Andrew also confirms that Tony will be reflecting on our scheme over the weekend, so I finish my note to him pressing that we have to do it all in one bill. It takes serious application to get right, because no Prime Minister has time to read minutes of more than two pages. As a result everything that goes to him has to be a miracle of compression. By the time I have finished my eight-point Memorandum it is a model of miniaturisation of which any Japanese engineer would be proud.

Monday 29 April

The press is pretty uncomfortable. Yesterday the *Sunday Times* broke a story claiming that we were about to cut child benefit to the mothers of children who are persistent truants. In their way of turning any story into one of process rather than substance, the press had divided into whether this was a conspiracy by Blair to float a kite or a conspiracy by Brown to shoot it down. Here and there, though, the central lunacy broke through of trying to cure the social consequences of deprivation by increasing the deprivation. There will be one almighty rebellion if any such legislation is brought to the House.

Gareth came round to talk over the latest moves on Lords reform. He was very exercised that we must include in the new package a measure to let the Law Lords go free and set up their own Supreme Court. 'It would be a dramatic gesture and would show we were serious about real reform, not just tinkering.' Personally, I totally agree with him, but if we take the Law Lords out of the House of Lords we take Derry out of the House of Lords, and that may prove a bridge too far. However, it is just possible that the Commons would come to recognise that it would be in its own interest to have an independent umpire to adjudicate between it and a democratic second chamber. Where else could we find a better umpire than a Supreme Court?

Tuesday 30 April

An historic day in Parliament, on which the Queen comes to address us on the occasion of her Golden Jubilee. There are only a few dozen of us left who were there when she came for the Silver Jubilee address.

The event itself is pure D'Oyly Carte. Gilbert and Sullivan could not have managed a finer theatrical coup than the march of the trumpeters of the Household Cavalry in gold and red heraldic regalia on to the balcony beneath the gable window, from which they blasted their fanfare of salute. Derry Irvine was dressed as if auditioning for a leading part in *Iolanthe*. He made a decent if rather formal address to the Queen. To my surprise he included a light-hearted reference to myself when he expressed the hope that the Queen's Jubilee year would be crowned by success with her racehorses, and prefaced it by saying, 'Unlike the President of the Privy Council I can claim no expertise on horse matters.' I just wondered if this was meant as an olive branch, and if there was a white dove flitting among the fourteenth-century rafters trying to find where I was sitting.

Afterwards there was a rather grand and crowded reception in the Royal Gallery. Almost the length of one wall is taken up with a painting of Wellington greeting Blücher in the midst of Waterloo, done in a style of heroic realism that would have met with Stalin's approval. The other wall is taken up with a painting of mirror proportions on the death of Nelson at Trafalgar. When President de Gaulle came to address both Houses of Parliament the original arrangements were for him to do this in the same Royal Gallery, but an equerry from his staff came to inspect the arrangement in advance and exploded that under no circumstances would 'mon Général' make his speech sandwiched between Trafalgar and Waterloo. That is why President de Gaulle was given the signal honour of addressing both Houses of Parliament in Westminster Hall from which we had just adjourned. However, today the triumphant patriotism of both paintings, while not exactly jolly, seemed entirely in keeping with the national event we were celebrating.

Wednesday 1 May

I wander along to the House of Lords to hear for myself what actually happens during their Topical Questions, about which the Conservatives are so excited. Today the Topical Question was on the press reports of child benefit being withheld in cases of persistent truancy. This is certainly one up for the House of Lords as the Commons has had no such exchange, and no opportunity to do so since the story broke a few days ago. The repeated question from several Tory interventions was, 'How can it help with poor education to make the poorest children even poorer?' It is an odd reversal of roles for the Tory Party to be representing compassion and the Labour Party to be imposing authoritarian compulsion. We are in danger of ending up with the *Daily Mail* vote while losing the *Mirror* vote.

Later I dropped in on Michael Martin for my regular bilateral. Michael was in good heart today as he had been rightly praised by everyone, including many Tory MPs, for the human warmth of his address to the Queen yesterday. He had come across as sincere, unpretentious and welcoming. If his speech benefited from simplicity it may partly have been because he persisted in his refusal to don a wig.

'Right up to the day before they were telling me I needed to wear a wig. I told them I don't have a wig, so they went away and reappeared with the last wig we had around the building, from the fifties. An enormous thing draped over a great big wire cage that you could have kept a budgerigar in. I told them I'm not wearing that.'

Thursday 2 May

The Cabinet is dominated by discussion of the grave situation in the Middle East, only marginally reduced in tension by the release of Arafat from siege. Tony asks us all to understand the domestic pressures on Bush not to intervene on behalf of the Palestinians. 'The US Congress is now more Likud than the Israeli government.' He then asks us to show understanding of the enormous hostility to any peace commitment among the Israeli electorate. 'Sharon rejected a UN inquiry into Jenin because of the public backlash against allowing Arafat out of siege.'

Both these observations are undoubtedly right, and reflect the very sophisticated knowledge Tony has built up of international affairs through his own first-hand contacts with the key players. Nevertheless, it is revealing that it is always the United States and Israel for whom we are asked to make allowances. He does not ask us to make allowances for the Palestinian leadership on the grounds, which are equally true, that President Arafat is universally criticised for having agreed to the exile of militants as part of the deal that got him out of house arrest.

I go down to Newham as Chair of the Cabinet Sub-Committee on e-Democracy to observe one of the first of Britain's electronic election counts. When we get there we are greeted by the local candidate for mayor, who turns out to be a Scot and has more vivid memories than I of when I addressed the Glasgow University Union over two decades ago. 'You demolished the opposition, but just when you were going to go we discovered that one of us had been sitting on your hat. We had never been so embarrassed.' I have absolutely no recollection of either this incident or the hat, and am discomfited that there are people around who remember me because of my association with a crushed hat.

Otherwise the evening would reinforce a technophobe's suspicion that electronic procedures have a malign tendency to go wrong. The company who provided the equipment come from the US and boast that they have just sold a package to the State of Florida to prevent President Bush stealing a second election by weight of hanging chads. They promise me that the result will be in by 9.45 p.m. Predictably, at 10.45 p.m. there is no sign of a result, or even much sign of a start to the count. This, it is explained to me, is the result of the delay in getting in the electronic cartridges from 'outlying polling stations'. Outlying? This is Newham, which measures about five miles by six across. I come from Scotland. I can tell you about outlying polling stations.

Tony Banks, one of the local MPs, sidles up to me and invites me to come to the Mayor's Parlour for a glass of wine, but I tell him I don't want to miss the count. 'Robin, you really ought to get out a bit more,' he advises me. He is, of course, right, and gives a knowing chuckle when, after another forty-five minutes, I give up and slip away. At least with the manual counts of ballot papers there is something to watch while you wait.

Friday 3 May

News from the electoral front is pretty good, all things considered. After five years in office we are still the party with the largest single number of councillors, which must be unprecedented in post-war history.

The success of all the new pilot schemes on new ways of voting is mixed. All the experiments in electronic voting have been a technical success and appear to have put up turnout by 4 per cent, which, to be fair, was the target. They are, though, overshadowed by the phenomenal success of the postal voting. Those councils which went for an all-postal vote ballot have reported turnouts of 50 per cent plus, including 61 per cent in Chorley, which exceeds the General Election turnout.

Andrew Adonis came round from Number 10 to discuss Lords reform in advance of next week's meeting with Tony. The good news was that Tony had read my minute to him and was now clear that we could not get away with doing it in two stages. We are going for broke with one joint committee and one bill.

But there was a bigger problem over the timescale of the operation. Gareth and I were both clear that the only vulnerable point of attack on the plan was that it was another way of delaying progress. We therefore wanted a finite timescale for the deliberation of the joint committee, especially on the options for the composition. As Gareth has said, 'We all try to think of something new to say about the composition of the new Chamber, but the fact is it has all been said. They could reach a conclusion within a month.' However Andrew, while as ever polite and diffident, stayed stubborn on this item. 'That's a key point you'll have to have out with Tony on Monday' was the nearest we could get to an understanding of our point of view. This is not a good omen. I want the joint committee to be seen as a way of restoring momentum, not derailing it.

Afterwards I took Gaynor out to lunch at the Gay Hussar which used to be a haunt of mine. Well, to be absolutely honest, the Gay Hussar paid for us to have lunch provided I sat to have my cartoon drawn by Martin Rowson and added to their gallery.

The proprietor asked me for my favourite anecdote of the Gay Hussar for their forthcoming book. That was easy. It has to be the day Roy Greenslade, then editor of the *Daily Mirror*, brought me for lunch to the Gay Hussar to make peace with me for their criticism of my reservations about the bombing that smashed up Baghdad in 1991. We had no sooner started the cherry soup than a waiter arrived to say that Mr Maxwell wanted to speak to him, which to my astonishment Roy waved away and said, 'Tell him I'm having lunch with an important MP and cannot possibly come to the phone.' Over the roast goose the same waiter appeared again and said, 'Mr Maxwell says it is very important he speaks to you now.' This time Roy responded, 'Tell him it's quite impossible. I'm having a very interesting conversation with a senior MP.' I was now not only astonished but immensely flattered that the editor of the *Mirror* preferred my company to a phone call from his proprietor. Finally, over coffee, the same waiter appeared and said, 'Mr Maxwell insists he must speak to you now.' At which Roy heaved a theatrical sigh and said to me, 'Do you mind?' Of course, I waved my hand and said, 'No, but you must, Roy.' After five minutes he returned and apologised profusely. It was only the next day when I opened my morning paper that I discovered Roy Greenslade had just been sacked. All the stage business about preferring to talk to me than to talk to his boss was part of the game-playing that surrounded the negotiations on the terms of his redundancy!

Tuesday 7 May

The day begins with an early meeting at Number 10 with Tony, Derry and Gareth to put the seal of approval on the new structure for the House of Lords. As with so many meetings called by Tony, he has already taken great care to square the key players on the central decision. There was therefore no argument about the issue of principle. We all know, although never say, that the dividing line in the room is between those who see the new plan as a way of making progress and those who see it as a way of halting progress.

Rather disarmingly, Tony begins by asking me, 'Nobody could accuse us of kicking the issue into the long grass now that we are setting up a joint committee, could they? After all, it would surely be improper of us to give a deadline to a joint committee.' He does not appear particularly pleased when I sweetly respond, 'When we appointed the joint committee last week to consider the Communications Bill, we did write into the remit a deadline of three months in which it had to report.' I can detect a silent consternation brewing in Derry at the very suggestion. We end with a compromise. There is to be no deadline on the work of the joint committee, but we will get it up and running as quickly as possible, starting with a statement in both Houses next week.

Wednesday 8 May

The text which Martin Sixsmith secured as part of his severance package has ignited the row all over again. We are all agreed that we cannot resist Opposition demands for yet another statement on the saga. With a heavy heart I ring Steve knowing that I will not be bringing welcome news. It is getting painful to see Steve yet again brought to bay at the Despatch Box with the Tory benches snarling for a kill. As a form of theatre it has all the parallels of throwing a Christian to the lions, only this time to amuse the mob in the Press Gallery.

Steve takes it with the patient resignation that has become his recent lot. We left it that we would see if there was an urgent question put down tomorrow by the Tories before he offered a statement, but I fear that means a statement is now a certainty.

Thursday 9 May

Stephen Byers made the statement with courage, and, in the circumstances, monumental calm. He was at his strongest when he challenged the Tories with being preoccupied by office gossip from within the DTLR, and blind to the real public interest in a rail system run for the passengers, not the shareholders. But the massed Tory benches did not want reason, they wanted blood. It was the House at its worst, and must have turned millions who watched it off Parliament.

In the evening Neil Kinnock dropped by for a whisky. He was in fine form. Ten years of no longer being used as a coconut shy by the press have restored his good humour and bonhomie. I told him of my recent visit to the Gay Hussar and we both reminisced about the victory celebration for the election of Michael Foot as leader when we filled the upper room of the Gay Hussar and finished up at midnight singing 'The Red Flag'. If only we'd known then what came next!

We talk about Romano Prodi's latest undiplomatic foray into UK politics by describing the government as 'paralysed like a rabbit in headlights before the euro'. I tell him that I could never understand why Tony backed Prodi rather than Wim Kok. Wim came over especially at the time to see Tony and they went, for the benefit of the photographers, on a train journey to Bristol. Tony was briefed by the Foreign Office to press Wim to run for President, but he never brought it up. Wim was far too much of a gentleman to bring it up himself. So he got off at Bristol and went home to the Netherlands with a clear message that Tony would not back him if he ran. As a result we've had five years of Prodi.

Friday 10 May

Start the morning with *Today* where I give a robust defence of Stephen Byers. The closest thing to being interviewed by John Humphrys is being in the boxing ring. His technique is to search for an opening where he can catch the other off balance and then keep hitting the same spot. Unwisely, Humphrys dropped his guard early on by admitting that 'some people say this is all Westminster village gossip'. I enthusiastically seized on this in agreement and never let him forget it or recover his balance in time to get in a punch. Afterwards, a beaming Des McCartan, my press officer, conveyed Number 10's official approbation of how well it had gone.

I call on my mother to put in hand arrangements for her ninetieth birthday. She is as bright and contrary as ever. When I proceed to talk about the party she interrupts with a classic mix of her wish not to be any trouble and her enthusiasm for fun: 'Oh, I don't want any party. Who's coming?'

Monday 13 May

The day we announce our new process on Lords reform. From two o'clock I start talking to the feature and leader writers who in fairness will not have long enough to turn round their columns by the time I sit down in the late afternoon. Moreover, I want to make sure they understand that I am very happy with the outcome. Half of what is fed to the public today as political analysis is not the result of what is said in a briefing, but the body language, the tone and the number of smiles.

It goes very well and after all I have a good story to tell. I stress two things. First, we have 'a route map' to finding a progressive centre of gravity for reform. Secondly, we have put Parliament in the driving seat for the journey, which fits our recent steps to strengthen Parliament, such as my package tomorrow to beef up the select committees. I express my enthusiasm about the prospects for progress by saying that the effect of the free vote is to 'put a stick of dynamite up the blockage across the road'. This produces raised eyebrows, and Don MacIntyre responds, 'By blockage I take it you mean the Lord Chancellor?' I brush aside such an unreasonable interpretation, but Des begs me not to use the phrase again. Nevertheless, the briefings went well and I was encouraged to hear that when Peter Riddell ambled through the outer office on his departure he expressed both surprise and delight at what I had secured.

Just before going into the Chamber I had a number of the ringleaders of the democratic option in to see me: Fiona Mactaggart, Chris Bryant, Joyce Quinn, Graham Allen and Tony Wright. The best way to get it off to a good start would be for a clear signal from the floor of the Chamber to the Press Gallery that those who most wanted a democratic second chamber were the most pleased. When the statement began, it quickly became clear that the supporters whom I'd briefed had worked hard in the short time since I saw them. The House of Commons signals its approval with what I guess was an Old Boys' cry of Hear Hear, but over the decades has become attenuated into a sort of low grumble in which only the two long vowel sounds can be detected. In the animal kingdom it is a noise that would easily be mistaken for a threatening growl, but among MPs it is the highest form of approbation. Today my supporters had made sure that it was heard often and loud during my statement. By and large, the reaction was positive even on the Opposition benches. It is very hard for the House of Commons to react to the promise of a free vote by saying that they don't want it. As a result I have rarely felt more comfortable with my afternoon's work as I walked the length of the table from the Despatch Box and out the door behind the Speaker's Chair.

My evening was anything but celebratory. Just before I sat down to dinner at home, Lorna rang to say that she is picking up negative vibes about the debate tomorrow on reform of nominations to the select committees. 'Everybody agrees now that it is down to your speech at the start of the debate,' she said. 'That's great, Lorna. The only problem is I'll be lucky if one in twenty of those who vote will be in the Chamber to hear my speech,' I replied. The call left me depressed, which in turn depressed Gaynor, and a deep gloom descended upon the dinner table that appeared out of place with what had been one of the best days for me in the Chamber.

Tuesday 14 May

I had allowed myself a lie-in before the tough day ahead, and after skimming the papers it was just gone seven when I wandered into the bathroom and turned on the radio as I reached for my toothbrush. I was electrified to hear them discuss the Lords reform announcement with a Tory MP and remembered I was due on air at half past seven. I dashed downstairs to the radio car. The great advantage of doing it from your own parking lot is that Jim Naughtie never suspected I still had my pyjama jacket on under the shirt I'd thrown over it.

Derry had done a most entertaining parody of being Derry Irvine on *Newsnight*, in the course of which he'd announced, 'I do not believe for a minute that the majority of the public want most members of the House of Lords elected.' Entirely predictably, this is thrown to me by Jim Naughtie as evidence that we are divided on the issue. I weave my way out of yet another story of division by praising Derry for his 'magnanimity' in admitting that the White Paper had failed to establish a centre of gravity, and his frankness in publishing the responses to the White Paper which did show that 89 per cent of those responding wanted a majority elected second chamber.

From then on the day was all downhill. Martin Kettle asked me yesterday during the briefing whether I was pleased with the outcome on Lords reform, and I had the foresight to reply, 'The first rule of politics is "never gloat". You never know what reverse is coming to you the next day.' How true, how very true. The debate on modernising select committees went extremely well. I was on my feet for forty-five minutes, partly because of a number of interventions from crusty backbenchers who had been put up to complain that I was handing over the choice of Labour representatives on the select committees from the Labour Party to the Tories, but I welcomed every chance to put the record straight.

We won the debate handsomely. Out of fifteen speakers, fourteen spoke in favour of the package. When I came to wind up I reminded them, 'I am a professional politician. Kind words in the Chamber are all very fine, but I'd much rather have votes in the division lobby.' We got through the bulk of the package to strengthen the resources and role of the select committees. However, we failed by a dozen votes to secure the reform of the system of nomination of select committees to make the final stage independent of party influence. Hilary and her deputy, Keith Hill, both voted with me, but every other member of the whips team who voted went through the other lobby. If that had been all they'd done we would still have won, but they also led an operation to persuade others to join them. Several recent ex-whips stayed outside the 'No' lobby crying 'Labour lobby this way', and pointing to the door just inside which stood several of the existing whips. Habit alone ensured that a large number of Labour MPs followed orders.

Despite all that, determined and courageous work by my colleagues on the Modernisation Committee ensured that we had a majority among the Labour MPs voting. We were defeated by the large majority of Tory MPs who voted in the 'No' lobby, which should have puzzled those Labour MPs who were directed into it on the advice that it was the Labour lobby.

I have often been asked since to explain why a majority of Conservative MPs voted to preserve the nomination rights of the government party. Entertainingly, Conservative spokesmen have also been asked the same question and have frequently floundered trying to come up with an argument they dare use in public.

It is easier to explain why a large minority of Labour MPs voted to keep the status quo. Most MPs are deeply ambivalent about their primary role. I include myself in that case of confused identity. MPs usually recognise that somewhere in their job description is a responsibility to protect the privileges and independence of Parliament. At the same time all MPs bar one are elected on a party ticket and came to Westminster not as independents but as partisans. This dual identity of MPs ensures a constant struggle between the perception of the role of Parliament and their sense of belonging to the party faction. On this vote a large minority of Labour MPs resolved that they would rather back control of committee membership by party than Parliament.

I think they made the wrong judgement but I can understand why government backbenchers came to that conclusion. I can barely begin to comprehend why the great majority of Conservative MPs came to the same conclusion. It must always be in the interests of the Opposition to have an independent, stronger Parliament, and it therefore should be easier for Opposition MPs to accept a collective role for Parliament at the expense of the party interest. The problem is that every Opposition sees itself as the next government. Its enthusiasm for an active, independent Commons is tempered by anxiety about whether it may prove too obstreperous once they get their own paws on power. The reform of the Commons, as on this occasion, often founders on the tacit understanding between the two front benches that what suits governments today will be just as convenient for the Opposition tomorrow.

In one sense the defeat had a valuable outcome. It taught those of us who wanted reform that winning the argument in the Chamber was not nearly enough. We also had to canvass the votes outside the Chamber. The impressive organisation that secured a majority for wider reform six months later was born that night out of the realisation that we had been beaten not by a better argument but by a more determined organisation.

4

Putting Parliament First

15 MAY–13 AUGUST 2002

Wednesday 15 May

A day of postmortems. The mood in the Modernisation Committee is subdued to a point of being cowed. I open the discussion by saying 'For me the clear lesson of last night was that we will not succeed on any proposal in which both Labour and Tory whips agree to mobilise against us. And I rather suspect that was the message we were expected to get.'

The Parliamentary Committee was a whole lot less civilised and much more brutal. Gordon Prentice went through the only too visible evidence of Labour whips trying to influence the way in which Labour MPs had voted. Gordon Prentice moved that the Parliamentary Committee formally instruct whips not to offer a view to backbenchers on a free vote, which was agreed unanimously.

I went straight from the meeting to another free-ranging discussion with Neal Lawson, Mike Jacobs and Matthew Taylor. Matthew Taylor has now blossomed into an original thinker. It is possible to see his father, Laurie Taylor, in him, in a way that was more difficult during all those years at Millbank when he was part of the Thought Police. Today he offers an interesting observation: 'The big divide in politics today is not left versus right, but Establishment versus populism. That's a large part of what's going on with the rise of the far right on the continent. The trick we've got to master is being in office without being in Establishment.'

I gather up Gaynor and we go together for dinner at The Brasserie in Brompton Road. We were in Paris from the moment we crossed the door, and it never fails to cheer me up. It reminds me that there are more important things in life even than reforming the House of Lords and Commons select committees.

Thursday 16 May

Disastrous news from the Netherlands. The new right-wing anti-immigrant movement has stormed from nowhere to become the third party, and my colleagues in the Dutch Labour Party have seen their seats almost halved. We discuss the arrival of the far right across Europe at Cabinet. There is total unanimity that we should not discuss it in terms as if it is about to happen here, and a broad recognition that part of the reason our colleagues across the Continent have been going down like dominoes is their failure to recognise popular concerns and unease on immigration, or to give priority to crime.

After Cabinet, Tony invites me to stay on for a chat. It is an early summer's day and he takes me out to his favourite sunny spot on the small terrace through the French windows from the Cabinet Room. Tony has deep Christian convictions, but they only just stay ahead of his tendency to worship the sun. One of the challenges of travelling south with him as Foreign Secretary was that he was forever placing himself in the hottest spot within half a mile. I deliberately place a wicker garden chair in the shade of the wall, prompting him to ask, 'Don't you like the sun?' 'Can't stand the heat. I am never happier than when I feel the crunch of snow beneath my boots.' People tend to forget that northern Scotland is actually on the same latitude as Hudson Bay and Stockholm.

He asked me what went wrong on Tuesday. I tell him about the operation against it. This is the rough trade of politics with which Tony himself has little first-hand experience.

I then put to him a kite that Meg had flown with me yesterday about the Joint Committee on Lords Reform. 'If you wanted to be really bold you could appoint Sir George Young as the Chair. He would command authority, and he would play to the great strength of our strategy, in that we are genuinely letting Parliament decide rather than the government decide. It would also have the low politics advantage that it would put the spotlight on the divisions between the Tories in the Commons and the Tories in the Lords.' In reply he was silent, and screwed up his face to focus on the distant sunny sky. Whether he was pleased with what he saw or appalled by it, it was impossible to tell. It all depends on whether he really wants the strategy for reform to succeed or to run into the sand.

At the lobby I'm perplexed with repeated questions about whether we might introduce a paving bill to hold a referendum on the euro whenever we feel like it. Perplexed by what prompts all these questions, I gingerly defuse the discussion by stating the obvious: 'I am doubtful whether anyone in Cabinet would want to go through the full parliamentary process without the certainty of a referendum.' Only afterwards do I learn that the press interest comes from remarks by Steve Byers over lunch with journalists. Number 10 will hate it if this story runs, if only because it will take them half of tomorrow to hose down Gordon. I long ago became very sparing about lunches with journalists when I realised that journalists buy you lunch because it is still one of the cheapest ways of getting a story.

Afterwards I race out to Heathrow to fly to Europe and dinner with Alfred Gusenbauer, the leader of the Austrian Social Democrats. A member of the Hungarian Social Democrats joins us for dinner. Curiously, as our sister parties ebb within the European Union, our counterparts are experiencing a resurgence across the candidate countries, and the Social Democrats are now back in office in Hungary.

My friend tells a hilarious tale over the asparagus about American detachment from world reality. When Hungary was seeking membership of NATO he had visited Washington and given evidence to the Senate Armed Forces Committee, then chaired by Strom Thormond, who was already in his nineties. He had felt he had been quite successful in making his pitch for Hungary to be admitted as a reliable partner, and was pleased when Senator Thormond asked him afterwards to come and have a quiet word. To his consternation, Strom said to him with a puzzled expression, 'When I was at school Austria and Hungary were the same country. When did you split up?'

Friday 17 May

I do a press conference with Alfred Gusenbauer in a gesture of solidarity and then scramble to catch a short hop over the mountains to Prague for a meeting of the PES to lick our wounds on our defeats by the far right. Jan Marinus Wiersma from the Netherlands conveyed the bewilderment of the Dutch Labour Party. 'We ran our campaign on our great economic record. We did not see until too late that economic issues were not what the electorate was bothered about. Fortuyn proved the more attractive precisely because he was not being responsible.'

When Greg and I reached Prague airport disaster awaited us. Apparently the new air traffic system in Britain had just crashed, and there was a minimum four-hour delay. I cannot comprehend how anyone could devise a new system for such a crucial purpose without the elementary precaution of including some back-up in the system. I told a rather bemused Czech airline attendant, 'I blame privatisation. Never let anybody privatise your air traffic control.'

When we finally got to Heathrow at midnight we found a scene of chaos that would have done justice to a war zone. The terminal was full of thousands of stranded passengers and the baggage hall full of more than a thousand abandoned suitcases which had missed their connecting flights. One of the British Airways staff told us that the airport hotels had put the price of the rooms for the night up to £450. Appalled at this profiteering I announced to a greatly entertained baggage hall, 'There ought to be a law against it.'

Sunday 19 May

Summer finally arrived with a bang on Sunday but we were limited in how much advantage we could take of it because poor little Tasker had pulled out a claw and had to be carried everywhere. For some unaccountable reason the vet hospital uses a bandage of alternating pink and fluorescent green, just to make sure that it catches the eyes of the rest of the world. As I cradle him in my arms round the park I get alternate looks of deep sympathy for the poor doggy and burning contempt for me as a suspected dog-beater.

Tuesday 21 May

I devote most of the day to preparing my lecture for the Hansard Society on Wednesday. I like to pace the room when I dictate to Rachel bent over her laptop. Yesterday I must have put in the best part of ten miles wearing out that carpet. I make the case that both MPs and journalists are victims of a culture of political reporting that has become too introverted and says too little about what goes on in the lives of their readers and our electors.

Anne Sloman, the PR and Parliamentary Head at the BBC, dropped by while I was in full flow. She in turn complained that the present rules prevented them from showing activity in and around the Chamber in a way that captured the buzz of the place, but she could not get the Broadcasting Committee to see the need for change. 'We've got to keep our camera trained on whoever's speaking at that particular moment. It's a bit like trying to film a football match when you can only show the player with the ball at the time.' She also let slip that on the night in February when they covered Stephen Byers' statement on Martin Sixsmith's resignation the BBC got its lowest ratings for a year everywhere outside the South East. I deliberately put this wonderful example of our introverted obsessions not being shared by the public straight into the speech the moment she had left.

Wednesday 22 May

I made a point of getting into the room for the PLP early. As Tony was speaking, seats at the top table would be at a premium. The other great advantage of getting early into the PLP is that Gareth Williams is always the very first to arrive, and since he and I traditionally sit side by side it gives me a good chance to catch up on developments with him. Indeed, paradoxically our whispered asides in front of a meeting of three hundred can be much more secret than any arranged meeting which might suggest to the observer that we were plotting, which is exactly what we do today sitting at the top table.

Tony is in good form. The press gossip about him facing dissent and mutiny could not be further from the truth. There may be individual issues on which the PLP has its doubts, but they have no intention of changing their leader. He has a particularly strong passage on Duncan Smith's attempts to reposition the Tory Party as a movement of social compassion. 'The Conservatives are offering themselves as a party of the vulnerable and the poor. Yet whenever they do a photo call in one of the deprived communities the result is to reveal themselves as wandering in a foreign land trying to speak to the natives in a language that is foreign to them.'

I went straight from the PLP to Buckingham Palace for the Privy Council. Gordon eventually emerges from the audience chamber where he has been giving the Queen the new gold sovereign struck in honour of her Golden Jubilee. When I enter I find the Queen is much taken with it, and I congratulate her. 'You have been more successful than most of the Cabinet, Ma'am, in getting money out of Mr Brown.'

Later in the day when I arrived at the LSE to deliver the Hansard Society lecture, I was much entertained to be met by an extremely courteous but worried security guard who insisted that I should know where the back exit is from the stage, 'just in case the audience should riot, sir'. The lecture seemed to pass off quietly enough, without at any point provoking the respectful and mildly intense Hansard audience to rip up the pews and fling them at the stage.

Friday 24 May

I am gratified to find an e-mail in my red box from the BBC *PM* programme detailing pages of positive comments on the interview I gave last night on the theme of my Hansard speech. By a margin of four to one the comments support my complaint that political reporting has dwindled to personality gossip and demand more substance and less spin from the press themselves. It's good to pack up a term knowing that I've hit a nerve with the press and a chord with the public.

Tuesday 28 May

I was in my constituency office when news came through that Stephen Byers was resigning. He made a simple, dignified and affecting statement, which again demonstrated the quiet courage he has shown in recent months. Steve has been a good minister and more radical than most. The appalling problem of the railways is not of his creation and within the industry he is given credit for getting to grips with it. But for all that he has taken such a pounding in the media that any balanced person would have concluded that the only sane course was to get back a life of his own.

Saturday 8 June

In the evening West Lothian Council threw a dinner to celebrate my neighbour Tam Dalyell's forty years as their Member of Parliament. He had just celebrated his forty years in the House with a big interview in which he lambasted Tony Blair as the worst Prime Minister during his time as an MP, which some felt a bit rich as his time in the House spanned all the Thatcher years. Michael Martin, as guest of honour, deftly turned his observation to humorous purposes in his speech when he expressed the view, 'Tam, I would regard it as an obligement if you were not to rank the Speakers under whom you've served in order of priority.'

Afterwards Michael, Tam and I stood together in loyal amity for the press photographs. It must be unique in the long history of the Commons for both the Leader and the Father of the House to come from the same small local authority area.

Tuesday 11 June

In the afternoon I appear at the Despatch Box for my monthly session of oral questions. Normally these are a doddle, but today they turn rather choppy as I get a roasting both to the front from the Tories and to the back from my own side over the Stevenson peers. These were the first batch of appointed peers to emerge from the new independent commission. Their announcement is no doubt still used in schools of public relations as an example of how not to go about public presentation. Matters were compounded by Lord Stevenson at the time of the launch observing that you could not appoint a hairdresser to the Lords because she would feel out of her depth. Anyway, today I get it thoroughly in the neck because one or two of them have not even spoken in the Lords a year after their appointment. I console myself that anyone listening to the unanimity with which the House tears into these appointed peers could not possibly be persuaded that any reform of the Lords will be stable if its members are all appointed.

Wednesday 12 June

The tabloid press and Tory broadsheets are now in full cry on the scent of a new perceived vulnerability of the Prime Minister. Yesterday Alastair Campbell withdrew Number 10's complaint to the Press Complaints Commission over claims by the *Mail on Sunday* and the *Spectator* that the Prime Minister had tried 'to hijack' the Queen Mother's funeral by getting a bigger role for himself in the ceremony for the reception of her coffin at Westminster Hall. Boris Johnson, editor of the *Spectator*, and of course also a Tory MP, is much quoted with claims of a 'humiliating climbdown'.

It all fits perfectly with the theme of my address to the Press Gallery. It is a classic example of the press preoccupation with process (how often did Clare Sumner ring Black Rod and what did she say to him?) rather than outcome (a dignified ceremony in which the Prime Minister was no more prominent than the Leader of the Opposition).

It is also a classic illustration of the extent to which the press are preoccupied with gossip about the titanic struggles between press officers, spin doctors and journalists, which are of no conceivable interest to the public in the real world.

I got out alive from the Press Gallery lunch, although the round of applause may have owed as much to a good lunch as to my speech. Many of those present would welcome it if their sub-editors allowed them to write more about content and less about gossip, and as for the rest my message came laced with enough humour for them to be able to swallow it. The Press Gallery has none of the extravagant proportions of the parliamentary suites over which it is perched. The bar where the victim of the day is taken first for his drink is a stark watering hole which would not be out of place on a street corner in Glasgow. The dining room to which you are then conducted has a low-slung ceiling and provides cramped quarters in which careful work has to be done with your elbow if your neighbour is to be given a decent chance to get at his plate. The journalists constantly complain about the provisions of the Press Gallery, but in truth I think many of the older hands have come to value its rather louche ambience which sends a signal that they may be in Parliament but they are not of Parliament.

Friday 14 June

I rang Alastair Campbell to share my vexation at the obsession of the press with the tale of Black Rod and the Queen Mother's catafalque. I had heard that he had appreciated my robust defence of him to the lobby, and he sounded thankful. Alastair has skin which is not just thick but armour-plated, but constant pinpricks leave their cumulative effect. I offer to help with the presentation of our case, and he immediately takes me up by volunteering me for *Channel 4 News* tonight and the *Today* programme tomorrow.

Saturday 15 June

Today went well. I enjoyed it. John Humphrys began his introduction by saying it had not been a good week for the government, and in my response I teased him by saying that I could not remember a Saturday when he had introduced me by saying that it had been a good week for the government. That made even John Humphrys laugh and got us off on a non-confrontational note which enabled me to correct the record of events.

Monday 17 June

A nightmare journey down to Westminster. Apparently one of the cabin crew had not turned up for work, and BA called for a dozen volunteers to go by later plane in order to get us down to the right ratio of crew to passengers. I was not regarded as helpful when I suggested that it would be quicker to call for a volunteer to join the crew serving breakfast.

I arrived just in time for my lunch with Sir Nigel Wicks, and assorted other regulators of public standards such as Sam Younger of the electoral commission, who meet occasionally to reinforce group solidarity.

Entertainingly, I discovered that Nigel still remembered me from his time as Private Secretary to Jim Callaghan as Prime Minister. I was flattered to hear that I was thought of as a troublemaker, and gratified to know that the trouble I created had been noticed in Downing Street.

We jointly commiserated that part of the problem with parliamentary democracy today is that troublemakers do not get promoted. In my day, those who caused trouble by asking sensible questions and pursuing independent lines of thinking got promoted on to the front bench. This was not simply the cynical calculation of Wilson that it would shut up the troublemakers, nor the more elevated concern of Callaghan to keep the front bench balanced as a means of promoting unity in the party. It was also a recognition that the most useful ministers were likely to be those members who had already shown a capacity for independent thought and initiative. How very different from today's culture in which promotion only comes from years of loyalty and a demonstrable capacity to master the party hymn sheets. If Parliament is a bit more dull today, it could be because any sign of an independent mind is regarded as rather dangerous and probably disloyal.

Wednesday 19 June

The press have a free kick today at Cherie for her observation that young people will only volunteer as suicide bombers if they feel that they have no hope. This simple statement of common sense is denounced by the press as justifying terrorism, and by Michael Ancram as 'causing massive offence'. It all made a much larger story because the same day a large bus bomb has been detonated in Israel, for which the right-wing press seem to hold Cherie personally responsible. I rang Cherie to express my personal solidarity and best wishes. She sounds genuinely pleased to be getting a message of support, and I assure her that nobody who knows her will fall for the libel that she sympathises with terrorism. The irony is that the Blairs' instinctive sympathy has always been with Israel, and if Tony is vulnerable to any charge of partisanship, it is that he does not emotionally identify with the consistent repression of the Palestinian people.

Thursday 20 June

At Cabinet there is an intense exchange of views about asylum seekers, which is likely to be the big issue at tomorrow's European Summit in

Seville. Tony has become identified with the proposal that the European Union should use the leverage of its development finance to punish those countries who do not cooperate in cutting the flow of asylum seekers. This has enraged Clare, whose strength is the clarity with which she single-mindedly keeps the focus of her development aid on poverty reduction. She has just described Number 10's proposal to use it as leverage over asylum seekers as 'a very silly idea'. My own worry is that from my experience in Europe I cannot see another government backing such an idea, whether silly or not. Chirac is forever looking for an opportunity to upstage us in African eyes, and will find this one a gift.

The penny does appear to have dropped somewhere in Number 10. The sound of retreat continues through the meeting of the lobby in the afternoon, where the Prime Minister's Official Spokesman stressed that the aim was to use development aid 'to reward rather than punish' countries who cooperate with us. This may be a mature recognition that we are not going to succeed in Seville, but I fear it comes too late to save us from being pasted for having 'failed' to get our objective.

Monday 24 June

In the early afternoon, I stroll along to the other end of Carlton House Terrace to the Foreign Press Association, to do the British launch of the *PES Yearbook*. It is organised by Peter Mandelson's policy network and features himself, myself and Charles Clarke. To my surprise, and to Peter's evident amazement, the upper hall is absolutely packed with journalists, including the cream of the Press Gallery, the BBC and ITN. It is apparent this has little to do with the *Yearbook*'s discussion of the finer points of social democratic values for the millennium, and much more to do with trying to get a story on the euro for the six o'clock bulletins. Peter Hain's comments at the weekend that the government now has a problem of trust, which will make it more difficult to win a euro referendum, appear to have been a better inducement for attendance than the official press release.

John Sergeant of ITN asks the first question, which not surprisingly turns out to be along the lines of whether we expect a referendum to be postponed in view of the government's current problems. Peter Mandelson, from the Chair, rather takes my breath away by responding, 'Robin, you are the most senior, you go first.' I give a recitation of the line that the referendum will be held if and when the five economic tests are met, and not at some arbitrary point in the calendar. John Sergeant then asks what the others on the panel think, to which I intervene to say, 'They agree with me' and they both loyally nod. I add, 'There, John, you have got your headline: "No Labour Split On The Euro" ', at which the whole room erupts in laughter at the ridiculousness of making a positive story into a headline.

Afterwards I walk across the park to the House, and get there just in time to take my place beside Tony for his statement on the Seville Summit. This is a tougher challenge for him than usual, as all the press are full of predictable headlines that he failed to get his way at Seville, and was rebuffed over his key objective to penalise those countries who do not cooperate more with us in halting illegal migration. His central defence is the perfectly creditable one, that in a gathering of fifteen nations you simply cannot get everything you want. However, the force of what he was saying was undermined by the way in which he said it. It was unmistakable that Tony was frustrated with the whole summit, rather fed up with most of his partners and wanted to get this statement over with so that he could get on with domestic issues where he was in charge rather than in the minority.

If ministers were worried a year ago that the government could not command enough trust to win a referendum they must now be in a state of settled gloom. Trust is the asset of which the government is most short in the wake of a war which has left two-thirds of the population convinced they were deceived. When I warned Tony the previous Easter that he could not attack Iraq and in the same year win a referendum on the euro, I had been more concerned that the predictable breach with our European neighbours would make it tough to persuade the British public to vote for closer union with the same countries. Certainly the buckets of vituperation emptied over the French for their opposition to the war would have challenged the greatest of spinmeisters to explain why the next logical step was to share a common currency with them. But in the event, the bigger obstacle to a successful referendum is that the credibility of the government has been a casualty of the war. This was poignantly demonstrated in Tony's visit to Tokyo in July 2003 for which he prepared his most forward statement yet that membership of the euro is firmly in the British national interests, only to see it wiped from the news by the subsequent question on the death of David Kelly the day before. And the government's desperate struggle to rescue any credibility from the controversy over weapons of mass destruction has made it impossible for Number 10 to contemplate the national roadshow they promised to sell the euro.

A commitment to Europe was one of the defining characteristics of New Labour and a central plank of their platform for a new centre ground on which they could make common cause with the Liberal Democrats and wet Tories. I have never doubted that the euro is for Tony an unusual case of conviction politics. During the last General Election, William Hague toured Britain with a digital clock warning of the hours left before polling day in which 'to save the pound'. Despite the blanket safety-first style of the campaign, Tony Blair was at his boldest in steadfastly refusing to rule out a referendum in the next Parliament. Ironically, we now look set to deliver the policy which William Hague put to the electorate of no euro referendum in this Parliament. This is an immense reverse not just for Tony Blair but for all of us who agree he was right when he said that Europe was Britain's destiny. Opinion polls on the euro are not uplifting reading for pro-Europeans, but our one trump card was that, although the majority against the euro may go up or down, there was always a majority who regarded membership of the euro as inevitable. When the Treasury trumpet in summer 2003 sounded an uncertain note on the case for the euro it blew away that trump card. The next poll found that those who regarded the euro as inevitable had slumped.

To be sure, the Treasury produced a whole dump truck of documents on its assessment, aptly summarised by *The Economist* as 'Five Tests and a Funeral'. They may have justified the conclusion that Britain should not join right now, but they did not explain why the Treasury could not announce a target date when Britain would be able to sign up. It may have been necessary to mine deep into the mountain of paper to realise it, but the supporting statistics established that Britain was now nearer convergence than some of the members of the euro at the time when they gave their commitment to a date for membership. The government will not shift public opinion on the euro until it shifts its position from pondering *if* Britain should join to announcing *when* Britain should join.

So long as the official policy is ambivalent as to whether Britain will join ministers are hobbled from proclaiming why Britain should join. I can testify to the pressures from many attempts to smuggle positive references to the euro into my speeches. On one celebrated occasion Number 10 instructed my private office to delete them just before I got up at the Despatch Box. Perhaps fortunately, no one had advised my press office, who dutifully distributed the original text, thus securing far greater publicity for the 'censored' passages than if I had been allowed to read them out – and even louder fireworks from the Treasury when they saw the next day's papers. It is remarkable that there is still a quarter of the population who consistently tell pollsters that they believe Britain should be a member of the euro as they never hear a minister argue that case without equivocation, and will not hear one do it until the government commits itself to a target date.

The problem with the national debate on the euro is that it is dominated by a preoccupation with the costs of joining. We cannot arrive at a balanced view until we give equal weight to the Sixth Test – what are the costs of staying out? The answer is already becoming alarmingly clear. Britain's share of Foreign Direct Investment in Europe has more than halved since the formation of the euro, as more and more companies come to the conclusion that there is not much sense in locating their production plant for the European market in the one economy where they must pay an exchange rate penalty to sell in the rest of the single market. Britain's trade with the members of the eurozone has also fallen behind the growth in trade between those members, which was entirely predictable as the euro was intended to stimulate trade between its members. This is a worrying trend in trade with what is by far our largest export market and after enlargement we will sell twice as much to the other members of the European Union as the rest of the world added together.

The economic costs of staying out are paralleled by its political price. Before I left the Foreign Office there was a prediction that Gerhard Schröder had given Britain until the end of 2002 to prove it was serious about the euro and, if by then we had made no move to join, he would revert to Germany's traditional partnership with France. That prediction has turned out to be more reliable than many recent ones on Iraq and the past year has seen a quickening tempo of Franco-German relations. It is inevitable that members of the euro will over time develop habits of consultation and coordination on matters that are of mutual interest to them, but which will leave Britain out of the loop. Britain cannot be at the core of Europe if it is outside the single currency that increasingly defines that core.

Tony Blair understood both the economic and the political importance of the euro. He was the political leader most likely to persuade the British people that their country will be stronger, not weaker, from sharing the same currency as its major trading partners. Personally, I believe Tony Blair will always regard his period in office as flawed if he does not seal Britain's place in Europe by taking Britain into the euro. It is his tragedy, and Britain's cost, that his loss of credibility over Iraq prevents him from even making the attempt.

Wednesday 26 June

I am to substitute at Prime Minister's Questions as Tony is out of the country. I wake up to hear on the radio that stock markets all around the globe are crashing as a result of the latest scandal of regulatory failure in the US. It is not difficult therefore to figure out what will be the vanguard of the Tory attack this afternoon – falling share values and shrinking pension funds.

I walk across the park to get in training at Number 10. The only perk about standing in for the Prime Minister at Question Time is that you are allowed the use of his empty office. My preparations are interrupted by the sight of Euan and a friend kicking a ball in the back garden, a charming reminder that the heart of the British government doubles up as a family home.

Contrary to popular myth, Tony is actually very indifferent to what the press say about him and his government, so long as the public say the right things about us. There is no television in his room, and it takes the press office three-quarters of an hour to come up with a transistor radio so that I can hear the news. I am, though, willed to concentrate by an astonishing array of photographs on his desk, of Tony with Cherie, of Tony with his teenagers, of Tony with baby Leo, of Tony with Clinton and assorted other global celebrities. It leaves me feeling rather inadequate at the memory of the modest pair of photographs on my desk – of Gaynor hugging Tasker, and Red Rum on the beach on which he trained.

Clare Sumner is my transmission mechanism to the government machine. This is a heavy burden to be thrust upon a twenty-nine-year-old, but there are many up and down Whitehall who have come to regret not treating her with the respect due to a fifty-nine-year-old Permanent Secretary. As a result, briefs of astonishing clarity, incision and accuracy appear within fifteen minutes at her command. I find that I lack the courage to tell her that I cannot keep up with the sustained paper flow that is generated by her enthusiasm to make sure I know the answer to every issue in which any of 659 MPs might have a fleeting interest for half an hour this afternoon.

At two o'clock we get into my car and transfer to Tony's suite at the Commons, where David Hanson, Tony's PPS, Bruce Grocott, his former PPS, Lorna and Ken, my PPSs, and assorted staff are waiting to put me through my paces. By this point the priority is not what I might be asked, but what I am going to get into my answer irrespective of the question. In a speech last night, Iain Duncan Smith announced that every Tory MP was going to spend a week with the 'vulnerable' in his constituency. This is just too good to miss, and David Bradshaw has come up with the punch line: 'A week with the vulnerable will not wipe out the memory of what they did to the vulnerable in eighteen years.' There is a visible start from the Number

10 team when Stephen Hillcoat arrives from my office with a glass of my traditional Talisker and water. However, they are reassured by the evident calmness of my team, who have seen both the ceremony and the results many times before.

Ken walks me the short length to the Chamber, where our side greet with loyal cheers their gladiator for the day. When I ask my opposite number, Eric Forth, when he is going to spend his week with the vulnerable, and could I come too, even his own benches erupt in laughter as even Eric's best friend would find it hard to claim he is overfond of spending time in his constituency.

I spent the last six months telling anyone who would listen, and a few who didn't want to, that the problem in the Commons is that we love the party political mud-wrestling and the public, while amused by it, find it hard to take it seriously. Unfortunately, I love the party political mud-wrestling myself. Afterwards Ken frogmarched me into the tearoom to parade me before colleagues, almost as if he was the proud parent of a son who had just graduated.

Thursday 27 June

The first meeting of the Cabinet Sub-Committee on Parliamentary Reform was a spirited affair. It quickly became clear that there are two principal camps. On the one hand are the reformers, who have firmly grasped that we simply cannot go on as before in Parliament. Pat Hewitt wickedly observed, 'Even if we are ministers now it would be dangerous to start to regard Parliament as a diversion from our real jobs.' On the other hand are those who regard all talk of reform as dangerously revolutionary. John Reid proved a fine example of the latter school: 'I am not here as a parliamentarian. I am here as a Labour politician.'

Friday 28 June

I wake in Vienna for the PES seminar on European security strategy. I begin the day with breakfast with Anna Lindh, the Swedish Foreign Minister, with whom I became firm friends in my last job. She taxes me with Tony's performance at the immigration debate at Seville:

'Tony was more right wing than Chirac. He kept going back time and again to press for penal sanctions on countries that did not cooperate in stopping immigration, even when it was clear he was isolated in the Council.' I loyally explained the nature of the English press and their fixation with immigration and asylum. However, I am not sure that I quite carried her with my explanation. Anna was robust in her Social Democrat principles: 'We will not beat the right by appearing to agree that they have the right agenda.'

Monday 1 July

The news from New York is grim. President Bush has just taken hostage the UN peacekeeping mission in Bosnia by refusing to extend its mandate unless every American soldier gets immunity from the International Criminal Court. There is a higher than usual degree of irrationality in this demand. Every American soldier in Bosnia is already in theory within the jurisdiction of the International Criminal Tribunal on the Former Yugoslavia, as a result of the architecture which the US itself negotiated at Dayton. There is, of course, not the slightest real·risk of American servicemen being brought before either the Tribunal or the International Criminal Court.

The real mischief is that the Bush Administration has once again pitted itself against all its allies. It is almost as if they are determined to prove that they have learnt nothing from last week's row over their unilateral demand that the Palestinians elect someone other than Arafat. Rather a rich demand that one, as whatever one's view of Arafat's performance in office, there is no getting away from the fact that his election was a whole lot more conclusive than President Bush's, without a hanging chad in sight. I go into the office more relieved than ever that I am no longer Foreign Secretary and have to pretend that everything is just fine between us and the White House.

Around 5 p.m. I cross over to my room at the Commons, only to discover that the second reading debate, that had been scheduled for the whole day, collapsed within fifty minutes with the result that the House packs up and goes home at 6 p.m. Mindful that colleagues keep telling me I cannot adjourn the House in the early evening because they have nowhere else to go, I ask Glynne Jones, my Private Secretary, to check how many members stay for dinner in the House. Then I go home myself and try to exercise a soothing restraint on Gaynor, who is bouncing out of the sofa and throwing soft objects at the television in a general effort to will Tim Henman through his current round at Wimbledon.

Tuesday 2 July

I have a fascinating hour in the morning with half a dozen junior ministers, whom we have chosen at random to act as a focus group on my proposals for modernisation. They are younger, keener and less world-weary than some of my Cabinet colleagues, and are gratifyingly enthusiastic about bringing the Commons into the twenty-first century – or at least the twentieth century. Des Browne volunteers, 'I have never been so tired in all my working life. Stopping Parliament at 7 p.m. has got to be sensible.'

Douglas Alexander, a rising star who will be in Cabinet before the party is in Opposition again, is scathing about the contempt of the rest of the world for the hours we work: 'Andrew Smith came up to do a constituency meeting for me with businessmen. To his credit he still came, even though he had been up all night taking a bill through the Commons. When he arrived he apologised for being late and explained that he had been up all night in the Chamber. He had expected to impress the audience, but all he got were amazed looks from sensible people who thought it was a crazy way to do business.'

Thursday 4 July

Jack was impressive at Cabinet outlining why the United States was wrong over the International Criminal Court. His clinching argument was, 'The only other countries they have got alongside them in resisting the International Criminal Court are China and Russia'.

Tony, though, was keen to play down the degree of disagreement with the Bush Administration. He stressed, 'I find it very easy to deal with George Bush.' At a personal level I am sure that is right, but it does require some pretty heavy-duty wallpaper to cover the growing political cracks. Nevertheless Tony is right when he warns that the right-wing agenda is to convince the public that Britain must choose between America and Europe. I am sure the right wing are wrong in believing that we can choose America rather than our immediate neighbours, but I am not so sure that they are wrong that the time has come when we will have to make a choice.

Fittingly, it is Independence Day. We could all do with a reminder that the US chose independence from us, and as a result we are two different sovereign states with different policies and different national interests. Eric Forth provides us with a timely reminder at Business Statement by turning up in an extravagant stars and stripes tie. I could not resist reminding him that it was a Tory Prime Minister who lost America in the War of Independence.

Friday 5 July

Nigel Sheinwald, who was Head of the News Department when I was at the Foreign Office, and is now ambassador to the European Union, called by for lunch. It would be strange if Our Man in Brussels was not worried about his country falling down the widening gulf between Europe and America. He was worried, but he has an unflappable good cheer which always prevents worry reaching a climax of panic. It was Nigel who had the challenging task of handling the media on the famous occasion when Netanyahu set up my visit to Har Homa then used it as an excuse to sabotage my trip to Israel. On the morning of Har Homa Nigel called at my room in the British residency with the news 'the British press is not all bad this morning'. The next morning on the plane on the way out of Israel, he came and sat beside me and began with the memorable introduction, 'Yesterday I said that the press was not all bad. This morning it is all bad.' When we got back, he got himself a T-shirt printed with the words 'I choreographed Har Homa'.

Monday 8 July

After the Business Managers have dispersed, Ben Bradshaw, who had replaced Stephen Twigg as my deputy, waits behind to share with me his anxiety over the decision Jack Straw is announcing today that we will allow the US to incorporate British avionics in the F-16s that they are exporting to Israel. He is visibly upset by it, as he regards it as a flat breach of our own domestic ban on the export of weapons to Israel, and he personally resisted it during his time as the junior minister responsible for the Middle East. All decisions on arms exports are a three-way tug between the Foreign Office, the DTI and the Ministry of Defence. In my experience the Ministry of Defence would sell any weapons short of nuclear warheads to anyone with money in the bank to pay, and famously on occasion has sold weapons to regimes which did *not* have the money to pay. The DTI under Steve Byers took its responsibilities seriously, and quite often together we were able to outgun the Ministry of Defence. With me out of the Foreign Office the MoD is now more often in the majority than the minority.

Friday 12 July

A day in the constituency. The high spot of the day has to be my visit to a community gymnasium, which has just been refurbished with a big council grant. It is a bustling, happy place, full of community activities from the pipe band to the trampoline club. The climax is my opening the new hall for the tae kwon do club. This is preceded by a fearsome display of kickboxing by my constituents, led by a six-foot Amazon who apparently kicks for Britain. I am presented with a calligraphic scroll in Korean, but get into boiling hot water when I hold it up for a group photograph upside down. The experts are willing to put up with being in the same photograph as an MP for the local paper, but are not willing to risk that one of the other clubs might spot that he can't read Korean the right way up.

Saturday 13 and Sunday 14 July

We went to Covent Garden to go around the outdoor clothing shops and kit ourselves out for the Hebrides. I leave Gaynor in the formidably capable hands of a former sergeant major to get herself kitted out with walking boots, and search out a new waterproof top for myself. The girl who helps me asks if I am going anywhere nice, to which I reply 'Harris'. She looks rather perplexed and finally plucks up the courage to say, 'I am not sure that top will be right for Paris.'

On Sunday Gaynor feels that she owes it to the retired sergeant major to try out the boots. We have a magnificent walk through the Missenden Valley in the Chilterns. On the final approach to Little Missenden, the Chilterns Way runs down a ridge through a broad cornfield, in which the path is reduced to single file with acres of ripening wheat to left and right. We stop off at the Red Lion for a pint before tackling the last leg back to the car, which is as well because Tammy has figured out he has done his statutory five miles. A bit of a union dog is Tammy, and at five miles always lies down flat and insists on being carried the rest of the way, to the great entertainment of the ramblers we meet going home in the evening shadows.

Monday 15 July

The day of Gordon's long-awaited comprehensive spending review. It is impossible to miss its dramatic, even triumphant, impact. He has presented a prospectus for a sustained investment in public services, of a kind which the Commons has not heard for a generation. I and the whole of the Labour Party thoroughly applaud it.

The rest of the day is spent with Rachel in my office struggling to finish the text of the report from the Modernisation Committee. She has worked so long and so late in putting the amendments to the paper over the past couple of weeks, that she claims to be thinking of calling her next cat 'Modernisation'.

Tuesday 16 July

I get light relief on my way into the Privy Council. The Palace find it convenient to combine the Privy Council with the presentation of credentials for the newest ambassador or high commissioner. It is a curiosity of London diplomatic life, presumably going back a couple of hundred years, that the monarch sends her carriage to fetch the new ambassador. This charming courtesy was never updated with the invention of the combustion engine, with the result that a couple of horse-drawn carriages leave the mews on every such day and return with a rather fazed ambassador.

When I arrived the recognisable horse carriages were at the door. When I went by the groom holding the horses, I asked 'Who is it today?' and was slightly surprised to hear the reply 'Tasmania'. As I went through the door, I muttered to the equerry, 'I wasn't aware that we had separate diplomatic relations with Tasmania.' He inclined his head with great delicacy and tactfully rejoined, 'I think he meant Tanzania.'

The business of the day is big in length but as usual short in substance. Bizarrely we pass an order for Guernsey to regulate 'electrically assisted pedal cycles'. I had anticipated the Queen asking about them, as she remains sharp about the business. I reply as briefed: 'I am advised that it assists in pedalling uphill, Ma'am', although I harbour the reservation that that won't be much help in Guernsey.

Wednesday 17 July

Yesterday Tony Blair fulfilled his commitment to give two hours of evidence to the Liaison Committee, making him the first ever Prime Minister to appear before an investigative select committee. He comes out of the morning crits rather well, as I was always confident he would. The members of the Liaison Committee, though, are thoroughly belaboured by all the press for not being journalists trying to get a story out of him. The reports point up the real dilemma we have in restoring respect for Parliament. Here we had a new, thoughtful, serious exploration of the big issues, but what the press had really wanted was drama and blood on the carpet.

At Prime Minister's Questions I take up my now customary seat beside Tony, to prompt him. He has a brilliantly crafted put-down for Duncan Smith, responding to a planted question from a Labour backbencher on the New Deal. Tony celebrates the success of our investment in the New Deal in getting young people back to work, and says that it would be 'such folly to take it out'. Having seen that Duncan Smith is about to intervene, he then adds with perfect comic timing, 'Talking of which . . .' – and then sits down. Duncan Smith is forced to rise to gales of laughter and derision from the Labour benches.

After Prime Minister's Questions, I had Ken Clarke in for a chat about progress on the Joint Committee on Lords Reform, of which he is a senior member. He is acute in his reading of the coded contributions within the committee: 'There hasn't been much real debate on the principles of reform. Instead, we've had the same debate played out over our schedule of work, with the reformers pressing for progress, and those who want as little reform as possible pressing for delay.'

Thursday 18 July

Most of the day is spent in a desperate effort trying to square the circles in my draft of the select committee report on modernisation. It is politically vital that modernisation does not become a purely government cause, which makes it all the more important that I get the Liberals on board. The problem is that they know that too. They won't come on board without some clearer commitment to consultation with them, and Hilary will jump overboard if I am too clear about consultation with them.

I craft a couple of carefully nuanced paragraphs on general consultation on the pace of the legislative programme and which bills might be appropriate for carry-over. I wander the length of the 'No' division lobby, and across the Members' Lobby to the suite of the government whips. These are among the most forbidding rooms in the Commons. They are sandwiched between two corridors and have no windows to the outside world, with walls that have been unusually neglected for the government's art collection. I am never quite sure whether the effect is contrived to intimidate the recalcitrant backbencher, or the inevitable consequence of the necessity of squeezing the whips into the nearest available space to the Members' Lobby.

Roy Stone, Hilary's principal official, is very affable, and surprisingly agreeable to my revised text: 'So long as it doesn't commit us to some kind of new structure such as a Business Committee, we have no problem with consultation in principle.' Relieved that I at last seemed to be on the home turn, I go back to my office knowing that I now only have to get the Liberals on board for the watered-down edition.

Friday 19 July

I take Gaynor to dinner at Livebait in Covent Garden, where my day starts to go spectacularly wrong as a result of my new medication to lower my blood pressure. I eat half a dozen oysters, immaculately presented in their shells on top of what looked for all the world like a cake stand. When I finish them, I am conscious of the world slipping away from me, as if I am the oysters and the rising tide of the sea is enveloping me. I say to Gaynor, 'I am afraid that I don't feel too well.' This proves prescient as they are my last words.

The next I know I am sitting on the floor surrounded by an awful lot of people. I have not been seriously worried about how I feel until I see the concerned looks on the faces in front of me. A girl in a summer frock is asking me polite but insistent questions which puzzle me until Gaynor explains that she is a GP, who had come in the hope of a quiet dinner. I am conscious that I have become something of a cabaret act for the restaurant.

Two wonderfully competent and tactful people arrive in green uniforms, and take me off in custody in an ambulance. I am given a choice of which hospital I want to go to. This seems a wonderful breakthrough. Our investment in the NHS must finally be breaking new ground if the patient gets a choice of which Accident and Emergency unit to go to. I select St Thomas' as the nearest thing Parliament has to a neighbourhood hospital, and we depart at an alarming pace. Just in case I think of bolting, I am strapped to a large electronic box on a trolley which whirrs every few minutes to monitor my presence and my plumbing.

NHS hospitals cannot compete on décor, carpets and cuisine, but in terms of personal courtesy and attention there is not a hotel in Britain with better staff. The only awkward moment arises when a male nurse breezes in and announces, 'I hear we need a catheter', but mercifully he turns out to have mistaken me for the man in the next bay. Eventually it dawns on me that I am being detained and will not be allowed home. The big downside to being admitted to hospital is that you shed your external persona at the door of the ward. Five hours ago I was a person of standing taking decisions on the contents of my government red box. Tonight I have the status of a toddler, being firmly told off by young girls in their twenties for getting out of my bed without permission. It is a valuable exercise in humility, which perhaps should be visited on politicians more often.

Saturday 20 July

Hospitals are not restful places. Paradoxically, I suspect that most patients are keen to get home to have a good night's sleep. I do not think I have been awake this early for months.

I have the joy of waking up in St Thomas' with the spectacular view of Parliament and Big Ben across the river. I pass my enforced confinement counting the windows and identifying every room behind them.

The paternal, authoritative figure of the cardiac consultant arrives. I find him perfectly charming, but it is obvious that to the nurses and junior doctors he is the big white chief. Unwisely I forget my place enough to interrupt one of his questions, and I am gently but firmly reminded that inside the hospital he is the one with status. However, the news is good. There appears to be no reason for me to remain.

It is a wonderful sunny afternoon as we drive back. St James's Park has never looked more lovely or the tourists more cheerful. There is nothing like a mild intimation of your mortal frailty for reminding you of the beauty of life. Once home, we have a frustrating weekend in which Gaynor works hard in trying to keep me inactive and rested while I try to explain to her that nothing makes me more stressed than doing nothing. However, I admit that as a result of her efforts I feel more rested on Sunday night than I have for a long time.

Monday 22 July

The neurologist at St Thomas' is engaging and helpful. He is keen to reassure me that there is nothing unusual in fainting as a result of medication to bring down blood pressure. He has a refreshing take on European history: 'Look at that picture of the three old men at Yalta. Every one of them with some condition of arterial degeneration.' At the end of extensive tests, including twenty minutes with my head strapped by multiple wires to a screen, it is pronounced that 'your brain is normal'. I try to conceal my disappointment at this conclusion.

A letter arrives from Clare Sumner, allegedly setting out the Prime Minister's views on my modernisation text as a result of perusing his weekend box. They look suspiciously similar to the views Clare Sumner had expressed to me herself last Thursday. I have grave doubts about whether Tony spent a couple of hours at the weekend wading through the ten thousand words of my text; I rather suspect that he has ticked off the covering comments from Clare.

I retaliate with a manoeuvre that has never yet failed. I responded that if the Prime Minister really insists on all these deletions, I must demand a meeting with him to discuss it in person, and within the next forty-eight hours. Private Secretaries hate having to squeeze in yet another diary engagement, and will readily compromise rather than persuade their boss to have yet another meeting.

Tuesday 23 July

The tactic once again has been a complete success, and this morning Clare is on the phone compromising.

Afterwards I chair the last meeting of the Cabinet sub-committee on the Modernisation Report. I have taken the precaution of circulating its recommendations to all the members of the Cabinet who are not on the sub-committee, which has elicited a few, broadly positive, responses. Tessa Jowell, bless her, simply sent back a copy of the recommendations with a tick against nearly every one of them. The meeting itself passes off rather well, as I have used the committee to try and create a corporate sense of ownership over modernisation. Even John Reid has come to accept that his role in the discussion is to be the entertaining but isolated voice of old-fashioned reaction. Today he is generous: 'We have given the proposals a good thrashing through. The result is that we have got a good balance between modernising Parliament and safeguarding the Executive.'

I make a point of saying three times that I would be looking for solidarity from colleagues on all those recommendations on which we agreed, and then ran up to my office to dash off a letter to the Prime Minister, confirming that I want a payroll vote on everything but the change in sitting hours, which I have had to concede as a free vote even for ministers.

Wednesday 24 July

Tony is the main item on the agenda at the weekly PLP meeting. It is traditional for the leader to send off the PLP for its summer break with a rousing résumé of what we have achieved, but Tony has always done much more with the PLP than go through the motions. Indeed, Jean Corston from the Chair reminds us when introducing Tony that this is the sixth time he has addressed the PLP since Christmas.

Tony is upbeat and bullish about all we have done. Indeed, he is so assertive that he sounds almost old Labour: 'Britain is the only country in the industrialised world which is expanding investment in health and education. We are also the only country increasing the number of public employees.'

There follow questions from nineteen MPs within fifteen minutes, on everything from the sale of fireworks to war on Iraq. Tony deals with all of them with great patience and occasional self-deprecation, as when he concedes in response to the question on some of the embarrassing results of the new mayoral elections: 'I have to confess that elected mayors was my idea, but was not my most inspirational idea.' He is robust, though, with those who press for a more leftist approach: 'If people yearn for a revolutionary Labour government, they will find that they have got no Labour government at all but a revolutionary Tory government instead.'

In the afternoon I held a meeting of officials from the Cabinet Office and the Parliamentary Draftsmen's Office, to vent my frustration at the difficulty in getting more progress on draft bills. Everyone agrees that if we can get away from the position of official bills being the first text that anyone has seen, to one in which most bills have first been scrutinised in draft, there will be immense gains for Parliament and everybody else. The problem is getting through the transition period in which the system has to produce both official bills for the present session and draft bills for the next session. I conclude the meeting by announcing that I want ten draft bills next session, and I hold them all personally responsible for delivering.

Thursday 25 July

Pat Hewitt rings seeking my support for a proposal that she and Alan Milburn have jointly prepared to create a new legal personality for Public Interest companies, which would enable public sector undertakings, such as hospitals, to achieve the freedom and independence of a company without any of the problems of private ownership and profit motive. It seems a novel way of providing a solution to our deep problem of how to retain the public service ethos while freeing the public sector from central control. Predictably, it is being resisted by the Treasury, who are incapable of letting go of their control. The big political problem with that is that they then produce the stultifying effects of public financial controls as an argument for private involvement. I promise her that I will write in and support their initiative.

Friday 26 July–Friday 9 August

As New Labour headed south for the sunbelt of Provence or Tuscany, I headed north to the Hebrides. You get a lot more weather for your money in the Hebrides.

The islands teem with wildlife, a demonstration that the most important requirement of animals is not an easy climate but the absence of humans. In one expedition, Gaynor and I climbed for almost two hours over a track in the cliffs before we were rewarded by the majestic sight of an eagle taking its kill back to its eyrie, and being ambushed on the way by crows mobbing it in the hope that it would let go. There was another memorable tramp at dusk when we were lucky to see within the same hour a sea otter rolling on its back in the loch, as if it was on a lido on the Riviera, a grey seal diving repeatedly in the tidal runs for its evening meal and a herd of deer trotting over the peat bog, with the brightly spotted calves of this spring at their heels.

On the last day, we went out with a local man in his boat. After twenty minutes, he pulled the engine and let us ride in peace on the sea. Like many landlubbers, I tend to think of the sea as an empty space with miles of nothing in every direction. Those fifteen minutes sitting at peace on the sea's surface were a revelation to me. The place was as busy as Piccadilly. Porpoises circled us, whales swam across our bows and puffins, guillemots, shags and gannets flew past us at every point of the compass with an earnest sense of purpose. It was a salutary lesson that there is as much life in the water as there is on the land.

Tuesday 13 August

Before we set off for the rest of the recess in Edinburgh I called Number 10 to register with the duty Private Secretary my deepening concerns over Iraq. While I was away, Tony had to answer a question at a press conference on whether Parliament would get a vote on a substantive motion before there was any war, and he had batted it away with the response that we should not break with the precedent that such debates take place on the Adjournment. I mildly demurred, pointing out that the precedents are more mixed, and that there was an adequate historical precedent for the House getting a vote on a substantive motion before the commitment of troops. The Private Secretary responded with the helpful gloss on her master's words: 'The Prime Minister was not ruling out a substantive motion, he just did not want to get boxed in on his options unnecessarily.' I can see that. The trouble is that, by not referring to the option of a vote on a substantive motion, Tony has given the press the impression that he has ruled it out.

On the tedious part of the drive up to Edinburgh through the endless junctions and contraflows with which the M6 navigates Birmingham, I share my anxieties with Gaynor. If I want to signal my worries on Iraq, the strongest platform for me on which to make my stand would be over parliamentary procedure. I will not get away with running my own foreign policy, but who better to stand up for the right of Parliament to take the decision than the Leader of the House? Anyway, I do not see how I can get through my forthcoming press conference on modernisation of the Commons without being asked

if a meaningful Parliament should not be allowed to decide whether
we go to war.

———⁂———

It is a curiosity of the British constitution that there is no formal
requirement on the Prime Minister to seek the authority of
Parliament before declaring war. He commits British troops to
action by virtue of the Royal Prerogative. It would, though, be
unwise for any Prime Minister to tell the Commons that it has
no say on the matter, with the result that by tradition Parliament
is allowed to debate the decision, although it is not allowed to
take it.

The most common procedure is a debate on the
Adjournment. A word of explanation is necessary here for the
great majority of sane people who have had the good fortune
never to have been involved in the minutiae of parliamentary
procedure. A motion for the Adjournment is literally a motion
proposing 'That this House do now adjourn'. It has to be moved
by a government minister, as one of the key ways in which the
Executive controls Parliament is by awarding itself a monopoly
over procedural motions. However, the government does not
actually want the Commons to adjourn as to do so would lose
the rest of the day's business. Therefore, if there is a division the
government and its party vote *against* the motion for the
Adjournment which the government itself moved. Conversely, if
there are rebels who wish to express their dissent at a proposed
war, they vote *for* the government's motion to adjourn. During
the run-up to the Falklands War a number of Labour
backbenchers did just that.

As a final twist in this corkscrew logic, it should be added that
the government really does not care much whether the House
adjourns or not, as these days the only business that follows is the
half-hour debate following the motion to adjourn in which by
convention a backbencher can raise a constituency or similar
issue. In reality the Adjournment Debate is a device to enable the
Commons to hold a debate without any risk of a serious division
at the end of it. The question of whether British troops are

committed to action ought to require the dignity of a more meaningful procedure.

The procedural convention that the Commons does not vote on military action is at odds with the political reality that no government could survive if it took the nation to war against a majority view of the Commons. The Opposition has the right to force a vote on a substantive motion in its name and can table a motion of confidence at any time. After the Suez invasion the Labour Opposition did indeed table a motion rejecting it, but was unable to secure sufficient support from government backbenchers to carry it.

The problem this time round was that the Conservative leadership was even more enthusiastic than the government about invading Iraq. There has been much huffing and puffing lately on Opposition benches outraged that the Prime Minister should have been guilty of overstating his case in the countdown to war, but at the time they were as keen as he to talk up the justification for war. When Tony went into the Despatch Box he knew that the only challenge he would get on Iraq from IDS was an attempt to outdo him in support for the Republican President and in denunciation of Saddam. He might have been much more careful with the hyperbole, and the debates in Parliament would have been more challenging, had the Tory leadership election been won by Ken Clarke, who expressed intelligent scepticism about whether there was genuine evidence that Saddam was a real threat.

Subsequent events would similarly have been more challenging. Every attempt by Conservative front-bench figures to exploit the embarrassment of the government over its failure to produce any weapons of mass destruction, or its inability to prevent security in Iraq from deteriorating, founders on their own complicity in the decision to invade. Iain Duncan Smith was much criticised for keeping his head down during these controversies, but in truth how can he exploit them without condemning his own failure to oppose the war that produced them? Michael Howard has hit upon the formula that he supported the principle of the invasion but is alarmed by the incompetence of the occupation. This though does not save him from conviction on grounds of opportunism. It was always predictable from past performance that the Pentagon would prove poor at nation-building skills, over the top at responding to any resistance with overwhelming force and insensitive in running reconstruction to provide profits in Texas rather than jobs in Iraq. Those who supported a Pentagon-led invasion cannot now walk away from the inevitable consequences of a Pentagon-led occupation.

Throughout the long period of the run-up to war in Iraq, a large majority of the public remained solidly opposed to a military solution but their concerns were not voiced by either official front bench in the Commons. True, Charles Kennedy and Menzies Campbell insisted with some courage in posing sensible doubts as to whether the juggernaut was rolling in the right direction, but their dissident voices only served to unite even more the Conservative and government benches. The time is long past when Tony Blair was going through his pluralist phase and went out of his way to find common ground with the Liberal Democrats as part of his project to establish a new centre-left consensus. Nowadays he is more likely to use them as a butt of jokes intended to get a laugh out of Conservative MPs who hate the Liberal Democrats more than the government. The nadir of Tony's speech on the eve of war was the gratuitous opening jibe that the Liberal Democrats were 'unified in opportunism'.

I was determined that a conspiracy between the two front benches should not cheat the public, and Labour backbenchers, of an honest vote on whether Britain should go to war. The first useful lever to hand was the parallel procedures of the US Congress. On Iraq it expected and secured a formal vote before the President could commit troops. I found that Number 10 was stumped for a reply when I innocently asked whether as a good ally we really could do any less than the US in consulting the legislature. The second source of help was that Jack Straw was just as robust on insisting on the right of Parliament to decide. Jack has been around the Commons as special adviser and MP for as long as anyone left in the Cabinet other than John Prescott and the Chamber holds no terrors for him. His strategy for putting before Parliament motions based on the resolutions of the Security Council worked well for the government in November when the Commons endorsed Resolution 1441. It came unstuck on the eve of war, because the government had no resolution from the Security Council to put before Parliament. In fairness that was not Jack's fault as no one could have worked harder to deliver agreement in the Security Council, but the Foreign Office had been set an impossible task by Number 10.

In the event the government tabled a lengthy motion into which they threw every possible reason they could come up with to justify war, except of course a UN mandate, and invited Parliament to support 'all means necessary to ensure the disarmament of Iraq's weapons of mass destruction'. By contrast, the amendment from the rebels in the name of Chris Smith was a model of brevity. It did not rule out military action but insisted it must be conditional on a second UN Resolution and on more time in which the weapons inspectors could finish their job. Tony Blair worked on Labour MPs by calling the waverers in to see him in small groups, and by all accounts laid on thick the threat from Saddam's weapons of mass destruction. Other senior figures, including even Cherie, worked the phones. One dissident became so fed up with pager messages to call assorted Labour luminaries that he sent colleagues a spoof pager message, 'Please call Bill Clinton re: tonight's Iraq vote.' I doubt whether all of those who were persuaded to vote for war that night would do so now that they know that there was no real and present threat from Saddam. Only twenty minutes after the vote one Labour MP who had supported the government could be found in the taxi queue already regretting what he had done.

But irrespective of the outcome, the very fact that a vote took place at all was a major advance. For the first time in the history of Parliament, the Commons formally took the decision to commit Britain to conflict. Now that the Commons has established its right to vote on the commitment of British troops to action, no future government will find it easy to take it away again. And one consequence of the controversy over the government's justification for the war is that next time the case for war will be more thoroughly tested by a more sceptical Commons. I may not have succeeded in halting the war, but I did secure the right of Parliament to decide on war.

—⁂—

5

We Did Good Work That Night

15 AUGUST–29 OCTOBER 2002

Thursday 15 August

I surprised myself, and everybody else, by joining a gym today. Well, that is not strictly accurate. I maintained my credentials as a supporter of public services by registering at the local municipal gym.

On the way back, I stopped off at the local newsagent and was intrigued to find that the *Spectator* front page was a cartoon of myself and Clare Short trying to stop Blair in a tank going to war. This turns out to be a trailer for a couple of articles against war by Gerald Kaufman and Mark Seddon. The latter piece credits me with being opposed to any active participation in a military attack on Iraq, which I suspect may reflect a conversation with Mick Rix since ASLEF are the landlords of the *Tribune* newspaper of which Mark is editor. When I buy it, the proprietor looks distastefully at the cartoon and asks, 'Do you not mind being drawn this way? In some countries they would be sent to gaol for such a cartoon.' I explained to him that in this country we don't take journalists that seriously.

In the evening, Elizabeth Smith had invited us to come as guests of Deutsche Bank to a Festival concert at the Usher Hall. Richard Goode provided a splendid performance of a Mozart piano concerto. Music means more to Gaynor than to myself. For me the main reward is to see her enthusiastic appreciation.

There is, of course, no such thing as a free concert, as the head of any corporate entertainment section will tell you, and afterwards Deutsche Bank took us off to dinner. I was favoured over my starters with a succinct summary of the dismal doldrums in which the financial sector was becalmed. I managed to break in when regret was being expressed that there was simply no take-over activity going on, to express the thought that while this may be challenging for those who live by commission from take-overs, it may not be entirely a bad thing for the rest of the economy and especially for those who work in the companies being taken over.

The rest of the meal was totally drowned out by my mobile, which went radioactive as the first editions hit the streets in London. Des McCartan, my Press Officer, rang first to say that he had been beset all day by Phil Webster of *The Times*, who wanted to follow up on the *Spectator* story about my views on Iraq. He had kept refusing to comment, but that had not stopped *The Times* running it as a front-page splash on the basis of a few sentences from 'a friend' of Robin Cook. It is one of the unconscious ironies of the press that they keep producing anonymous 'friends', whom you would cheerfully strangle if you ever found out who they were. Des was now getting bids from every breakfast channel for me to expand upon the views of my 'friend'. The calls had even included one from a New York radio station, where they were only now limbering up to the main bulletins of the evening, and had rung to ask 'if Robin could come on to explain his opposition to President Bush's foreign policy. And, by the way, do you know who this Gordon Brown is and where we could contact him?' I put it to Des: 'If I give any interview on the record, I would be pushed into expressing full support for the government line. It is much better that I don't do anything that forces me to deny the damn story, and we let it run without any comment.'

Friday 16 August

I wake up to hear Tony Lloyd on the *Today* programme responding to John Humphrys' questioning on my views with commendable honesty: 'To be candid, John, I do not know the answer.' If only all my friends had taken the same rigorous standard of scientific accuracy.

The *Times* article itself is reasonably restrained and as balanced as I would expect from such a respected reporter as Phil Webster. The actual quote from the unknown friend is that 'Mr Cook has no intention of leading a Labour rebellion on Iraq. He will make his interventions in Cabinet and not elsewhere.' However, in the hothouse of today's press, even such a modest seed swiftly mushrooms and metamorphoses into a much more sensational story. Des tells me that this morning we have already had fourteen different bids from BBC channels alone.

Tuesday 20 August

Most of the day is spent on a visit to the constituency. We begin with the opening of a plant for Terahertz, a company formed to turn a technological breakthrough in photoelectronics at Heriot Watt University into an industrial product for a global market. Over coffee, the Chair of Scottish Enterprise warns me that we will be lucky if we again see a mass production facility such as NEC or Motorola come to the UK. They will be looking for mass production in places like China where they can get the advantage of an ambitious but cheap workforce. The future of our electronics industry is in the higher valued added products such as the present one. As if to confirm the point, the Chief Executive of the new company enthuses to me on their sales to the new factories in China, while the rest of the room laments the competition that those factories represent.

Friday 30 August

I fly down to Birmingham where the PES members of the Convention on the Future of Europe are holding a caucus to hammer out a common line. Before dinner I had a drink with Klaus Hensch, the influential German MEP, who was still delighted with his visit in late July to London, where he had been given access to both Tony and Gordon, the latter giving him a full hour. 'I now know all your plans for the euro,' he surreptitiously confided in me, glancing to the left and right to make sure that we could not be overheard. Trying not to sound too fascinated, I asked what he had learnt. 'You will make an assessment of the five tests in June, then you will have your referendum in October.'

At dinner I sat between Giuliano Amato, the cosmopolitan former Prime Minister of Italy, and Jan Kavan, with whom I had shared platforms during his long years of exile in the Communist era and with whom I worked well when we were both Foreign Ministers. Jan is now preoccupied with representing the Czech Republic at the forthcoming meeting of the UN General Assembly, of which this year he is President.

He had a fascinating tale of his visit to Washington to prepare for the General Assembly, where he was briefed by William Wood, the State Department's Head of their UN Section. 'To speak to you frankly, Mr Kavan, we are pleased that the Czech Republic is going to chair the General Assembly, but we are glad you are no longer the Foreign

Minister of your country. You were more close to the UK than you were to the US.' Jan was startled with the diplomacy of telling him that the US was glad he was no longer Foreign Minister. I was just as startled that the State Department was keeping lists of people who were too close to the UK, given that we are supposed to be their own closest ally. It got better. After Jan had expressed his country's reservations about a unilateral attack on Iraq, Mr Wood triumphantly seized on his comments as further evidence of his unsoundness. 'That's just why we're glad you're no longer Foreign Minister. Your thinking is closer to that of Robin Cook than to Tony Blair.'

Both Jan and Giuliano are much exercised by the immediate dilemma facing every European state – whether to accede to the unilateral demand by the US for an assurance that they will never hand over American service personnel to the International Criminal Court, an undertaking contrary to their treaty obligations to the court. Jan is troubled about whether small countries such as the Czech Republic can resist the US demands, which were forcibly put to him by his State Department interlocutor on the basis that 'no US citizen is going to be tried by a Belgian', which may raise legitimate doubt as to whether he is capable of correctly identifying in which European country The Hague is to be found. Even while we are talking, an Italian MEP leans over Giuliano's shoulder to tell him that Berlusconi has just announced that Italy will give the US such an undertaking, breaching what had hitherto been a united resistance by the European Union. Giuliano turns back to me and says, 'It shames me that Italy should have been the first to give in.'

The preoccupation of our own dinner table with the difficulties of living with Bush is mirrored in the wider ambience of the gathering. On the plane down I had resolved that in view of my growing anxieties on Iraq I should take on the distressing unilateralism of the current administration in my speech to the dinner. 'We are in a unique period in the history of the world, in which there is one global superpower without a rival, and yet it is also a superpower whose President does not accept global responsibility. Whether it is Kyoto or Johannesburg, whether it is the International Criminal Court or the Chemical Weapons Convention, whether it is the Middle East peace process or Iraq, their instincts are unilateralist rather than multilateralist. The world today needs a strong, united Europe that can provide an alternative vision in international forums.'

This passage provoked the strongest spontaneous applause from the audience. Greg told me afterwards that Roger Liddle, who was at his table marking the occasion for Number 10, did not join in the applause and observed at the end that it was 'a bit anti-Bush'. I hope Number 10 is going to grasp that it is becoming increasingly difficult to be pro-European social democracy and pro-Bush at the same time.

Tuesday 3 September

Tony gave the second of his new monthly press conferences to the Press Gallery. He promises 'the fullest possible debate' in Parliament, and stresses the importance of building broad international support for action at the UN. I am, though, haunted by the fear that Tony still sees this as an issue of manipulating press and public opinion, and has not grasped that on the substance of the issue the public and he are so far apart that he cannot win this one. Over the years, those employed to support him at Number 10 have become accustomed to the Blair magic working, and I fear that there are none left among them prepared bluntly to tell him that this time it cannot work.

Wednesday 4 September

I arrive at the office early and get down to work on what I am going to say at tomorrow's launch of the Modernisation report.

Iraq is not mentioned in the report but will certainly be mentioned in the press conference. I agree on the phone with both Paul Tyler and Nick Winterton that we should avoid the press conference being derailed by Iraq, but you do not have to be a rocket scientist to craft a relevant question on Parliament's right to debate the issue. I have long, protracted discussions with Des and Greg on how I should handle this. I am firm, even ruthless, that I have to be upfront on Parliament's right to take the decision. We would be treated with derision if we produced a package of measures to strengthen Parliament and excluded any role for Parliament on whether British troops went to war.

Number 10 are obviously nervous about what may happen tomorrow. Alastair Campbell rings to check that I have got the transcript of Tony's

Sedgefield statement, and I assure him that I will make full use of it, particularly the commitment to 'the fullest possible debate' in Parliament.

Thursday 5 September

It is as well that I spent as much of yesterday preparing my answers on Iraq as on Commons reform. I wake up to find that the big story on *Today* is the growing demands for the recall of Parliament to debate Iraq. After the seven o'clock bulletin, Charles Kennedy gives a sensible interview in which he calls for Parliament to be recalled to hear a briefing from Tony on his talks with Bush.

Much of the point of Parliament being recalled for debate is undermined by an interview with IDS, who is slavishly loyal to the Republican ideologues. He offers full and uncritical support for military action against Iraq, and comes close to giving the impression that the only real issue for debate is why the Prime Minister has not already attacked Iraq.

We get off lightly at the press conference. The first half dozen questions are on Iraq. I close them down with courtesy, on the grounds that this is not a press conference about foreign affairs. However, I take care first to trail my prepared thoughts on the central importance of Parliament debating Iraq, by saying that it is 'inconceivable' that Britain could go to war without the consent of Parliament and 'reminding' the press that the 1991 Gulf War was preceded by a vote on a substantive motion, not a motion for the adjournment. Number 10 would almost certainly rather the world was not reminded of the precedent, and will decode what I was up to, but cannot come back to me and say that when the Prime Minister promised 'the fullest debate' in Parliament he did not actually mean one as broad and as full as last time.

The story on the recall of Parliament, though, is not going so well. In my own comments I have tried to avoid getting into the corner of rejecting recall but kept the question open by talking about keeping it under review. However, by the end of the lunchtime bulletins it is plain we are losing on this one, and I call Jonathan Powell at Number 10 to press on him my concerns. I find Jonathan very sympathetic. He tells me that there had been a meeting this morning between Tony, John

Prescott and Jack Straw. As far as Number 10 was concerned, the heat had gone out of the issue when IDS had rung Tony to say, 'I am not calling for a recall at present', a view which deepens the eccentricity of his behaviour over this issue. When I put it to Jonathan that we would be better to recall Parliament before IDS does get around to demanding it, he agrees. We both agree that I should speak to Tony and Jonathan arranges for a phone call tomorrow.

I am intrigued by this morning meeting and ring John Prescott to get his version. I find he also is very sympathetic on the question of recall. 'Tony was claiming that the press are whipping this issue up. I told him that was true, but that the press were bound to do that. If you ask me where he is on the issue, he is focused at the moment on pushing Bush to go the United Nations.'

I responded that that would be helpful, but we also need to ask what happens next. If the UN says no, we cannot then go ahead with military action without being in even greater difficulties with the public and international opinion. John responded, 'Yes, but at the moment Tony is taking one step at a time.'

Friday 6 September

The press is as good as it gets. Even the *Mail* hedges its bets by praising me in its editorial, for saying it was 'inconceivable' that Britain would attack Iraq without the agreement of Parliament. Tony has not been so lucky. The *Mail*'s front page covered remarks by Tony that are prominent in every other paper, that Britain must be ready to pay 'the blood price' for its close alliance with the United States. Close inspection of the text reveals that Tony did not use the words, but was unwise enough to say yes when Michael Cockerell, in a TV interview, asked him if he agreed with Robert McNamara that Britain's 'special relationship' meant being prepared 'to commit themselves to pay the blood price'. If he had a better sense of Labour history, Tony would have known that Harold Wilson's answer to McNamara's question was no, and that he refused President Johnson's request to send British troops to Vietnam. The overall impact is disastrous as it positions Tony exactly where he does not wish to be, namely paying in British blood for his relationship with Bush.

In the late afternoon we drive up to take Gaynor's parents to dinner. Halfway up the M40 I get the promised phone call from Tony. He confirms John Prescott's view that he still sees the whole issue as built up by the media, and has not yet grasped the extent to which he is in real difficulty with the wider public: 'I never used the words "blood price" and anyway that interview was back in July.' This is all very true, but the fact remains that in his head he heard Michael Cockerell ask whether the relationship with the US was special, and he was not attuned to the extent that too many in Britain think that under Bush the special relationship comes at too high a price, whether in blood or any other coinage.

On the recall of Parliament, he begins with his reluctance: 'I have nothing new to say.' I comment that this shouldn't put him off. People are not demanding that he come up with something new to say, but that he should say in Parliament what he is saying everywhere else but Parliament. Slightly surprisingly, Tony claims that the pressure for recall will fall away after his meeting tomorrow with Bush. I stress to him that it will be a real surprise if recall is going to go off the agenda, but I am happy that we'll consider the issue next week.

Sunday 8 September

The reports from Washington don't quite match Tony's faith that his meeting will take the steam out of the demands for a recall. There is, though, a welcome stress in what both he and President Bush said on the importance of building an international coalition through the UN.

I am struck this weekend by the totally impossible schedule we demand of Prime Ministers. Since he came back from his break last weekend, Tony has flown to Johannesburg to make a big speech; returned overnight and the next day given a major press conference in Sedgefield; flown the following day to Sweden to take part in the General Election; flown to Spain the very next day to attend the wedding of the daughter of Prime Minister Aznar. On Saturday he flew to the US and back for a face-to-face meeting with Bush, and on Sunday he went to Balmoral for his annual residence with the Queen. It is hardly surprising if Prime Ministers find it very difficult to get the right perspective when they are never given a minute to sit still and think. I do think that two centuries later we could at least spare the Prime Minister the annual pilgrimage to Balmoral. Reputedly it was valuable to the relationship between Disraeli and Victoria, but Disraeli was not quite under the pressures of a modern Prime Minister, and was certainly not expected to pop over the Atlantic and back again in one day in order to see President Ulysses S. Grant. I suspect that the Queen, who is eminently reasonable, would be happy to dispense with it, but probably labours under the misapprehension that the Blairs would be disappointed.

Monday 9 September

I woke up to find that the *Today* programme was very excited by the IISS study of Saddam's military capacity. It sounds as if it has been carried out with their characteristic thoroughness and I am sure that its seventy-five pages are hemmed in with adequate scientific caution and caveats. Most of these, though, seem to have been rubbed off in the process of dealing with the wider media. Great excitement is being aroused by their observation that Saddam could produce a nuclear weapon 'within months' if only he could find a way of getting his hands on the fissile material. This does rather overlook the most pertinent point, which is their observation that they haven't got any fissile material and no national means of producing any.

British Energy has been forced to admit that its nuclear reactors cost more to produce electricity than the market price will pay, and as a result have had to plead with the government for a £400 million handout to avoid collapse. It has taken twenty-five years to be proved right on my speeches in the House in the seventies that nuclear electricity properly costed was not competitive. The only pity is that it took privatisation to flush out transparent costings which confirmed what many of us had long suspected.

Tuesday 10 September

At the end of the day Meg and Greg, my special advisers, asked if they could see me to find out if I was really resigning and if they would be out of a job. I was frank with them that I did not want to resign, and I did want to see through modernisation of the Commons and reform to the Lords. But the bottom line was that I would find it hard to stay inside the government if we were alone with the US in attacking Iraq without a fresh UN mandate. The meeting was a salutary reminder that other people would also be affected by any decision that I might reach.

Wednesday 11 September

It is a glorious, bright day and I dismiss Nigel and the car to walk across the park for my meeting at Number 10 with Tony.

I open up with the recall of Parliament. The decline in demand for a recall, which he had predicted would happen after his visit to Bush, has not materialised. On the contrary, it is even easier to detect the swelling opinion gathering itself into a tidal wave about to crash all over us: 'Recall is inevitable, and the longer we put it off the more grudging we appear and the less credit we will get for it when it happens.' To my surprise, Tony readily agrees: 'This is not a national emergency as no decision has been taken or is about to be taken, but I recognise the case for having a recall because there is such a big national debate.'

I moved immediately to follow up the breakthrough and asked how we made it public. Tony suggested that we get in Alastair and Jonathan, which on one level I regretted as it broke the tête-à-tête atmosphere, but that was outweighed by the value of getting his agreement to the recall thoroughly buttoned down. While we waited on them arriving, I reminded him that the two previous military engagements in Iraq were preceded by a substantive motion in the Commons and that it did not seem to be possible to avoid that the third time around. For a second time he surprised me by readily agreeing: 'I have no problem with a substantive motion if a decision is taken, but a recall debate is not the right time for it.' All four of us then resolved that there was no point in delaying the announcement, which would merely result in more demands by tomorrow. Tony would write to the Speaker today and Number 10 would put out his letter this afternoon.

We then moved on to the substance of policy on Iraq. I grounded my main line of attack on the deep unpopularity in the country of

Britain taking part in any military intervention in Iraq. Tony was optimistic that he could turn public opinion around, and that the majority would back intervention if there was a Security Council resolution in support of it.

He attaches great importance to the forthcoming dossier, although I myself fear that the main response will be one of disappointed expectations. He is particularly enthusiastic about a report they have that at a cabinet meeting Saddam has said that Iraq must get nuclear weapons to pose a threat to the West. Tony then added, 'Given the poor state of his conventional forces, it is not surprising that he wants to get his hands on nuclear weapons.' This is a curious aside. If Tony himself recognises that Saddam's conventional forces are much weaker than they were before, it is going to be difficult for him to be convincing that Saddam is now a greater threat to his region. And in any case there is no evidence that he has got any nuclear weapons with which to threaten us.

Nor was Tony just optimistic about domestic opinion. He was also hopeful that he could turn around international opinion. When I said that the bottom line was that he should not end up being the only other country to join the US on military intervention, he was quick to assure me that from his conversations he believed that others will be with us – he specifically named France, Italy, the Netherlands and Denmark. I refrained from pointing out that this was no help to me in the Social Democrat family as all those governments were now right wing and the product of recent defeats for the left. The discussion was good-humoured. At the end Tony said, 'I can put you down, then, as unenthusiastic.' I responded by saying, 'All I ask is that every morning you remember what happened to Anthony Eden.'

It took until the late afternoon to get the press statement cleared at Number 10, and I then did a stand-up for the cameras on College Green just in time for the early evening bulletins. As soon as we announced the news, I rang Graham Allen, who had shown characteristic enterprise in making Heath Robinson arrangements for a voluntary recall of Parliament meeting in Church House, in the event that there was no formal recall. He was delighted by the news and had only one reservation: 'My problem is that I have committed myself to four thousand vol-au-vents which I will now have to eat on my own.'

Thursday 12 September

The day begins with the *Today* programme. I suspect Number 10 will hate my references to a vote in the House and a substantive motion, in both the 1991 and 1998 military interventions in Iraq.

Sure enough, just before I headed off to the Eurostar, Jonathan Powell rang to say that Tony wanted to speak to me by phone tomorrow. He sounded a bit crestfallen when I told him that I would be chairing the Praesidium of the PES but of course I would be happy for Tony to ring me on my mobile. I doubt if they relish the idea of giving me a call when I am in the presence of an influential body of opposite numbers from Europe.

Friday 13 September

The call from Tony came through first thing in the morning. He was half-apologetic and began by explaining that people were telling him that I had a problem with there being no vote in the recall debate. I quickly reassure him on that point, as it plainly would be a mistake to have a substantial motion when there is no decision yet to debate. 'However, I don't see how we can avoid a vote if intervention is going to happen and we should avoid being positioned in public as if we are against a motion.' He readily agreed. 'Look, Robin, if you have a problem with this, remember that my door is always open. Come and talk to me about it.' Now it was my turn to agree. I repeated the anxiety that I had expressed earlier in the week about the depths of public feeling: 'I don't know that you understand just how strong the feelings run on this issue.' I ended by stressing that my worries were for him as well. 'I think you have been a great Prime Minister. I want you to have the opportunity to go on being a great Prime Minister.' 'Well, so do I,' he responded. And on that note of amity we ended.

The problem, of course, is that when Tony Blair and Bush talk about going to the UN they are talking about two very different concepts. Tony has not entirely lost hope that the UN process might provide a diplomatic solution and he really would want it to work in order to spare him the domestic and international tension of a military attack. Bush, by contrast, would be aghast if the UN process produced a successful result in terms of getting Iraq to comply with its obligations, as by definition that would leave Saddam still in place. For the time being there is still a licensed role for me trotting alongside the juggernaut for war, privately asking rational questions about whether this is the direction in which we all want to go.

The meeting of the Praesidium which had brought me to Brussels was, for a change, quite upbeat about the latest news from the electoral battlegrounds. After a year of ignominious retreat, there was a mood that the corner was turning. Schröder's strong campaign, ironically on a populist opposition to war on Iraq, has now got the SPD three points ahead in today's opinion poll.

This naturally led on to a political discussion on Iraq. It would probably be fair to characterise the discussion as one of unease rather than outright hostility. Social Democrats find it impossible to contemplate defying a resolution of the United Nations, but equally on today's evidence we will find it impossible to summon up enthusiasm for military intervention. Charles Clarke made a sensible and balanced contribution, in the course of which he let slip the revealing observation of Tony's that 'the United States has as many arms as the next nine biggest nations, and we have got to reflect that in the way we handle them'.

—⁓—

Tony Blair deserves credit for persuading President Bush that he must take Iraq to the United Nations for multilateral agreement. It is the only point in the whole saga where it is possible to pinpoint a clear instance where British influence made any difference to US policy on Iraq. The resistance Tony Blair had to overcome should not be understated. The powerful Neo-Con faction within the Bush Administration was flatly opposed to the UN route as a matter of political principle. It was fundamental to their ideology that the US should retain unilateral freedom over its security interests and that it should not be constrained by any requirement to seek the agreement of others. As the Neo-Cons called all the shots on other aspects of Iraq policy it was a substantial achievement by Tony Blair to see them off in the struggle for Bush's ear on whether to go to the UN.

There was, though, no merit in asking the UN for a decision on Iraq unless the US and UK governments were willing to abide by the result. Only six months after Bush went to the UN and sought their views on Iraq, he was proceeding to war ignoring the views that had been clearly expressed by a majority of the Security Council. This left Tony Blair in the uncomfortable position of urging our European partners to preserve the form of multilateral process by endorsing a decision that the US had already taken on a unilateral basis.

A rational interpretation of the events of the summer of 2002 would be that Tony Blair succeeded in convincing President Bush that they would secure more international and domestic support for an attack on Iraq if the President put the issue before the UN. The gain from this approach was that the US submitted to a UN process. The downside was the implicit guarantee that Britain was committed to join the US military action.

I do not know whether Tony ever made that deal explicit rather than simply implicit, but it would have been consistent with his previous conduct towards Iraq if he had given the US President a private assurance. I had seen a minute of January 1998 to Tony Blair from John Holmes, his then international Private Secretary, written during the confrontation with Iraq over weapons inspections, which reminded the Prime Minister that he had already assured President Clinton, 'If a Resolution were unachievable, there would certainly be support here for further action.' On that occasion Saddam's subsequent refusal to cooperate with the weapons inspectors provoked unanimous condemnation by the Security Council. Tony Blair may have bargained on history repeating itself five years later, and it certainly would have been in line with his own previous practice if he had given President Bush a private assurance of British support.

The subsequent refusal of the UN to provide cover for military action came as a very unwelcome surprise. Tony Blair had given himself some wriggle room by asserting that military action could not be stopped by 'an unreasonable veto'. This left interesting room for debate on who was to define when a veto was unreasonable and whether all of the thirty-odd times the US had cast its veto were so reasonable. But the implication was clear. Britain might ignore a solitary veto, but it could not ignore the opposition of a majority on the Security Council. Yet throughout the countdown to war a majority of the elected members of the Security Council *and* a majority of its permanent members remained opposed to war. There was an unhealthy self-delusion within the government in those last weeks that all their problems were the making of President Chirac. In truth, the issue of a French veto – whether unreasonable or not – never materialised because there was no prospect of Britain ever mustering a majority for war.

Those who wanted war subsequently claimed that by refusing to agree with them the UN had somehow failed to rise to its responsibilities. On the contrary, the Security Council admirably discharged its role by backing the UN weapons inspectors and by refusing to sanction an unnecessary breach of international peace and security. It was all the more impressive that some of the poorer, weaker members stood their ground despite a coercive campaign of bullying and bribery by the US and UK. History may be puzzled that the British government could not muster the same independence of spirit as Cameroon or Mexico.

When I went to my first UN General Assembly as Foreign Secretary I met an official of an NGO who volunteered that, as a result of the commitment to the UN of the new Labour government, he was again proud to tell others around the UN precinct that he was British. I used the incident at the end of my speech the next week to the Party Conference to warm applause from a Labour Party that has always regarded the UN as an international extension of collective bargaining. It was not possible by the time of the war on Iraq to find British citizens working for the UN who were still proud of their government. Ian Martin, who had earned respect for Britain and praise from Tony Blair for his courageous role as the UN Administrator in East Timor, resigned his membership of the Labour Party, protesting, 'I do not know of any British citizen working for the UN or other multilateral agency who is not appalled at the UK's position.'

—⁓—

Monday 16 September

As I was getting ready for bed, I listened to the midnight news and was startled to hear that the lead item was the report of Kofi Annan that he had just received a letter from the Iraqis accepting the return of the UN weapons inspectors without any conditions. This is quite a climbdown by Saddam, who until now had regarded the return of weapons inspectors as something to be bargained for in exchange for the lifting of sanctions. It is almost certainly true that he has only made this unconditional offer under duress of a military strike, but that does not alter the fact that we cannot credibly proceed with a military strike now that he has met our key demand. This may be bad news for the White House and the Pentagon, but it has to be good news for the rest of the world.

Tuesday 17 September

When I got into the office the first thing I did was to ring Jonathan Powell to express my strong view that we could not simply bat away the latest offer from Saddam to let in the UN weapons inspectors: 'Tony is entitled to real credit for securing this offer. But the more grudging we are in responding to the offer, the more difficult it becomes to claim any credit for it.' I found Jonathan very receptive to my argument, but there was a catch. 'We have to be careful of how our statements will play in Washington, and we therefore should not get too far in front of the Americans.' At this, I must confess, I got a bit impatient, and broke in, 'I assure you that there is nobody in Washington who is now asking themselves how anything they say will play in Britain. They are single-minded in focusing on their own domestic audience.'

Jonathan promised that he would report my views to the Prime Minister, and I am sure that he did. I am not so sure, though, that they were the views which were in the ascendancy. Later in the day I was passing through Number 10 on my way to chair the LP Committee in the Cabinet Office. It is one of the many curiosities of the unplanned nature of the old buildings at the heart of the British government that for those of us with offices on the St James's Park side of Whitehall, the short cut to the Cabinet Office is by going through the door of Number 10, through the Prime Minister's eighteenth-century town house, and out of the connecting door into the Cabinet Office. Emerging from the eighteenth-century domestic elegance of Downing Street does not catapult you into the modern age, but actually represents a step back into history as you find yourself in a corridor lined with Tudor bricks in the gallery from which the courtiers once watched fighting cocks take one another on. Not so far away from the occasional exchanges in modern Cabinets, I suppose. This time as I passed through Number 10, I bumped into Alastair Campbell and again expressed the view that we should not be too grudging in our response and thereby deny ourselves the credit for having pushed Saddam into being encouraged to make the offer. Alastair, as always, was no-nonsense in his reply: 'I cannot agree with you. We are playing a long game.' Presumably the long game is to contrive an assault on Iraq whatever Saddam does.

In the late evening I rang Madeleine Albright. She herself was deeply sceptical about the current war drive, but was candid about the absence of a clear democratic challenge to it: 'I cannot tell you how difficult it has become over here to present an alternative perspective since September 11th last year. Any questioner is simply branded as unpatriotic.' I recognise both their dilemma and Bush's political strategy. His strategy for the mid-term Congress elections is to keep America in a permanent state of mobilisation.

Madeleine did come up, in a genuinely puzzled voice, with the question, 'Just what does Tony Blair think he's doing?' The Democrats rightly regard President Bush as very ideological. As Madeleine put it, 'He is not just Reagan, he is Reagan squared, Reagan cubed.' She stressed that they have always liked Blair and hoped we do not end up with problems down the line if the Democratic Party succeed in getting back into the White House in a couple of years.

Wednesday 18 September

Late in the afternoon, Michael Levy called on me at my office in Carlton Gardens. It was our first chance to catch up since the summer recess. Michael has done a pile of work behind the scenes in trying to get the key players in the Middle East back into the peace process. It is one of the gross injustices of the past couple of years that for all his efforts, including paying for his own fares back and forth, Michael gets only abuse from the media. In part, it is a cultural problem. It may seem odd to those who only know Wapping and Fleet Street that the Prime Minister should send a close friend as an envoy, but to the countries of the Middle East it seems the most natural way of doing business, and Michael's strength there is precisely that he is known to be close to the Prime Minister.

Thursday 19 September

The day began with a call by Benedict Brogan, the recently elected Secretary of the Press Gallery. He is a bright young journalist who is as impatient with the traditionalist ways of the Press Gallery as I am with the Commons. The Press Gallery occupies the least revamped part of our rambling Victorian pile. The corridor from the gallery is so crowded with overworked scribes that shortly after the war it became dubbed 'the Burma Road'. The name has so passed into official usage that Benedict has just received a circular from the Sergeant-at-Arms informing him that there are plans to 'repaint the Burma Road'.

Afterwards, Geoffrey Bowman, the new First Parliamentary Counsel, came round to present a very intelligent paper on how we expand the numbers of the Parliamentary Draftsmen. It is an extraordinary, but little known truth, that the real bottleneck on government legislation is not the Commons, nor even the House of Lords. It is the brute fact that there are fewer than fifty Parliamentary Draftsmen working for the government. They each have a positively Stakhanovite commitment to their job and in the past session we got one bill published in time only by its draftsmen sitting up through the night putting the finishing touches to it. But if we are going to improve the quality of legislation, and if I am going to succeed in getting bills published in draft, we simply have to increase the capacity of the team. We resolved that I will minute the Prime Minister on Geoffrey's proposal to increase its capacity by a quarter over the next three years.

At the end of our meeting it emerged that the timetable for finalising the Queen's Speech was dictated by the necessity to give a week's notice to the craftsmen who inscribe it on to goatskin. I exploded at the idea that in the twenty-first century we are still using the technology of the fifteenth century. 'Does the Queen read it from goatskin?' I asked. 'No, she reads one of the versions on printed white cards.' Ben Bradshaw intervened to explain that in 1997 one of the first proposals for modernisation that we had made was to scrap the goatskin copy, but this had been dropped as a result of opposition from an MP on the constituency grounds that it would put out of work some of his electors whose special skill it was to inscribe on goatskin. 'I cannot believe that I am sitting here hearing this,' I concluded.

I rounded off the afternoon with an interview with Rachel Sylvester from the *Daily Telegraph*. Des, who for a professional journalist is wonderfully trusting, had been assured repeatedly by Rachel that the interview would be on modernisation, but being more cynical than Des I am not at all surprised that half of it was on Iraq. Rachel is not a seeker after truth but after stories.

Saturday 21 September

A rare treat as I have engineered a morning riding in Windsor Great Park. We pause before cantering in front of the deer herd to debate whether the rut will have begun, when our discussion is conclusively terminated by the unmistakable sound of a stag bellowing his challenge. We resolve that discretion is the better part of valour and canter in the opposite direction.

On my way back I stop off at the service station on the M4 to pick up a *Daily Telegraph*. The interview itself is unexceptional, but, as I feared, Rachel has lived up to her reputation with a highly coloured account on the front page, in which my praise for Tony Blair on his commitment to go to the UN is morphed into 'a warning' to Blair that he must go to the UN. On my way into town, Des calls me to say that the *Observer* have just rung to say that they are 'getting a lot of incoming traffic' criticising me for saying too much on Iraq. I tell him to be philosophical and say nothing. I doubt whether all this traffic is incoming rather than outgoing, and the Sunday papers are only too obviously in search of a row story.

Sunday 22 September

Somebody else in government has not been quite so philosophical in avoiding comment. The *Sunday Times* quotes an alleged colleague describing me as 'a chancer' and the *Observer* quotes presumably the same source expressing the Orwellian thought that I have 'unhelpful opinions'. No doubt he thinks I should be sent off for compulsory re-education.

I take the precaution of touching base with Number 10. The duty officer is very sympathetic: 'I read the transcript of the interview and thought that you made a Herculean attempt to deflect her questions.' I say that we will do what we can to hose down the story, but that he ought to ring the MoD press office to warn them that we cannot stop reports of a row on our own.

Monday 23 September

The day of the much-heralded Cabinet meeting on the eve of recall. It is a curious but unremarked feature of our constitutional arrangements that not only does Parliament not sit for three months over the summer, but neither does the Cabinet sit when Parliament is absent.

Personally, I found it a grim meeting. Much of the two hours was taken up with a succession of loyalty oaths for Tony's line. Estelle Morris, though, was frank, even pained, in her contribution. She bravely reported that, in the opinion of the people she had spoken to, what has changed in the past year to make war imminent is not what has happened in Iraq but the election of George Bush in the United States. 'The question we have to answer is "Why us?"'

Only Clare and I openly questioned the wisdom of military action. Clare set out a solid philosophical objection grounded in the Catholic doctrine of a Just War, and concluded that this would be an unjust one. I said that for me the most difficult question was 'Why now?'. What has happened in the past year to make Saddam more of an imminent danger than he has been any year in the past decade? I close my contribution by stressing the vital importance of getting approval for anything we do through the UN. 'What follows after Saddam will be the mother of all nation-building projects. We shouldn't attempt it on our own – if we want the rest of the international community with us at the end, we need them in at the start.'

There really was no answer to the question 'Why now?'. Geoff Hoon made an attempt to respond to me but his answer only served to confirm the difficulty of the question. 'The key issue in answering the question "Why now?" is September 11th,' he said. The problem with this, of course, is that no one has a shred of evidence that Saddam was involved in September 11th.

In summing up, Tony put rather more stress on the US than the UN. 'To carry on being engaged with the US is vital. The voices on both left and right who want to pull Europe and the US apart would have a disastrous consequence if they succeeded.' The one good development in an otherwise depressing meeting was that Jack volunteered that we should have a vote on a substantive motion before any action. His solution, which I think is very intelligent, is that we should take the kernel of any Security Council resolution and turn it into a motion before the House. So much for the ignoramus who was briefing the Sunday papers at the weekend that I was out of order in even talking about a substantive motion.

John Prescott came in at the end to stress that none of us should brief the press afterwards, and I loyally walked straight past the press corps ignoring their shouted questions, only to find that the *Evening Standard* reported that I had maintained 'an ominous silence'.

Tuesday 24 September

The House was packed for the recall debate; even the front bench was tightly packed. I got a glimpse of the irritation of the war party with my public doubts when Hilary expressed her appreciation that I had lost a stone as we otherwise would not have squeezed in, and Adam

Ingram, a Defence minister, asked me how I had done it. 'Basically by starvation,' I replied. To which he cheerily responded, 'I'm sure many of our colleagues would be only too happy to help you with that.'

Tony, as ever, was fluent, calm and in command of the House. For its part I thought the House did itself credit by a dispassionate and serious exchange, which must have appeared so much better to the public than the usual petty points-scoring of Prime Minister's Questions. Jack Straw's speech was refreshing for its extended and powerful emphasis on working through the United Nations. He stressed that this was not simply a dry, formal requirement, but one which sprang from the fact that the United Nations charter and declaration of universal rights embody our values, and that we can only uphold them by upholding the UN.

Afterwards I went over and sat next to him and congratulated him on a good speech, and then added, 'You do realise now you are thoroughly impaled on the UN route?' To which he responded with a twinkle, 'Yes, I am glad you noticed that.' I suspect that there is some tension behind the scenes between the Foreign Office and Downing Street about the extent to which the UN can be the only route.

After the opening speeches we adjourned for a meeting of the Parliamentary Committee in Tony's room. Chris Mullin put it to Tony that, 'No one outside Texas has confidence in Bush. I will understand if I have to wait until your memoirs to find out if you agree.'

Tony was open in his reply, saying that he found Bush 'easy and very open' to deal with, but he did show an understanding of what clearly is the wider opinion on current US policy. 'The problem with the US is that they worry about what concerns them, but don't worry about what concerns others, as we saw over Kyoto.' At the end of the meeting, I had a private exchange with Tony about the dialogue I am setting up through the PES with the Democratic Party. He was keen to know what they thought of him, and was not surprised when I reported Madeleine's perplexity at his stance.

—❦—

This was the Parliamentary Debate in which the Prime Minister presented the now notorious Dossier on Iraq's Weapons of Mass Destruction. I had been familiar with previous secret reporting on Iraq, and when I came to read the dossier I was surprised that there was so little new material in it. There was no new evidence that I could find in it of a dramatic increase in threat requiring urgent invasion.

At Cabinet I described the dossier as 'derivative'. What I was expressing was the extraordinary degree to which the bulk of the document was derived from what we know about Saddam's arsenal of chemical and biological weapons as it had been in 1991. It was never in any doubt that during his long war with Iran, Saddam deliberately developed chemical and biological weapons as his military response to the human wave assaults of his opponents. Certainly the US and UN governments of the time could not have doubted it as they helped Saddam to develop that capacity. What was doubtful was whether the arsenal that Saddam possessed in 1991 was any guide whatsoever to the state of his capacity in 2002.

For a start most chemical or biological agents that Saddam had retained for a decade would long ago have degenerated to the point that they were of no operational use. This is a principle of science well known to those who wrote the dossier. Go to your own medicine cabinet and you will find that every chemical and biological substance in it has an expiry date. Government ministers alarmed the public by claims that Saddam had ten thousand litres of anthrax solution unaccounted for since 1991. They never added that the standard life of liquid anthrax is three years and by now the substance would be in the words of Scott Ritter, the former UN inspector, 'harmless useless goo'.

It is not even clear that Iraq had achieved the technical performance to ensure the standard life of its agents. Last year the US Defense Department published its assessment of Iraq's weapons technology and revealed, 'When the Iraqis produced chemical munitions they appeared to adhere to a "make and use" regimen. They had to get the agent to the front promptly or have it degrade in the munition.' Their conclusion was that the shelf life of Iraqi chemical agents was numbered in weeks, not decades.

Yet half of the text relating to Iraq's weapons capacity is drawn from the period before 1998. Much of the remainder depends for its claims of present capacity on historic capabilities. Thus the reader is warned, 'Most of the personnel previously involved in the program remain in the country.' It is hard to see how Saddam could have avoided this charge other than by expelling his scientists and if he had done so the authors would no doubt have added that to the list of his human rights abuses which made up the final chapter. Stripped of the historical résumé, the aerial photographs and the inset boxes on technical terms, the dossier was very thin on new evidence on the current position. Notoriously such claims that it did advance have turned out to be spectacularly wrong.

It is a measure of how modest was the new evidence available to those seeking to justify war that what little they had they repeated often. Thus, the claim that Saddam could deploy weapons of mass destruction within forty-five minutes was repeated *four* separate times. In the aftermath of war this claim was proved false as not only were chemical or biological weapons never fired by Saddam's forces, but none could be found anywhere, never mind within a forty-five minute radius of the artillery emplacements. Even before the war, Dr David Kelly, the government's most authoritative expert on Iraq's biological weapons, regarded it as so risible that he and his close friend Tom Mangold laughed at the impossibility of arming and firing such a warhead within forty-five minutes.

As a result of the Hutton Inquiry the public – and MPs – know much more about the background to the forty-five minute claim than we were told at the time. We have learnt not only that the intelligence was uncorroborated and came from a single source, but that he in turn was reporting hearsay from another uncorroborated, single source. When Dr Brian Jones, formerly of the Defence Intelligence Staff, gave evidence to Hutton he offered the opinion that the source did not appear to 'know very much about it' and may have been 'trying to influence and not inform' UK policy. But even more damaging was the revelation by John Scarlett, Chair of the Joint Intelligence Committee, that it was always known inside the government that the forty-five minute claim applied only to battlefield munitions and small-calibre weaponry. This was a limitation that the government chose not to share with the readers of the September Dossier, with the result that the press next day reasonably reported the claim as covering missiles and other real weapons of mass destruction, giving the impression which the government wanted that Saddam was a greater threat than intelligence suggested. At the Hutton Inquiry Geoff Hoon denied that the government had any duty to correct this 'distortion' by the press. I can understand why ministers made no attempt to correct the press reports. To do so would have provoked immediate complaints by the press that the dossier had been misleading.

Other claims have not received the same attention, which may be as well for the government as they have proved equally unfounded. Thus, the dossier warned that Saddam had rebuilt plants to manufacture chemical weapons. By definition, such a production facility would require substantial buildings covering a large surface area. There is nowhere on the face of the globe that has been more intensively mapped by aerial surveillance than Iraq, but no such rebuilt weapons plant has ever been found. The dossier specifically cited the chlorine and phenol plant at Falluja 2 as one of the installations that had been 'rebuilt'. Hans von Sponeck, who was once the UN Coordinator on Iraq, visited the site with a German TV crew in July 2002 and reported, 'They are indeed in the same destroyed state which we witnessed in 1999. There was no trace of any resumed activity at all.' No one has ever explained why a site that was filmed as destroyed in July surfaced in the dossier as back in production by September. Through the Hutton inquiry we have since learnt that the MoD expert on chemical weaponry had warned against inclusion of the claim that Iraq was manufacturing phosgene for military purposes and believed its retention in the dossier was 'a pretty stupid mistake'.

But the most egregious claim of all was that Saddam had attempted to reconstitute his nuclear weapons programme. A nuclear weapons programme requires large industrial plants, employs a workforce of thousands, and emits telltale radiation signals. None of these has been identified before, during or since the war. The conclusion to the section on nuclear weapons is a masterpiece of false suggestion. It reports that, 'The JIC judged that while sanctions remain effective Iraq would not be able to produce a nuclear weapon.' Logically, the entire section could have stopped here with the reassuring ending that the policy of containment was working. However, what Number 10 needed from the dossier was not reassurance but alarm. Thus there follows a fanciful leap into the realm of fantasy. 'We therefore judge that if Iraq obtained fissile material and other essential components from foreign sources ... Iraq could produce a nuclear weapon in between one and two years.' This language is frightening. But as evidence that Iraq was a threat it is pathetic and the authors must have known it. Given off-the-peg fissile material 'and other essential components', any of three or four dozen industrialised countries could probably produce a bomb in a couple of years. The key barrier to manufacturing a nuclear bomb is precisely the problem of acquiring the rare, expensive fissile material of weapons-grade quality.

The dossier did not come up with a shred of evidence that any country was even remotely contemplating the sale of weapons-grade fissile material to Iraq. What it did allege was that Iraq had sought to buy natural uranium from Niger. This would still have left Iraq requiring the best part of a decade and specialised industrial plant and technology to refine the natural uranium into weapons-grade material. Nor would they have got away with such a process under the present regime of containment and sanctions. In any case it simply was not true.

The most baffling of all the background events to the dossier was that the CIA warned British intelligence that this claim in the draft was wrong and yet the authors persisted in printing it. The CIA knew what they were talking about as they had sent a former US ambassador, Joseph Wilson, who had served both in Iraq and West Africa, to investigate the allegations. He had reported that 'there's simply too much oversight over too small an industry' for a sale of uranium to Iraq to take place without it becoming known to the international consortium that ran the mines and therefore to the International Atomic Energy Agency. Nevertheless, the Bush Administration repeated the claim of a Niger connection, most famously in the President's State of the Union Address, prompting Joseph Wilson to observe, 'Based on my experience with the Administration in the months leading up to the war, I have little choice but to conclude that some of the intelligence related to Iraq's nuclear weapons program was twisted to exaggerate the Iraqi threat.'

If the Bush Administration was guilty of twisting the intelligence on Niger, then so was the British government. The Niger claim blew up in their faces when Mohammed El Baradei, the Director General of the International Atomic Energy Agency, reported to the Security Council that the documents that had been supplied to him by a Western intelligence agency to prove a Niger connection were forgeries, and crude forgeries at that. The IAEA report which he submitted came to the conclusion, 'We have found no evidence or plausible indication of the revival of a nuclear weapons programme in Iraq.'

Number 10 has since taken refuge in the claim that it has other intelligence, separate from the forged documents, that proved there had been a Niger connection. However they have so far been unable to tell the rest of us of what exactly it consists, as it allegedly comes from the intelligence agency of another country that apparently is so self-effacing that it does not want the US to know it helped with the information. As someone who was familiar for four years with the way our intelligence agencies operated, and the extent to which they cooperated with other agencies, I simply cannot make any sense of this. Niger is a small country in which only a finite number of other countries can be represented by their agencies without intelligence staff meriting their own entry in the residential census. France certainly, but they vigorously deny the story. Spain and Italy possibly, but their Prime Ministers would be on the next plane to Washington if they really had the information that could rescue President Bush from his embarrassment over the Niger claim. The longer the British government delays producing the additional intelligence, the greater is the suspicion that the real reason it is kept concealed is because they know it is not convincing.

Intelligence is supposed to be the evidence on which ministers reach decisions on foreign and defence policy. It is not meant to be the propaganda by which ministers sell a policy to a sceptical public. Nor are intelligence reports suited for the purpose. In my years at the Foreign Office I regularly saw the assessments of the Joint Intelligence Committee. They would normally arrive in the red box for the weekend and were readily identifiable by their distinctive green covers. Green is the colour much favoured by the Secret Intelligence Service, and Cummings, the original and eponymous 'C', who founded MI6, instituted the practice that only the Director could write in green ink so that his marginalia could be readily recognised.

Politicians are prone to dogmatic texts that supply a single-minded statement of their own certainty. The JIC Assessments by contrast were refreshingly balanced, almost academic in their detachment. It was a common experience to put down a JIC Assessment more perplexed than when you picked it up as it had fairly presented you with the intelligence evidence on both sides of the question. And they never claimed certainty. One of my predecessors at the Foreign Office observed that a report did not become more true by being stamped 'Secret', and the authors of such reports were well aware of it themselves. A witness at the Hutton inquiry proudly observed that intelligence officers were careful about the subtle nuances between whether intelligence showed, suggested or indicated. I grew to respect the caution of the SIS and I would regard it as monstrously unfair to the men and women who serve in the agency if they were now made the fall guys because of the way their work was used to produce the September Dossier. The dossier did violence to their craft in two ways. First, it painted only a one-sided picture, whereas every JIC Assessment I saw would honestly present any contrary evidence that might be inconsistent with the final conclusion. Secondly, it defiantly proclaimed a certitude for its claims that was at odds with the nuanced tone of every JIC Assessment I read.

Acres of newsprint have been expended on whether Alastair Campbell 'transformed' or 'sexed up' the original drafts. In truth it suited Number 10 to throw itself into a vigorous combat with the BBC denouncing the suggestions that they had deliberately cheated. There was a crudity to that charge that made it easier to rebut. Andrew Gilligan provided Number 10 with the great gift of an opportunity for displacement behaviour. By alleging that ministers knew that claims in the dossier were wrong he enabled them to turn the debate into a question of whether they had acted in good faith without ever answering whether they had acted competently. Personally I never doubted that Number 10 believed in the threads of intelligence which were woven in to the dossier. But that does not alter the awkward fact that the intelligence was wrong and ministers who had applied a sceptical mind could have seen that it was too thin to be a reliable basis for war. Number 10 believed in the intelligence because they desperately wanted it to be true. Their sin was not one of bad faith but of evangelical certainty. They selected for inclusion only the scraps of intelligence that fitted the government's case and gave them a harder edge than was justifiable. The net result was a gross distortion. Although every individual claim could be sourced to an intelligence report, the overall effect was to present a false picture of an Iraq bristling with real weapons of mass destruction that have turned out not to exist.

In his foreword to the September Dossier, Tony Blair asserted Saddam was 'a current and serious threat' to the UK national interest. Yet only a week before he had been minuted by Jonathan Powell, his chief of staff, warning 'the document does nothing to demonstrate a threat, let alone an imminent threat from Saddam . . . We will need to make it clear in launching the document that we do not claim that we have evidence that he is an imminent threat.' It was wise advice. Unfortunately it was also unwelcome advice, as accepting it would have undermined the whole point of the dossier which was designed to prove that Saddam was an urgent threat.

Sir Jeremy Greenstock, our ambassador to the UN, and a first-class diplomat, was subsequently to observe of the other members of the Security Council, 'Almost none were ready to accept the British and US evidence that Saddam had weapons of mass destruction.' In the absence of any discovery of real weapons, the scepticism of those other UN members looks a lot more sound than the alarmist rhetoric of the September Dossier.

Sunday 29 September–Wednesday 2 October

New Labour has modernised the Party Conference faster than it has modernised Britain. One consequence is the complete inversion of the traditional dynamics of conference votes. Previously the platform relied upon the trade unions to keep some grip on sanity, and to put down the more implausible constituency resolutions. Today, it is the constituency delegates who are the loyalists and who stick by the platform even when the unions are rebelling.

Tony's speech went down well with this audience. It was not the kind of platform oration that would have gone down well with the rumbustious conferences of twenty years ago, but Tony has complete mastery over the modern conference. He was confident, conversational and candid. This was not the same young man who over a decade ago was thrown into evident disarray when he turned over a sheet of his conference speech and found the next one missing.

Late on Tuesday afternoon I was on my way to address a fringe meeting and, as I emerged at the bottom of the stairs in the Imperial foyer, Alastair Campbell with superb aplomb stepped forward, relieved me of my briefcase, and instructed me, 'Go out and welcome Bill Clinton.' I went to the front door, where an American security agent barked at me to get out of the way. When I explained that I had been sent out to greet the former President, there was a hurried conference through lapel microphones and I was then instructed on the precise spot where I could greet Bill and she could keep her eyes on me. Nobody knows better than Bill how to work a crowd. He greeted me warmly, moved effortlessly through the Imperial foyer shaking hands, touching elbows and smiling to cameras. The one hundred carat sincerity of his tone carries him through such improbable observations as 'I just love Blackpool', made only five minutes after arriving in it. When I left him outside Tony's room, he contrived to be both confidential and sincere in thanking me for taking the trouble to greet him. What a shame that the founding fathers of the American Revolution did not allow their Presidents to run for a third term and spare us President Bush.

As always, one of the most cheerful events was the reception of Britain in Europe. Curious, really, since we don't have that much to be cheerful about. In my impromptu address I said that this was the fourth year that I had spoken at this reception, and I hoped we would not be meeting for another four years and still find ourselves outside the euro. In his speech to conference, Tony used very strong language on the euro, in he which promised that if economic conditions were right, we would 'go for it'. He also described Europe as 'our destiny', but at some point even Tony is going to have to confront the tension between seeing Europe as our long-term destiny and loyalty to the United States as our immediate priority.

On my last night in Blackpool I had a long, frank exchange with Will Hutton. In order to find any corner in which we could be frank, we were obliged to get out of the Imperial and pace the extended car park at its front. This had the consequence that I became part of the tour of the illuminations at the front, and found myself breaking off our deep analysis to wave to passing busloads of Labour voters.

We were both clear that the fundamental issue was whether the Iraq crisis would bolster multilateralism through the UN, or completely sabotage it and clear the ground for America's increasing unilateralism. If action was taken under the authority of the UN, then those of us who are multilateralists would have little option but to uphold the authority of the UN. Crunch time, however, would be if the US brushed the UN aside. Will's last words were 'Don't underrate the value of a principled resignation. The need for a UN resolution is not some arid question of process, but a central issue of whether we can fashion a world government by multilateral agreement.'

Now that I have left the Foreign Office I am not usually away for such an extended period, and when I got home Tammy and Tasker gave me a rapturous reception, launching themselves from the sofa to kiss me and flinging themselves on the floor to have their tummies tickled.

Thursday 3 October

In the afternoon I was given a Foreign Office briefing on background. The Foreign Office is often being accused of being Arabist, but their diplomats are paid to acquire expertise in their special region, and it is a strength, not a weakness, for Britain that we have a better understanding of the Arab world than the US State Department. I sometimes think that Tony ought to worry about parallels with Suez, because it brought down a sitting Prime Minister blessed by a comfortable majority in the House. The Foreign Office is more subtle. Suez lost Britain influence in the Arab world for a generation and in their dark moments they fear the experience could be repeated if we go into Iraq on the coat-tails of the US and without the backing of the UN.

Tuesday 8 October

The Cabinet sub-committee met this morning to discuss tactics on how we proceed on the modernisation proposals. I was nervous that some colleagues might take the opportunity of a discussion of tactics to reopen questions of substance, and took the precaution of meeting in advance with John Prescott, who is a potential key ally.

John is the most solid team player in the Cabinet and was positive about my proposals. On the way back through the maze of corridors which link the many different buildings of the Cabinet Office, I said to him that I was sorry he had decided to give up foreign travel although I understood why, given the vicious criticism in the media. The truth is that John did a genuinely good job in promoting to the world Britain's position on the environment, spectacularly so in the case of Kyoto where he was instrumental in getting agreement. Yet all that he got for his pains was criticism for travelling abroad or, apparently worse, eating meals while he was abroad.

At the end of the meeting Alan Milburn, John Prescott and I had an exchange of views on foundation hospitals. There will be a report in tomorrow's *Guardian* that Gordon has won his battle to prevent them getting freedom from borrowing constraints, and I was relieved to hear from Alan that the Treasury had not got it all its own way.

Alan was eloquent on the need for the NHS to decentralise: 'The state's responsibility is to provide the guarantee of free health care, but the state has to get out from being a monopoly producer.' If Herbert Morrison had won his arguments in the Attlee Cabinet, we would have ended up sixty years ago with the kind of devolved, localised health service which Alan is now proposing, and old Labour would already be fiercely attached to it.

Wednesday 9 October

This is the day of the long-prepared gathering of socialist leaders at Downing Street. We have a good turnout of the party leaders from all the other European Union countries, even if these days few of them are actually in government. We hold the meeting and discussions in the state dining room in order that lunch can be served to us while we talk. Its décor is simple and in keeping with the general ambience of Number 10 as the town house of a successful merchant. Each place has its own individually etched silver under-plate. The one at my place rather eccentrically shows an heraldic lion holding a cricket bat, presumably designed at a time when the English cricket team did rather better than this year.

I invited Göran Persson to start the discussion, in order to get us on to an optimistic note by describing his recent election victory in Sweden. Interestingly, he attributed his own success to their success in keeping their core supporters on side: 'We are in trouble when we lose touch with our core voters.' I rather wished I could read the mind of Tony Blair sitting to my right, as I have frequently warned him that our message is too often honed towards the aspirant voter and not often enough towards the core voter.

The discussion on social democracy was thoughtful, but there was no disguising the fact that the real interest of those present was to hear what Tony was going to say on Iraq after the lunch. He was candid with them on his strategy of keeping close to Bush in order that he can keep Bush close to the UN. Mark Durkan, the new leader of the SDLP, had often been out of the room taking calls about the imminent collapse of power-sharing in Northern Ireland and began his contribution with a self-deprecating line that, as a result of his repeated suspensions as a minister in the Northern Ireland Executive, 'I have had more sackings than Roy Keane.' Though the representative of possibly the smallest party in the room, he nevertheless struck the most critical note about Tony's strategy: 'We should not go to the UN just as a badge of legitimacy.'

Antonio Gutteres wound up the discussion on the agreed priorities of all of us at the table: 'Disarm Iraq. Strengthen the UN. Maintain multilateralism.' So far, so good. He then went on, looking straight at Tony, 'But if we fail in that strategy, the consequences will be grave.'

Friday 11 October

Poul Nyrup Rasmussen, the former Prime Minister of Denmark, has attracted a high-octane attendance to Copenhagen for his seminar on social democracy and globalisation. The result is a stimulating, almost heady discussion. Pascal Lamy, the European Commissioner, gave a lucid and precise expression of our problem: 'Historically, the success of social democracy in the past century was to promote a compromise between labour and capital, between the state and the market, and between commercial competition and social solidarity. Globalisation has unhinged the balance by taking away all the domestic levers by which we maintained the compromise.'

This provoked Peter Mandelson to rebuke Pascal in an intervention which began with the rather Panglossian observation, 'Globalisation offers all the best the world can offer.' He then warned, 'we must not sound as if we believe that there is a tension between labour and capital, or competition and solidarity', at which point Pascal interrupted: 'Yes, that is what I believe.'

Saturday 12 October

In the evening, we had a real musical treat when we went to hear Simon Rattle conduct the Berlin Philharmonic Orchestra with his interpretation of Mahler's Fifth. Although it begins with a funeral march, Simon Rattle had brought out the life-affirming qualities of the symphony and the exuberant finale brought the Festival Hall to its feet for a longer standing ovation than Bill Clinton got at the Labour Conference. In the end he offered as an encore Satie's *Gymnopédie*, which was probably psychologically sound as it cooled the audience down and was the only way that he could get them to go home to bed. In our case, Gaynor was too high with the drama of the piece to contemplate sleep. Instead we had a Thai dinner then danced in the kitchen to the jazz music I had selected for my desert island. It is going to be a dismal island without her.

Monday 14 October

I told Gareth that Meg was very depressed about the meeting of the Labour Lords which she attended last week, as so many were hostile to introducing elections. I asked him whether opinion was turning against reform. 'I don't think they were committed to reform in the first place,' replied Gareth with a twinkle. He confirmed my view that if reform is going to come to the Lords, it must come from the Commons.

The day was rounded off by a visit from one of the researchers from *Desert Island Discs*, who wanted some colour for my forthcoming interview. There was an entertaining passage when she asked what will be my choice of luxury and I responded by saying that I would like to take my Scottish terriers with me. There was a long face at this, and a patient explanation that the rules state that the luxury must be inanimate. However, apparently there is some body that considers appeals against the rules, to which she will put my request. I was left with the sense that my desert island is as hidebound by rules of procedure and protocol as Whitehall.

Wednesday 16 October

Tony addresses the PLP at our first meeting of the new term. He makes some acute observations on the need to modernise the public services 'for a modern world in which the public thinks of themselves more as consumers'. There are then a succession of questions from the floor on Iraq. Malcolm Savidge makes the point most intelligently and ends on a warning note: 'Many of us want to be loyal to the leadership. But loyalty is a two-way street. We want to work with a leadership that is loyal to our country, our party, and our principles.'

Unfortunately, in the pressure of responding to a score of questions, Tony forgets to respond to the planted question he was softballed on what he thought of answering Prime Minister's Questions earlier in the day. In the corridor after the meeting I bump into David Hanson, his PPS, who promises he will get Tony to express support at the meeting in the afternoon of the Parliamentary Committee. In the event, Helen Jackson reminds him that he had not entirely done justice to the question at the morning meeting, and very helpfully Tony begins by saying, 'I support the modernisation package. If people want to start earlier I have no objection.' It may not be a ringing declaration, but it will sound that way by the time I've passed it on.

At Prime Minister's Questions Duncan Smith tried to capitalise on the A-level controversy, which would have been fine if he had not gone on to demand that we scrap the new AS levels. Tony had seen that one coming, and responded that the AS levels had been thought up during the Conservative government, when they had been promoted, as it happened, by Eric Forth. This provoked much ribald humour. It was to be expected that the Labour benches would find it comical, but what made this an extraordinary affair was that the Tory benches appeared to find it just as funny, even though the joke was at the expense of their leader. Eric himself pulled a funny face and held his fingers to his temple as if pointing a gun to his head, provoking even more merriment at the very moment when his leader was struggling at the Despatch Box to restore some sense of his gravitas. I have never before seen the front bench on either side of the floor treat their leader with such open disloyalty. Unfortunately, Duncan Smith proceeded to deliver himself the *coup de grâce* on his performance, by asking whether A levels were worth the paper they were written on. Tony, with an unerring eye for the killer punchline, seized upon it and turned it into tomorrow's press story by accusing him of denigrating the work of tens of thousands of students who had worked hard to gain their A levels.

We attach too much weight as MPs to these gladiatorial bouts. William Hague performed very impressively at Prime Minister's Questions but still sank like a stone in public estimation. However, his performances were crucial in maintaining his hold on Conservative MPs despite all the problems outside. Duncan Smith's problem is that his poor performances in the Chamber are merely reminding Conservative MPs of how badly he is doing outside the Chamber.

Thursday 17 October

Lloyd Axworthy, the former Foreign Minister of Canada, dropped by in the early morning to say hello. He is a decent man with sound instincts and we did a lot of useful work together on human rights and conflict resolution. He is anxious to compare notes with me on where we now both stood in relation to Iraq, or more accurately in relation to a US Administration which was breaking all the international agreements that he and I had worked for. He was astonished when I told him that, at a personal level, Tony felt that he had a warm relationship with Bush.

Lloyd particularly wanted my advice on the International Criminal Court, as the US are pressing all their allies to bilateral assurances not to surrender any US servicemen to the ICC if asked. It is extraordinary that the whole of Europe has buckled under to a demand which clearly undermines the ICC, while Canada, despite its intimate relationship with the United States, so far has firmly refused.

At Business Statement I began teasing Eric about yesterday's exchanges on the AS levels, and said how relieved I was to see the architect of the AS levels still in his place: 'There were some concerns on our side of the House about his welfare overnight. We are delighted that he did not wake up to find his appointment was not worth the paper it was written on.'

Friday 18 October

I got away just in time to get to my constituency for lunch at the local police station. They were forthright in their view that they also could do with the discretion over enforcing the law on cannabis, which is about to be extended to the English police. As one senior officer expressed it, 'In my thirty years in the force, I have never yet had to wrestle to the ground somebody who had been smoking cannabis.' A previous chief superintendent once told me that most of the teenagers in my constituency did not know that cannabis was illegal, because it was so widely available and in common use. There probably is no other single issue on which the agenda of most of the press is more out of touch with the reality of life among the young people of Britain.

Monday 21 October

I rounded off the evening with a meeting with Phil Woolas, who has just been appointed to my team as its whip. I was encouraged to regard his appointment as an olive branch from Hilary, as Phil is known to be a stout supporter of the change in sitting hours. I was even more encouraged by his description of the recent whips' meeting: 'Hilary told us all we were in a no-win situation on sitting hours if we voted against change. If we defeated the change, we would be blamed by those who wanted earlier sittings. If we failed to defeat it, we would then be seen as impotent. The one thing the Whips' Office cannot afford to be seen as is impotent, and we would be better to let it go through.' I have to admire Hilary. It was the one argument that might convince the more conservative members of her team to tolerate change.

Wednesday 23 October

At the weekly meeting of the Modernisation Committee, the clerk, George Cubie, circulated the latest results from a survey of members' views on sitting hours. There has been an impressive response to it, with five hundred MPs replying. The bottom line is that there is a majority of seventy for earlier sitting hours, but this disguises a sharp cleavage in opinion between the two sides of the House. There is a two to one majority for change among Labour MPs, but a three to one opposition to change among Conservative MPs.

I shamelessly exploited this party difference when I subsequently addressed the PLP. Martin Salter, who has an excellent sense for where our colleagues are at, had urged me last night to make the point that Tory MPs are more likely to want to work in the mornings, as that is when they look after their business interests. By the time I was finished, I had convinced half my audience that earlier sitting hours would not only make Parliament more effective, but it would also be a victory in the class war.

The Parliamentary Committee was notable for the formal rites on the experiment in election of mayors. Last week saw disastrous results, and in three out of four posts up for election our party candidates were beaten by figures from outside the political mainstream. Far from increasing turnout, the move to election of mayors has actually resulted in a turnout half the level of those who participated in the elections of old-fashioned councils. John Prescott, who has very recently taken over in charge of local government, was blunt and dismissive in his burial service: 'We have had the experiment, and it is over now'. It was, of course, Tony's own pet idea. It is a dramatic example of how the politics of North America often do not travel well across the Atlantic.

In the evening, I took Gaynor to the reception to celebrate Harriet Harman's twenty years as MP. While Gordon was making a worthy speech in praise of Harriet, a dramatic rumour started to circulate, by whispered exchanges round the back of the room, that Estelle Morris had just resigned. By the end of the speech, there were two meetings going on in the hall, those at the front who were dutifully listening to Gordon, and those at the back who were excitedly muttering about Estelle.

As it was Harriet's reception, most of the women MPs were present. Margaret Hodge, who is Minister at the Department of Education, volunteered that every morning there would be another pile of press cuttings on Estelle's desk which for the last few months had been grim reading. I remember those piles well. You're in danger of losing your sanity until you realise there's nobody else in the length and breadth of Britain who is reading all of these critical cuttings except yourself. The best way to keep perspective is to stop reading them. There was a broad consensus among the women that Estelle's decision was in part a reflection of gender. Women find it more difficult to handle unremitting negative coverage. There were also stories circulating about the intolerable practice of the press in approaching any of Estelle's relatives or friends for gossip. The great irony is that the press keep demanding all politicians behave as human beings, but seem to forget this will never happen until they start respecting the fact that politicians are human beings too.

Afterwards, I saw Estelle giving her resignation interview on television. She was candid, dignified and self-deprecating. There is something deeply wrong with public life in this country if somebody as decent and human as Estelle felt so uncomfortable with public life that she felt she had to leave the Cabinet.

Tuesday 29 October

I am already well prepared with my speech to open the debate on the modernisation package. However, unusually for the Chamber I am also closing the debate and I have not yet given that any thought, although the nature of the Commons means it is likely to have the larger attendance. Most of it will take care of itself in that I can respond to the points raised in the debate. I do, though, need to have ready the final couple of minutes of peroration in order to go out on a climax at the stroke of ten o'clock. If you speak beyond the stroke of ten o'clock, you have actually talked out your own business and there will be no vote. On the other hand, if you finish a few minutes in advance of ten, any other member of the House can get up and make a speech in which they get the last word. It is a legend of the House that on one occasion Anthony Crosland simply dried up with five minutes to go and had to repeat himself like a record with the needle stuck. It is therefore worth getting it right, and I spend an hour making sure that I have a two-minute peroration which I can turn to as soon as the digital clock hits 9:58.

After I have finished, Ken Purchase, my PPS, comes round to walk me down to the Chamber. Ken has worked with me as PPS for ten years now, in which he has given me both loyalty and lots of frank advice. It suddenly strikes me that I have never asked him what he is going to do himself. He looks almost insulted when I do ask him: 'You don't need to ask. You need to win this and I'll be voting with you.' I was moved by his loyalty as I knew many of his close friends would be in the other lobby.

I try to smooth over the divisions behind me on my back benches, by making a speech that is as tribal as I dare, given that I desperately need the few Tory rebels who might come over to us in the vote on sitting hours. I point out that the House had sat in mornings and afternoons until the invention of gas lighting at the end of the eighteenth century, and suggest to Eric Forth that, 'It might help you to come to terms with early sittings if you were to think of it not as modernisation, but as a reversion to tradition.'

One of the best speeches is made by Edward Leigh, a Thatcherite Tory with whom I normally do not have much cause for agreement, but on this occasion he makes a candid and forceful speech urging members to face up to the degree of change we must embrace if Parliament is to live in the present and not the past. Rather brutally, he asks the House what is the point in our speaking in the evening if nobody is listening?

The length of time for wind-up is settled by consensus between the two front benches. Eric Forth insisted that we should both reply for twelve minutes as he had a lot to say. In the event he speaks for only eight minutes, leaving me with longer than I had bargained for. Just before I rise, I hiss to Graham Allen on the bench behind me that I will need an intervention to keep going, and he handsomely obliges. In the event I manage to reach my peroration at just the right moment to sit down with a few seconds to spare. I am therefore spared the ignominy of being pulled down by the rear of my jacket, which is the obligation on the duty whip to prevent government business being talked out by government ministers.

There follows nearly three hours of voting. By the end of it, we have made a clean sweep on all our proposals for modernisation: a shorter period of notice for Question Time; more draft bills; carry-over of bills from one session to the next; September sittings; an annual calendar for the parliamentary year; shorter speeches to enable more members to speak in debates; and, yes, earlier sitting hours.

The last of these is much the most contentious. We carry the vote for a change on Wednesdays by a comfortable margin of almost eighty votes, but we always knew that Tuesday would be a much tighter proposition. Shortly before the result Phil Woolas tells me that we have lost, but when the tellers line up before the Table the figures show that we have scraped through by a majority of seven. It produces gasps of delight from the modernisers on our side. For the first time in this whole long exercise, I have a real sense of achievement. We have made an historic change in the procedures and working conditions in the House. In the next division lobby one of the women MPs tells me, 'You have saved me from having to get out of politics at the next election.' Hilary had done an honourable job with the whips, and at the end of the day the majority of them voted with us. In testimony to the need for the reform for which we had just voted, the end of the sitting did not come until half past midnight.

We did good work that night. The reforms went about as far as the market could bear, as the occasional cliff-hanger in the voting lobbies confirmed. Parliament as a result merits a little less its description by one commentator as Hogwarts-on-Thames. For a start most of its business will now be conducted in the hours of daylight rather than darkness.

A major reason why the House was willing to think so radically about its procedures was the large intake of new members in 1997. Parliament is so steeped in venerable tradition, that our image obscures the refreshing reality that a majority of today's MPs have only been elected since 1997. They came from work environments in which information technology was taken for granted, flexible working practices were commonplace and the hours were sane. Many of them reacted with incredulity to the discovery of how they were expected to work in Westminster.

One valuable gain from the large turnover in membership is that it has permitted a substantial rise in the number of women MPs. Parliament has always been recalcitrant about acknowledging that the majority of the population are women. It was not until 1917 that the House could be persuaded to take down the metal grille in front of the Ladies Gallery, enabling women to be seen as well as to see. Within my lifetime new women MPs had to be advised not to push open doors marked 'Members Only' as this remained the original marking on the Gents. I am no fan of Margaret Thatcher, but her remarkable achievement in becoming the first woman Prime Minister and remaining the longest serving Prime Minister for over a century, could only be appreciated if you saw her sit on the Treasury backbench surrounded by a sea of male MPs beside her and behind her. Even today the surge in women MPs has established the new high water-mark at only a sixth of the total membership of the Commons and within the Conservative Party the proportion of their MPs who are women still has not reached a token tenth. We have a long way yet to go before the Commons comes anywhere near to representing the balance between the genders in the electorate.

Even so the arrival at Westminster for the first time of a three-figure number of women has helped humanise the place. The

Palace of Westminster was built in a conscious echo of the Pall Mall gentleman's clubs and the Chamber, especially after dinner, can be an intimidatingly masculine environment. For the first time there are enough women to subvert that macho culture and to challenge whether ritual male display behaviour is really the best way to conduct political exchanges. As a result we are edging towards a House of Commons which may no longer approach its big debates with all the finesse of a rugby scrum. It was the Labour women MPs who encouraged me to stay ambitious about my programme for reform in the dark moments when I might have been tempted to scale back.

The representations from colleagues of both genders was never inspired by a wish that their job was easier. It would be a truly eccentric candidate who ran for Parliament in the expectation of an easy job. What MPs did demand was that their job should be made more effective. In that respect the change in sitting hours was one of the less important reforms. More valuable in strengthening Parliament's role of scrutiny were the decisions to make question time more topical by cutting its period of notice, to reduce the pressure to rush bills through Parliament by enabling them to be carried over to another year, and to increase the research staffing of select committees. Yet even the change to the sitting hours was motivated by the objective of restoring Parliament as the forum which set the political agenda of the day. I was often infuriated by the media obsession that the change in hours was about getting MPs home to bed. There is no reason why MPs should apologise for insisting on a reasonable night of rest. I served in the 1974 Parliament when all-night sittings were a common occurrence and I thought then it was a daft way to conduct our business. I have seen an MP woken up by his neighbour on the bench because the Chair has just called him to move his amendment. This is not a sound working method to produce the best laws for the nation. But the real issue is not the time at which the Chamber stops sitting but the hour at which it starts up. Under the previous sitting hours, statements of major developments in government policy would be relegated to mid to late afternoon. None of the experienced politicians in the Commons would voluntarily opt for such a late hour for a press conference on an important news story. If Parliament is to be the fulcrum of political debate, then it must start at an hour when its proceedings have a better prospect of setting the media agenda.

I am realistic about the challenge of getting a fair hearing for Parliament. In Disraeli's time, when the print media curiously had later deadlines than today, the majority of column inches in *The Times* were reports of yesterday in Parliament. I do not aspire to restore that news balance and I am not even sure that I would buy such a newspaper, but the press now have no excuse for not covering the full day's events in Parliament. There is already one encouraging example of the earlier hours putting Parliament back in the news agenda, although I appreciate it is not one which government welcomes. As a result of the earlier closing time it is now possible for the press to report, analyse and comment on any interesting votes in the Commons. Thus the subsequent division on Lords reform dominated the next day's editorials in a way which would have been impossible in the previous era when the divisions did not start until the leader writers had gone home. It must be right to rescue decisions in the Commons from the comparative secrecy of a vote late at night, even if it is at the expense of some embarrassment to a minister and on that occasion to myself.

For the future I expect the theme of reform in the Commons to be the strengthening of its committees. At their best the select committees enable members of all parties to perform as members of a legislature scrutinising the Executive rather than always acting as supporters or opponents of the government according to party identity. Tony Blair's admirable decision to answer questions before the Liaison Committee of their Chairs is testimony to the growing status of the select committees. Yet the debilitating weakness of the whole structure is that the only power of the select committees is to issue a report. The Commons remains a plenary Chamber with a committee system rather unconvincingly bolted on as an optional extra. The many MPs who now spend half their time on committee work will increasingly demand that it has a more direct impact on public policy.

I did not manage to secure all the measures of modernisation which I had sought. I still believe that the balance of power between the Executive and Parliament will remain too firmly tilted in favour of government until MPs win a say on the agenda of their proceedings through some form of collective Business Committee. And famously I failed to save the goat. The Queen's Speech will still laboriously be copied on to goatskin before the monarch's annual visit even though she sensibly chooses to read the printed version. But we made as much progress as was possible in a single Parliament and have left openings to be pursued by others willing to take up the baton for reform.

6

Moving Apart

30 OCTOBER 2002–4 FEBRUARY 2003

Wednesday 30 October

I had too much adrenalin in my circulation to sleep particularly well, and found myself back up by 5 a.m. trying to discover what the press had made of last night. In truth it was too late for all but the very latest editions. *The Times* very fairly made the point that even the tiniest NGO would know not to produce a major news story at an hour when all the British press had already gone to the printer. At least that complaint now belongs to history.

Prime Minister's Questions brought me back down to earth with a thump. I successfully fed Tony a number of useful lines, but was baffled that all my prompt lines in response to IDS's question on top-up fees were ignored. There was no mistaking the obvious conclusion from Tony's reticence and body language that he was a man seriously thinking of introducing top-up fees. The Labour benches went quiet and thoughtful, and for the first time since the summer recess the Tory benches felt they had something to cheer.

Afterwards, before the start of the Parliamentary Committee, I raised with Tony where he felt we were going on university fees. He was obviously troubled by the difficulty of carrying the party with him, but it was equally obvious that he has been lobbied by the dozen top universities and bought their argument that they need the right to raise extra funds if they are to be competitive in a global market. I was left reflecting that there may be something in the press speculation that Estelle Morris resigned in part because she and Number 10 were at odds on the issue. The problem is that Tony has such an exaggerated respect for those who are successful that he is very susceptible to mistaking their arguments of self-interest for the national interest. It is simply not in his nature to say to the country's top twelve university vice-chancellors that they have got it wrong.

Thursday 31 October

At Cabinet there was much discussion on the row with France at the weekend European Summit, which has since prompted Chirac to cancel the forthcoming Franco-British Summit. Jack was at his most ironic: 'It was an interesting summit and a privilege to be in the room.' As he fairly said, 'Tony does not do rude.' The reason Chirac was upset was not that Tony was rude but that Tony stopped him from railroading through his private deal with Schröder, to delay reform to the Common Agricultural Policy.

My own suspicion is that Chirac was glad of an excuse to get out of a Franco-British Summit in which the press would have wanted to know who got the upper hand in the well-advertised differences between him and Tony over Iraq. This morning, Clare Short reopened the issue by asking, 'Is it our interpretation of the current draft Security Council resolution that it gives authority for force?' Tony was surprisingly unequivocal in responding: 'I have always said that we would go back to the Security Council before any action.' So far, so good, but left hanging in the air is a hint of menace that unilateral action would follow if the UN did not agree to multilateral action.

Immediately afterwards I got a plane to visit my mother. On the way back I found myself sitting next to Timothy O'Shea, the new Vice-Chancellor of Edinburgh University, and we naturally fell to discussing top-up fees, of which he is a vigorous opponent. 'They will make only a marginal difference to the revenue of universities, but will have a big impact on their ability to attract students. I keep telling the vice-chancellors of the top dozen that they are wrong.' 'Yes,' I responded, 'but I think they have got their message through to Mr Blair.' 'I know,' he said, nodding assent.

Sunday 3 November

On Sunday we settled down to listen to my *Desert Island Discs*. Gaynor was touched that I had chosen Mahler's Fifth to remind me of our tough and our good times together. A positive endorsement came from Christopher, who rang up to express the sort of backhanded compliment which so often comes from your sons: 'Your choice of music was not as excruciatingly embarrassing as I had expected.'

Monday 4 November

Last time, I had complained that the meetings of the Legislative Committee were always held in the Large Ministerial Room. Despite its grandiloquent title, this is more of an underground bunker, occupying territory that must have been designed by the Victorians as the foundations of the building. Today the secretariat responded to my complaint by going to the other extreme. We were in the Moses Room, a very grand committee room adjacent to the Lords' Chamber. The room gets its name from two large Victorian oil paintings of episodes in the life of Moses. As it happens, we were considering the Alcohol Licensing Bill and one of the ministers before us was Kim Howells, who achieved notoriety over the weekend for his observation that the latest Turner Prize exhibition was 'conceptual bullshit'. John Reid demonstrated his streak for creating mischief by putting as the first question to Kim, with mock innocence, 'So what do you think of the paintings, Kim?'

Back in the Chamber, the House was debating the Adoption of Children Bill, which has come back to us from the Lords without the provision allowing unmarried and gay couples jointly to adopt. The Tories put a three-line whip on to support the Lords in the idiotic hope that this will be embarrassing to us, but it has spectacularly blown up in their own faces, as many on their own side simply refuse to be whipped against unmarried couples and gays. I went into the Chamber to hear John Bercow, who has resigned from the Shadow Cabinet in protest at the decision. It was an impressive performance. Unlike so many in the Chamber these days, he did not read the speech but spoke with only a few notes which he left lying on the bench beside him. I dropped him a note welcoming him back to 'the Business Statement repertory company'.

Tuesday 5 November

Des drops by in the late morning with a broad grin, to let me know that Iain Duncan Smith has summoned journalists to make a personal statement. This is a mystifying choice of language. In parliamentary terms, you only make a personal statement when you have resigned or if you are about to be suspended from the House for being caught with your hands in the till. In the event, IDS walks on to the television screen to announce that he knows last night's rebels are out to get him, and he is not going to put up with it. I paraphrase, but only slightly. Then he walks off the television screen without saying what he is going to do about it. I am left totally baffled that the leadership of the Conservative Party has not yet grasped that if you summon the press to an emergency briefing, you have to deliver them some line of action you are taking if you are going to convince them that you are in control of the story.

In the afternoon, I got a call from Jan Kavan, who is now engaged full-time as the Czech President of the UN General Assembly. He wanted to know what Tony would do if there was no agreement within the UN. I wanted to know how genuinely the US was engaging with the UN. Jan had met President Bush privately, and had been heavily alienated by the contrast between the public rhetoric of the President's speech and the private contempt of Bush for the UN: 'He kept saying he was putting a ball in the UN's court, but he did not trust the UN to take action. He kept saying that Saddam is Hitler, and the UN is like the League of Nations.' Not for the first time, I am puzzled that so often people whom I respect come away from a meeting with Bush alarmed at his shallowness, while Tony repeatedly assures us of his genuine regard for the President.

Wednesday 6 November

I woke up to dire news on the radio from the US, where Bush has swept the Democrats aside in the mid-term elections. For the first time that I can remember we have a Republican President, a Republican Senate and a Republican House of Representatives. The big danger is that Bush will draw from this the conclusion that keeping America in a permanent state of mobilisation is a smart electoral strategy. Whether it is going to be as smart in its impact on international affairs is a much more doubtful proposition.

John Reid addresses the PLP on his new role as Chairman of the Party. It is an effective speech which begins with some good jokes at the expense of the current difficulties of the Tories: 'When Tony appointed me, he told me that my two tasks were to raise the morale of the Labour Party and to destroy the morale of the Tory Party. Two weeks into the job, I have already completed one of those tasks.' I was impressed that he had quickly grasped that the central problem in the party is that we have not done enough to motivate its members: 'We have convinced the intellect of the party, but we have not aroused the passion of the party.'

The crisis over Duncan Smith's leadership has created such a high-noon atmosphere around Prime Minister's Questions that the actual event itself is something of an anticlimax. There is immense pressure on IDS to redeem himself, but there is also an intense amount of pressure on Tony to outperform him. When Tony joins us on the bench, he is unusually attentive in checking his briefs. I whisper to him, 'Relax. You are always so good at this.' He smiles back but responds, 'I am not always good.' However, he was good at the end of the day. Now that I am charged with the task of being a sort of front-of-stage prompt, I am astounded at the amount of work that is demanded of him to be ready for Prime Minister's Questions. It took me two hours this afternoon simply to read the brief on every political story of the past few days which might just possibly be raised, so that I am able to hiss two or three lines for his replies, but he has such a formidable mastery of the House now that he does not need them.

Thursday 7 November

At Cabinet, I reported that the Opposition choice of topics for the debates on the Queen's Speech appeared to be dominated more by the crisis in the Tory Party than by the political debate in the country. For the first time that I can remember in thirty years, they have chosen that there should be no debate on economic affairs, to deny a platform to

Michael Howard who is widely regarded as a potential replacement for IDS.

Equally surprisingly, they have opted to have no debate on foreign affairs, although Jack underlines just how out of touch that decision is with current reality, by reporting that we are on the verge of agreement to a resolution in the Security Council on Iraq. Geoff Hoon follows this up by observing that the most difficult dilemma for Saddam in the text is that he will be obliged to make a declaration of his weapons stockpile within thirty days: 'He will be forced either to demonstrate that he is a liar, or expose himself as a threat.' I wish Geoff could try a little harder to conceal his relish for the military solution. Jack evidently felt the same, as he intervened again to stress that the resolution will not provide a hair trigger for attack. Pat Hewitt, who occasionally strikes a thoughtful note of caution on the whole subject, intervened to state the obvious, namely that half the country thinks this is a war about oil not about weapons of mass destruction.

I was one of a handful of MPs who stayed throughout the afternoon in the House until we received the summons to come to the Lords for the official prorogation, where we are informed in elaborate, flowery language, which has changed little since the Middle Ages, that the monarch is pleased to let us go. I and my colleagues from the Commons stood beyond the bar at the end of the Chamber, while Derry and the leaders of the other political parties in the Lords sat together on the woolsack to receive the message from the Palace. Although the language of the occasion is frozen in the Middle Ages, their attire did not stagnate until the eighteenth century. For some unaccountable reason of protocol they all wear cocked hats, and there is much doffing and donning of headgear to register that they are in their place and that they have understood the message. It is pure *Monty Python*.

Friday 8 November

We had a rare political meeting at the Cabinet. It began with a presentation from Philip Gould on the consensus from his sixty focus groups over the past year. Apparently we are ahead on all issues, with the single exception of asylum, which explains why David Blunkett is being encouraged to appear more draconian on asylum than the Tories could ever possibly manage.

There followed a genuinely thoughtful table round. Indeed, it was so good that Peter Hain, who was attending his first political Cabinet, said that he was surprised how good it was since he had been told that Cabinet meetings were boring, to which Tony demanded with mock severity, 'Who told you that?'.

Tuesday 12 November

Most of the day is spent working out my speech for the PES Council in Warsaw, but I take light relief from the exercise by attending the rehearsal in the House of Lords for the ceremony of the Queen's Speech. Somehow it all seems even more absurd that we are pretending to be great medieval barons when everybody is dressed in civvy suits. The Earl Marshal has brought along his Duchess to role play for the Queen, and gently rebukes Derry and I for walking too fast through the Royal Gallery at a pace which disrespectfully leaves our substitute monarch well behind.

I am developing a new affection for Derry, who is putting up a stout defence of the independence of the courts and the civil liberties of the accused, against the efforts of David Blunkett to rebalance the criminal justice system in favour of getting a conviction. Derry has just revealed figures which show that out of every hundred crimes, only one ends in an acquittal, but seventy-five never result in anyone being charged. This would suggest that if we wanted to address reality, we should be looking at the problems in investigations rather than in trials, but of course it does not address the politics of the issue since to the *Daily Mail* the police are heroes and the judges are villains.

Wednesday 13 November

The day of the Queen's Speech.

I wander along to the far end of the building to take my place in good time for the arrival of the Queen at the House of Lords. I am confronted with a resplendent Bruce Grocott, whom I remember as an

MP who blended into the tearoom with an unassuming and unassertive dress sense. Transplanted to the House of Lords and appointed as Chief Whip, he is today in full fiery-red Napoleonic uniform, complete with a magnificent headdress of tumbling ostrich feathers which would be surely more appropriate as an ethnic tradition in the Kalahari. Andrew McIntosh looks similarly like something out of D'Oyly Carte and reassures me that he has just been down to the cellars with his eighteenth-century lantern to examine them for any barrels of gunpowder. It is good to know that in the face of yesterday's taped threats from Osama bin Laden our vigilance against international terrorism is in safe and reassuring hands.

As ever the Queen reads the speech with impeccable clarity and careful neutrality of tone. I am pleased that I have wedged into the Queen's Speech our commitment to bring forward more bills in draft for earlier scrutiny, but I note that the Queen hesitates momentarily before embarking on the mouthful 'pre-legislative scrutiny'.

Thursday 14 November

The morning cuttings bring a surprisingly mixed bag of reviews of the ceremony surrounding the Queen's Speech. Even the *Daily Star*, which rarely comments on the latest political events, has a lengthy editorial denouncing it as 'a daft ritual'. I get the impression that we may be entering a new phase in public sensibility in which impatience with the Ruritanian pomp outweighs respect for ancient tradition.

Cabinet begins with yet another posed photograph of the membership, necessitated by the most recent reshuffles. It is only six months since the last group photograph, but already we have lost Steve Byers and Estelle Morris. The attrition rate is beginning to resemble that of the trenches.

Friday 15 November

A day in Warsaw at the biennial Council of the PES. The lunch, with the party leaders, comes alive when the Commissioner for Enlargement, Günter Verheugen, reflects rather too candidly on the problems of taking Turkey seriously as an imminent candidate for membership: 'The problem with Turkey is that the politicians are accountable to the military, rather than the position in a true democracy where the military are accountable to the politicians.' Denyz Baikal, the leader of the Turkish socialist opposition, responds furiously and at length, insisting that Turkey must be treated as an equal.

I have to admire the finely honed diplomatic skills of Tony, who, as it happens, is sitting next to Denyz. With gravitas he assures Denyz that Turkey will be treated as an equal, and then goes on very sweetly to suggest that it would help if Turkey was to remove its veto in NATO on cooperation with the new European Security and Defence Force. Of course, everyone in the room knows that Turkey hasn't done that because the military won't allow the politicians to agree. It is a brilliant stroke, which says to Denyz that Tony is on his side, while at the same time telling everyone else in the room that Günter was right.

Tuesday 19 November

In the afternoon, I had a call from Pat McFadden, who has taken over from Robert Hill as the political fixer at Number 10. I have known Pat since he was active in the Labour student movement, and have always felt very comfortable with him. He was open with me that there is now a structural problem within Number 10, in that the political unit is being expected to fix problems that arise from the lack of politics in the policy unit. The problem is that the policy unit tends to listen to managerial obsessions and to be deaf to political concerns.

We both agreed that the kites being flown on top-up fees for universities are a good illustration of the problem, and I observed to him that 'Tony's great historic achievement for the Labour Party is to enable it to break out of electoral dependency on dwindling numbers of the manual working class, and to colonise the expanding middle classes as Labour's natural territory. I can't think of a more comprehensive way of undoing that legacy than telling middle-class parents they'll have to pay up to £10,000 for their sons and daughters to get the university education that they used to get for free.'

Thursday 21 November

Before he starts the meeting John Prescott takes me aside and asks me if I could stand in for him at the British Irish Council tomorrow, where he was supposed to be standing in for Tony. John is totally immersed in the looming fire strike, on which there are key talks throughout the day, and I readily agree to take it on as there is no responsible way in which he could leave London at the present time.

Immediately after Business Statement, we made a small piece of Commons history with the first of the new consultations with other parties on the shape of the legislative programme. There has been a running battle all week between my office and the Chief Whip's Office as to what I can tell them, or indeed whether I should be telling them anything. After hard bargaining, I was finally authorised to table a single sheet listing all the bills confirmed for this session and the likely period of their introduction. In a giant stride for parliamentary openness, I also got authority to disclose which ones would be introduced in the Lords and which in the Commons.

Towards the end of the afternoon, Neil Kinnock dropped by for a general chat. I stood next to Neil on the Embankment outside the Festival Hall on election night in 1997, when we all left the party to greet Tony, who with perfect timing arrived with the dawn. He went quiet and tense as Tony addressed us all, and I could see he was reflecting on what might have been. I put my hand on his shoulder and asked him if he was all right, to which he silently nodded in response. I don't imagine we would be contemplating war if Neil was at Number 10, and certainly not if Glenys was there as well.

Friday 22 November

The British Irish Council was hosted by the Scottish Executive in New Lanark, the model mill town built by Robert Owen, one of the early forerunners of socialist thought. Two hundred years ago he provided nursery education from the age of three, a crèche for working mothers, a free health service and compulsory insurance for welfare. It was a brilliantly chosen venue for the major theme of social exclusion.

I reminded Bertie Ahearn that he had been the occasion of one of the most embarrassing episodes for me as Foreign Secretary. We were both in Istanbul at a grand gathering when word came through that Cherie was pregnant with Leo. I had been locked up all morning with Madeleine Albright and Igor Ivanov, the Russian Foreign Minister, and was totally oblivious to the news. When I came out of the conference room, Bertie flung his arms around me and said, 'Great news for Tony.' I hadn't a clue what he was talking about, but assumed there must have been a breakthrough in the Northern Ireland peace process, and innocently replied, 'Yes, Tony's been working very hard for this for a long time.' I could see from Bertie's face that I had not said the right thing.

In the car on the way to the airport, I spent most of the time briefing myself for *Any Questions* by phone with Phil Bassett, head of the Strategic Communications Unit at Number 10. I was struck by how much the tone at Number 10 on the fire dispute has hardened. Only yesterday, John Prescott was being allowed to sound a reasonable man trying hard to find a reasonable solution. Today, the briefings coming out of Number 10 are of resolve and determination to face down the other side. Personally, I think John Prescott's line was one around which we were more likely to gather public sympathy.

In the event, *Any Questions* passed off without any casualties. I was helped by the presence on the panel of Ken Clarke, who was breezily frank in confirming that no government could agree at four in the morning to sign an uncosted cheque because there was a gun at their heads.

Monday 25 November

Hilary was missing from the Start the Week meeting of Business Managers. It was only later in the day that I discovered what had kept her in the precincts. Today was the debate on Iraq, and Michael Martin had dropped a bombshell by announcing that he was going to ignore the pointless and supportive amendment put down by the Conservatives, and select the more critical amendment by the Liberal Democrats. This is another assertion of the independence of the

Speaker, as by convention the Chair always selects the amendment of the Official Opposition, who had deliberately put down an amendment this time that we could accept. The result was to leave both Labour and Conservative whips in a state of equal consternation, but with the entirely democratic outcome that there was now a genuine choice for those rebels who wanted to take it. As if that was not enough innovation for one day, the Speaker had rendered the Labour whips incandescent by also granting an urgent question on the firefighters' dispute to IDS, which required Tony to answer it in person. This is the first time I have ever known the Prime Minister obliged to answer such a question, and it is a twenty-two carat innovation by Michael, who is probably now having pins stuck in a wax effigy of him in the Whips' Office.

I missed the debate on Iraq myself, as I flew up to visit my mother in hospital. I got back in time for the vote, in which there were fewer rebels than might have been expected if there had been a similar vote during the recall debate back in September. Part of this is to the credit of Jack, who had struck the right tone in his speech of respect for the UN.

It was evident from the government's approach to this and other debates on Iraq that Number 10 had abandoned the long-standing Western strategy of containing the threat from Saddam in favour of military action. This came as unwelcome news to me as during my years at the Foreign Office I had administered, with the full support of Number 10, a policy of containment designed to keep Saddam in a tight cage from which he could not escape and no weapons could get through. There were problems with containment. Even after we lifted all restrictions on the volume of oil Saddam could sell officially through the Oil for Food programme, he continued to smuggle large volumes of oil in order to use the illicit income for his own priorities rather than for the UN's humanitarian purposes.

But in its central purpose of hobbling Saddam's military ambitions containment did work. Indeed, all that we have learnt in the aftermath of war is that containment was successful to a degree that even I would not have dared to hope. Saddam's military formations were so weakened that they made little attempt to defend Baghdad and famously no weapons of mass destruction have been found, nor are expected to be found. We had succeeded in our security objectives of thwarting Saddam from converting his technical nuclear, chemical or biological capacity into actual weapon systems and had so reduced his conventional forces that they could not defend their own capital city, let alone threaten any of their neighbours.

Emotionally, however, it is understandable that Tony Blair had to believe that containment had failed. How can you begin to persuade yourself that war is necessary and just if you still believe that the policy of containment, which it is replacing, was a success? Geoff Hoon was probably more honest when he told the Cabinet that Resolution 1441 marked the end of containment, but nobody openly told the Security Council when they voted on it that they were voting for the end of containment as the agreed international strategy.

Nor would it have been easy to explain to the Security Council why they should bring down the curtain on containment, as there was no evidence it was not working. One reason why I rejected the war hysteria that gathered pace in 2002 was that I had seen no credible evidence up to the time I left office in 2001 that there was any increase in the threat from Saddam, nor any need for urgent military action to disarm him. On the contrary, our more pressing problem was resisting international opinion, especially in the Arab world, that was increasingly sceptical whether after a decade of sanctions Saddam could be a threat to anybody. As part of the effort to prove that we were being reasonable, we had considered in 1998 the possibility of closing the dossiers of the UN weapons inspectors on Iraq's nuclear and long-range missile capacity and in these two issues moving from intrusive inspection to the second phase of ongoing monitoring to prevent rearmament. This reflected our confidence that Saddam had neither an active nuclear weapons programme nor long-range missiles, which has since been proved right on both counts by the failure to discover either in Iraq.

More recently Britain had brokered a change to the basis on which sanctions on Iraq could be lifted. The previous position had been that sanctions could only be lifted when all the disarmament obligations on Saddam had been fulfilled. At the time that resolution had been crafted no one had foreseen sanctions lasting for a decade, or that the process of guaranteeing disarmament would be so complex. Therefore, we proposed an interim position that sanctions could be suspended if there was evidence of real progress in good faith towards disarmament. It proved exceptionally challenging to get consensus on the new position between those who wanted no change and those who wanted no sanctions, but after tortuous negotiations, and with US agreement, it was adopted as Security Council policy in late 1999. This was not a step that would have been taken by Western powers or by the Security Council if they really believed the security threat from Saddam was growing, rather than diminishing.

There are few cheaper rhetorical tricks in the armoury of the war party than the claim that those of us who believed invasion was the wrong action were therefore in favour of no action. On the contrary, we had pursued vigorous action to ensure containment, which we now know to have been a success in drawing the teeth of Saddam as a security threat. In a decade of containment, UN inspectors had disarmed more weapons than were destroyed in the first Gulf War, including forty thousand chemical shells.

Tight and effective embargoes on Iraqi imports had prevented Saddam reconstituting his programmes for weapons of mass destruction and had denied his conventional forces a single new weapon system or any state-of-the-art military technology. The years of containment are the only period in Saddam's rule in which he was not at war with one or other of his neighbours, and, by the end of it, his military was in no position to threaten any country of consequence. The strength of his conventional forces was less than half of what they were when he had invaded Kuwait.

Just before I left the Foreign Office, I wrote an article in February 2001 in which I concluded: 'Too many commentators overlook the fact that Britain's robust approach has contained the threat that Saddam poses. Since the UN imposed the policy of containment, Iraq has not used chemical weapons against the Kurds of northern Iraq, or against Iran, and it has not invaded its neighbours – all of which it did before. As a result, there is no high risk of his being able to attack us.' When I left the Foreign Office in June 2001, neither I, nor, as far as I am aware, anyone else in the government, imagined that Iraq posed a real and present danger to Britain's interests. Yet, less than two years later, the same government had concluded that we must immediately invade Iraq to remove just such a danger.

What had changed in the interim was not the military capacity of Saddam, but the policy of Washington. The new Bush Administration did not select Iraq for a victorious campaign because they really believed Saddam was a threat, but because they knew he was weak. Ironically, what had rendered him weak was the very policy of containment which they so much derided.

Tuesday 26 November

Martin Schulz came over to join me for lunch. Martin is currently the leader of the German group in the European Parliament and it was a useful opportunity to update me on the state of my old contacts in Germany. Most of them appear to have come to a rather sticky end in a German government that has had almost as many casualties as our own. The week after the election I visited Bonn, where the SPD was still in opposition and keen to talk up their links with the successful Tony Blair as an electoral asset. Oskar Lafontaine, who was then the party leader, greeted me in front of every television camera in Bonn with a great bear hug that made the evening TV bulletins in Britain, much to the discomfort of Alastair Campbell. Alastair is not strong on foreign contacts, and for months afterwards at summits would say to me, 'No hugging foreigners, please.'

Later, Jack Cunningham called round to brief me on the state of play in his Joint Committee. They have reached an agreement on the content, if not the language, of their interim report on the composition of a reformed second chamber. Unfortunately, they reached agreement by including just about every possible option which the laws of arithmetic permit. They have included each of the quintiles (which surprisingly add up to six, not five, as they include both 0 per cent and 100 per cent) and for good measure have thrown in half-and-half. It is further proof of the difficulty in establishing a consensus on what a reformed second chamber should look like. The risk is that with so many options we will end up with no one choice commanding a convincing majority in the Commons, which of course is exactly what the opponents of democratic reform are hoping for.

Wednesday 27 November

The business in the Chamber was dominated by Gordon's pre-Budget report. His statement demonstrated how much better Britain is doing than other countries in the context of a grim economic climate around the globe. Justifiably he went big on the commitment we have shown to boosting the income of pensioners, which everyone behind us knew was the result of his redistributive instincts rather than Tony's caution.

Tuesday 3 December

I call on the Speaker for our weekly chat. He is feeling a bit bruised from the battering he had received from the whips over the two decisions he had taken last week, which were both seen as unhelpful. In many ways, the Speaker gets the worst of both worlds. On the one hand he is supposed to stay aloof from the broad membership of the House, and Michael feels keenly his inability to wander down to the tearoom and spend time with his old mates. On the other hand, his isolation up in the great tower of his residence does not protect him from the Chief Whips on either side ascending by the lift and beating him about both ears with their own partisan agendas.

In the evening we vote on the Communications Bill. I take in with me a handful of the plastic calendars which the Clerks' Office has just produced, setting out the sitting and recess dates for 2003. To the outsider it may appear a modest advance, but in terms of parliamentary procedure it is revolutionary and is the first concrete benefit from the votes that we carried a month ago. Part of the contempt with which all previous governments have treated Parliament was their refusal to tell Members of Parliament when their presence might be required more than a month in advance. I handed around copies to those MPs who were most active in supporting the modernisation package, starting with Margaret Moran, who first gave me the idea by showing me the equivalent annual calendar for the Canadian Parliament.

Wednesday 4 December

Gordon Brown addressed the PLP following his presentation of the pre-Budget report last week. It was a vintage Brown performance. He is the most successful Chancellor Labour has ever had. On top of that he has also been the most redistributionist Chancellor we have ever seen, at any rate since Lloyd George's first Premiership. Today, he emphasised the revolution he has carried through by means of tax credits: 'Britain now has tax rates that range from +40 per cent to –200 per cent.' The impact of these on low income households is dramatic, but is never written up in the press because sub-editors only write about their own social class and don't know anybody trying to get by on £10,000 per year. Shrewdly, he chose to finish with the leading role he has played on rolling back the debt of the poorest countries. And then, in a way that only someone with his wide reading could do, he brought his peroration to a close with a quote from Tom Paine, which is certainly the first time I have heard his name invoked at a PLP meeting.

Gordon was greeted with thunderous applause. And yet he does not inspire affection in the way that Tony does. With Gordon, you feel a bit of sympathy with Queen Victoria's comment on Gladstone that she always felt as if she was being addressed as a public meeting. So it was today. At no point in an extremely intelligent and interesting address did you ever feel that he was sharing a confidence with you.

Thursday 5 December

When my turn came in Cabinet to announce the business of the House, I was able to report that between the Queen's Speech in mid-November and the Christmas recess at the end of December, we will have introduced seventeen government bills for a second reading in one or other chamber. It is a striking demonstration of the success of our efforts to get bills ready for the start of the session. Margaret Beckett, my predecessor, generously interjected, 'That must be a record.'

After Business Statement, I got back to my office to receive a frantic message from the Number 10 press office that I was advised not to turn up for today's lobby. Apparently, the official spokesman had taken such a battering at the morning lobby that they did not wish to inflict the experience on a Cabinet minister. The mischief stems from today's *Mail*, which has published e-mails between Cherie and a convicted con man, which purport to show that he helped her buy a student flat for Euan. The press are now going through a familiar phase of having their cake and eating it. Cherie is damned for associating with a con man who cannot be trusted, while at the same time every allegation by the con man is solemnly reported as gospel truth by the same press.

Monday 9 December

The press are still thrashing about trying to find some issue of substance to justify their preoccupation with the relationship between Cherie Blair and the con man. Today they have taken up the idea that it was improper for the Blairs to instruct their blind trust to buy a flat for their son to attend university. I began my morning chat with Hilary by lamenting how grossly unfair it was to Cherie: 'Are they really suggesting that the blind trust should be left to get on with finding the flat, and should have refused to tell the Blairs where Euan would be staying as it would breach the rules on disclosure?'

Tuesday 10 December

In the evening I called at Number 10 to see Tony, who had asked me round for drinks before Christmas. The poor man has to work his way through so many different contacts before Christmas that he has to start a clear fortnight in advance. I was taken up to the private flat, which involves a tramp through Number 11 as the Blairs have swapped flats with the Chancellor.

Curiously for a man who is setting out on his Christmas drinks season, Tony had no whisky in his drinks cabinet, but he did produce a good cognac of 1975 vintage. If this is a present from Paris, I can only assume that relations have been repaired since his much-publicised rift with President Chirac. I offered my deep sympathy for the wholly unreasonable press treatment of Cherie. He thanked me but quickly wanted to move on. One of the remarkable strengths of Tony is his sheer resilience, and despite a press onslaught on his family that would have paralysed a lesser man, he led into an animated conversation on how we were performing politically.

I asked him if we will have a referendum on the euro next year, and he replied, 'If it is up to me, yes. It is not a decision we can keep putting off. The longer we delay, the greater will be the penalty we will pay.' I agreed with him: 'I am struck that despite all the help you gave Schröder in the election, he is back in business with Chirac and the Franco-German relationship is as strong as ever. Nobody on the Continent will consciously decide to ignore us because we are outside the euro, but we will just drift to the margins as we become the last people they phone up.'

I offered to make a speech attacking the euro if he thought that would help bring Gordon round to being more enthusiastic. Tony laughed. He responded, 'Even the Treasury officials can't find what's going on over the economic assessment, never mind us here at Number 10.' I asked if he had yet seen the ministerial floor of the new Treasury, and he said he hadn't. 'You really ought to go there. It is terribly symbolic. The Permanent Secretary has a moderate-size desk at one end of the open-plan space, and towering above it is a great enclosed glass bunker which has three times his space and ten times more privacy from where Ed Balls can keep an eye on the Permanent Secretary through the glass.'

Before I left, I put down a marker on Iraq. 'Whatever happens, don't end up being the only one taking military action alongside the US. However multilateral the decision may be in the Security Council, it is the image of you alone with President Bush that people will see.' When I mentioned military action, he held up a hand with two fingers crossed and interjected, 'It may not come to that.'

I got back to my room behind the Speaker's Chair in the Commons to be greeted by the news from my staff that Cherie was about to make a personal statement. Sure enough, just after seven she appeared live on Sky to make what was a moving and effective statement.

Wednesday 11 December

At Prime Minister's Questions, Iain Duncan Smith chose to recite the latest smears on Cherie. It demonstrated yet again that the man does not have the stature to be a credible alternative Prime Minister. A Heseltine, or even a Thatcher, would have had the insight to recognise that there was nothing they could usefully do to add to the damage we have suffered at the hands of the press, and that the sensible strategy for them was to be seen to rise above it all. Instead Duncan Smith took off his shirt, got down in the gutter and rolled in the mud.

I hissed to Tony as he got up, 'Just stay dignified', which he did with magnificent composure. I was more practical help later on in feeding him a comparison between our record on local authority spending and the Tory cuts. On the whole I felt we left the Chamber well ahead on points, which is a striking comment on Tory incompetence given the mauling we are getting in the press.

Thursday 12 December

At Business Statement, Eric Forth banged on at considerable length about Cheriegate. He did not even bother to make it appear balanced by including a question about anything else. My style at Business Statement is to remain urbane and to score points for appearing unruffled, but this time I felt that passion was called for in defence of Cherie.

After the exchanges, I had Eric round to talk about various items of housekeeping, such as the questions rota. Before we got down to business, I twigged him about the decision of his party to run with the Cheriegate allegations. As always, Eric was engagingly frank. They have never forgiven the *Daily Mail* for backing Blair in '97 and, now that illicit affair is over, they are ruthlessly determined that there will never be any daylight again between them and the *Mail*. Few people outside Westminster understand that Paul Dacre has exercised more influence over political positions over the past decade than any politician elected by the public.

I got back home after a late dinner just in time to catch *Today in Westminster*, and hear it reported that I had given 'a staunch defence' of Cherie Blair.

Friday 13 December

I struggled out of bed for an early train to Newcastle where I had promised Ronnie Campbell, the MP for Blyth, that I would open his new constituency offices. On the train I bumped into Stephen Hepburn, the MP for Jarrow, and solicited a tale about Ronnie that would come as news to his party members: 'Tell them he keeps Tony supplied with stotty cakes. They are a big, round northeast flatbread. Tony had a reception for the northeast members, and sure enough Ronnie turned up with a stotty cake to give to Tony. Of course, the cockney policeman had never seen a stotty cake, and was very suspicious. Ronnie had to put it through the metal detector, just in case it was going to explode in the middle of the reception.'

Wednesday 18 December

At the Modernisation Committee we took evidence from Geoffrey Bowman, the First Parliamentary Counsel. I wanted colleagues to come face-to-face with the extraordinary pressure on the Parliamentary Draftsmen – or 'Drafters', as Geoffrey carefully styles them – and Geoffrey's urbane understatement convinced them far better than any high-blown rhetoric would have done. He described how for a dozen years when he drafted the Finance Bills he would expect to work seven days a week for three months, taking off only Sunday afternoon. With few resources, they do a remarkable job and their work has been much plagiarised by the new democracies of the East. Geoffrey tells us that Azerbaijan copied one of their bills word for word. They were able to identify it as a copy because it even included the clause on its application to Northern Ireland. When he left, I had another dozen allies in the room for my campaign to get more resources for the Parliamentary Drafters.

At the Parliamentary Committee, Gordon Prentice, despite being one of Tony's most outspoken critics, expressed his admiration for how calm Tony remained: 'When my friends ask me whether what is going on gets Tony down, I tell them, "No, he just looks incredibly relaxed." How do you do it?' Tony responded that there is just no point in getting worked up about it. I don't know how he does it either. The paradox is that as politics has become less ideological, its coverage has become more sensationalist. It needs an unusually calm and confident person to stay sane at the helm of Number 10. Most people would crack up in the first month.

Thursday 19 December

At Cabinet we have an extended discussion on pensions strategy, following Andrew Smith's statement to the House yesterday. I am struck by the extent to which our strategy is based on encouraging older workers to remain in employment for longer. This makes perfect sense in an era when people not only live longer but are fitter and healthier for longer. However, it also underlines how readily we have adjusted to taking full employment for granted. It was only twenty years ago that Labour's strategy was to encourage workers over fifty to retire in larger numbers to provide jobs for the young unemployed.

Friday 20 December

A day of seasonal shopping, shoving, shouldering and spending. I returned with the perishables as a successful hunter-gatherer in the early afternoon, to find my many bags viewed with grave suspicion by half the Israeli security service, who were there to protect their Foreign Minister's lunch with Jack. I descended deep into the bowels of our residence. This time I needed the capacity of the industrial-scale freezer in the official kitchen. Here I was surprised to find a caterer after two in the afternoon, still stirring the gravy. 'Gosh, their talks must be going badly if they have not yet started lunch.' To which she replied grimly, 'Not half as badly as the lunch if they don't start eating it soon.'

Both my sons came round to stay with us over the weekend. They are punctilious in making sure that they have two Christmas family experiences, one shared with their father and another with their mother. They have even negotiated a brotherly compact that they give each other two gifts, one placed under the tree of their father and the other under the tree of their mother. They function so well together as a family unit that they are a standing rebuke to their dysfunctional parents.

Wednesday 25–Friday 27 December

War is much in the air, even if this is the season of peace on earth. Press and radio bring every day fresh evidence of preparations for an attack on Iraq. Everyone appears resigned to the fact of war, but nobody appears convinced by the need for war. I think Tony was right to cross his fingers when we discussed the possibility of averting a war. The political problem is that the more the war is perceived as a priority of Washington, the less it can be sold as in the best interests of Britain.

On Friday night we went to Polly Toynbee's annual party. It was a select gathering of what is left of the media intelligentsia in Britain. Paradoxically, although Labour is in the ascendancy and the Conservatives are in trouble, there was an atmosphere of a threatened minority meeting clandestinely to swap covert liberal values. Polly did come up with an hilarious tale from her experiences in researching her book on low pay, for which she has undertaken low-paid jobs. Earlier this year she applied for a job as a cleaning lady which had intrigued her as it mentioned there would be a need for security clearance. When she turned up for the appointment, it transpired she was being interviewed for the job of cleaning the function rooms on the floors beneath my flat at Carlton Gardens. She didn't get the job, but some weeks later Alan Rusbridger, the *Guardian* editor, took a senior government official out for lunch and was taken aback when his guest upbraided him, 'I think it was jolly underhand of your paper to try to infiltrate one of your reporters into a sensitive building. Fortunately we were able to spot what you were up to in time.'

Tuesday 31 December

There is a wonderful story in the papers today that Donald Rumsfeld has been exposed as visiting Saddam twenty years ago as Ronald Reagan's special envoy, and arranged for him to get US exports to help his war against Iran. I suppose it would be too much to expect Rumsfeld to moderate his extravagant rhetoric about the evil of Iraq, now that we all know the part he played in equipping it. Curiously, only the *Mail* splashed it on the front page, but the *Mail* is pursuing an intriguingly anti-war line, which is going to be more uncomfortable for IDS than for Tony, given that IDS is way out in front of us in his enthusiasm for war.

Wednesday 1 January 2003

As I sat at my desk in the bay window, and watched the dusk settle over the spires of the Palace of Westminster, I resolved on two objectives for the new year, which would be a firm measure of progress on modernisation: first, to ensure that the changes we have already set in train are seen as a success, and that I meet my objective of persuading even those who voted against them that they actually had supported them; secondly, before the end of the year to have got a bill which we can introduce on reform of the House of Lords.

In return for these high-minded civic commitments, I also promised myself one lifestyle change which will make the cycle of my week more pleasant and less stressful: I will give up my regular rendezvous with the Press Gallery. Their only interest is in sensationalising anything I say, and my only interest is in avoiding giving them such a story. The net result is that I succeed if I am boring, and fail if I am interesting. I don't like to be boring, and I like even less what they do with anything I say which is interesting.

Thursday 2 January

There is a big negative reaction across the press to Tony's New Year message, which has been widely reported for its grim warning of the 'difficult and dangerous' year ahead. It certainly was sombre. Presumably its tone was chosen to reflect the frequent predictions of the press that 2003 will be a difficult and dangerous year for Tony, which makes it a bit rich for them now to complain that he was not more cheerful. Yet I can't help wondering whether Tony, or more plausibly Alastair who will have written the text, has not misjudged the public mood. When the public are worried about the future and feeling insecure, they want a leader who will tell them how it is going to be put right, not a Prime Minister who tells them they are right to be worried.

Monday 6 January

When I take the dogs out in the early morning, I wear headphones so that I can keep up to speed with the *Today* programme. This morning I am rewarded with a brave interview by Jack Straw, who is gaining in confidence in his new role. This morning he virtually admitted that he was the Cabinet minister quoted at the weekend as saying that the odds against a war have lengthened to 60/40 against. This is certainly what the nation wants to hear as they take their dogs for their morning constitutional, but I am not so sure it will go down well with the occupants of Number 10, and it will be even less popular at the Ministry of Defence, who are just about to announce troop deployments to the Gulf with every appearance of 100 per cent enthusiasm for a conflict.

Tuesday 7 January

This is the first week with the earlier hours for which we voted back in October, and the *Today* programme has asked me on to talk about modernisation. They have also warned Des that Derry will be on an hour before me, and helpfully suggested that I might like to listen to him, from which I deduce that the bulk of the interview will be on Lords reform rather than Commons reform.

Derry is as incorrigible as ever. As far as it is possible to tell from my radio set, he managed to keep a straight face while telling the nation that 'the centre of gravity' for reform now was gathering around 20 per cent as the elected element. With Olympian disdain for consistency, he then asserted in the same answer that opinion was polarising between an all-appointed House and an all-elected House. I was therefore not at all surprised when, after a few perfunctory questions on modernisation, Jim Naughtie said that he now wanted to turn to Lord Irvine's comments on Lords reform. I did my diplomatic best to reconcile the impossibility of agreeing with Derry's claims, and the undesirability of being seen to disagree with him too publicly.

Derry's downbeat assessment of the prospects for real reform rumbled on through the day. Not surprisingly they featured large at my oral questions, where Andrew Mackinlay asked me to tell the Lord Chancellor that Lords reform should not be kicked into touch by him or anyone else from the House of Lords. I drew laughter from the Chamber when I prefaced my response by saying that 'I shall reflect on the precise terms in which I might convey that message to the Lord Chancellor.'

I escaped from the Chamber just in time to get a mug of coffee to take down with me to the LP Committee. Our big headache today was the Mental Health Bill. It is running late because the Parliamentary Drafters who should be working on it are running late on the Water Bill. And they are running late because we had to take them off the Water Bill back in November because the Criminal Justice Bill was running late and needed their help. And so it goes on as we endlessly juggle around far too few people to draft so much legislation.

I hear the midnight news while I brush my teeth, and discover that Geoff Hoon has said that it does not help for Jack to say that war is less likely. I go to bed mystified as to whom Geoff imagines he is helping by making such an observation.

Wednesday 8 January

We had our first session of Prime Minister's Questions at the new time of midday. None of the dire predictions about the event losing all its character turned out to have any substance. Tony was as well briefed as ever despite the unconvincing anxiety which the Opposition had professed as to whether he would have time to prepare.

Not surprisingly, Iain Duncan Smith asked Tony whether he agreed with his Defence Secretary or his Foreign Secretary about the prospects for war in Iraq. Tony saw him off perfectly satisfactorily within the context of the parliamentary exchanges. However, the difference between their two perspectives in truth reflects an even greater gulf between their respective opposite numbers in Washington, Rumsfeld and Powell.

The issue was further explored at the Parliamentary Committee. This time there appeared to have been a degree of coordination between them, in that several raised the same issue of our strategy towards Iraq. Helen Jackson opened up the discussion, wanting to know what our exit strategy is if we cannot get the UN to agree on a further resolution. Tony was commendably robust that the next step was down to the inspectors: 'The inspectors are going to have to certify that there has been a breach of the UN resolutions.' The effect of this robust support for the UN was marred by his confidence that they will report a breach. 'It is only a matter of time before they find something.'

For the first time ever, we finished business at 7 p.m. In the division lobby there was much backslapping from sympathetic colleagues congratulating me on the change. Des Browne said one of the kindest things I have heard since entering government. Mentioning my appearance at the Despatch Box he said, 'You wear the House like an old waxed coat.' I went home with a real sense that, after some challenging years going around the rest of the globe, I had come home to Parliament.

Thursday 9 January

I went round early to get on with preparations for Business Statement, and found a rather shocked Des waiting for me with the front page of the *Mirror*. It was entirely given over to a demand that Jack Straw must resign, based on the claim that Tony had authorised Geoff Hoon's attack on Jack. The same story appears in the *Express* and the

Mail with the same quotes, which obligingly all three papers ascribe to the Ministry of Defence. Personally I don't believe it for one minute. Tony is preoccupied with preserving an image of unity and would never sanction one colleague publicly attacking another, but it does look as if Jack is now getting the same treatment from one of the junior ministers that was visited upon me in the Sunday press last autumn.

In her indomitable way, Clare Short raised the issue at Cabinet to deplore the attacks on Jack, and I came in to add that Jack had been doing a great job in keeping the Iraq crisis in the UN track, and that is what we should keep telling the press.

The main business for Cabinet was my paper on the legislative programme for the third session. In my opening remarks I firmly warned that the programme was now full, and suggested as a discipline on discussion that any colleague who wanted to add a bill to the programme should also nominate the bill he wanted taken out. This warning proved very effective, possibly too effective. The net result was that no colleague suggested yet another bill, but an unhelpful discussion on Lords reform, which is in the programme, expanded to fill the vacuum. David Blunkett, who is still smarting from his many defeats at the hands of the second chamber, urged that we must take a collective view on the kind of second chamber we actually wanted. I responded with studied patience that we had committed ourselves to a free vote six months ago and could not now go back on that. As the discussion had largely gone his way, David seized the moment to ask that all those in favour of an elected second chamber raise one hand. Tony intervened good-humouredly to ask me not to rise to the bait, and pointed out that we would never get agreement among us on a single view for Lords reform. More worryingly, he pronounced that he would be making his own view clear before the vote, which will at the very least shade the extent to which Labour MPs will see it as an entirely free vote.

When I got back to my office I had a meeting with the backbench Labour members, who were working as a team to canvass support for the democratic options on Lords reform. I reported on the morning's discussion in the Cabinet, in which a number of voices had argued for an all-appointed Chamber. Chris Bryant succinctly expressed the disbelief of those present with his observation, 'Let me get this straight.

The Cabinet is not proceeding with the White Paper option for a second chamber with only 20 per cent elected because that did not provide a large enough democratic element . . . So now they want to go ahead with a second chamber with nobody elected?'

Sunday 12 January

A bright, clear, cold day. The lake in St James's Park was frozen over, and the ground frost crunched under our feet. Beautiful but threatening. The political climate is also getting frosty. Last week's stories of splits between Jack and Geoff have set the press off with new confidence spotting a Labour rebellion over Iraq behind every arras. Tony may be right, and inspectors may eventually come up with a discovery, but for the time being it is hard for either public or party to understand the case for a military assault on Iraq to disarm it when the inspectors can't find any of the weapons we are supposed to be disarming.

—⁂—

I t is still possible to find loyal ministers who will grimly defend the invasion of Iraq as the right decision in international policy. It is becoming hard to find any who do not resignedly accept that the war has been an unmitigated disaster for Labour in domestic politics.

This was not the expectation of those who got us into the war. It seems almost cruel now to remind them of their promise that victory in Iraq would be followed by a 'Baghdad bounce' in the polls in Britain. Nobody can now be found to own up to being the source of the extensive briefings that in the wake of victory the Prime Minister's status would be so strengthened that he could press ahead even more boldly with all the measures of public service reform that his party may still not like but would no longer dare deny him. In place of those heady expectations reality must have been a sore disappointment. Instead of Baghdad bounce, Labour bombed in the local elections with its worst results since taking office. Brent East produced Labour's worst by-election result for fifteen years. Instead of a rejuvenated Prime Minister, the polls have registered a record slump in Tony Blair's personal ratings. Instead of basking in public approbation, the government is in the throes of a crisis of public trust.

It is curious that a political organisation that tracks public opinion as obsessively as New Labour should have decided on Iraq that what the public thought could be discounted. At one Cabinet meeting I drew attention to a recent opinion poll in which Labour had dropped ten points in one month and warned that our belligerence on Iraq was hurting our political support. Nobody disagreed with my analysis. But there was no change in policy to lessen the political damage.

Number 10's belief that it could get away with ignoring public opposition to the war was based on two calculations. The first was that when the war started a majority would swing behind our troops. The polls did indeed produce majority support for the war once it had started but this reflected public support for British troops in action and it was hubris of Number 10 to read them as support for the Prime Minister who had got Britain into the conflict.

The second calculation was that the war would be short and the political fallout would be equally short. Forget those feeble excuses that the looting and disorder which followed victory were the result of the Coalition Powers being caught by surprise because the fighting finished faster than expected. White House and Number 10 banked on a quick war. If anything, it took them longer than they had bargained to overcome the resistance on the road to Baghdad. Tony Blair once enigmatically assured me that there were ways in which the war could be concluded quickly. On another occasion, when I shared with Hilary Armstrong my worries that it would be difficult to fight a local election campaign at the same time as fighting a war, she responded that Tony had promised her it would all be over by polling day.

The big blunder at the top was the assumption that the political fallout would be over as quickly as the war. I believe Tony genuinely expected that delivering victory in Baghdad would wipe the slate clean on the political controversy over whether the

war was justified. Perhaps his own political experience had led
him to assume that victory would be all. I met Tony Blair for the
first time in 1982 at the Beaconsfield by-election where he was
our candidate. I had been sent down by party headquarters to
support him at a press conference on the disastrous state of the
economy. What was more obvious on the day was the disastrous
state of Labour campaigning. The press conference was a positive
parody of Labour Before Mandelson. Tony and I sat behind a
trestle table in a largely empty hall. An optimistic party official
had laid out neat rows of about thirty plastic chairs which
contained two visibly bored local journalists. Labour was never
going to win Beaconsfield in any year of the last century and
certainly not in the very month that Margaret Thatcher had
liberated the Falklands. Afterwards I dropped Tony a note
consoling him with the thought that in the circumstances Labour
could not have won even with Rear Admiral Sandy Woodward
as our candidate.

I have often wondered in recent years whether that formative
experience of being turned over at the polls by a governing party
led by a war hero has not left Tony Blair too inclined to associate
military victory with political popularity. Iraq, though, was not
the Falklands, where British territory had been invaded and
where victory was followed by a jubilant welcome from the
liberated islanders. The war on Iraq was preceded by deep public
opposition precisely because there had been no such compelling
reason for military action. It has been followed by prolonged
political fallout as the public came to terms with the realisation
that there had been no imminent threat from Saddam and that
the coalition forces had no clear idea of how to run the country
they had just conquered.

At his press conference before departing for his summer holiday
after the war, Tony Blair was to complain that Iraq had dominated
the political scene 'for about a year'. As a result there has been an
immense diversion of the time and energy of himself and his
ministers from domestic priorities and a massive distraction of the
public from the very real domestic achievements of his government.
Part of the political cost of the year of Iraq was that it created in the
public mind an image of their Prime Minister as preoccupied with

fixing the world rather than running Britain. The irony is that this political damage to the Labour government was a self-inflicted wound. It could have been avoided by listening to the majority who were opposed to the war.

—〰—

Monday 13 January

On Monday I normally have sandwiches in my room with Meg, Greg and Ben Bradshaw. Today we have a valuable discussion on how I should develop the Modernisation Committee's inquiry into reconnecting with the public. Greg shows an enthusiastic tendency to suggest some more populist forms of consultation. He is particularly keen that we take evidence from Ms Dynamite, a young pop star who has expressed an interest in entering politics. I know the limits of my skills at chairmanship, and they stop short of moderating a question and answer session between Sir Nicholas Winterton and Ms Dynamite.

Friday 17–Monday 20 January

A long weekend in Italy at a meeting of the PES Praesidium in Florence and then the Socialist International Council in Rome. The offer of a double international meeting on their territory was eagerly grasped by the Italian left who are locked in a battle with Berlusconi, which is not just about how the government should be run but whether the media should be free and the courts independent. In Florence, they were warm in their hospitality and on the last day opened up the secret passage by which the Medicis used to cross the river from the Pitti Palace to the Uffizi without being seen, but keeping a watchful eye on the populace at the same time. In this suitably conspiratorial setting one of the members of the Italian Senate shared with me the observation that Berlusconi's coalition had won every one of sixty-one seats in Sicily and added drily, 'That does not happen by accident.'

The discussions on Iraq were sombre, both in the PES Praesidium and even more in the wider Socialist International Council. As I was in the Chair at the PES discussion in Florence I was able to hold us together in a spirit of tolerance, if not unity, which helped set the scene for the replay of the same discussion in Rome. But there was one stark conclusion that stood out as clearly as the Bargello Tower over Florence. The European left will go along with the strategy just as long as it is seen to be driven by the United Nations. If we once step outside the UN mandate the British Labour Party will have nobody on the European left for company.

Friday 24 January

Jim Devine rang to warn that he could not keep quiet on Iraq any longer. Jim has been my election agent for twenty years and has loyally kept my base secure. But as a union official he is also a media figure in his own right. Every general election we make the same bargain that he will get as much airtime in the Scottish media for me as for himself, and every time he fails to deliver. He said he was coming under a lot of pressure to speak out and could not support a drift to war without UN authority. We both knew that anything he said might be seen as a signal from me, but in fairness to Jim I could not ask him to stay silent any longer.

Tuesday 28 January

Most of the day spent putting together my speech to the Parti Socialiste which I have to deliver on Friday in Paris. But I am drawn out of my shell at the end of the day to attend the Channel 4 Parliamentary Awards. The ground floor of the Channel 4 building has been converted into one giant set for the occasion. It is a law of all grand TV occasions that you must have a large live audience and as a result they have invited many more people than they have tables for. Over drinks I get much ribbing from Martin Salter and other colleagues that they qualify for standing room only on the terraces. To my astonishment Channel 4 produce John McCririck to do one of his over-the-top displays to camera as the introduction to my award for delivering modernisation. Afterwards I learn it was as much of a surprise to him as he had been instructed by his employers to turn up, but only told why ten minutes before going onstage. The award itself turns out to be a large oblong of solid glass which will come in handy if we ever need a doorstop.

Wednesday 29 January

At Prime Minister's Questions Tony slammed a big fat torpedo into our joint strategy on Lords reform. He had an unerring aim and I was left sitting silently beside him for the rest of Question Time contemplating the wreck of democratic reform sinking beneath the horizon. Only last week I had begged him not to express any preference among the options before the House. I thought I had convinced him with the clinching argument that he would get panned by the press for coming out in support of a House of Cronies and panned a second time over because he would not have been able to convince a majority of Labour MPs to vote with him.

The opening had been perfectly teed up by David Clelland, who has consistently opposed any direct election to the second chamber and was a logical choice for Number 10 to approach. I have sat with Tony through enough Prime Minister's Questions to tell the unscripted answer from the prepared text, and there was no mistaking that this time the offence was premeditated. Indeed, I suspected Alastair Campbell's hand in the carefully crafted antithesis at the heart of the answer: 'The key question of election is whether we want a revising chamber or a rival chamber. My view is that we want a revising chamber.' It was a clever pitch in that it presented reform as a threat to the Commons and thereby conjured up a common interest of both government and Commons in resisting reform. In reality the Commons faces a more immediate threat from the determination of the government to keep it in its place, than from too much democracy down the corridor. But the damage has been done. It is impossible to square the spirit of a free vote with the Prime Minister advertising how he wants his party to vote.

Thursday 30 January

It did not take genius to predict that Eric Forth would major at Business Questions on the Prime Minister's views on Lords reform. I had already made up my mind that if it was acceptable for the Prime Minister to express forcefully his view between the options it must also be acceptable for the Leader of the House. Eric is fairly unflappable, but even he looked as if I had taken his breath away when I replied with heavy irony, 'It is my personal and very humble opinion that by removing the 20 per cent elected element, and substituting zero, we will not restore the public confidence that was missing the first time round.' I did my best to dismember the Prime Minister's antithesis by agreeing that we did not want a second chamber that was a rival, but that the Commons did need a second chamber that was a partner in restoring respect for Parliament.

Friday 31 January

I woke up in Paris to find that *Libération* runs a front-page headline denouncing Tony and the other European leaders who have just signed a statement of support for military action on Iraq as 'Bush's eight mercenaries'. In all the circumstances I found it challenging to make a speech in front of the television cameras that did justice to the common position of the European left while not totally losing touch with the perspective of the British Labour government. The speech suffered as a result and remained a bit flat.

As soon as I decently could I slipped away to the neighbouring room and rang Number 10 to let off steam on Lords reform. Pat McFadden was the unfortunate soul at the receiving end. I bitterly protested that the effect of Tony taking a public position had made it impossible for me to state my well-known position without it appearing a calculated rebellion. The press reaction to my comments at Business Questions had portrayed me as a rebel disagreeing with the Prime Minister. Pat advanced the novel argument that people had wanted to know how Tony was going to vote. Since Tony drops in for only 5 per cent of all votes I found it implausible that people expected him to vote at all, but I had the tact to keep this thought to myself.

Instead, I said that I was very angry at what had happened and they would have to recognise that simply repeating what I had been saying for the past year was going to create a story of Labour splits which was not of my choosing. A rather browbeaten and weary Pat at the other end assured me that I had made it perfectly clear that I was angry and he would tell Tony.

Sunday 2 February

Gaynor's birthday. We spend it driving up to Kenilworth and back for a celebration lunch with her parents. On the way to lunch, Sally Morgan had rung from Number 10 to say that Tony would like to speak to me in the evening. I cheekily inquired whether this is part of the 'resignation watch' about which I had read in the papers, but she assured me that he only wants to brief me on how he got on at Camp David with Bush. I didn't believe it at the time.

The call comes through when we are stopped at a service station on the M40 on the way back. Disconcertingly, I find myself talking to the Prime Minister of Great Britain about the prospects for world peace or war staring through the windscreen at an overflowing litter bin. Tony begins with one of his disarming chuckles, followed by 'Look, I'm very sorry if what I said brought you a lot of difficulty.' I responded, 'It's not giving *me* any difficulty', but that, as I predicted before he said it, the inevitable consequence is that the press report as a split and rebellion even the simple restatement of my well-known and long-held views. He assures me that it will be a genuinely free vote and says a couple of times that he is quite relaxed about it. In return I assure him that whatever the press might be speculating, it had never entered my head to resign over this issue.

He has obviously not had an easy time on his US trip. He was encouraged that Bush had been as strong as he had ever heard him on the Middle East, and got the impression that Bush was willing to push the Israelis into making peace. On the negative side, he had found Bush what he described as 'hard over' on the problems of getting a second resolution through the UN. 'I had to convince him that it would not be so difficult and that getting a second resolution in the event of a material breach would be much easier than the first time around. But they are afraid of disappearing down the swamps and marshes of the Security Council process.'

Monday 3 February

The *Guardian* has done us proud with a good front-page article stressing that Blairite ministers like David Milliband and Brownite allies such as Douglas Alexander are coming out for a largely elected second chamber. Meg tells me that it is the work of Michael Jacobs, who had persuaded the *Guardian* to take up the theme after the Fabian conference which the *Guardian* jointly sponsored. It is a helpful signal that the momentum may be with us.

The same cannot be said of Hilary. At the routine Start the Week meeting, I had the temerity to remind her of the decision of the Parliamentary Committee that whips should not campaign on free votes and got an affronted response. She could not have been more blunt that the whips felt that Tony's intervention not only made it permissible for them to campaign for his position, but obligatory that they delivered for him.

Tuesday 4 February

The day starts early with a round of the breakfast broadcast programmes. They mostly go well, primarily because no interviewer can think up a good reason why electing people to Parliament is wrong.

The only awkward moment came on *Breakfast* TV, not because of the interviewer but because of the girl working the camera, who began to gesticulate wildly the moment I went live on air. For a ghastly minute of conversation, I thought she must be trying to tell me that there was something truly alarming about my appearance such as a spider on my collar. The interviewer was into the second question before I realised that the girl was trying to summon an assistant to work the camera while she rushed to answer the door. It subsequently turned out that one person in the whole of the BBC suite at Millbank was responsible for answering the door, working the camera and operating the remote radio studios.

For the debate I had made a deliberate decision not to have a typescript speech, but to speak, as I did before joining government, from handwritten notes. The problem with a full text is that it can come between you and the audience. By contrast, working from a few notes leaves you free to keep your eyes on the audience rather than the page. It was the right decision because the chamber was full of members with strong views on the subject, and I was better able to let the interventions naturally fit into the argument I was developing than if I was working from a prepared script. I appealed to the House to 'bring down the curtain on the longest political indecision in our history' and ended with a strong plea to members to keep faith with democracy.

The best speech of the debate which followed came from Estelle Morris, who was speaking for the first time in the Chamber since her resignation in October. She spoke with a simple and persuasive conviction that only an elected second chamber would feel right to the people outside Parliament.

The votes had a sense of excitement as no one really knew who was going to win. The sense of suspense was also laced with nervous gossip of the dark rumours circulating about the activities of the whips. In one division, Greg Knight, Eric Forth's deputy, told me that one of our ex-whips had been approaching Tory MPs and telling them that the best way to give the government a bloody nose would be to vote for an all-appointed house as that 'would force Robin Cook to resign'. Tory MPs had not been taken in by the argument that voting for the Prime Minister's preferred option was the best way of embarrassing his government.

Despite all these efforts, we comfortably defeated the option of an all-appointed chamber by almost one hundred votes with a narrow margin of Labour votes on our side. I had not expected to win the wholly elected option and was personally surprised that the majority against it was a mere seventeen votes. It was evident from the faces of the tellers as they stood before the mace to announce the result that it had also come as a surprise to the whips, and not such a pleasant one either. However, I did expect that we might win the next vote on an 80 per cent elected chamber and I had a real pang of disappointment when the clerk handed the result to the teller for the noes to read to the House. We had lost by a mere three votes.

By the end of the evening, every single option had been defeated. It was little comfort that the biggest defeat of all had been for an all-appointed House. However, at such moments the House respects the member who can retain his sang-froid. When Eric Forth got up on a point of order to demand to know what we intended to do next, I rose with such coolness as I could muster and said, 'We should go home and sleep on this interesting position.' This provoked a gale of laughter which blew away the tension and enabled me to execute an orderly retreat to Room 4, where Lorna passed round the Scotch and Chardonnay to a small group of our closest allies. Fortunately we had set up an operation to analyse the division lists as soon as they came down from the Table Office and within an hour were able to dispatch a couple of our lieutenants up to the Press Gallery to put the best gloss on the results, and in particular to stress that a majority of Labour MPs had voted against an all-appointed House.

The House of Lords will never reform itself. In the course of its debates in parallel with the Commons, there were a few brave speeches which recognised that it is insupportable in the democratic era for one of the two chambers of Parliament to have not a single elected member. But the tone of most contributions was overwhelmingly complacent and occasionally revealed a superior disdain for the elected politicians in the Commons as the rough end of the trade.

Lords reform will only happen if the Commons insists upon it, and that night MPs passed up the opportunity to do so. It is possible to put a positive gloss on the voting figures, and I did my best to do so over the next couple of days. It is also the case that some MPs simply got lost in the thicket of differing options and competing percentages. Infuriatingly, three Tory reformers had intended to support an 80 per cent elected chamber but got confused among the multiple votes and by mistake voted against it. Had they recorded their vote correctly we would have secured a majority in favour of, not against, that option.

But no amount of footnotes can obscure the central fact that the Commons had the historic chance to modernise the House of Lords and chose not to do so. The awkward truth is that the present arrangement suits many MPs just fine. They relish the fact that the Commons enjoys undisputed primacy and that so long as the Lords has no legitimacy it will have no real powers. For all the publicity that surrounds each government defeat in the Lords, most end not in confrontation but compromise, and the number of times post-war government has been obliged to resort to the Parliament Act can be counted on the fingers of one hand. The constitutional reality is that Britain has a unicameral parliamentary system concealed by an elaborately colourful, but pathetically irrelevant second chamber.

The real tension today within our political system is not an imaginary tussle between Lords and Commons for primacy, but the struggle to make the Executive more accountable to scrutiny in Parliament. The real danger to the Commons is not some fanciful erosion of its powers by the Lords, but the crumbling public esteem for Parliament which undermines its authority. In the present mood of public disenchantment from the political system, Parliament cannot afford a second chamber which lacks relevance, legitimacy and representativeness. The Commons needs a modern second chamber as its partner in restoring public confidence in parliamentary democracy and respect for parliamentary scrutiny.

Tony Blair's intervention brilliantly positioned a democratic second chamber as a threat to the Commons rather than a challenge to the Executive by warning that it might become a rival. He thereby conscripted enough, though not most, Labour MPs to voting for a wholly appointed Chamber. Such a Chamber will not demand any scrutiny that will trouble the Executive and will therefore not offer any hope of restoring public respect for parliamentary democracy. It is Parliament that is the loser from this outcome and only government that gained.

The Commons cannot defend its primacy by denying legitimacy to the Lords. Nor is it necessary. In its retreat from Empire, Britain has covered the globe with bicameral systems in which the lower House retains unequivocal primacy. We could readily repatriate such an arrangement for ourselves, in which the primacy of the Commons was guaranteed by law and constitution, not by the preposterous illegitimacy of the Lords. Half the second chambers in parliamentary democracies around the world are entirely elected, and half of the remainder are largely elected, but almost invariably their Parliaments manage to ensure that the second chamber is subordinate to the first from which the government is formed.

The Preamble to the 1911 Parliament Act explained that reduction in powers of the Lords was necessary because 'a Second Chamber, constituted of a popular instead of a hereditary basis . . . cannot be immediately brought into operation'. I doubt if Lloyd George, who wrote it, ever imagined that a century later the House of Lords would still lack a popular and elected basis. I remain hopeful that one day there will be a courageous government that will bring the Lords into the democratic era and provide for its members to be chosen by the ballot box rather than patronage. Sadly, it will not be a Blair government that carries out that modernisation.

7

The Final Break

5 FEBRUARY–17 MARCH 2003

The press are not nearly as bad as I might have feared. Even the *Daily Mail* in its editorial praises me for 'a magnificent *tour de force* for democracy' although quickly adds it never thought that I was someone it would salute. Tony gets a dire press, as I had warned him he would, following what is reported as his humiliation at being defeated in the vote on an all-appointed House. However, there is no disguising the raw and awkward truth that the biggest loser of all is the House of Commons which has shown that it does not know what to do when asked to make up its own mind.

I rang Number 10 and insisted on speaking to Tony. I did not want to find myself at Prime Minister's Questions again faced with another surprise announcement from Tony. We agreed on the holding line that it was now for the Joint Committee to consider how to take forward the process of reform.

Famously, Tony returned yesterday from the Anglo-French Summit in order to vote down Lords reform. At the Parliamentary Committee he was surprisingly optimistic about Chirac's mood on France and gleeful about the impact of his famous letter as one of eight European leaders supporting Bush: 'It has obviously got home to Chirac that it might not be us who are isolated in Europe, but himself.' I am sure Jacques did his bonhomie best, and nobody does diplomatic glad-handing better than the French. However, I couldn't help suspecting that Tony was now so desperate to believe that Iraq would turn out all right that he was getting guilty of wish fulfilment.

Afterwards I crossed over to Downing Street to see Tony on my own. He again repeated that he was totally relaxed about the choices that people had made in a free vote, and wanted me to know that nobody would be barred from promotion because they voted a different way from him.

He was sensitive on two points. First, he conceded that he had taken a battering in the press and mischievously demanded to know how I could explain away my great offence of being praised by the *Daily Mail*. Secondly, he instantly agreed with my warning that yesterday he had

286 The Point of Departure

got himself into the lobby with the wrong people. All the young modernisers were in my lobby and all the old-machine tribalists were in his lobby. He responded that he knew that this was a legacy of yesterday's votes which he had to address.

Afterwards Alan Milburn dropped by to talk to me about the delays to the bill setting up the foundation hospitals. In truth, he is running so late up against the wire that in any other circumstances I would be telling him that we should pull the bill. However, I like Alan, I agree with the policy of decentralising and localising the NHS, and in any case we both know that the delays are caused by the resistance of Gordon to the policy not because of any indolence within the Department of Health. After we had reached agreement on the revised set of deadlines, he asked his officials to leave in order to give me his private advice in the wake of the votes on Lords reform. 'First, don't do anything foolish by resigning. Second, don't show you are defeated. You had better find a way forward that shows you are still in control of the project.' It was well meant and it was well received.

Thursday 6 February

At Cabinet, Jack is beaming with satisfaction about the relative success of Colin Powell's presentation yesterday to the Security Council, which he attended. Justifiably, he highlights how Powell's transcripts of Iraqi commanders being instructed to conceal nerve agents had 'given colour to the mendacious character of the regime'. However, in a comment which revealed the thin ice on which we are skating, he began with the admission that 'Powell's presentation went better than I or Powell expected'.

One issue on which we may have already fallen through the ice is on the rather laboured attempts to prove that Saddam and al-Qa'ida are in the same camp despite the mountain of evidence that they heartily loathe each other. Tony, who has made much of trying to merge Saddam and world terrorism in the public mind, half-acknowledged the poverty of evidence when he described it as 'a changing picture' with the two thrown together on the principle that 'my enemy's enemy is my friend'.

At Business Statement there was a lot of inevitable banter about Tuesday's debacle on Lords reform, but I welcomed the opportunity to get on record the reality of the arithmetic of the votes on Tuesday, in particular that almost a hundred more MPs had voted for one or other option for a largely elected House than had supported an all-appointed House.

After the Business Statement I fitted in a workout at the gym, before catching the train north to address Stephen Hesford's constituency party in the Wirral at a dinner they held in the stadium of Tranmere Rovers Football Club. It was a warm, friendly gathering. The events of the past week have increased my popularity among the party. I am that political stereotype the party loves best – an heroic failure.

Back at the Adelphi Hotel where I was put up for the night, I found myself listening on the late-night news to the latest shambles in our propaganda campaign on Iraq. Our latest 'intelligence-led' dossier on the dangers Saddam poses to the world turns out to have been largely lifted from an academic thesis a decade out of date. There is an almost entertaining, comic Inspector Clouseau quality to this bungling incompetence, but the serious consequence is to damage Tony's credibility when he asks the public to trust him that the intelligence he sees is serious.

There never was a shred of evidence found linking Saddam to al-Qa'ida, despite a desperate hunt for it by the intelligence services of three continents. In his presentation the day before to the Security Council, Colin Powell had produced satellite images of what looked like Portakabins in a remote mountain valley and claimed these were weapons laboratories of an al-Qa'ida unit operating in Iraq. Nothing more was ever heard of these claims after the valley was overrun in the early stages of the war and no laboratories or chemical agents were found. More to the point, the valley was deep in the northern territory of our Kurdish allies and well beyond any control of Baghdad. Even President Bush has been forced recently to admit that he has found no evidence to link Saddam to 9/11.

Nor is it any accident that there was no evidence of complicity between Saddam and Osama bin Laden. Foreign Office contacts with Iraqis discovered that they were indignant to be compared with al-Qa'ida whom they regarded as an enemy rather than an ally. These feelings were heartily reciprocated by al-Qa'ida. On the eve of the invasion a tape allegedly from Osama bin Laden bracketed 'the socialists in Baghdad' along with the unbelievers in America as legitimate targets of the true believers. Saddam was no fundamentalist and had an obsession with the coercive authority of the secular state that was at the other end of the ideological pole to the nihilism of al-Qa'ida. He was more Stalin than Osama bin Laden.

However, leaders in both the US and the UK did not let the facts on the ground get in the way of their allegations on the airwaves. Donald Rumsfeld asserted that he had 'bullet-proof evidence' of an al-Qa'ida link. We are still waiting on him to produce it. The speechwriters of his President were rather more circumspect. Rather than allege a link between Saddam and al-Qa'ida, they simply suggested it by repeatedly popping them into the same sentence. It was a technique adopted by Tony Blair for his address to the nation on the eve of war when he warned, 'Dictators like Saddam, terrorist groups like al-Qa'ida, threaten the very existence of such a world. That is why I have asked our troops to go into action tonight.' Tony was far too clever to allege there was any affection between Saddam and al-Qa'ida. But he deliberately crafted a suggestive phrasing which in the minds of many viewers must have created an impression, and was designed to create the impression, that British troops were going to Iraq to fight a threat from al-Qa'ida.

In a powerful speech to the Commons before it voted on war, Tony Blair majored on the risk that weapons of mass destruction in the hands of rogue states and fundamentalist terrorist organisations might come together to pose a unique threat to Western security. It was the first time I heard his speech from the back benches rather than sitting beside him, but even at that greater distance it was impossible not to be impressed by the passion with which he spoke and his evident conviction in his case. Regrettably, the logic of the speech did not measure up to its delivery. Despite many years of association with Hamas, Saddam has never shown any propensity to share a chemical or biological capacity with them. As for al-Qa'ida, he would very properly calculate that any weapons of mass destruction he supplied to them would be as likely to be used against himself as anyone else. Tony Blair's case for war rested on the assumption that at some point in the future Saddam might behave in a way totally different from the way he has behaved for the past thirty years.

What none of us knew at the time was that only a month before the Prime Minister had received an assessment that 'there was no intelligence that Iraq had provided CB materials to al-Qa'ida'. Even more startlingly, the Joint Intelligence Committee warned that 'in the event of imminent regime collapse there would be a risk of transfer of such material'. We had to wait until the report of the Intelligence and Security Committee six months later before we learnt of these warnings. Tony Blair was entirely within his rights to set aside this advice, but it is extraordinary that he should make the risk of the transfer of CB material to terrorists a centrepiece of his case for war, when he had just received an intelligence assessment that war might make such transfer more, not less, likely.

A glimpse of the dangers to the world from the post-war anarchy of Iraq is provided by the comprehensive looting of the al-Tuwaitha nuclear facility. This site was secured and subject to regular IAEA monitoring, up to the point of Iraq becoming the responsibility of the Coalition Powers, who astoundingly took no steps to protect the site. The result was that the local population helped themselves to the plant equipment and nuclear material, with dire consequences for their own health. In a purple passage to the packed Commons, Tony Blair warned of a terrorist organisation acquiring the capacity to develop a dirty bomb from radioactive material. Can we be confident that the looting of al-Tuwaitha has not conferred precisely that capacity on al-Qa'ida?

The Intelligence and Security Committee also revealed that the Joint Intelligence Committee had assessed that the al-Qa'ida threat 'would be heightened by military action against Iraq'. This assessment chimed with common sense. The occupation of Iraq both increased anti-Western sentiment in the Arab world and brought within reach a wider number of Western targets. Sadly, this JIC assessment, unlike its intelligence on weapons of mass destruction, has proved only too accurate. Suicide bombings against US and UN targets have become all too common in occupied Iraq. George Bush has even dubbed Iraq the new 'central front' in the war against terrorism, which is curious since he had previously claimed that the invasion of Iraq was a victory in the same war. We are left with the unpalatable conclusion that the occupation of Iraq has brought about a major reverse in the war on terrorism, and that international terrorists who previously were excluded from Iraq have been presented by the West with a new opportunity for their malign message and a fresh stage for their atrocities.

The publication in the summer of 2003 of the Congressional investigation into the events that preceded 9/11 has highlighted that there is one country in the Middle East with extensive links to al-Qa'ida. It is not Iraq, but Saudi Arabia. Osama bin Laden's family fortune came from Saudi Arabia. The hijackers he recruited were overwhelmingly from Saudi Arabia. His ideology of hatred and violence is derived from the Wahabi sect who have their epicentre in Saudi Arabia. Immediately after the invasion of Iraq, al-Qa'ida demonstrated its continuing ability to operate in Saudi Arabia with the bombings of foreign compounds. Very sensibly, neither the US nor the UK have proposed invading Saudi Arabia. Were they to do so they would be confronted on the other side by the latest British Aerospace warplanes, kept battle-ready by an extensive ground staff of British Aerospace personnel under the largest single arms deal in British history.

The biggest diplomatic challenge in the region is how to encourage from within the peaceful transition of Saudi government to a more inclusive, and therefore more stable basis. Any military threat from outside by the West would only strengthen the prospects of the fundamentalists coming out on top. Yet the commendable choice of the diplomatic path towards Saudi Arabia, despite the many links of that nation to al-Qa'ida, exposes the opportunism of using the threat of terrorism as justification for war against Iraq which had no such links.

Tuesday 11 February

Either Tony was deliberately taken in by Chirac last week or he wilfully failed to read the signs right. The big story of the day is that France and Germany have produced their alternative plan on Iraq based on more intensive inspections, and in the meantime have vetoed NATO strengthening Turkey's eastern border with Iraq. I am blessed if I can see in any of this the anxiety on the part of Chirac that he is becoming isolated, which Tony claimed to detect last week.

Wednesday 12 February

Jack Straw addressed a packed PLP on Iraq. Jack's presentation is workmanlike, serious and neither plays to the gallery nor seeks an ovation. Curiously, he gets most heated not about Saddam but about France and Germany, whose governments he describes as indulging in 'fantasy and denial'. From the floor, Anne Campbell made the shrewd point that she understood why we had to be bellicose to scare Saddam, but the problem was that the same rhetoric terrified her own members.

Prime Minister's Questions were also dominated by Iraq. Indeed, the focus in the House was so much on Iraq that a few colleagues who raised other matters sometimes apologised for it first. What was novel, though, was the way in which Tony has shifted the terms in which he justifies military intervention. For the first time he argued that war would be preferable to sanctions because of the suffering and malnutrition that comes in the wake of sanctions. Not surprisingly, some of the anti-war members were heckling that he had never before shown any interest in the suffering of the Iraqi people from sanctions. For years as Foreign Secretary I loyally defended sanctions on the basis that the suffering was not the result of the UN policy, but of Saddam's refusal to cooperate with us on humanitarian relief. It does rather stick in my gullet now to be asked to swallow all those words and accept the suffering from the sanctions which we ourselves imposed as the reason why we now have to bomb the same Iraqi people.

Thursday 13 February

On the way into Cabinet I find David Blunkett seething at the over-the-top reaction of the forces of law and order to the latest security alert at Heathrow. The papers are full of photographs of tanks and troops in combat fatigues mingling at Heathrow with tourists trying to get to their mid-term holidays. Helen Liddle complains that Pringle's annual fashion launch on Monday is up the spout because every single US buyer, including Bloomingdales, has cancelled their flights after seeing the tanks at Heathrow. Yet another striking example of the lack of solidarity we can expect from the ally for whom Tony Blair is putting his political future on the line.

Tony strikes a rather more conciliatory note about France and Germany than Jack had yesterday. He warns that we should not so alienate them that we cannot rebuild bridges and expresses the hope that we will still 'get everyone on the same page'. I intervene to describe the powerful anti-war sentiment I have found in Europe on each of my three recent visits, and go on to express my concern at our tumbling rating in the weekend opinion polls. I get a laugh when I add, 'I am tempted to say this is a result of justified public outrage that we screwed up the Lords reform, but I don't quite have that brass neck.' The truth is that it is Iraq, unusually for an international issue, that is hurting our public support. I offer three messages for how we should conduct ourselves if we are going to reconnect with the public:

'We could stop appearing to force the pace on the war. The public will only follow us if they believe we are reluctant about conflict and will not support us if they think we are keen on it.'

'We need to find a distinctive British tone in which we address the Iraq crisis. We should stop always appearing as the US and UK axis.'

'We should stick to the UN like glue. If tomorrow Hans Blix asks for more time for the inspectors, he must get it. If we depart from the UN process we will be committing suicide, and suicide is a sin.' At the last point Tony had the good grace to smile. He is well enough versed in Catholic doctrine to know it was a shaft aimed to strike home with him.

After I escaped from the Chamber, I set off on the journey to

Abergavenny where I addressed the annual dinner of the Monmouth CLP. Monmouth is as near to Blairland as you will find in Wales. It is a highly marginal seat that we won in 1997 and only just held on to in 2001. Yet even here I found the party in revolt over Iraq and giving its centrist Labour MP, Huw Edwards, a thunderous ovation when he announced that he will be going on Saturday's march.

Friday 14 February

The news from New York is electrifying. The latest report by Hans Blix registers a lot of progress in cooperation from Iraq, fails to identify any evidence of weapons of mass destruction and expresses confidence that with time more progress can be made. What Hans Blix was in effect confirming was that the UK strategy of applying pressure on Saddam to cooperate on disarmament, through the dual track of UN inspectors on the ground and the threat of force across his border, is working rather well. However, far from being welcome news to Tony, this will be his nightmare come true. The truth is that he does not want the UN inspections to work. He needs them in order to prove that Saddam will not cooperate and that he is therefore justified in going to war as Sancho Panza to George Bush's Don Quixote. The ghastly dilemma he now faces is that without Hans Blix denouncing Saddam there is little chance of getting a majority in the Security Council for military conflict, and therefore even less chance of getting a majority among the British public.

—⁓—

The more difficult it has proved to find actual weapons of mass destruction, the more the war party have shifted their ground to justify war not on the claim that Saddam was a threat but on the truth that he was a brutal tyrant. This was not of course the basis on which the war was sold to Parliament and public. The motion on which Parliament voted to authorise the use of troops does not even mention Saddam's abuse of his people, but remains fixated with the threat from his alleged weapons of mass destruction and long-range missiles. To discover a new humanitarian basis for war now that we find he had no weapons to disarm does not, as one commentator expressed it, merely move the goalposts, but transports the entire football field, stadium and all.

Nor had the Western powers ever worried much about Saddam's abuse of human rights before they wanted popular support for the war. During the long years in which they armed him as a bastion against Iran, they did not want to know what he was doing to the people of Iraq. Even in the last year they showed no interest in the proposals within the UN General Assembly that weapons inspectors should be accompanied back into Iraq by human rights monitors. There is a particular humbug in the indignation that has been produced over the discovery of mass graves. The majority of these appear to date from the Shia uprising after the Gulf War when Washington incited the local people to revolt and then did not lift a finger to protect them from Saddam's vengeance. Tony Blair himself never once suggested that we should displace Saddam on humanitarian grounds throughout his first five years in office. It was the advent of George Bush to the White House that prompted the discovery that changing the regime in Baghdad was an urgent necessity.

Saddam was a psychopath. The world is not short of leaders who have ordered others to carry out killings. Saddam was unusual in that he had no compunction about killing in person. The legend is that he killed his first man while he was a child and he continued to do so even when he was President, on one occasion reputedly producing a revolver in cabinet and shooting a minister who had the impudence to disagree with him. Saddam did not practise his brutality casually. What made him so chilling is that he consciously built his political strategy on the methodical and ruthless use of terror as a means of control. His sons were worse. When Saddam found that Iraq's prisons had no room left for the burgeoning number of political prisoners, Qusay solved the problem by shooting the 15,000 prisoners with the longest sentences to make space for more.

Personally I would support the UN asserting its right to mandate military intervention in the case of major and persistent violations of humanitarian law. It is a fair criticism of the UN that it is founded on the rights of states rather than the rights of people, which is understandable given its origins in the aftermath of a world war precipitated by the aggressive seizure of other states by totalitarian regimes. However, in elevating the sovereignty of the state to an absolutist principle the UN has made it more difficult to override national sovereignty when the citizens of a country need protection from their own government. As a result the UN has often felt unable to intervene in the more common form of conflict in the modern world, which now tends to be a war of oppression within states rather than a war of aggression between states. The contemporary challenge to the UN is whether it can develop the rules and procedure for intervention on humanitarian grounds and assert its right to protect peoples when their own government is unwilling or unable to discharge that basic responsibility.

A new doctrine on the basis for humanitarian intervention is emerging in response to that challenge. The report of the International Commission on Intervention and State Sovereignty (ICISS) established the broad consensus on the rules that should govern humanitarian intervention. The threshold for intervention must be a grave breach of humanitarian law such as genocide or ethnic cleansing. Military intervention should only be adopted as a last resort after all attempts to find a peaceful solution have been exhausted. Any intervention must command the support of regional opinion and must obtain multilateral authorisation. The ICISS Report concluded that the Security Council is the most appropriate body to authorise intervention, but, recognising that five separate vetoes can be a recipe for stalemate, it also recommended that the permanent members should agree to confine their veto only to cases of intervention where their own vital state interests are involved.

The requirement for regional support and international agreement should not be dismissed as some kind of legal formality. It is essential to prevent humanitarian intervention being abused as a cloak for otherwise naked aggression. After all, at the outset of the last world war Hitler annexed Czechoslovakia to 'protect' the citizens of the Sudetenland. By all means let us accept the principle that grave breaches of humanitarian law justify military intervention, but let us also recognise that the decision to authorise such use of force cannot be left to individual nations.

The other reason why a decision on humanitarian intervention must be collective is to avoid the use of force becoming arbitrary. If we attempt to displace every regime that offends the Universal Declaration of Human Rights, we shall be in a state of permanent conflict that will exhaust the resources of even the US military. But identifying the worst offenders as the candidates for intervention cannot be left to a unilateral decision by countries whose choice may reflect their own national agenda rather than humanitarian criteria. Why is Saddam such an offence to humanitarian values that he must be overthrown by force, but the ageing military regime can be left in place in Burma to continue its career of internal repression and displacement of the ethnic communities and mountain tribes? Why is it intolerable for Saddam to be left in charge of Iraq but acceptable for Robert Mugabe to remain in control of Zimbabwe? Could the number of lives saved provide an objective test of the priority for humanitarian intervention? If so, top of everyone's list for military action should be the Congo, where three million people have been brutally killed in a decade and unknown thousands raped. Yet the West can mobilise a quarter of a million of its best fighting troops to take over Iraq, but can only muster a few thousand for a limited province of the Congo. Unless humanitarian intervention is the result of a collective process based on objective criteria, there will always be the suspicion that Washington picked on Iraq, not because it was the strongest case for humanitarian intervention but because it provided the best opportunity to reorder the politics of the region and to safeguard the energy supplies of the US.

A world governed by rules rather than by force requires an agreed forum to regulate the use of force. That forum can only be the UN. Tony Blair came to the same conclusion in his Chicago speech, which was his contribution to the debate on humanitarian intervention: 'If we want a world ruled by law and by international cooperation then we have to support the UN as its central pillar.' But when it came to Iraq Tony Blair backed a war launched by a unilateral US decision rather than international agreement, and in doing so took us further away from a world ruled by law. Nobody in their right mind would dispute that Iraq is a better place without Saddam. But the world is most certainly not a safer place now that we have reasserted the unilateral right of one state to invade another. As Kofi Annan observed to the autumn's UN General Assembly, such a right 'represents a fundamental challenge to the principles on which, however imperfectly, world peace and stability have rested for the last fifty-eight years' and 'could set precedents that resulted in a proliferation of the unilateral and lawless use of force'.

—— m ——

Saturday 15 February

John Nash designed our residence at Carlton Gardens with a big, sweeping, bold frontage and from its projecting windows we have a commanding view of The Mall. All afternoon I watched thousands walk back and forth to the demonstration in Hyde Park against the war. As I looked out from my window that February afternoon, I was catching a glimpse of the largest demonstration in British history. Greater than the Chartist marches to demand a reformed Parliament. Greater than the Suffragette demonstrations for votes for women. I recognised many of them as the kind of people who would have marched with me against cruise missiles twenty years ago – young people with bright woollen scarves and clumsy mittens to keep out the biting cold. But most of them were different. They were ordinary people in their everyday clothes, from every walk of life and every age group in Britain. Large numbers of them, I suspect, had not voted Labour until Tony Blair became leader and may not now vote Labour again as long as he remains leader. The great irony of his current position is that he is destroying the new base that he almost single-handedly built for Labour among the new middle classes.

Sunday 16–Wednesday 19 February

On Sunday I made a flying visit to Edinburgh to see my mother, and got back in time to pick up Gaynor and drive up to the hotel in north Norfolk where we had booked ourselves in for a short break during the parliamentary recess. It was an atmospheric Victorian shooting lodge in which it is claimed Lillie Langtry was always accommodated while Edward VII was up at the big house beyond the deer park. I suspect that if Lillie Langtry were to have eaten and slept in all the commercial establishments which now claim a connection with her, she would have had little time left to do any acting.

We went for long tramps on three successive days and pottered in and out of the parish churches that provide witness to the medieval wealth of Norfolk's wool industry. As it was February we seemed to have the place largely to ourselves, which were probably the best circumstances in which to appreciate its tranquillity. We walked for most of a day on a path that traversed the reed beds of the Broads and met only one other couple, but had the constant company of waterfowl, wild geese and hovering hawks. The sea of reeds bending in the wind at human height was just right to give a serene sense of enclosure without claustrophobia.

The hours together on our country walks gave me time to talk through my dilemma with Gaynor. That afternoon walking through reed beds I came to the clear conclusion that I could not stay if Tony embarks on a military conflict without a fresh UN resolution. If the inspectors report that they cannot do their job, and if the Security Council then passes a resolution accepting that Saddam is in material breach, then and only then would I be prepared to justify military action. Indeed, in those circumstances I would accept that it is important that the authority of the United Nations is upheld. But if we embark on military action without that multilateral agreement, then it is not Saddam but we who will be undermining the authority of the UN.

Thursday 20 February

We drove back from Norfolk in time for me to spend the afternoon in private meetings at our flat. An old friend from the Foreign Office called first. He observes that, since the Blix report, Jack has been talking even faster than usual, which is always a sign with him that he knows he is under pressure. I find him much more resigned to the inevitability of war than when we last met before Christmas. Indeed, thinking appears now to have moved on to focus on the aftermath of war, about which there is real anxiety in the Foreign Office that the stark simplicity of the US plans for a protectorate will collide with the ancient complexities of the region.

I shepherded my friend down the lift, while I myself used the stairs in order that John Scarlett, who had come to brief me, would not see my visitor. The presentation was impressive in its integrity and shorn of the political slant with which Number 10 encumbers any intelligence assessment. My conclusion at the end of an hour is that Saddam probably does not have weapons of mass destruction in the sense of weapons that could be used against large-scale civilian targets.

I rounded off my meetings with a couple of beers with David Clark who used to work for me as a special adviser at the Foreign Office. As a committed European, David is much more exercised at Tony's continued prevarication over the euro: 'We are always asking the wrong question. What is the cost of joining? Nobody asks the equally important question – what is the cost of not joining?' He reacts with dismay when I tell him that Tony has said in terms to me that there will be no referendum this year. For myself, I just do not see how we can ask the British public with a straight face to vote to join France and Germany in the euro after we ourselves have made Iraq the biggest issue in our foreign policy, at the expense of our relations with France and Germany.

Friday 21 February

I went across to Brussels to chair a special meeting of the PES Praesidium on Iraq. I opened the meeting by saying that I had never known a world situation which was so tense or had so much capacity to go wrong: 'For the past six years since the Amsterdam Summit we have talked about developing a Common Foreign Security Policy. Today, far from having achieved a common position, we have a deep division within Europe on how we should respond to the gravest international crisis so far this century.'

The discussion that followed was serious, thoughtful and free of gesture politics. Martin Schulz, the leader of the SPD group in the European Parliament, acutely brought out the dilemma that ran through much of the discussion, namely that we must avoid the UN becoming the most strategic casualty of the crisis: 'We cannot play the US card of saying that we would only agree with the UN if the UN agrees with us.' Everything went swimmingly until I produced the two-page statement which I had painstakingly drafted on the train on the way over. At this point the meeting fractured into two equal groups of those who could not accept any language about supporting the UN if it authorised force as a last resort, and those who could not agree to a text which did not recognise that force must be available as a last resort. At the end I was forced to wind up the meeting with the conclusion that there were just too many different national perspectives for us to agree on a common European position.

Saturday 22 February

It was a wondrous, happy day out at Kempton. Chris and I regularly used to attend the Racing Post Chase meeting as a way to celebrate my birthday. Indeed, this had become so much a matter of habit that one of the waitresses today actually stopped me to wish me a happy birthday.

My hosts asked me to come down to the paddock for the first race, which was among the ones they were sponsoring, and I found myself drafted in to advise the woman whom they had asked to judge the best-turned-out horse, and who, it transpired, knew little about racing. When she asked me what she should be looking for, I gave the familiar response that 'the perfect racehorse has a head like a lady's maid and an arse like a cook's', at which she exploded in laughter, somewhat to the surprise of the horses parading around us.

Monday 24 February

In the afternoon I went into the Chamber to make a short Business Statement, announcing that we will debate Iraq on Wednesday. The media have already built this up as some kind of high noon which will be the last chance to vote on military action and it was clear to me that the priority was to reduce the potential for rebellion by reducing the dramatic sense that this was a last chance for a vote before conflict. Before I went into the Chamber I carefully prepared a few phrases and early in the exchanges recorded: 'The motion will not be a trap. No MP need fear that support for it will be interpreted as support for any specific military action. The House will have other opportunities in the future to debate Iraq and if necessary to vote on military action.' This all went down well; however, Tam Dalyell mischievously got up to observe that I had referred to a trap – 'What trap exactly did you have in mind?' A question which I thought it wise not to attempt.

When I got back to Room 4, I found Des waiting with a report from the Press Gallery where he had been observing the action. He tells me that there was no problem in the Press Gallery for myself, but the story that the gallery were going away with was that I had not given any guarantee that there would be a further vote before military action. I demurred that I had been pretty blunt that we wanted and intended to have such a vote before military action. 'Yes, but I think there's somebody stirring the story in the press that after Wednesday we will have the authority to proceed to conflict.' I suspect the MoD are again being at best disingenuous to the press. As I said to Des, I cannot be confident that other elements in the government are being entirely frank with *me*, never mind the Press Gallery.

Joyce Quinn and Chris Bryant called to talk about tomorrow's meeting of the Joint Committee on Lords Reform. We came up with the most positive strategy we could devise, which was that the committee should simultaneously explore the option of a largely elected House, which is favoured by the Commons, and an all-appointed House, which is favoured by the Lords – which at least keeps democratic reform on the agenda. Chris had a very interesting piece of gossip from his conversations with Number 10, and had been told that Tony had 'not been well advised' over the debate on the options for reform. Apparently the whips had promised Tony that if he came out in favour of an all-appointed Chamber, two-thirds of the PLP would vote for it. In the event, of course, most of the Labour MPs who voted had voted against it. It was gratifying to know that Number 10 as well as myself had felt raw and bruised by the events of that night.

Tuesday 25 February

Today Tony made his statement on Iraq to the House. He was at his most effective. He was convincing and passionate about his own belief in the correctness of his course of action. He was understanding and conversational in responding to the beliefs of others who disagreed with him. It is an unusual combination which goes a long way to explain his unique effectiveness as a political communicator. Other politicians when they are sincere about their views tend to be equally passionate in duffing up the critics of those views.

However, no amount of skilled presentation could conceal the immense confusion that we are in over the role of the UN. Tony knows that he desperately needs the blessing of the UN if he is to have any chance of carrying domestic opinion with him, but since he knows that Bush will go to war whatever the UN says, Tony's attempt to wrap himself in the UN flag is fatally hobbled by his inability to say that the UN will have the last word.

In exchanges with the backbenchers, Tony at one point clearly laid out the nexus of issues which have brought him to his present conviction. The argument runs that proliferation, plus unstable states, plus terrorism adds up to a new and serious threat. This is a way of linking action against Saddam to the response to 9/11, and avoids the irritating evidence that Saddam had no link whatsoever to 9/11 and has no link with al-Qa'ida. But it does still leave unanswered why Iraq is the focus of so much effort. Whatever else we might say about the Iraqi regime, it is not unstable. Indeed, the problem with Saddam is that the regime is proving only too damn stable.

In the evening I dropped by on the tenth anniversary party of *Renewal*, a thoughtful leftist magazine, which was born out of the Labour Coordinating Committee who had been an important part of the coalition in taking on the Trotskyists and exposing their intellectual bankruptcy. It was a nostalgic occasion full of many old friends whom I had not seen for most of the intervening decade. They were the people who had paved the way for Tony to secure the leadership in 1994, but tonight the only topics they wanted to talk about was why Tony was so keen on Bush's war against Iraq and why Tony had torpedoed my plans to democratise the House of Lords. Gordon Brown made a solid speech in which he set out a coherent, thoughtful case for Labour's values of social justice and received a warm ovation. Pretty nearly everyone in the room was among those who had scuppered his own ambitions for the leadership in 1994 by throwing their support behind Tony. But if you had taken a vote between them tonight, Gordon would have won by acclamation.

It would be a mistake, frequently committed by the media, to exaggerate the disaffection with Tony in the party. The wider membership are appreciative of his electoral success. No previous leader has secured in successive elections a majority capable of sustaining a Labour government for two full Parliaments and none has survived in office for such a long consecutive period. These are no mean achievements given the demoralisation of the left after three crushing defeats by Thatcher and a fourth, unexpected, defeat by Major.

However, it was strikingly evident at that evening's reception that the members disappointed with what Tony has delivered in office are the very people who would still describe themselves as the real modernisers within the party. When he ran for leader, Tony Blair had sparked their enthusiasm because he had the courage to take on the powerful vested interests within the party machine and to spell out the radical changes they must accept to make Labour relevant to modern society. They are now mystified how that iconoclastic courage has been replaced in office with a caution about offending the Establishment and a hesitance about challenging the political values inherited from the Conservative era.

Their discontent has become acute since the last election because of the timidity and ideological vacuity of the second term. We have been busy in office. No one is more aware than myself that we have rammed through Parliament a record volume of legislation establishing new highs in the number of pages added to the statute book in a single session. But, equally, I know from frequent attempts to do so how baffling it is to capture this cornucopia of legislation in a coherent political vision.

Although a staunch advocate of the principle 'underpromise and overperform', in the case of his second term Tony Blair himself oversold its promised radicalism. Repeatedly he assured the party and the public that in a second term Labour would be more bold. In this he was consciously summoning up the experience of the Thatcher era. It was Margaret Thatcher's second term in office that defined her distinctive place in history. All the major characteristics of Thatcherism reached their high-water mark in her second Parliament – privatisation of all state utilities, victory over organised labour symbolised by her defeat of the miners, and the sustained promotion of individualism rather than social cohesion. Even her eventual nemesis, the poll tax, was invented in her second Parliament. Whether you supported or loathed the results, it was impossible not to admire the energy of her second term, nor to fail to see its powerful ideological clarity. No one who lived through the Thatcher years was in any doubt at the time that they were witnessing radical surgery on British society.

Simply to state the achievements of Thatcher's second term raises a series of question marks over Tony Blair's second term. Where has there been the innovation that can compare in its boldness with those of Thatcher? Which part of the Establishment has felt the least bit challenged by the last couple of years in the way that they were consistently discomfited by change under Thatcher? And where is there a connecting doctrine that we can describe as Blairism which can remotely match Thatcherism in coherence and vision? There have been genuine historic achievements of the Blair governments, but all of them were introduced in his first term. The dour, uninspiring slogan of his second election, 'The Work Goes On', aptly foreshadowed the determined air of consolidation rather than advance which has been the hallmark of the Blair second Parliament. In historic terms New Labour appears to have shot straight from the Thatcher first term to the John Major years of technocratic managerialism and missed out on the intervening high tide of political innovation.

There have been two seismic landslips in electoral support in the past half century. The first propelled Margaret Thatcher into power with successive record majorities in Parliament. In a decade in office she smashed every political consensus and single-mindedly wrenched to the right the parameters of political debate. It was the Thatcher era that finally demolished the post-war settlement within which previous governments had operated with varying degrees of enthusiasm. It was accurately dubbed by Stuart Hall 'the great moving right show'.

The second seismic electoral movement returned New Labour with majorities that exceeded even Thatcher's. But unlike Margaret Thatcher, New Labour has chosen to operate within the conventional orthodoxy they inherited rather than challenging it. Margaret Thatcher transformed the political culture of Britain by identifying the centres of strength of the left and then ruthlessly planning a strategy to marginalise and destroy them. New Labour has approached the Establishment power centres of the right by incorporating them or by appeasing them, rarely by confronting them. Tony Blair has halted and reversed the electoral advance of the right, but he has failed to displace their ideological hegemony by building a new centre-left consensus around social cohesion.

—⁓—

Wednesday 26 February

I rang Göran Persson, the Swedish Prime Minister, and Paavo Lipponen, the Finnish Prime Minister, to sound them out about the pressure for a meeting of the PES leaders. I found them both distinctly lukewarm which, frankly, was a relief to me as I can see no good coming out of a meeting which some parties want more to advertise their disagreement with Tony Blair than to seek a common position.

On the way into the House I met Jack Straw coming up the back stairs which we all use when our ministerial cars drop us off. 'I have told Tony that I will have to be much more blunt in my speech that there will be another vote and that MPs don't need to take today as their last chance.' And indeed he was. He was commendably robust in saying that it was as much in the government's interest as the interest of the House that any future vote on military action should be before the start of hostilities. Thereafter he made a well-argued speech, carefully crafted to provide maximum appeal to our backbenchers, with much detail on Saddam's brutal rule. Like virtually everyone in the Foreign Office building, I suspect Jack would much rather be looking for a diplomatic than a military outcome.

It was a good debate. One of the best speeches was from Ken Clarke, who expressed all the rational doubts that we ought to be hearing from the Conservative front bench if it was really attempting to fulfil its role as an Opposition in voicing the division in the country. He expressed the unspoken thought at the back of most of our minds when he said that he could not rid himself of the suspicion that the timetable was driven by military rather than by diplomatic deadlines.

I missed the announcement in the Chamber of the vote on the motion, by a classic case of bathos. I was in my room discussing with Alun Michael how we could find a positive way to handle the Ragwort Bill being introduced as a Private Members' Bill. I was taken aback when the result flashed on the monitor screen and showed that 199 members had voted against the government, the majority of whom must have been Labour. In my thirty years in the House I have never known such a large government rebellion.

Thursday 27 February

The morning papers are full of comment on last night's rebellion, which by common consent was the biggest government rebellion since Gladstone introduced his Home Rule Bill. Every newspaper has an editorial reflecting on what this means, most of them agreeing that it has shown that Parliament has come to life again. I can't help feeling some sense of satisfaction at the acres of editorials and commentary, as none of them would have been possible if we had not modernised the hours and brought forward the vote to seven o'clock. In the old days when the rebellion would have been consigned to 10 p.m., it would have been too late for the next day's papers and too old for the day after. In that sense the reforms have certainly helped to put Parliament higher up the media agenda, although I do not anticipate that this is an argument which would endear itself to Number 10 at the moment.

After Cabinet I had a conversation with Sally Morgan about the draft which I prepared for Tony on our options on how to take forward Lords reform. The crux of it was my conclusions from the stalemate on votes in the Commons that an all-appointed second chamber would not get through the Commons even with his support, but that a largely or wholly elected Chamber would not get through the Commons against his opposition. In short, I made plain that the key to progress was that he needed to shift his position. Sally was commendably candid that Tony was not up for shifting his position and was not looking for an ambitious plan for Lords reform. She pressed on me again the option of a short, simple bill that abolished the remaining hereditaries and put the appointments committee on a statutory footing. I wearily and patiently explained to her yet again that this would be resisted in the Commons, and the Lords, as doing no more than creating an all-appointed House by the back door, and, far from being simple, would be a nightmare during its passage through Parliament.

Business Statement was notable for the repeated attempts by the Tories to get me to admit who had ministerial responsibility for the crushingly embarrassing government dossier that turned out to be a plagiarised academic thesis of a decade ago. The short answer to this, of course, is the Prime Minister, but because this is also such a crushingly embarrassing answer, I am under strict instructions to avoid saying so. Therefore there follows a protracted period in which the Opposition pack snap at my heels while I show Olympian disdain and lecture to them about not playing party political games at a time when we should all be rising to the dignity and gravity of a serious international occasion.

In itself it is nothing but the kind of mildly amusing sideshow which the Commons stages for its own entertainment. However, the fundamental truth which it revealed is that the Conservatives are desperate to find ways to distance themselves from us on our position on Iraq, which is the government policy currently the most unpopular. Last night's rebellion must have brought home to them that if they could only find a way of wriggling off the hook of support for our position, they could just grasp the almost unimaginable prize of defeating Blair in the Commons.

Friday 28 February–Monday 3 March

The weekend was absorbed in moving my mother into a nursing home.

The logistical arrangements were frequently interrupted by calls on my mobile from Gordon and Hilary about the date on which we would hold the Budget. In the end I finalised the date of the British Budget from the car park of a nursing home. It is to be 9 April. Gordon has helpfully dug up figures to prove that there have been more than twenty April Budgets in the last fifty years. This is fine until you scratch the statistical series and discover that this will be only the second one in the last twenty years. The truth is that Gordon does not want to compete for publicity for his Budget with a shooting war in Iraq. I don't blame him at all for what is an entirely rational decision. The only problem, of course, is that we can't offer that explanation, which would only confirm that the Chancellor now believes that war is inevitable.

Wednesday 5 March

Prime Minister's Questions was notable for the confidence Tony expressed about getting a second resolution. I don't know whether this is calculated bravado to keep Saddam wary, or whether he is in a state of denial about the mounting evidence that they can't get a second resolution on the present terms.

I saw Tony privately shortly after we left the Chamber. He remains in surprisingly good humour despite the disaster that is staring him in the face. He even began with a joke: 'They gave me a whole briefing on what to say if asked about the extermination of the ruddy duck. I said, what I'm worried about is the ruddy French.'

I started first by observing that he'd gone out on a limb and the first piece of advice that I would offer is that he had to stop climbing further out on it, especially on Friday when Hans Blix presents his next report: 'Britain has got to be seen on side with Blix. You will never carry British opinion with you if it is we who are seen to be sidelining the work of the inspectors.' He responded by predicting that Blix will say that Saddam has done some work on disarmament but is not cooperating enough, and that Britain will then say that is why Saddam is in breach of the UN resolutions and why we must now take action. He suggested that on Friday Britain may propose a new deadline for Saddam and I responded that I was not against setting a deadline, but it must be seen logically to arise from what Blix said. If he needed months, we should be prepared to give him until the autumn. Tony was quite frank in that he could not deliver that: 'I don't know if I could do that. Left to himself, Bush would have gone to war in January. No, not January, but back in September.'

I expressed my concern about the hard-line right-wingers around Bush and warned him that many of them would regard it as a bonus in the present crisis if we were driven from office and replaced in Britain by a Conservative government. He laughed and said, 'Regime change is for Baghdad. It is not for here.'

The most revealing exchange came when we talked about Saddam's arsenal. I told him, 'It's clear from the private briefing that I have had that Saddam has no weapons of mass destruction in a sense of weapons that could strike at strategic cities. But he probably does have several thousand battlefield chemical munitions. Do you never worry that he might use them against British troops?' 'Yes, but all the effort he has had to put into concealment makes it difficult for him to assemble them quickly for use.' There is logic to that response, but it is a logic that does not make a case for war but for a process of containment that prevents him from holding weapons in usable mode.

When I left Tony I went back to my office to brief Greg and Meg, who were keen to know that I had not resigned from the government since they last saw me. As a result I was late in getting into the Parliamentary Committee. I understand that the first question was where we were on Lords reform. Tony and all eyes automatically turned to my seat, which was empty, at which everybody laughed and Tony said, 'Obviously Robin and I need to talk about this.' We were, of course, meant to talk about it at our meeting that afternoon, but we had used it to talk only about Iraq.

—ɯ—

This was an honest exchange between two colleagues who were both open about the gulf widening between them. Others have complained that Tony was not level with them, but during the build-up to war in my experience he was always candid about his intention to be with Bush when the war began. The candour of the conversation, though, did not make me any more comfortable with what I was hearing. There were two distinct elements to this exchange that sent me away deeply troubled.

The first was that the timetable to war was plainly not driven by the progress of the UN weapons inspections. Tony made no attempt to pretend that what Hans Blix might report would make any difference to the countdown to invasion. Only two weeks earlier Tony had said in his speech to the Glasgow Conference, 'I continue to want to solve the issue of Iraq and weapons of mass destruction through the UN.' Today he was telling me that the solution was not going to be disarmament through the UN, but regime change through war.

In the event Hans Blix submitted a report that Friday which was among the most positive that the Security Council had ever received from its weapons inspectors. On cooperation he reported that, 'One can hardly avoid the impression that there has been an acceleration of initiatives from the Iraqi side.' On disarmament he reported the destruction of more than thirty missiles: 'We are not watching the breaking of toothpicks. Lethal weapons are being destroyed.' And on the amount of further time he needed to resolve 'the key remaining disarmament tasks', he estimated that he needed only months. Had he been given those extra months we would have learnt by now that Saddam had no actual weapons of mass destruction, and we would have discovered it without a war and without the British, American and Iraqi casualties of the invasion and then the occupation.

Tony is entitled to full credit for persuading President Bush to delay the attack long enough for the UN inspectors to go in. But since both Tony Blair and George Bush were determined that the confrontation should end in invasion it is a puzzle what point they saw in resuming inspections. I suspect Tony promised Bush that the inspectors would come up with the evidence that Saddam was a threat and thereby strengthen the case for war. If Tony himself believed half the allegations he included in the September Dossier, he must have expected the inspectors to find some of the chemical weapons he claimed were ready to be fired in forty-five minutes, or at least one of the chemical weapons plants he claimed had been rebuilt. He sounded completely confident when he said in January that it was only a matter of time before the inspectors found something.

By the end of February that confidence had gone. The success of the inspectors in securing cooperation and in dismembering missiles had been greeted in Washington not with satisfaction but consternation. There was no prospect of obtaining agreement in Washington to a further delay in the attack because of the growing danger that with more time the inspectors may be able to prove that Saddam was no threat and that there was no case for war. Hans Blix himself shrewdly sensed what Washington wanted from him: 'They would say I was too compliant with the Iraqis when in reality they meant I was not compliant enough with what the US wanted.'

The second troubling element to our conversation was that Tony did not try to argue me out of the view I expressed that Saddam did not have real weapons of mass destruction that were designed for strategic use against city populations and capable of being delivered with reliability over long distances. I had now expressed that view to both the Chairman of the JIC and to the Prime Minister and both had assented in it.

At the time I did believe it likely that Saddam had retained a quantity of chemical munitions for tactical use on the battlefield. These did not pose 'a real and present danger to Britain' as they were not designed for use against city populations and by definition could only threaten British personnel if we were to deploy them on the battlefield within range of Iraqi artillery. I had now twice been told that even these chemical shells had been put beyond operational use in response to the pressure from intrusive inspections. I have no reason to doubt that Tony Blair believed in September that Saddam really had weapons of mass destruction ready for firing within forty-five minutes. What was clear from this conversation was that he did not believe it himself in March.

This in turn begs another chain of questions. If Number 10 accepted that Saddam had no real weapons of mass destruction which he could credibly deliver against city targets, and if they themselves believed he could not reassemble his chemical weapons in a credible timescale for use on the battlefield, just how much of a threat did they really think Saddam represented? I have long been puzzled that the contentious claims in the September Dossier were quietly dropped by ministers as war drew nearer. In the debate on 18 March, no minister claimed that Saddam had weapons of mass destruction ready to be fired in forty-five minutes, or that he had rebuilt chemical weapons plants, or that he had sought uranium from Niger. Yet in that debate the government had its back to the wall and outside the Chamber the whips were deploying every technique of persuasion available in their armoury. Why then did ministers not repeat inside the Chamber their strongest lines on the threat from Saddam unless they themselves had come to recognise they were disputed?

They had been given plenty of cause to come to doubt their own claims. The scepticism about the September Dossier which has surfaced from within the UK intelligence community is a pale reflection of the raging controversy in the US. There the case against Iraq had been subcontracted to the Office of Special Plans which had been set up by Donald Rumsfeld to find the right kind of intelligence. The official agencies who had been marginalised by this development struck back. The Defense Intelligence Agency reported that there was 'no reliable information' that Iraq possessed or was producing chemical weapons. CIA veterans subsequently protested to the President at what they described as 'a policy and intelligence fiasco of monumental proportions'. At the State Department Greg Thielmann, who had monitored Iraq's WMD programme for the Bureau of Intelligence and Research, resigned in disagreement with the official line in the same month that the British government presented its dossier.

Colin Powell invested four whole days before his presentation to the Security Council in March grilling the CIA on the reliability of the intelligence he was going to deploy. By the end of it he had decided not to use the claim about the Niger connection on uranium and he made no mention of weapons of mass destruction ready for firing in forty-five minutes. Given the intimate relationship between State Department and Foreign Office it is implausible that his cautious scepticism did not become known in London.

Then there were the investigations carried out on the ground by the inspectors. Very properly, both the US and UK governments passed the weapons inspectors our intelligence leads on where to look for evidence of weapons of mass destruction. It led to not a single discovery. Hans Blix was scathing about the useless character of the intelligence fed to him: 'I thought, "My God, if this is the best intelligence they had and we find nothing, what about the rest?"' There are only two possible explanations. For reasons that appear incomprehensible we chose not to give the UN weapons inspectors our best intelligence. Or that we did, in which case we already knew before the war that our best intelligence was badly wrong.

The public controversy over the September Dossier has focused on whether Number 10 really believed in its claims at the time of its publication, and whether all of its claims were sourced in reliable intelligence. There is, though, another and even more disturbing question. Did Number 10 still believe in its own claims six months later and how many of those claims had been undermined by subsequent intelligence and analysis? This in turn leads to the gravest of political questions. The rules of the Commons explicitly require ministers to correct the record as soon as they are aware that they may have misled Parliament. If the government did come to know that the State Department did not trust the claims in the September Dossier and that some of even their own top experts did not believe them, should they not have told Parliament before asking the Commons to vote for war on a false prospectus?

—m—

Thursday 6 March

Jack Straw was absent from Cabinet as he is already pre-positioned in New York to lobby the Security Council. In his absence Tony gave an account of the latest negotiations. He was surprisingly upbeat about the prospects of getting the six swing votes on the Security Council behind our latest wheeze of producing a new deadline within which Saddam must comply. He even expressed a hope that Russia might abstain and France might not veto. This was not just surprising but manifestly unrealistic. One of the dimensions of the present crisis that worries me most is that Tony believes so much in his case that he has difficulty recognising that others do not agree with him.

Afterwards I found my day surprisingly light of diary engagements. This is partly because the current preoccupation with Iraq has slowed down any other initiatives within the government machine. Even if it all ends peacefully we will have already paid a high penalty in lost progress on other political fronts.

Friday 7 March

I spent the day at the office where I watched Hans Blix on television give his latest, and possibly last, report on the progress of inspections. It was a carefully balanced, painfully honest report. But that, of course, is not what the US and UK need. Number 10 desperately wanted Blix to lay into Saddam and to report no progress, in order that they could mobilise the Security Council for war.

I caught the train north to Wolverhampton to address the local party of Ken Purchase. Nothing New Labour about Wolverhampton Labour Party. While the more middle-class sections of the party may have a three-course dinner as the big social event, in Wolverhampton they relax with a karaoke machine and a very good curry. Most of the questions were about Iraq and every single one of them was hostile to military action. My answers were well received, but not as well as Ken's spot on the karaoke machine. I had not previously suspected Ken of being really quite a fine jazz singer.

Saturday 8–Sunday 9 March

Saturday was a rare treat. Gaynor drove up and joined me for Cruft's in the Birmingham NEC. So many dogs to see and so little time! We enjoyed it but on the whole felt that we were glad we had decided not to take up showing with Tammy and Tasker. Every Scottie we saw was beautifully groomed and immaculately styled, but some of them in their cages were looking listless and bored. Our two rascals may look the doggy equivalents of Just William, but we would rather have them scruffy and happy than pretty and bored.

I was invited to award the trophy for the Best Terrier, and although that went to a Kerry Blue, the top Scottish terrier at least came in fourth, which pleased us. When we got home there was a lot of suspicious sniffing around us by our two, and big accusing eyes turned on us to make us feel guilty at fooling around with other dogs.

Monday 10 March

A dramatic day. Indeed, the Labour Party cannot survive too many dramatic days like this one.

I woke up expecting to find Andy Reed's resignation the top story, but found that he had been obliterated by Clare Short announcing that she *will* resign if there is no second resolution. For good measure, she also describes Tony Blair as 'reckless', and repeats it five times. Meg, who heard the original interview, tells me that Clare sounded under great strain throughout it and was obviously in real anguish about the position in which she and the party both found themselves. As a result Meg was very sympathetic towards what Clare had done. I suspect that there may be a difference in gender perception. I fear male colleagues may be less generous. It is a sign of Tony's weak political position not that Clare said these things last night, but that this morning he has not dared remove her from the government. When Hilary came in I could not resist teasing her by asking if Tony was going to dismiss Clare, and got a brisk response: 'No, he's far too busy today.' She then added, with a hint of a smile, 'Reshuffles take so much time.'

There was only one real issue for discussion at Business Managers.

When do we have the debate on Iraq? Hilary readily agreed that we
needed to have a debate as soon as any second resolution was agreed
in the Security Council. She was less ready to agree that we needed
a debate with equal expedition if a second resolution is rejected, but
could not seriously argue against the logic of that position. There
was a suggestion that we could announce next week's business
without a debate on Iraq, but that I could subsequently change the
business if necessary. I was brisk with that idea: 'I will be killed on
Thursday morning if I go in there without announcing a debate on
Iraq.' In the end we agreed that we should have a debate on Iraq next
week.

The House of Commons was in a febrile, almost histrionic, state as
a result of the great events of the day. In the division lobby the talk was
that Tony had been slow-handclapped by a TV studio audience of
women. Labour MPs spoke about little else than the mystifying crisis
into which we had got ourselves so soon after a landslide victory.
Much of it was necessarily gloomy, but there were brighter flashes in
the dark. I took Gaynor and Peter to dinner in Portcullis House and
found Martin Salter, Peter Bradley and Alan Whitehead at the
neighbouring table. Martin leaned across to tell us that the whips had
been asking tonight if Labour MPs would be for France or against
France. To demonstrate where their prejudices lay on the war, they had
set up a game of *boules* in the Portcullis corridors and had been talking
loudly to each other in French.

Tuesday 11 March

The morning press are not kind to Clare, but there is no escaping the
fact that she has shaken some trees and left Tony's perch looking
distinctly vulnerable.

Sod's law, but today happens to be my monthly time for oral
questions. I welcomed the chance firmly to say on the record again that
the reality is that it is 'inconceivable' that the government could go to
war without the support of Parliament and putting it on record that 'I
attach the highest importance to the right of the Commons to vote
before there is any conflict.' Sadly, we finished just before Andrew
Mackinlay's question suggesting that Lords ministers should come to

the Commons to answer questions. In my brief it tells me that the last time any member of the Lords appeared in the Commons chamber was 1604 when two Lords who were parties to a private bill attended and 'were sat on stools with their heads covered'. A treatment which most of the house would find an attractive basis under which to invite Derry to answer questions.

Afterwards I talked to Jonathan Powell and asked him to press on Tony my own view that if he gets no second resolution he can have no military action. I told him that it is one of my duties as Leader of the House to warn him that if he comes to the House with no UN resolution he may well be defeated if he persists in going to war: 'He will be dependent on Tory votes for rescuing him from a Labour rebellion. Given the choice between voting for consistency and integrity or for Blair's head on a pole, many Tories may vote for the latter option.'

The desperation of our position becomes public thanks to the bottomless capacity of Donald Rumsfeld to put his foot in it. This afternoon he startled a press conference by sharing with them the possibility that Britain may not be able to take part in military action from the start because of the difficulty in handling its Parliament. I can't help feeling gratified that Parliament has come centre stage in this world crisis after years in which the commentators were inclined to write it off as irrelevant.

Jack Straw, when I speak to him about possible dates for a debate on Iraq, sounds genuinely worried. I suspect that half of the Foreign Office is on valium as they stare into the precipice into which the crisis is bulldozing every international partnership except the transatlantic one. Jack is a shrewd politician and is keen to know my reading of the balance of votes in the House. I tell him that the latest estimate is that 160 Labour MPs would rebel if there was no second resolution. His response is instant and crisp: 'We cannot get ourselves into the position of depending on Tory votes.' I ask him if Tony understands that he cannot go for military action without a second resolution, and get a surprising response: 'Tony is just focused on getting a second resolution. He is not thinking about what we do if it fails.'

I go along to the Speaker's residence, conscious as I take the lift up to the flat that this may be my last visit as Leader of the House. I am frank with Michael about my troubled state of mind. He is very sympathetic and wants me to know that he would be sorry to lose my support if I were to go. Unusually, we shake hands, then I go down in the lift with the sense that I am already on my rounds of my leave-taking.

Wednesday 12 March

At short notice it was decided to put up Jack Straw at the PLP. Famously, the pager is the favoured means of communication of New Labour and a message was instructed: 'The Foreign Secretary at PLP at 10 a.m.' Unfortunately this was transmitted as 'Phone Secretary at PLP at 10 a.m.' and Alan Howarth, the Secretary of the PLP, arrived harassed from answering a phone that had been jumping off the receiver for the past hour. Before Jack could speak, Diana Organ, who won Forest of Dean in 1997, got up to attack those who were trying to turn concern over the war into a challenge to Tony Blair's leadership. When she denounced a call for a special conference to vote on the leadership as 'outrageous', she was greeted with spontaneous and rumbustious applause.

On my way down the back corridor from Room 4 to the Chamber, I bumped into David Curry, one of the most rational of the Tory MPs and therefore, of course, consigned to their back benches. In reference to Clare Short's outburst he said wryly, 'I bet you lot are glad you don't have William Hague at the Despatch Box against you today.' It was a fair comment. Hague would have eviscerated us with merciless wit over Clare's remarks, and was always a serious threat because he was capable of finding an original line which we were not expecting. IDS as usual floundered around with neither wit nor originality, and was easy for Tony to brush aside.

Madeleine Albright rang up from Washington wanting to know how I was getting on. Like all of us she is worried about the alarming extent to which the Atlantic is widening, and has persuaded the Aspen Institute to fund a gathering of former Foreign Ministers from both sides to explore how we get our continents back in touch. She spent her first decade as a child in Europe and is totally impatient with the crass anti-Europeanism in some Republican quarters: 'They have even taken French fries off the menu in Congress,' she exclaims. 'You have now got to ask for freedom fries!'

At the end of the day, John Prescott dropped by for my agreement to emergency legislation on the fire dispute. Afterwards he asked me about my intentions over Iraq, but he has known me too long to try to talk me out of it. As he left I reminded him that he and I were the only survivors of Kinnock's original Shadow Cabinet in 1983. Soon he would be the only one.

Thursday 13 March

I am not out of the house before Jack Straw calls me to urge me not to resign. Jack and I go back a long way and were the two junior members of Peter Shore's Treasury team in the early eighties. I got the impression that he clearly wanted me to stay out of concern for me as a friend.

The case he put to me was rather legalistic. He went over how resolution 1441 gives us all the legal authority we require to launch war. I responded that my problem was the political and diplomatic absurdity of a unilateral war even if it were legal.

I saw Tony before Cabinet. I found him half-amused, half-furious with IDS. He had given IDS a briefing in Privy Councillor terms and, to his dismay, IDS had walked straight out of the door and disclosed to camera that the Prime Minister thought a second resolution now 'very unlikely'. Since the fiction that Tony still hopes to get a second resolution is central to his strategy for keeping the Labour Party in check, it is not welcome news that IDS has told the world that not even Tony believes this.

I began by joking: 'I'm getting so many regular checks from colleagues that I'm beginning to think I'm on suicide watch. I wouldn't be entirely surprised if someone came along and took away my belt and shoelaces to keep me out of harm's way.' He laughed and said – and I think he meant it – 'I hope it doesn't come to that.'

I was frank with him that my mind was made up, and that I would not mislead him into thinking that he could persuade me to change it. However, I was equally clear that I was not running any other agenda, or lending myself to an attack on his leadership. 'You have been the most successful Labour leader in my lifetime. I want you to go on being leader and to go on being successful.'

At this point his body language visibly softened as his muscles relaxed and he leaned back into his sofa. After that he was open, almost philosophical. All he said confirmed my impression that he is mystified as to quite how he got into such a hole and baffled as to whether there is any way out other than persisting in the strategy that has created his present difficulties.

He told me that he was going to call a special Cabinet meeting when the process in the UN was complete, and I promised that I would make no public move while he was still working for a result in the UN.

After me he was seeing Clare, which had the effect of delaying Cabinet for fifteen minutes. When we began, Gordon launched a long and passionate statement of support for Tony's strategy. The contribution was rather marred by an outspoken attack on France: 'the message that must go out from this Cabinet is that we pin the blame on France for its isolated refusal to agree in the Security Council'. I spoke after him and began by reminding colleagues that when this was over the first priority must be to repair the divisions with Europe, and in the meantime we should not make that job more difficult by sending out messages that attack France or any other European country. I applauded Tony, Jack and Jeremy Greenstock for the effort they had put into getting agreement at the UN and their 'ingenuity' in finding new initiatives when all seemed lost. 'However, the intensity of our efforts to get agreement in the Security Council means that we cannot now pretend that it does not really matter if we fail to get agreement. In the meantime, we should avoid saying that we will take military action even if we fail to get a resolution, as we need some flexibility to consider what we do if we find ourselves in that position.' At this last point, John Prescott nodded and I suspect that half the Cabinet agreed with me even if no one else said so.

At Business Statement I began with a short statement promising that there would be a debate on Iraq as soon as we knew the outcome in the Security Council. I got that in first as I knew that otherwise I would be drowned in a tidal wave of impatience when I announced the business for the fortnight, which did not include a single reference to Iraq. I nearly got through the hour without taking any hits, partly because those against the government line now suspect that I am on their side, and did not bowl as hard as they might. Unfortunately, towards the end Julian Lewis produced one of his typically well-researched questions which slightly threw me and I finished my reply to his question whether collective responsibility would apply in the forthcoming debate on Iraq by saying that 'collective responsibility will apply to all who are in the Cabinet at that time'. The last phrase produced gasps from the Tory benches and I was immediately irritated for letting my tongue run on.

When I got back to my office there was a message from the Foreign Office to say that Jack would be very grateful if I could represent the government at the funeral on Saturday of Zoran Djindjic, the Prime Minister of Serbia, who was assassinated yesterday. I readily agreed as I had worked with Zoran for years. We cooperated closely when I was Foreign Secretary and he was in opposition. It is a terrible irony that throughout those years he managed to avoid being assassinated by Milosevic, only to be killed now that he has brought Milosevic to the bar of justice. There is also something of an irony in that my last official engagement representing the government will be attending a funeral.

Friday 14 March

The papers are full of prominent reports that I had 'put down a marker' on my position at yesterday's Cabinet. I take the bull by the horns and ring Alastair to suggest that I come round to discuss a joint strategy for handling the media that minimises the damage to the party. Alastair occupies a pleasant and airy corner room with windows in two directions to Horse Guards Parade. If it wasn't for the dark wood panelling which gives it a very nineteenth-century feel, it would be an altogether more pleasant room than the Prime Minister's.

Sally Morgan is already with him. I begin by saying that I had not planned on ending up in this position, but I didn't imagine that they thought they would end up in this fix either. They both nodded agreement to that. I get the strong impression that Number 10 is as bewildered as anyone else how we ended up in this crisis. I explained to them that my mind was made up, but I was willing to discuss how we handle my departure with as civilised a form as we could agree.

Alastair suggested that we agree the text of my letter of resignation and Tony's letter of acceptance, and that we negotiate a tone that is regretful but warm rather than bitter and hostile.

He told me that Tony would be travelling to the Azores on Sunday to meet Bush and made no bones about the fact that this was to seal the plans for war next week. When I expressed surprise at the Azores, Alastair told me that 'Bush wanted to come to London, but we had to talk him out of that.' I can understand why the idea of Bush arriving in London right now must have appalled Number 10. He would have been an immediate focus for protests and it would be impossible to get the British press to treat Bush with the deference and respect which he gets in the Rose Garden. Yet it sums up our basic dilemma that we fear it would be a public relations disaster to have a visit from the President who is the ally upon whose coat-tails we are about to go to war.

In the course of the day I pick up from my contacts that the Foreign Office are equally depressed. In some ways they have more right to be frustrated, as they have several times tried to warn Number 10 of the dangers of Tony's strategy. Apparently Jack Straw wrote last summer warning the Prime Minister that we could end up in a diplomatic stalemate.

Among the open fury with the French for their treachery there is also private impatience with the US for its cack-handed diplomacy. Part of the problem in getting international support is the fact that Powell does not travel any more. He has been terrified of leaving Washington ever since he went to the Middle East and was stabbed in the back by Sharon ringing up Cheney to brief him against Powell. This is a problem for Britain as well because Foreign Office influence on Washington is limited by the fact that the State Department itself has little influence over what is happening in Washington.

Saturday 15 March

I got up in the middle of the night to fly to Belgrade for the funeral of Zoran Djindjic. It was a moving occasion to see the vast Orthodox cathedral crowded with silent mourners. The cathedral itself is something of a symbol of the paralysis which gripped Belgrade under Milosevic. It has been under construction for a generation and is still incomplete. The walls are unfinished and no lighting or heating has been installed. There was a sense that the service was being held in a building site. Adrian Nastase, the Romanian Prime Minister, who was standing next to me, suggested that it made an appropriate metaphor for Zoran's work against the nationalist–mafia complex, which also remains unfinished.

After the service we adjourned to one of the ugly rectangular boxes which Tito built to house his government. Over the trays of vodka I got the chance to catch up with old colleagues from my days as Foreign Secretary, many of whom had already read in their national press speculation that I might resign. Joschka Fischer wanted to know how Britain had got into this cul-de-sac and I found that I could not give him an explanation that satisfied even myself. He underlined the degree of European opposition to military action by observing to me that 'you and I are not pacifists'. Indeed we are not and we worked together closely on behalf of Britain and Germany during the Kosovo campaign, but neither of us can support this one.

Monday 17 March

I began the day by ringing Michael Martin to warn him that I would want to make a personal statement on my resignation. He and I had worked well as a partnership over the last couple of years and we were both sorry it could not continue. After that I contacted Frank Dobson and Chris Smith, who have been good friends and allies over the years, and asked them to sit with me when I made my first speech from the back benches for twenty years.

Tony had asked to see me before the special Cabinet in the afternoon. It was a very civilised affair. He had given up on trying to talk me out of resignation. Anyway, I had come armed with the final edition of my resignation letter signed and sealed. I in my turn had given up on trying to talk him out of going to war. Bush was set on going to war and paradoxically the forty thousand British troops in Kuwait had become hostages to ensure that Tony was obliged to go to war alongside him.

I focused instead on what would happen next. 'The people around George Bush will come up with another military venture. Next time don't get so committed that you can't draw back.' I felt that he took the point about staying out of future conflicts more willingly than he had absorbed my many repeated arguments against military action on Iraq. I got the impression he was a man who was genuinely puzzled as to how he had got into his present dilemma. I suspect he had never expected to find himself ordering British troops into war without UN backing. The root problem of the last year has been that Tony was so convinced of the case against Saddam that he never doubted the rest of the world would come to see it his way and had therefore left himself no other way out.

It was Tony who suggested that I should not attend the special Cabinet meeting. It had been my intention to make one last appeal to colleagues. I had even prepared in my mind a short speech on the text: 'Just because we have marched up to the edge of the precipice, does not mean that we have to jump over it to demonstrate our credibility.' However, I had been making interventions against the war over the past year and, frankly, I was as relieved not to have to make a final one as my colleagues no doubt were to be spared it. It did, though, leave me with a logistical problem. I had long ago decided against 'doing a Heseltine' and walking out of the Cabinet to announce my resignation straight to camera. I was a parliamentarian and I wanted the first statement of my resignation to be to the Commons. But the pavement outside Number 10 was crammed with journalists and cameras jostling for a foothold on the pavement. If I walked back out of that door before the Cabinet meeting even started I might as well have worn a placard saying I had resigned. Instead, I walked along to the press wing and called on Alastair for the last time. Together we arranged for one of his assistants to let me out down the back stairs and for my driver to be waiting by the side door.

All that was left now was to get my resignation speech in ready order. But that was not difficult. This was a speech that had been brewing inside me for two months. I was only glad that at last I could speak honestly.

8

A War Without Victory

The people of England have been led in Mesopotamia into a trap from which it will be hard to escape with dignity and honour. They have been tricked into it by a steady withholding of information. The Baghdad communiqués are belated, insincere, incomplete. Things have been far worse than we have been told, our administration more bloody and inefficient than the public knows . . . there has been a deplorable contrast between our profession and our practice.

T. E. Lawrence, Letter to the *Sunday Times*, 1920

From Liberation to Occupation

On 9 April 2003 the US Third Infantry Division occupied Baghdad. The toppling of Saddam was given graphic expression by the felling of an outsize statue of him in the central square. This should have been the signal for the release of 'the explosion of joy and relief' which Paul Wolfowitz, number two at the Pentagon, had promised would greet the invading troops. Instead, it was the prelude to an orgy of looting in which hospitals were stripped, centres of administration were wrecked, the power network was vandalised and museums trashed. The volume of copper wire stripped from the electricity system was so great that it dented the world market price. The first seeds of Iraqi cynicism must have been sown by the discovery that the Ministry of Oil was one of the very few public buildings secured by US forces.

A year to the day after Saddam's statue was pulled down the square in which it had stood had to be sealed off by razor wire and US tanks to prevent it being used for a protest against the occupation. A loudspeaker blared a warning, 'This area is completely sealed off by the coalition troops. If anyone tries to get close to a military vehicle they will be attacked.' US forces are largely confined to heavily fortified frontier posts, from which they venture out only in armoured convoys. As a result of growing casualties the number of such forays has been sharply reduced, a retreat which the US command presented as a victory by citing the corresponding drop in attacks on patrols as evidence of progress.

Donald Rumsfeld had predicted that US troop levels would fall to 30,000 within a few months of the invasion but a year later has increased it by about the same amount, mostly by extending the tour of duty of reservists. The strategy of recruiting Iraqis to take over control of security was derailed when in Najaf and Fallujah the Iraqi police melted away and the Iraqi army refused to fight. The Coalition Forces have lost control over even the most basic asset of an occupation force – its supply routes. Both the highways to Jordan and to the Gulf are frequently interdicted by rebel and bandit action. Even the surprise decision to bring forward the handover of power to the new Iraqi government was dictated by anxiety that the terrorists may have plotted a spectacular for the official date of 30 June.

The crisis of security in Iraq can be traced to a fundamental miscalculation in Washington. In their arrogance the Neo Cons assumed that the citizens of a Muslim country, with strong pride in their ancient culture, would welcome its occupation by foreign troops from Western countries. The Bush strategy was built on the shaky proposition that the Iraqis would be so glad to see the back of Saddam that they would be pleased to be occupied by the people who had liberated them. The first leg of this proposition was sound. As the recent report on Iraq of the UN High Commissioner for Human Rights expressed it, Saddam's regime was 'a brutal, murderous, torturing gang that preyed on its own people'. However this did not make Iraqis regard US forces purely as liberators and not also as conquerors. They were both relieved to be freed from Saddam, and humiliated at their conquest by a Christian army. A consequence of the Pentagon's misplaced confidence was a wilful failure to prepare their troops in the skills they needed to make themselves welcome. The rank and file US personnel were dumped in a distant country without any training in its foreign culture or local customs, without any language skills and without any ability to distinguish friend from foe among its population. It is not surprising that the natural reaction of ordinary soldiers was to regard this strange environment as a hostile place in which every hand was turned against them. Nor did the Pentagon listen to those who warned that Iraqis had a long tradition of resisting foreign occupation. Incredibly the US occupying forces were despatched with no training in counter-insurgency. When the predictable insurgency mushroomed one colonel lamented, 'We are not trained to fight a war like this.'

At the best of times the warrior ethos of the US army does not lend itself to peacekeeping. But in Iraq the US forces were hindered from ever attempting the transition from war waging to peacekeeping by frequent assurances that they were the central front in President Bush's Global War on Terrorism. A year after the invasion Donald Rumsfeld was still justifying civilian casualties on the grounds that the US army was fighting a war. Any war requires an enemy and every day since the invasion Iraqi civilians have found that some of them have been cast in that role. The responsibility for this goes right to the top. President Bush, Dick Cheney and Donald Rumsfeld deliberately cultivated the notion that the invasion of Iraq was a logical response to 9/11. As a result 60% of the US public, and no doubt a similar proportion of the US military, believe Iraq was responsible for the attack on the Twin Towers. During the invasion one journalist embedded with US Marines reported a conversation with a soldier who carried inside his jacket a photo of Ground Zero to remind him it was 'pay back time'.

The result of this mixture of vengeance, incomprehension and hostility is a mindset which led too many US combat troops to regard as fair game all Iraqis – or 'hajis' as they called them in an expression reflecting the widespread Islamophobia among the 'liberators'. Some service personnel did rebel against the carnage they witnessed. Staff Sergeant Massey of the Marines complained to his commanding officer that he felt they were committing genocide and retired from the army. Sergeant Massey reckoned his platoon killed half a dozen civilians a week.

To his credit Sergeant Massey was at least keeping a count. The most contemptible aspect of the conduct of the Coalition Forces is that they regarded the death of Iraqis with such indifference that they have not even counted them. Those human rights NGOs who have attempted to estimate the number of Iraqi fatalities put the number of civilians killed in the war and subsequent occupation at over 11,000. Extraordinarily not one of these killings has resulted in a single US soldier being charged or disciplined. This has in turn sent a message throughout US forces that senior command regard Iraq as a free-fire zone. The result is that the slightest suspicious activity provokes immediate lethal force, without pause for further investigation. In May the US Airforce mistook an open wedding party for a clandestine gathering of foreign fighters. Over forty civilians were annihilated in the subsequent bombing raid. Despite the irrefutable evidence of a dozen small children and a popular wedding singer among the dead, the Coalition Forces refused even to admit there had been a mistake.

Much of Iraq is still a tribal society. Its culture ensures a powerful solidarity from all members of the same tribe and extended family in response to an attack on any one of them. As a result every Iraqi death has fuelled increasingly aggressive resistance to occupation. Unfortunately the American doctrine of overwhelming military force does not lend itself to isolating and defusing the sources of resistance. On the contrary the standard response has been to meet resistance by escalating the violence and deploying helicopter gunships and armoured artillery, which make no distinction between combatants and civilians. The punitive code-names, such as Iron Hammer and Resolute Sword, picked for such operations by the high command betray that even senior officers see their objective as intimidating Iraqis rather than winning them over. The Coalition Forces thus became mired in a downward spiral of resistance provoking a heavy-handed military response, which in turn stimulated even greater support for resistance. As Kofi Annan presciently observed, 'Violent military action by an occupying power against inhabitants of an occupied country will only make matters worse.'

The nadir of the occupation came at Fallujah when over three weeks in spring US marines attempted to storm a city that was a centre of Sunni resistance. The trigger for the assault was the brutal murder of four American security guards and the indignity heaped on their corpses before camera. Unfortunately the scale of the military response treated every one of 300,000 residents as if they were all guilty of the murders. In launching an attack by missile, gunship and tank General Kimmitt announced that its objective was to 'pacify that city'. Irony is not General Kimmitt's strong suit.

The operation was a military failure and a political catastrophe. Around a thousand of the residents were killed during the siege. Local doctors reported that the majority of the dead they saw were women and children, although not every casualty made it to hospital as US firepower kept access to it closed for much of the time. Médecins Sans Frontières complained that in breach of the Geneva Convention US snipers were deployed on the hospital's water tower, preventing use of its operating theatres. Other US snipers took up firing positions in the minarets where they appear to have followed rules of engagement of firing on anyone who moved. Among those killed by sniper fire was a woman hanging out her washing, and an elderly woman who was still clutching her white flag when aid workers found her body. Lee Gordon, a British journalist who volunteered to accompany the evacuation of severely wounded, reported that even ambulances were repeatedly targeted by snipers in clear violation of the Geneva Convention.

Inside Iraq the number of fatalities and the suffering of the living under siege in Fallujah provoked outrage. It produced the unity of Sunni and Shia which had long been an objective of the Coalition

Authority, but in protest against the occupation rather than in support. Even the members of the Iraqi Governing Council, although hand-picked by the Pentagon, were moved to condemn the operation. Adnan Pachachi denounced the conduct of US forces as 'illegal and totally unacceptable' because it was 'inflicting collective punishment on the residents of Fallujah', which is a further breach of the Geneva Convention. Fallujah may prove to have been the tipping point at which moral authority irrevocably slipped away from the military occupation. In the month after the siege the Coalition Authority conceded that its own private polling found that 82% of Iraqis disapproved of the conduct of its military forces. An even larger proportion, 92%, described the Coalition Forces as 'occupiers', and a meagre 2% described them as 'liberators', even less than the 3% who wanted Saddam back.

It is an open secret that the British military in Basra are as dismayed as everyone else with the counter-productive behaviour of US forces. One serving officer even complained that US forces view Iraqi people as 'untermenschen' (under-people). Sir Michael Jackson, the Chief of Defence Staff, hinted at these tensions when he asserted, 'we must be able to fight with the Americans. That does not equal we must fight as Americans'. There are a number of serious allegations under investigation into the conduct of individual British servicemen, but as a general rule British units have applied military force with more restraint and have given greater priority to winning the confidence of local people. As a result, their sector over the past year has largely been spared the growing insurgency throughout the other Arab regions of Iraq. However there is an obvious tension between the determination of No 10 Downing Street to stand shoulder to shoulder with the US Administration on the international stage and the hope of our military that they can keep their distance from the provocative tactics of US forces on the ground in Iraq. It is also further embarrassing evidence of Britain's junior status in the partnership that our military and our diplomats have been ignored when they have urged the Pentagon to show more restraint. In May a leaked document from within the Foreign Office pleaded for a 'need to redouble our efforts to ensure a sensitive and sensible US approach to military operations'.

Tony Blair repeatedly dismisses the resistance as the work of 'fanatics and terrorists'. An open letter from fifty-two former ambassadors has characterised this description as 'neither convincing or helpful'. A less diplomatic response might be that it reveals Downing Street as in denial.

We will never make a success of our presence in Iraq if we refuse to come to terms with reality. The widening resistance has its roots in the resentment of ordinary Iraqis at the humiliation of occupation. Daily in Iraq some of its citizens will experience an assault rifle being pointed at them on their own streets by a nervous, suspicious soldier of one of our partners in the coalition. Tens of thousands of Iraqis have been held without any legal process in the new gulag of detention centres run by the US military. Whole communities know of families whose homes have been trashed by US troops who sometimes enter by driving their armoured vehicles through the wall. It does not need 'fanatics and terrorists' to foment an insurgency in such circumstances. If it was happening on our streets we would be in resistance also.

Privatising Iraq

Paul Wolfowitz visited Iraq shortly after its conquest to survey the victory of the Neo Con strategy. He had to travel inside a convoy of armoured vehicles watched over by Black Hawk helicopters, no doubt lest he was overwhelmed by 'the explosion of joy and relief' which he had predicted. While there he was moved to admit 'some of our assumptions turned out to be wrong'. One of the key assumptions which proved unreliable was that the reconstruction of Iraq would pay for itself out of oil revenues. Wolfowitz himself had given wildly inflated estimates to Congress of the likely oil revenues, which one industry expert alleged as 'total fabrication'. It was though a widely shared delusion at the time of the invasion. I recall Tony Blair assuring Cabinet that rebuilding Iraq would be easier than Afghanistan because of its oil wealth. In the event it has proved much harder than he imagined to tap that oil wealth. At the time of writing the oil flow from Iraq is still less than was achieved before the invasion by an Iraq handicapped by sanctions from importing any new technology. In April BP announced that it was abandoning Iraq. In the words of its Chief Executive, John Browne, 'We need a government, we need laws and we need decisions. We have not got any of that yet.' Over the next two months insurgents blew up the two pipelines connecting Iraq's oilfields to the outside world, making it even harder to restore the previous level of oil exports. The consequence is that the reconstruction of Iraq is proving very expensive indeed. The sums that the US and other partners have now committed to Iraq are much bigger than the total amount pledged to Afghanistan, a larger and poorer nation.

It is said that when Colin Powell tried to talk President Bush out of the invasion he quoted the notice in many china shops, 'You break it, you own it.' Despite his warning the Bush Administration proved lamentably unprepared for the task of running the country they had insisted on conquering. The planning for war had been meticulous and exhaustive. For a year the military forces of both countries had refined their tactics and tested them out in war games. But the job of winning the peace did not receive anything like the preparation that was given to winning the war. The world's most powerful military machine shifted whole formations of tanks and heavy artillery to Iraq, but could not deliver a comparable volume of emergency generators to keep the power supply working. This summer the proportion of the Iraqi population with access to clean water is still 10% down on the period before the war and the Coalition is expected to miss its own targets for electricity generation to meet peak demand in the sweltering summer. A clear majority of Iraqi males remain unemployed.

One explanation for the poor performance on reconstruction is that the American companies who are awarded the contracts by the Coalition Authority bring in their own specialists who are accustomed to advanced technology, rather than utilising Iraqis who are skilled at fixing the old systems. The natural instinct of the US administrators is to fund large-scale contracts rather than local projects. Thus the traffic lights do not get fixed and the sewage system breaks down, but contracts for long-term infrastructure are signed. By definition companies with the scale to match the size of the contracts tend to be American. Reconstruction has so far been more conspicuously successful in producing profits in Texas than jobs in Iraq. The first company to get its feet under the table was the oil conglomerate Halliburton who secured a monopoly on providing fuel to the Coalition Authority. It was awarded the original short-term contract without any competitive tender, on the basis that there was an urgent need for the supply and it then secured repeated renewals, again without any competitive bids. The US Army has since complained of overcharging. When I observed to Madeleine Albright that it was incomprehensible to a European that a company could secure contracts for billions of dollars without competitive tendering she replied, 'It is incomprehensible to an American also.' A document leaked from the Pentagon this summer revealed that the Halliburton deal had been 'coordinated with the Vice President's Office'. Dick Cheney had been Chief Executive of Halliburton until being picked by Bush for Vice-President.

It was a prime objective of the Neo Con strategy to exploit the takeover of Iraq to introduce free market ideology to the Middle East. Therefore many of those picked to work for the Coalition Authority were political staffers rather than specialists with experience of development work. They used the absolutist power of the Coalition Authority to impose on Iraq a fundamentalist version of Republican economics. Paul Bremer, the US head of the Coalition Authority, laid down a legal base for foreign companies to buy up all Iraqi state assets, other than the sensitive oil reserves, with no restriction on the amount of profit they could repatriate. Joseph Stiglitz, the Nobel Prize-winning economist, warned that this could create the conditions for 'Russia-style asset-stripping' and wryly added, 'Of course it is nothing we would do at home, because we're actually quite protectionist.' The Coalition Authority has now gone out of business, but part of the deal with the new Interim Government is that they will not amend any laws pending the election of a more permanent government. As a result there will be at least a further year in which the Bremer decrees will provide carte blanche for the sale of assets, without any test of its legitimacy in Iraqi opinion.

A key component of a successful market economy is the requirement for independent audit to enforce integrity. Yet Paul Bremer has shown no enthusiasm for applying that requirement to the operations of the Coalition Authority. At the time of the invasion Tony Blair promised that the oil revenues of Iraq would be put to the benefit of the Iraqi people. The first UN Security Council Resolution provided that the Development Fund created by oil revenues would be disbursed by the Coalition Authority but audited by independent public accountants to ensure it was applied for the good of Iraq. It was not until the subsequent October that an Advisory and Monitoring Board was established and not until May of this year that the new Board was able to persuade the Coalition Authority to appoint auditors. At the time of writing KPMG have still to make a full report on the use to which the Coalition Authority has put Iraqi oil revenues, but Paul Bremer and his staff have already moved on from Baghdad and can no longer be held to account. If the oil revenues have indeed been put to the benefit of the Iraqi people it is hard to fathom why the Coalition Authority has shown so much foot-dragging over proving it.

A large part of the reason why the occupation has lost legitimacy and popularity among the Iraqi people is the failure of reconstruction to demonstrate real improvement in the standard of living of their families or the quality of life on their streets. Frustrated expectations have fostered sympathy and tolerance for the resistance to the occupation. Violence and insecurity from insurgency have in turn hampered reconstruction, which is proving much tougher than the pre-war pipe dreams of those who planned the invasion. An ironic admission by the Coalition Authority of its problems came in a brochure for a business conference in London which advertised it as 'An excellent opportunity to do business in Iraq without having to consider the current security risks of visiting the country.'

Weapons of Mass Disappearance

The swelling insurgency and faltering reconstruction has fuelled a loss of faith among many of the commentators who enthusiastically urged on Britain to invade Iraq. Michael Ignatieff, for example, has complained, without his usual elegant prose, 'The Americans screwed it up.' Those who supported the war in good faith have every right to feel betrayed by the incompetent and ill-prepared occupation. But they also need to recognise that every justification they made for the war has disintegrated.

The claim that Saddam had a handy arsenal of weapons of mass destruction has become the butt of satire for stand-up comedians the length and breadth of Britain. We have found no nuclear material. No chemical agents. No biological samples. No delivery systems. Nothing. It is not for want of trying. The first search party went in with the US forces. It was dubbed, in classic example of military jargon, the 75th Exploitation Task Force, and for months before the war had been assembling biologists, chemists, computer experts and special forces to locate the weapons of mass destruction over which we had gone to war. By June they had retired from Iraq, baffled by their inability to uncover any of the weapons which they had been equipped to trace. As one of their officers expressed it in a candid, idiomatic expression, 'We came loaded for bear country, but we found no bears.' At an early point of the occupation a Kurdish leader complained that it was difficult to find a US officer with whom to negotiate because they were all too busy trying to qualify for a medal by being the first to discover a weapon of mass destruction. General Conway, Commander of the US Marines in Iraq, was blunt about both the scale of the effort and the paucity of the result: 'It's not for lack of trying. We've been to virtually every ammunition supply point between the Kuwaiti border and Baghdad, but they're simply not there. We were simply wrong.' Unwilling to admit they were wrong Washington and London launched the Iraq Survey Group to carry out an even more intensive search. The man appointed to front it up, David Kay, was chosen because he was a hawk who had robustly insisted before the war that Saddam had weapons of mass destruction. To his credit David Kay was honest that he also drew a blank and succinctly admitted, 'We were almost all wrong.'

Washington has since turned on Ahmed Chalabi who had been the Pentagon's pet Iraqi exile and the source of many of their fantasy claims about Saddam's weapons capacity. It was Chalabi who was the origin of Colin Powell's presentation to the Security Council that Saddam had mobile chemical weapons laboratories which no one can now find. The immediate cause of the breach is reported to be the claim by US intelligence that Chalabi had been feeding genuine US secrets to the Iranian intelligence service. It is alleged that Chalabi told an Iranian agent that the CIA had cracked their codes, which, in a touch of farce, the agent then reported to Tehran in the code he had just been warned the Americans had cracked. But the real mystery is why the Pentagon ever took seriously Chalabi, who is wanted in Jordan to serve a sentence of hard labour for major bank fraud. We turn out to have gone to war on false intelligence largely fed to us by a man who would not have survived a background check for a job with a used car firm.

It seems almost cruel to remind those who sold the case for war of what they claimed at the time. But it is necessary because they appear to be forgetting it themselves. President Bush was both definite and apocalyptic: 'Saddam is building and hiding weapons that could enable him to intimidate the civilised world.' Donald Rumsfeld went one better, 'We know where they are.' On the eve of war Tony Blair was equally specific that Saddam had the real thing: 'Saddam has chemical and biological weapons.' At the last minute the title of the September dossier was changed from Saddam's Programme for Weapons of Mass Destruction to Saddam's Weapons of Mass Destruction to convince the reader that the weapons already existed.

Now Tony Blair tells us that he hopes to come up with not actual weapons but evidence of Saddam's intentions to develop weapon programmes. We always knew that left to himself Saddam would try to acquire any weapon system going. That after all is why the West put in place a strategy of containment based on a mix of sanctions and UN inspections to frustrate his intentions. We now know that containment was an unqualified success in denying Saddam a single weapon of mass destruction. The case that George Bush and Tony Blair made for war was that containment had failed and that we must launch a pre-emptive strike before Saddam used his imaginary weapons. Indeed the claim that Saddam already possessed weapons of mass destruction ready for use was central to their argument that military action must be taken urgently. As Donald Rumsfeld warned in alarmist terms, 'Within a week, or a month, Saddam could give his WMD to Al Qaeda.'

Lord Hutton was factually correct to acquit Tony Blair of lying over the intelligence on Saddam's weapons. I never imagined that Downing Street would have committed itself to a flat untruth. But neither were they candid with the British public, as the evidence paraded before the Hutton Inquiry copiously demonstrated. Nor did Downing Street reveal the unfolding intelligence which cast doubt on the September dossier. Indeed it was not until a year after the war that the Government admitted that a Joint Intelligence Committee assessment had warned that 'intelligence on the timing of when Iraq might use CBW was inconsistent and that the intelligence on deployment was sparse'. This revised assessment was dramatically different from the September claim that Saddam had weapons of mass destruction ready for firing in forty-five minutes, but it was not shared with Parliament before the vote on war. The intelligence agencies had good reason to doubt their own claims before the invasion because the leads they kept feeding the UN Inspectors kept drawing a blank. Hans Blix has since observed, 'This shocked me. If this was the best (intelligence), what was the rest?'

If Saddam had no weapons of mass destruction there was no urgent need to invade Iraq. George Bush and Tony Blair could have given Hans Blix the extra few months for which he pleaded to finish his job and prove Saddam was no threat. What created real urgency in Washington to start the invasion may have been the dawning realisation that Hans Blix was about to remove their pretext for war.

Unfortunately for Downing Street, the one-dimensional endorsement of the government case by the Hutton Report encouraged it to be triumphant when it would have been wiser to have been conciliatory. That hubris may explain why in the Commons debate on the Hutton report Tony Blair stumbled into fresh controversy by letting slip that he had never realised before the war that the chemical weapons described as ready at forty-five minutes notice in the September dossier were only battlefield munitions and not missiles. I was astonished by his reply as I had been briefed that Saddam's weapons were only battlefield ones and I could not conceive that the Prime Minister had been given a different version. My briefing took place in February at my residence at Carlton Gardens where I was visited by John Scarlett, Chairman of the Joint Intelligence Committee. We spoke together for almost an hour and as always I found him professional, dispassionate, and frank in his replies. When I put to him my conclusion that Saddam had no long-range weapons of mass destruction but may have battlefield chemical weapons he readily agreed. When I asked him why we believed Saddam would not use these weapons against our troops on the battlefields, he surprised me by claiming that in order to evade detection by the UN inspectors Saddam had taken apart the shells and dispersed them with the result that it would be difficult to deploy them under attack. Not only did Saddam have no weapons of mass destruction in the real meaning of that phrase, but neither did he have usable battlefield weapons.

I put these points to the Prime Minster a couple of weeks later. The exchange is recorded in my diary on 5th March 2003. Tony Blair gave me the same reply as John Scarlett, that the battlefield weapons had been disassembled and stored separately. I was therefore mystified a year later to hear him say he had never understood that the intelligence agencies did not believe Saddam had long-range weapons of mass destruction.

I have been told that Tony Blair does not recall me telling him that Saddam had no long-range weapons. But did *nobody* else tell him? How often did he meet before the war with the Chief of Defence Staff who would certainly have known the weapons the enemy was believed to possess? Why did Tony Blair himself never ask John Scarlett whether he was talking about long-range or battlefield weapons? Given that the Prime Minister was justifying war to the nation on the grounds that Saddam was a serious threat to British interests, he showed a surprising lack of curiosity what that threat actually was. We are asked to accept that from September to March the Prime Minister was allowed to think that Saddam had long-range chemical weapons, while the intelligence agencies assessed he had only battlefield weapons, despite the Joint Intelligence Committee sending up to Downing Street three separate assessments on Saddam's weapons capacity. This must represent the most extraordinary failure of communication in the history of the British intelligence agencies.

An Own Goal on Terrorism

Tony Blair deceives himself if he really imagines the insurgency across Iraq is all the work of foreign terrorists and fanatics. It is undeniably true that there now are fundamentalist terrorists in Iraq, but that only demolishes another justification for the war – that it would be a blow to international terrorism. On the contrary our invasion allowed terrorists into a country from which they had been kept out, by disbanding all its security apparatus and leaving its borders open for the best part of a year. One supporter of Al Qaeda expressed his gratitude to the Coalition Forces for overthrowing their enemy Saddam and thereby enabling them to operate in Iraq. We have created the perfect conditions for Al Qaeda to thrive in Iraq – poor security, a hostile population with a sense of grievance, and a rich range of accessible Western targets. Few days go by now without an Al Qaeda-style suicide bomb being detonated in Baghdad or elsewhere in Iraq.

At first the Neo Cons brandished the new terrorism inside Iraq as evidence of how cunning their strategy had been. Their theory was that Coalition Forces were the 'fly paper' which was attracting terrorists into Iraq and diverting them from elsewhere. This was not a theory that was ever going to commend itself to the foreign workers in Iraq, many of whom have left rather than be the fly paper, but it also could not be made to fit the facts. The year since the Coalition Forces conquered Baghdad has been punctuated by terrorist attacks from Riyadh to Madrid and from Istanbul to Jakarta. The initial instinct of Washington was to deny the evidence of their eyes and ears. In April the State Department announced that since the invasion terrorist attacks had fallen to a thirty-year low. Subsequently they had to admit they had made a mistake over the way they had compiled the figures and that in fact there had been a big increase in terrorism. The respected International Institute for Strategic Studies concluded in their Strategic Survey that 'overall, risks of terrorism to Westerners and Western assets in Arab countries have increased since the Iraq war', which is precisely what the Joint Intelligence Committee warned the Prime Minister would happen.

Any serious strategy to defeat international terrorism would begin by denying it popular legitimacy. Instead Iraq handed Al Qaeda a massive propaganda gift. Richard C. Clarke, until recently National Coordinator for Security and Counter-Terrorism in Washington, concluded his book with the observation, 'We did exactly what Al Qaeda said we would do. We invaded and occupied an oil-rich Arab country that posed no threat to us.' The massive and fascinating Pew Global Attitudes Project put figures to the subsequent growth in public hostility in twenty countries around the world. It found that 'favourable opinions of the US have slipped in nearly every country for which trend measures are available' and bluntly warned that 'the bottom has fallen out of support for America in most of the Muslim world'. In terms of public diplomacy the attack on Iraq has been the equivalent of shooting ourselves in the foot.

This rise in public hostility to the West has a direct read across to Western concerns on terrorism. The Pew Project found that in ten out of the fourteen countries where comparisons were possible, public support for the war on terrorism had declined. This drop in public concern is reflected in the expression of alarm by Ambassador Arias, Chair of the UN Counter-Terrorism Committee, that there has been a loss of momentum in the fight against terrorism and that people were 'sleeping again': In the wake of 9/11 a global coalition willingly signed up to tackle a common enemy in international terrorism. As a former Foreign Secretary I was impressed by the extraordinary achievement of recruiting Russia, China and most of the Muslim world to a common cause with the US in fighting the same threat. That grand coalition was a precious asset. It has been shipwrecked on the rock of our stubborn insistence on invading Iraq and as a result we are more, not less, vulnerable to the threat from international terrorism.

From Guantanamo to Abu Ghraib

There remained one last line of defence for those who joined the clamour for war. There may have been none of those weapons of mass disappearance, and terrorism may have got worse, but at least nobody could deny we had brought democratic values and human rights to Iraq. Then the barbaric photographs from Abu Ghraib prison demolished even that claim to superior moral values. No image could have more flatly contradicted the claim that the invasion had been waged to bring human rights and individual freedoms to Iraq than the gloating trophy photos of its citizens hooded, manacled, naked, with electrodes attached to their genitals or excrement smeared on their backs. With savage irony this catalogue of imported barbarism came from within the very prison that had been notorious as the symbol of the brutality of Saddam. It is necessary to remember the estimate of the Red Cross that seventy to 90% of those who passed through Abu Ghraib since the occupation had no connection with terrorism and were there by mistake.

The most chilling feature of the snapshots was the happy grins with which the tormentors went about enjoying their work. It all too clearly revealed that they had settled into the supremacy of colonialists and the contempt for natives that accompanies it. Part of the problem with colonialism is that it brutalises the occupiers also, who cannot admit to themselves that the people they repress by force are human beings like themselves. The shot of Specialist Sabrina Harman posing with a satisfied smile over a corpse provided an unforgettable illustration that torture degrades both abuser and victim. In fairness we should also applaud the courage of those individuals who rebelled against the prevailing culture of abuse, such as Joseph Darby who blew the whistle on the practices by reporting them to the Army's Criminal Investigations Division, or William Kimbo, a Navy dog handler who refused requests to use his dogs to intimidate detainees.

Since the Abu Ghraib scandal broke the Pentagon has determinedly presented it as isolated abuse by 'a few bad apples'. This defence is risible. The Red Cross reports that ignited the controversy was blunt that the ill-treatment was 'systematic' and its Director of Operations, Pierre Krahenbuhl, insisted, 'We are dealing here with a broad pattern, not individual acts.' The US Army's own official investigation into Abu Ghraib concluded that the guards had been instructed by military intelligence 'to set the conditions' for the subsequent interrogations and had been ordered to 'manipulate an internee's emotions and weaknesses'. Similar techniques of hooding, sleep deprivation, and sexual humiliation have surfaced in use by US forces from Guantanamo to Kabul. It is simply not credible that a unit of reservists from trailer parks in the Appalachian Mountains happened to come across these practices on the Internet and decided to try them out. Somebody instructed them how to apply those techniques to break down the resistance of detainees.

There is copious evidence that in the autumn after the invasion the Pentagon was panicked by the scale of a resistance they had failed to predict and ordered a more aggressive approach to gathering intelligence from alleged suspects. The driving force behind the intensified efforts to wring information from the detainees in Iraq came from Stephen Cambone who had been personally chosen by Rumsfeld for the new post of Under Secretary of Defense for Intelligence at the time of the invasion. Following the high-profile bombing of the UN headquarters and the Jordanian Embassy in Baghdad he took the decision, endorsed by Rumsfeld, to order General Geoffrey Miller, the commander of Guantanamo, to Baghdad to introduce the approach to interrogation that had been honed inside that legal black hole. The man who personally carried the instructions to General Miller in Cuba was General Jerry Boykin, a fundamentalist who on his return achieved notoriety for a speech of staggering Islamophobia in which he characterised the US as 'a Christian nation' engaged in a holy war against 'Satan'. Brigadier Karpinski, who was then the commander of Abu Ghraib, has provided a graphic illustration of General Miller's attitude to the Iraqi detainees, 'They are like dogs. If you allow them to believe they are more than dogs you have lost control.' When the scandal of the photos broke it was General Miller, of all people, who was ordered back to take charge of Abu Ghraib. His arrival was presented as a mission to clean up the Iraqi prison system, but in reality his priority must be to contain exposure of the political responsibility for the system of interrogation. That may prove a tough assignment. The trail from the abuse in Abu Ghraib back to instructions from political appointees of the Bush Administration may yet provide the most explosive fallout from Iraq.

International Law: Collateral Damage?

A striking feature of the Abu Ghraib scandal is that no one has come forward with a scrap of valuable military intelligence produced by all that degradation, deprivation, and violence. This is not surprising. Since the days of Torquemada it has been known that torture tends to produce not the truth but what the tormentors demand to hear. The point is confirmed by the evidence of Saddam Saleh, one of the row of naked, hooded prisoners in the photograph of Lynndie England mocking their sexual organs. After eighteen days of torture he agreed with anything his interrogators wanted. 'Whatever they asked me for I just said, "Yes". I was desperate.' They asked him if he knew Abu Musab al-Zarqawi, an Al Qaeda leader: 'I said yes, but I'd never even heard of him before.' Eventually Saddam Saleh was released with no charges, having been held for weeks with no legal process.

It was the absence of legal accountability in Abu Ghraib that enabled its abuse to take place. The precedent was set in Afghanistan when the Bush Administration resolved that the fighters they shipped to Guantanamo Bay were not prisoners of war, entitled to humane treatment under the Geneva Convention, but 'unlawful combatants' who were outside any lawful protection. By the time of the invasion of Iraq the Pentagon had taken a further step away from international norms with a report that concluded, 'criminal statutes are not read as infringing on the President's ultimate authority' and that therefore the President had the 'inherent constitutional authority to sanction the use of torture'. Not surprisingly the document was classified by Rumsfeld's office as 'not for foreign eyes'. The abuses at Abu Ghraib were a scandal waiting to happen given the escalating contempt for international humanitarian law by the Bush Administration. As Amnesty International observed in its latest Annual Report, 'The current framework of international law and multilateral action is undergoing the most sustained attack since its establishment half a century ago.'

The same cavalier approach to the requirements of international law is to be found in the origins of the war. Given that every political justification for the war has collapsed, it is difficult to see how the legal basis for the war can remain sold. Here we enter dark and obscure territory. Downing Street has persistently refused to release the full legal opinion it received from the Attorney General on the case for war and as recently as May of this year insisted to the Parliamentary Ombudsman that it was exempt from the Code of Open Government. What has seeped out about the legal debate within government is disturbing enough. It is known that Sir Peter Goldsmith, the Attorney General, initially warned the Prime Minister that a second UN Resolution would be advisable to provide sound legal cover for military action. It was only when it became evident that there would be no second resolution that he submitted a revised opinion arguing that there was a legal basis for war without it. However it was not the Attorney General himself who drafted the new advice, as he invited a professor of international law to write the opinion for him. What made this procedure all the more curious is that the professor he chose, Christopher Greenwood, was one of the small minority of experts in international law who believed that an invasion would be legal without a further resolution and had already gone public with that view in *The Times*. His opinion may have convinced Downing Street, but does not appear to have convinced everyone at the Foreign Office, which is the major centre of expertise in government in international law. Elizabeth Wilmshurst, the Deputy Legal Advisor to the Foreign Office, resigned on the eve of war and subsequently stated 'the conflict in Iraq was contrary to international law'.

A brief summary of the Greenwood/Goldsmith opinion was published as a parliamentary answer. There is not one word in that answer offering a legal basis for war on the grounds of removing Saddam. It is explicit that the authority for military action turned entirely on the material breach of the UN resolution passed twelve years previously because Iraq had 'not fully complied with its obligation to disarm'. But we now know that Iraq had fully complied with its obligations to disarm its weapons of mass destruction. If Iraq was not in breach of its obligations how could we have legal authority to invade it? This legal advice was offered in the same month as the war, and by then there had been three separate assessments by the Joint Intelligence Committee qualifying the claims in the September dossier, and the UN Weapons Inspectors had already reported that there were no weapons of mass destruction at any of the sites identified by Western intelligence. In those circumstances how could Sir Peter Goldsmith be certain as a matter of fact that Iraq was in breach of its obligations? Or had Downing Street not shared with him the emerging doubts on intelligence that was available to the Prime Minister?

It was a Labour Government that in 1948 played a crucial role in founding the UN on the principle that no nation should invade another without international authority. The heart of the controversy over Iraq is that a subsequent Labour Government has demolished that principle, and in doing so, undermined the system of international law in a way which, in Kofi Annan's words to the UN General Assembly, 'could set precedents that resulted in a proliferation of the unilateral and lawless use of force'.

The West and Islam

One reason why starting a war in Iraq appeared a curious priority for the region is that there was already a bloody war in the Middle East. President Bush offered Tony Blair a promise that after the conquest of Iraq he would turn his attention to the existing war in the region and put momentum into the Roadmap to peace between Israel and the Palestinian people. This never appeared a credible promise. The same Neo Cons who plotted the invasion of Iraq were also committed as a matter of ideology to Israel's right to its biblical lands. Paul O'Neill, Bush's first Treasury Secretary, has recorded in his memoirs that at the very first meeting of his National Security Council President Bush announced 'a tilt back towards Israel'. When Colin Powell warned that the consequences for the Palestinians could be 'dire', Bush replied 'Maybe that's the best way to get things back in balance.' There never was any realistic prospect of the Bush Administration applying pressure on the Israeli Government pursue a negotiated settlement rather than a military victory.

Prime Minister Sharon understood this full well. He also knew that the elimination of Saddam reduced the pressure on him within the region. As a result he has become even more aggressive since the fall of Baghdad in his pursuit of an illusory military solution. The Israeli army has conducted intrusive operations with escalating levels of violence, such as the invasion of Rafah refugee camp, and the policy of demolishing Palestinian homes has been accelerated. Extra-judicial killings have been stepped up with the assassination of two successive leaders of Hamas, and Sharon has announced that he is no longer bound by his pledge to President Bush not to target Yasser Arafat. This escalation of the conflict is a tragedy for the Israeli people also. They need security from the suicide bombers, but will achieve peace only through a negotiated settlement that is just to both sides. President Bush's response to Ariel Sharon's intransigence was to invite him to the White House and endorse his objectives. Standing beside Prime Minister Sharon, President Bush announced to a startled crowd that Israel should expect to retain major settlements on the West Bank but that the Palestinian refugees should not expect to return to their homes. In half an hour in the Rose Garden, President Bush cremated the Roadmap which called for both these issues to be settled by negotiation in the final phase of the peace process. Two days later Tony Blair was wheeled out to the Rose Garden by President Bush to endorse the new line, which he dutifully did. For some people it was a moment which represented the nadir in Britain's subordination to the foreign policy agenda of the Bush Administration. It appears to have been the event which tipped fifty-two former ambassadors into signing their open letter to Tony Blair expressing their dismay that he had endorsed 'new policies which are one-sided and illegal and which will cost yet more Israeli and Palestinian blood'.

In the Commons debate on the eve of war Tony Blair had said that in return for its support on Iraq, Britain asked Washington to 'recognise the over-riding importance of restarting the Middle East Peace Process'. The failure of President Bush to keep his own promise, and the inability of Britain to hold him to it, has repercussions that spread much wider than the betrayal of the Palestinian people. A crucial condition of securing Arab tolerance of the invasion of Iraq was for the West to remain at least even-handed in the other war in the region. Instead we have occupied Iraq on a strained interpretation of its obligations under one set of UN resolutions, but have unilaterally announced that another set of resolutions placing obligations on Israel are 'unrealistic'. Such blatant double standards rob our two countries of any credibility. We are now identified on the Arab street with both the unpopular occupations in the region.

The failures of the occupation in Iraq have had a profound impact on Muslim opinion going well beyond its borders. Fallujah has become a modern symbol throughout the Arab world of the repeated invasion of their region by the West. While I was Foreign Secretary I visited Amritsar, which was the scene of the worst atrocity of the British Raj, when an army detachment shot three hundred and seventy-nine Sikhs (unlike the Coalition Authority, the British Raj at least took the trouble to record the number of its victims). Eighty years later the scene of the massacre is preserved by a moving garden of commemoration. Three times as many people were killed in Fallujah, and their deaths will also be remembered for generations by Arabs. The degrading treatment in Abu Ghraib of naked detainees was carefully calculated to inflict maximum humiliation on people brought up in a culture of sexual repression. The consequence is that the pictures of those practices has triggered a wave of anger and indignation across all Arab communities who share the same culture.

It is ironic that a war that was partly motivated by a strategy to ensure security of access to oil reserves has instead contributed to record world prices for oil, reflecting increased instability in the region. The year since the invasion of Iraq has been marked by a new wave of terrorism in Saudi Arabia where there have been persistent and daring attacks on the expat compounds. There were already grounds for profound concern about the stability of the Saudi kingdom. Anomalously in the twenty-first century political power and economic opportunity remains in the hands of a royal family that with each successive generation is expanding and becoming more expensive. Meanwhile a coincidence of interest in change has developed between the educated middle class that is frustrated by its exclusion from political power and the urban poor that has an acute sense of the injustice of its poverty side by side with royal affluence.

Princes of the royal family have vainly attempted to buy the popular legitimacy they lack by patronising the fundamentalist Wahhabi sect which is the dominant local strain of Islam. They first funded Usama bin Laden when he was waging jihad against the Russians in Afghanistan, and then earned his hatred by renouncing him when he turned the organisation they had helped build against the Americans. The perverse result has been that the militant and intolerant message of the Wahhabis has been exported throughout the Muslim world on the back on Saudi oil wealth and has also become the animating spirit of a violent oppression to its royal patrons whose corrupt, luxurious lifestyle is seen as an affront to fundamentalist values. A rational priority for Western strategy in the Arab world would have been to promote a peaceful transition in Saudi Arabia to a more inclusive form of governance and to counter the violent ideology of the Wahhabis. The war on Iraq was not merely a diversion from that priority, but provided a positive incitement to new levels of violence inside Saudi Arabia and supplied a popular struggle in the region for Wahhabi fighters.

The great challenge of this century for the West is whether we can forge a relationship with the Muslim world of tolerance, mutual respect for each other's cultures, and recognition of our common interest in securing peace and prosperity. In four short years the Bush Administration has set back the prospects for success in that project by a generation. Ironically Britain, because of its historic ties and its modern Muslim community, was well placed to be a bridge between the West and Islam, and Tony Blair, who has shown a personal interest in the correspondences between Islam and Christianity, would have been a good architect for such a project. The tragedy of the Iraq war is that by making the international perception of Blair's Britain indistinguishable from that of Bush's America it has disabled us from helping build a positive relationship between the West and the world of Islam.

An Unrequited Special Relationship

Part of Tony Blair's problem in struggling to explain exactly why he embarked on George Bush's adventure in Iraq is that he cannot be honest about his real reason for taking Britain to war – that he did it to keep on the right side of Washington. The more President Bush sinks in public esteem in Britain, the less Tony Blair dare admit he went to war to stay in with the White House. His difficulty in converting his private reason for supporting the war into public justification for it is the stark impossibility of establishing that Britain ever received anything in return for committing to combat a third of the British army. The Bush Administration still blithely sabotages most priorities of British foreign policy from implementing the Kyoto Protocol to setting up the International Criminal Court, slaps 40% tariffs on our steel industry until obliged to withdraw them by the WTO, and humiliates Tony Blair by torpedoing his personal commitment to the Middle East Peace Process. It is essential for a British Prime Minister to have civil working relations with any President of the US, but the total identification of Tony Blair with George Bush would only make sense if they shared the same domestic values and had a common international vision. It was always going to end in tears when one partner came from the mainstream of European social democracy and the other from the right-wing extremes of the Republican Party.

It was not in Tony Blair's nature to spell out bluntly to someone as powerful as the President of the United States that he had got it wrong. Christopher Meyer, who as British Ambassador to Washington sat through the meetings between Blair and Bush before and during the war, has since complained, 'I don't think we had always enough candour in private.' A strong feature of Tony Blair is his total freedom from political ideology, which continually springs unwelcome surprises on the Labour Party. It appeared natural to him to assume that as an electorally successful politician, George Bush would be equally pragmatic. It is only recently he has grasped that he is dealing with an administration packed with ideologues who are happy to pocket Britain as an ally, but have nothing but hostility and contempt for even Tony Blair's lite version of left of centre politics. I once tried to warn him that the Neo Cons around Bush would regard it as a bonus if the war brought down a Labour Government but could not convince him. Last November Tony Blair faced down strong public criticism in order to facilitate a state visit for President Bush, an honour that had not been extended to any previous President in the Queen's long reign. One of Bush's entourage was Karl Rove, his top adviser on political campaigns, who took time off to meet at Westminster with Liam Fox, Chairman of the Conservative Party, and the two strategists have since maintained a close liaison. Blair may have helped Bush defeat Saddam, but the ideologues in his administration are now helping Howard in his attempt to beat Blair.

There were not many lighter moments in the dark history of the Iraq war, but one hilarious interlude was the discomfiture of the Republican Right at discovering their Administration had inadvertently funded a study by the National Science Foundation into the psychological origins of right-wing opinion. It concluded that the reactionary world view is the result of a set of neuroses rooted in 'fear and aggression, dogmatism and the intolerance of ambiguity . . . This intolerance of ambiguity can lead people to cling to the familiar, to arrive at premature conclusions, and to impose simplistic clichés and stereotypes.' For good measure the study noted that President Bush displayed the signature personality of preference for moral certainty and dislike of nuance, and one of the authors speculated this may explain why he had ignored intelligence that contradicted his belief in weapons of mass destruction.

This atmosphere of paranoia and dogmatism in the Bush Administration has prompted successive refugees to escape and write about how awful it was on the inside. Their witness has illuminated the magnificent obsession of the Bush team with Saddam. Paul O'Neill has revealed that in the second week of his administration President Bush chaired a discussion on Iraq at which he instructed General Shelton, Joint Chiefs of Staff, to 'examine our military options'. Even a lengthy meeting on economic policy was closed by Bush with the chillingly irrational observation 'Until we get rid of Saddam Hussein, we won't get rid of [economic] uncertainty.' What is clear from O'Neill's account is that the Bush Administration was determined to occupy Iraq long before the attack on the Twin Towers. The hideous truth is that after 9/11 they did not view international terrorism as a threat as much as an opportunity to secure support for the invasion of Iraq within domestic opinion. This may now have backfired on them with the finding of their own commission on 9/11 that there was 'no credible evidence' to link Iraq to those attacks.

The central objective of Tony Blair's approach on Iraq may have been to stay close to America, but ironically he finds himself identified with a costly occupation which most Americans now reject. This has prompted some of them to question whether Tony Blair has really served them well. John Kerry has pointedly said his priority as President would be to rebuild relations with France and Germany. The *Atlantic* magazine ran an editorial in May under the heading 'The Tragedy of Tony Blair' which complained that America would have done better with 'a candid friend, brave and clear-eyed enough to tell the all-powerful one when it was in error'. In ducking out of challenging the irrational preoccupation of President Bush with Iraq, Tony Blair not only failed Britain, he let down the American people.

The Political Reckoning

This summer the Bush Administration has given ground on just about every one of their major policies on Iraq. It may be too late to recover the credibility of the Coalition Forces after a year of spectacular miscalculations in the conduct of the occupation, but the shift in approach is welcome all the same. They have abandoned heavy-handed tactics such as the siege of Fallujah or 'the mission to kill or capture' Muqtada al-Sadr in Najaf. They have given up on their ambitions for a permanent military presence in Iraq and have accepted the end of 2005 as an exit date. They have handed over much wider sovereignty to the Interim Government than they had previously contemplated, including control over prisons and oil. They have courted UN endorsement for the appointment of the new Iraqi ministers and have pleaded for more international involvement. And the Interim Government is exploring the mobilisation of units of the old Iraqi army, which Paul Bremer disbanded against British protests. None of this would have been imaginable before the spring.

It would be good to put these somersaults in policy down to British pressure, and I am ready to believe that our government has lobbied for all of them. But what has compelled the Bush Administration to shift tactics in Iraq is the pressure it is under in the presidential elections in the US. The American press have concluded that President Bush deluded them over the case for war and have turned on him with aggressive exposures of the error in intelligence and the mistakes of occupation. Three times as many US service personnel have been killed in the course of the occupation as during the invasion and as a result a clear majority of American voters now believe that the war in Iraq was not worth it and almost two to one believe that America is 'getting bogged down'. George Bush has been forced to change course because he is desperate before November to come up with something – anything – that can be presented as a success for his decision to invade Iraq.

Tony Blair's determination to stand shoulder to shoulder with President Bush has inevitably left him sharing the same political problems. He cannot shrug off the photo albums from Abu Ghraib as actions of the US military. We went in to Iraq in a common enterprise with the US military and are jointly and severally liable for abuses that are committed in the name of the Coalition Authority of which we are partners. It was a leaked Red Cross report into torture in Algiers that provided the turning point in French support for the war of occupation. It was the account of the fatal beatings at Hola camp that broke British support for the colonial war in Kenya. The Abu Ghraib photos have similarly destroyed the legitimacy of our presence in Iraq not only among its population but among many British voters as well.

The Iraq war has cast a long shadow over British politics that extends well beyond the division over the merits of the invasion. The yawning gulf between the claims that were made before the war and the reality exposed after the war has prompted even people who supported military action to doubt the competence and credibility of the Government. Writing as the weapons of mass destruction started to prove elusive David Aaronovitch warned, 'If nothing is eventually found I will never believe another thing I am told by our Government. And more to the point, neither will anyone else.' Many citizens have indeed come to that conclusion. The result is a crisis of trust in the Government, with the number of voters who regard it as honest more than halving. Once lost, trust is difficult to regain and its absence infects the credibility of the Government across the board, including the domestic agenda.

This June the local elections delivered what John Prescott characterised as a kicking. A succession of ministers were refreshingly open that Iraq had been a major factor in the electoral drubbing. A number of departed councillors were equally blunt in blaming the loss of their activists and their voters on a war for which they had no responsibility and which many of them had opposed. This is a far cry from the fabled Baghdad Bounce which was predicted last year, when Downing Street still expected military victory in Iraq to bring in a harvest of votes from an admiring nation. The Labour Government is the victim of a tragedy of Greek proportions. It has delivered record investment in the NHS and a dramatic drop in waiting lists; created two million jobs and wiped unemployment from the political agenda; taken a million children and a million pensioners out of life below the poverty line. Yet its remarkable domestic progress has been buried by anger over the Government's decision to join George Bush's war on Iraq.

Labour needs closure on what is turning out to be the most controversial action in British foreign and security policy since Suez. It is hard though to see how the continuing controversy can be resolved without some form of catharsis, and Downing Street has stonewalled every invitation over the past year to concede that its handling of Iraq was anything less than morally sound and technically perfect. It is an immense irony of Iraq that so far the only ministers to have resigned over the debacle were those who opposed war, and the only people to lose their jobs because of it are media figures at the BBC and *Mirror* who criticised it. Tony Blair, at the time of writing, has not even admitted the intelligence was fundamentally flawed. On the contrary whenever he speaks about Iraq it is all too plain that in his heart he remains convinced that he was right, and if only Britain can 'hold its nerve' and 'see it through' the position in Iraq will get better and public perceptions of whether the war was justified will shift. For the sake of the people of Iraq I sincerely hope that his optimism about their country this year is better founded than it turned out to be last year, but I doubt whether that alone will heal the wounds which the war has inflicted on British politics. Nothing that happens now will change the history that the war was launched on a false prospectus, the occupation was ill-prepared and the brutality at Abu Ghraib was a disgrace.

If Tony Blair wants to win back those whose support he has forfeited because of Iraq, he must convince them that lessons have been learnt. A sensible starting point would be to ditch the new doctrine of pre-emptive strike. If Iraq in reality had no weapons of mass destruction, we had no right to attack it in order to pre-empt their use, and Tony Blair needs to rule out repeating the error of launching a war for which the only basis is dodgy intelligence. Then he could recommit Britain to the pursuit of multilateral solutions to issues of peace and security. For the Kosovo campaign we had the backing of the great majority of the Security Council, all of NATO, the whole European Union and every single one of Serbia's neighbours. On Iraq we passed none of those tests of international opinion, and Tony Blair must confirm that Britain will never again commence military action which is neither in legitimate self-defence nor with international support. The last step goes beyond the particular case of Iraq. Tony Blair needs to assert that British foreign policy will be run by London, not Washington. If George Bush should be re-elected it will be all the more important that Tony gives a clear signal that second time around he will give more weight to public opinion in Britain than Republican instincts in the White House.

At the Labour Conference after the war, Tony Blair was unrepentant in insisting, 'I would take the same decision again.' That is precisely what worries those who could not vote Labour in June because of his decision last time round. If he wants them to come home to Labour he must find a way of assuring them that Iraq was unique, and that if they vote for him next time they will not find that they have paved the way for another unnecessary, unpopular war made in Washington.

9

Where Do We Go From Here?

It would be easy to end the book on the previous chapter, but that would be an evasion. Iraq has provided a catharsis for the Labour Party. The repercussions of the shock it has provided have released healthy questioning of New Labour thinking on issues that come much closer to home than foreign affairs. It would be wrong to conclude this account of how I drifted apart from New Labour without offering a personal statement of the new directions which would furnish the centre-left with a radical but popular vision.

There is a consensus from top to bottom of the Labour family that we urgently need that new sense of direction. As I write the briefings are loud in their promise of renewal of The Project. This indicates a welcome recognition of the change that must be made if the government is to recapture momentum and the Labour Party is to mend the erosion of its political support. The only troubling element is the implicit assumption of both those placing the briefing and those lapping it up that the renewal of a mass party is the business of the man at the top. This is revealing evidence of the way our democracy is no longer perceived as a process belonging to the many who participate in it, but the property of the few celebrity politicians. Political parties do not achieve renewal by reshuffling staff in their leader's office, but by changing the culture, priorities and direction of the organisation. In fairness to Tony Blair, the paradigm shift that Labour needs cannot be achieved by one member, but needs the contribution of all.

The first modernisation of Labour a decade ago was a success because it caught a tide among members and supporters who were impatient of electoral failure, tired of sterile debates on old remedies and hungry for imaginative, novel solutions. Any credible renewal of that project must now capture the current tide of opinion in its centre-left constituency. It is not an ebb tide from modernisation. It is convenient to the leadership to characterise their critics as traditionalists who want to revert to old tribal beliefs, but in reality few members have any nostalgia for the eighties. Those who are most disappointed by the timidity of the second term are those who were most supportive of modernisation. The litmus test of any renewal is whether it can energise and motivate the very people who supported the modernisation of the Labour Party but now feel disillusioned that in government there has not been the same radical boldness brought to the modernisation of Britain.

Renewal must be about more than reviving party political support for Labour. It must also offer a prospect of giving politics back a sense of excitement, and rekindling the dwindling interest in the political system. That means a return to value-based politics. A large part of New Labour's current problems is the perception, which it has brought upon itself, that it is good at producing a spate of performance indicators, public service agreements and delivery targets, but less strong at generating vision, values and ideology. There is common sense in Tony Blair's constant emphasis on better services. No government should expect to be re-elected if it cannot prove that it has provided better hospitals and better schools. But although it is necessary for politicians to be competent managers, it is not a sufficient condition for a successful political movement. Political choice is about the kind of society in which voters want to live, and the good society is defined not by its pass rate on performance indicators, but by the values that shape it.

The crucial issue for the centre-left, and for British democracy, is that we put values and ideology back at the heart of political debate. Margaret Thatcher gave ideology a bad reputation by creating the impression that conviction politics meant turning a deaf ear to any contrary opinion. New Labour's excessive pragmatism is a reaction to her excessive dogmatism. But it is perfectly possible to maintain personal convictions within an ideology of pluralism that is respectful of other opinions and values. It is not only possible, it is essential. Ideology provides political parties with cohesion and gives government direction. Value-based politics are crucial if we are to revive the confidence of the public in parliamentary democracy.

What follows is a very personal statement of what I see as the central values that the centre-left should offer in the twenty-first century as the basis of a good society. They incorporate values such as equality and democracy which are embedded in the roots of the centre-left in the eighteenth-century Enlightenment, but they also embrace values such as pluralism and cosmopolitanism which must be part of any progressive response to the modern world. It is not a manifesto and it is therefore not a programmatic list of policy prescriptions, although it does point up a number of priorities. If we first establish a clear vision of the society in which we want to live, it will be easier then to identify the policy steps that will build its foundations.

Margaret Thatcher famously observed, 'There is no such thing as society.' In context, what she meant was that society has no independent personality of its own and therefore cannot be expected to feel any obligation to look after those who will not look after themselves. In that sense she had a point. Society is only as good as its individual members, and a society entirely consisting of Margaret Thatchers would certainly not place a high priority on support for their weaker neighbours. But, fortunately, the range of human instincts and emotional incentives is richer and more diverse than can be satisfied by her brand of individual materialism. The great mass of humanity would not relish a life without the society of others. The human being is a sociable animal. We derive our sense of identity, of status and of self-esteem from our association with others, and for that we need a cohesive society.

It is not police and law and courts that make societies strong. These are essential attributes of society, but they address its malfunctions. What makes a society strong is its sense of social cohesion, the belief of all its members in their basic equality. That is why progressive political forces who value society treasure those institutions which reinforce the sense of equality – an open democracy in which everyone's vote is of equal worth; a free Health Service in which patients get equal treatment depending on their medical need; an education system in which everyone can develop their full potential. Each of these assertions of human equality is a valuable balance to the unequal relations of the market economy. Commercialising the provision of public services through privatisation or marketising them through health charges or education fees erodes this public realm.

Equality, though, is meaningless unless the opportunity to participate to the full in society is a reality for every citizen. Social cohesion is only possible if all members of society believe in its basic fairness. That cannot occur while large numbers know that they can barely afford subsistence and are hopelessly priced out of the consumerism that much of the population takes for granted. I remember a jawdropping conversation in the 1997 election with a constituent who worked as a security guard and told me that he was really looking forward to the minimum wage, not to increase his income, but to enable him to make ends meet on sixty hours' work a week instead of his present eighty hours, and to spend the time saved with his family. I did not attempt to convince him that he was then living in a fair society.

Social fairness is the natural complement to civic equality. Both should be part of the core values of a centre-left party. Fairness in the distribution of income and wealth is an essential feature of a good society. The citizens of fair societies tend to enjoy better health, to suffer less crime and to benefit from wider opportunities through greater social mobility. And fair societies are more open societies, in which citizens mix in the same public spaces and share broadly comparable life experiences.

Despite these powerful attractions of a fair society, New Labour is curiously diffident about proclaiming its commitment to fairness. Its commitment is real enough. This government has been the most redistributionist since Lloyd George's and has brought about a real boost to the weekly income of the poorest households. But Labour keeps such progressive policies under the counter in a back room where members who know where to find them can slip in and admire them while the spin doctors are not looking. There are profound political handicaps from this strategy of trying to deliver social justice by stealth. Labour misses the opportunity to consolidate its core support among the very voters who have benefited most out of this government, because they rarely hear its ministers talking about what Labour has done for them. It is commonplace to come across less well-off families whose weekly budget has been immensely improved by the new system of tax credits, but have no idea that this is not the result of the obscure working of the tax system, but the direct consequence of a deliberate political decision. It would be a bitter irony if they first discovered how much they owed to Labour when an incoming Conservative government took it away.

The wider political handicap is that Labour is committing large amounts of public funds to fighting poverty without any effort to convince the public that this is the best investment they can make in the health of their society. Ultimately, this is not a sustainable strategy. The post-war settlement established by the Attlee government survived for a generation because it was founded on consensus support for a welfare society. The post-Thatcher settlement established by the Blair government will be more fragile, and potentially more ephemeral, if it is not built on consensus support for a fair society.

The immediate problem from the failure to mobilise public opinion for a campaign against poverty is that, despite progress under Labour, so much remains to be done. By European standards Britain is still spectacularly unequal in the spread of household income. Germany, France, Italy, Benelux and all of Scandinavia have managed to avoid the extremes of poverty and wealth which characterise Britain, while for the most part achieving higher average incomes. Mobility between the social classes in Britain may actually have peaked in the heady days of the sixties and seventies and may now be declining. A recent study by the LSE concluded that children born to low-income households in 1970 were more likely than children born in the fifties to be trapped in the same low income and poor job prospects as their parents.

It is no criticism of the good start that Labour has made in its measures against poverty to recognise that we will only deliver European standards of fairness if we are prepared to be even more bold. The first step must be to make more ambitious use of the National Minimum Wage. It was a valuable innovation and a logical complement to Labour's strategy of encouraging unemployed claimants and single parents back into the workplace, which required many to enter low paid jobs. But the numbers benefiting from the protection of the National Minimum Wage are barely half the two million which was expected at the time of its introduction. A step change in the level of the minimum wage is necessary if it is to fulfil its intended scope, and entirely justified if it is to provide an adequate subsistence income.

The next step must be to sustain the expansion of child benefits and tax credits to families with children. This government deserves credit for increases that set new records by British standards. We must shed the British double standard that labels spending on welfare benefits as wasted, but expenditure on health or education as a valid priority. There is an entire library of literature on the correlation between poverty and ill-health. Switching spending from welfare to health may increase the capacity for surgical procedures, but only by producing a less healthy population. The same is true of education. The association between poverty and educational low attainment is one of the fixed poles of social statistics. If we are serious about widening opportunity then we could usefully amend the famous Blair mantra to 'Education, education, and child poverty reduction'.

The market economy is without rival in releasing initiative and rewarding innovation. It therefore is a powerful mechanism for wealth generation. Left unchecked, though, the market economy creates two fundamental problems. The first is that it can be inimical to the values of equality and fairness and therefore corrosive of social cohesion. The second is that an unregulated market is not a stable device for perpetual motion. Success accumulates market power which then destroys competition, and failure can also be cumulative and end in recession. For these reasons, political debate since the Industrial Revolution has repeatedly turned on how to manage the economy to promote its own efficient functioning and to protect the wider interests of society.

In the present generation the balance between social intervention and the free market has been unhinged by the dominance in orthodox economic theory of an aggressive market fundamentalism. The neo-liberal consensus dictates that maximising shareholder return is the prime objective of business organisation, that individual self-interest is the sole motivation of economic activity, and that social institutions, such as governments, should shrink to a minimalist role of light regulation, non-interference in markets and low taxation. This neo-liberal fundamentalism inverts the common-sense order of priorities. In its ideology, society exists to provide the framework for the economy, rather than the economy existing to sustain society. Goods and services are produced to provide profit, rather than profit providing the means to the production of goods and services. Part of the malaise of Western democracy is that this economic consensus commands no public consensus because it offers no account of the economy as a means of meeting human needs. Outside its citadels of Wall Street and Chicago University, the new economic orthodoxy is reviled by popular unrest and buried under bestsellers denouncing it. There can rarely have been a moment in the history of political thought when its dominant economic thesis was regarded with such popular distaste.

Neo-liberalism provokes a populist reaction against it because it offers such a determinist and stultifying account of the richness of human behaviour. Most of us are motivated by a complex web of incentives. Financial reward is part of it, but so also is job satisfaction, social status and obligation to our colleagues. Few of us would volunteer that it is only greed that gets us out of bed in the morning. Traders in Wall Street itself were humbled by the New York firefighters attending the burning Twin Towers who performed remarkable acts of heroism not for financial reward but out of duty to the public and solidarity to their colleagues.

The neo-liberal prescription not only lacks popular appeal; it is also short on practical examples of its economic success, perhaps because it undervalues human capital. Its nostrums of low taxation and deregulation when applied by the Bush Administration have resulted in rising unemployment and the largest Federal deficit since the last neo-liberal Administration under Reagan. The World Bank discovered in the mid-nineties that those countries on whom they had visited Structural Adjustment Programmes of neo-liberal priorities had turned in lower growth rates than those countries that had been spared them. The reality is that wealth generation is a social activity requiring corporate companies to organise collaborative endeavour. Sustainable growth requires a stable society, collective investment in social capital such as education and transport, and public regulation to ensure common standards of probity, safety and consumer protection. This is even more important in the modern knowledge economy. For creative companies at the cutting edge of innovation the skills, initiative and teamwork of their staff are more valuable assets than their financial capitalisation, and the quality of the national education system is more important to their location than the relative level of company taxation.

There is therefore an opening for an alternative economic analysis that can both command public support and more comprehensively account for the many diverse ingredients that are part of economic success. The challenge to the centre-left is whether it can fill that vacuum. For one brief moment the stakeholder economy surfaced as an organising principle of the Third Way. The stakeholder economy recognises that success of a commercial enterprise is not solely the creation of its shareholders. Its workforce, suppliers and local community all make a contribution to its success and also have a stake in the prosperity of the enterprise, with which these days they are more likely to have a longer-term relationship than most shareholders. The stakeholder economy provides a positive rationale for the constructive role of trade unions in organising the collective views of the workforce as social partners with management.

It was an exciting interlude in which the possibility emerged of a coherent left prospectus for non-marketised relations and a credible alternative to the short-termism of shareholder value. It was also a brief interlude. The concept had surfaced in a speech by Tony Blair in Tokyo and was evaporating by the time of his stopover in Singapore. New Labour had already discovered that sticking to such a radical departure in economic thinking would require them to challenge both the business establishment and the conventional wisdom that shareholder value is the paramount measure of commercial efficiency. Those of us who had been put up in the media to promote the new line were perplexed to find that it was we who somehow seemed to be off message.

This retreat was disabling because it left New Labour with no distinctive economic narrative. A coherent centre-left project requires an economic analysis that incorporates its social ethos and reflects its commitment to fulfilling human needs. It must start from the proposition that the economy is not the property of any single set of participants in it, but it is a public good which requires to be managed in the public interest. Embracing such a proposition would help New Labour find the confidence to be ambitious where at present it has been cautious.

In the first place it could be more robust in defending the case for public regulation than credulously accepting the neo-liberal demands for deregulation. This government on coming into office accelerated the fast-track mechanism introduced by their predecessors to facilitate the parliamentary process of deregulation. As the Tories never tire of reminding us, the total number of such deregulation orders is tiny (currently less than fifty) compared to the thousands of regulations on the statute book. The explanation for this is not that the mechanism is faulty, but that upon examination most regulations turn out to serve a valid public interest. Nobody was louder in his demands for less regulation than Ken Lay, Chief Executive of Enron, and nothing better demonstrated the public interest in more regulation of accounting standards than the ignominious and expensive collapse of his company.

The immediate priority for more regulation in the public interest is in pension provision. This is currently a classic case where the operation of the market is producing an outcome that it is contrary to the public interest. It is entirely logical in its own interest for an individual company to reduce the cost of its pension contributions, and if its rivals are also cutting that cost the market will exert downward competitive pressure on pension provision. But the net result is a big social problem as Britain faces a population living longer on less. There would be wide public support for more regulation to protect pension rights and to discourage companies from reducing their corporate contribution to pension funds at the very time when the demand on those funds is increasing.

New Labour should also be more ambitious in promoting public intervention in the protection of the environment. The market is incapable of respecting a common resource such as the environment, which provides no price signal to express the cost of its erosion nor to warn of the long-term dangers of its destruction. Yet every participant in the market will experience a loss in their quality of life if the cumulative effect of their activities is to degrade their common environment. Strategies to preserve and to restore a healthy environment cannot be subcontracted to the operation of the market but require conscious political decisions.

Environmentalism is not anti-technology. On the contrary, it needs technological innovation to deliver its goals. Traditionally, regulation has sought to encourage incremental change on short-time horizons but it is possible that we may have a better prospect of stimulating innovative solutions if we focus on securing step changes within a longer target period. The California mandate requiring the motor industry to produce cars with zero emissions over a decade is an encouraging example of what is possible. At the time the mandate was adopted in the early nineties no one knew how to produce commercial cars with zero emissions but the regulation has obliged the motor industry to find the new technological solutions that otherwise would not have been explored.

Lastly, a recognition of the social character of wealth creation should induce some healthy scepticism of the new Atlantic culture of ascribing heroic status to top executives. This has found its most unpopular expression in the award to a few chief executives of extravagant pay packages, that in some cases exceed not just the salary of the Prime Minister, but the ministerial pay bill of the entire Cabinet. Perhaps we should admire the altruism of the companies who shell out such gold-plated packages as there is no objective evidence that their corporate performance is any better as a result. Indeed, there is some evidence that it may even be worse. One study concluded that throughout the nineties most of the ten US companies with the highest paid chief executives actually turned in a performance below the national average. Even when an executive is sacked he is paid a bonus for failure that looks like a lottery jackpot, with sometimes the added insult that his pension is secured by plundering the same company pension fund which, while a manager, he had claimed could not meet its commitments to his workforce.

Looting on this scale has no commercial justification. It simply reflects the powerful bargaining position of the chief executives who extract it. It is a classic abuse of corporate power which comprehensively destroys any sense that the people at the top are partners in the same team as the rest of the workforce. This is a case where a more robust approach by New Labour would be welcome in Middle England which pays for this greed out of their shares and would support measures to discourage it.

Modern society welcomes diversity. Conformity is no longer valued as a virtue, but originality and self-expression are admired. People are more mobile between the communities in which they live and the jobs in which they are employed, and as a result are more open-minded in their social attitudes. Our political system needs to adapt to the greater pluralism of opinion in the society it seeks to represent. The British people have already decided for themselves that they want a pluralist society. Forty years ago, at the time of the first Wilson government, a majority of electors would say they strongly identified with a specific political party but today only one in seven are willing to express that commitment. For most of the population a political party is just for polling day, not for a lifetime. The paradox is that in Wilson's time the Labour Party was itself more pluralist than now and its senior figures had distinctive views of their own which mirrored the spread of opinion across the broad church of the Labour vote. By contrast New Labour aspires to a uniformity of view that is badly behind the times for the individualist, diverse, pluralist society it seeks to govern.

New Labour's stress on discipline is an understandable reaction to a media that is constantly hovering ready to pounce on the slightest hint of independent thinking as evidence of a split. As a result New Labour has drawn itself up into the political equivalent of the regimental square of the army of the British Empire. The problem is that this is an essentially defensive strategy. It baffles the press in its search for mischief, but does not enable Labour to enthuse the public with a new political vision or to demonstrate that they have elected politicians with passionate beliefs and original minds. As a result the electoral challenge for Labour is not winning next time, but persuading enough people to vote to make the victory legitimate. An essential part of renewal must be for New Labour to permit its MPs to throw away their pagers and to encourage its ministers to speak more often from the heart than from the party line. I do not dispute that in the short run there will be some difficult passages with the press, but in the long run confidence in parliamentary democracy will only revive if the voters believe that politicians are saying what they think, rather than suspect they are saying what they are told to think.

Election to government on a dwindling turnout is not adequate for Labour because we need the legitimacy of popular support if we are not simply to sit in office, but to redistribute power and wealth to the many from the few. A number of natural consequences flow from the commitment of the centre-left to a pluralist democracy.

The first is that Number 10 needs to rediscover some of its original enthusiasm for working with other parties. Paddy Ashdown's diaries tellingly record how the promises of cooperation made in Opposition faded as Tony Blair discovered the security of a large parliamentary majority. For a while there was an effort to pioneer new working relations across parties but today the Joint Cabinet Committee no longer meets and Tony Blair relies on machine politics to deliver the Labour majority. This is a perfectly satisfactory way of getting business through the Commons, where the Labour machine has an invincible majority. It is much less satisfactory as a means of changing the political culture of Britain to establish a new foundation of centre-left values, which is unlikely to be achieved on a purely party political basis.

Where Labour disagrees with the Liberal Democrats we should be robust in asserting our differences. But where we have common ground, such as on the constitution, public services or Europe, we should not be afraid to demonstrate to the public that we are willing to work with like-minded people beyond our own party.

The next consequence of our commitment to democracy must be a continuing priority to modernise our constitution. I have already written in previous pages on the importance of a largely elected second chamber as a partner to the Commons in restoring public respect for Parliament and do not need to rehearse these arguments again. An equal priority must be to revive local democracy which has been under siege for a generation, first as a result of the assault of Thatcherism on any centre of resistance and subsequently from the disastrous experiments of Blairism with the option of the mayoral model in place of existing councils. The crucial issue here is not so much to introduce yet another change in structure, but the restitution to local government of the freedom which once enabled local democracy to pioneer the introduction of new forms of public service provision, such as comprehensive education. A distribution of power which deprives local democracy of their role as pathfinders and confines them to the function of administering the policies of central administration will leave Britain with less possibility of creative solutions and a more uniform political culture.

A healthy democracy also requires independent political parties. Parliament needs political parties before an election to provide candidates standing on a broadly consistent platform and after election to supply government and Opposition. Political parties need cash. Indeed, they need cash more than ever, partly because the decline in the number of volunteer activists has created pressure for more professional paid staff. If we want independent, political parties that put the public interest first, then we should join the rest of Europe in the funding of political parties from the public purse. The danger of funding by private donations is not the corruption of government by donors hoping to buy favours. The real problem is the more subtle corruption of political debate as parties are obliged to adopt political programmes that cannot be seen to challenge the interests of the wealthy or of big business. The extent to which money, and the wealthy backers who provide it, now disfigures US democracy is an awesome warning of the risks from not introducing an impartial and capped source of political funding. If we want political parties to pay equal attention to the interest of the many in society then we must rescue them from their growing dependency on a few very wealthy backers.

But the acid test of any commitment to pluralism is whether we are prepared to allow Britain a proportional electoral system that returns a pluralist Parliament. It is a test which the supposed modernisers in Number 10 have been markedly reluctant to apply to themselves. True, this government has covered the map of Britain with other institutions elected on systems of proportional representation – Scotland, Wales, Northern Ireland and London – but Westminster remains the odd one out. The increasing pluralism within the electorate has rendered the first-past-the-post system a liability to the legitimacy of Parliament. Only half a century ago, in 1951, over two hundred Members of Parliament were still elected with the support of a majority of their electorate. In the last General Election not a single MP was elected by a majority of their electors. Most people in Britain are represented by MPs for whom they did not vote, and all MPs represent constituencies most of whose electors did not vote for them.

The damage, though, from the present system is not confined to its inability to produce a Parliament that reflects how the nation voted. Even worse is its disabling effect on political debate. The reason why every election campaign is fought only on the issues that matter to Mondeo Man, Worcester Woman and the rest of the Pebbledash People is that they are the only electors whose votes really count. Increasingly, the campaigners hone their message to the 1 per cent of the electorate whose swing votes in the target constituencies decide which party is in government and which in Opposition. It puzzles me that many of my colleagues who complain that Labour's core voters are ignored also stoutly defend the first-past-the-post system which is the reason why core voters are neglected.

The image, language and policies of the Labour leadership are angled to the right because they know that the only electoral battleground that matters is for the centre. A more pluralist electoral system that obliged them to fight for every vote would promptly produce a more diverse campaign pitch. The programme of Sweden's Social Democrats is radicalised by the knowledge that proportional representation obliges them to look to the left as well as to the centre for votes. Their record vote in 2002 was entirely built on a swing to them not from the centre but from the party to the left of them. We also will only secure pluralist politics if we adopt a pluralist electoral system that obliges politicians to take every voter equally seriously.

Globalisation renders the modern world a challenging place. Most of humanity derive their sense of identity from affinity with others of the same ethnic roots, of the same regional culture or belonging to the same revealed religion. Unfortunately, many assert their identity by celebrating differences from other groups, and feel threatened at a time of accelerating commercial, cultural and electronic contact with people on the other side of the globe. Hence the phenomenon that the growth in foreign contact is paralleled by a rise in religious fundamentalism and ethnic tension.

As the international dimension increasingly dominates politics, the old dividing lines between left and right will evolve over the twenty-first century into a parallel divide between cosmopolitans and chauvinists. Reactionary political forces will be distinguished by their attempts at isolation from the modern world and their nostalgia for a false, romanticised past world. They will resent the pressures to reach international agreement as a threat and are more likely to detain than welcome the stranger in their midst. By contrast, progressive political forces will be outward-looking and comfortable with building international partnerships. They will welcome foreign contacts abroad and at home as enriching rather than threatening.

It is no longer possible to separate into neat compartments domestic and foreign policy. Economic prosperity turns on growth in trade, and technology transfer comes with success in attracting inward investment. Security depends on the strength of military alliances and regional structures to maintain stability. Even issues that once were regarded as the very stuff of domestic politics, such as the struggle for law and order against organised crime, now need to be tackled with international cooperation. Only a cosmopolitan approach which makes a success of relations abroad is likely to produce success in resolving challenges at home. I still hear discussion of British foreign policy in terms of the pursuit of narrow national interest, as if we were living in the age of Metternich or Palmerston. In reality, in today's interdependent, interconnected world, the interest of the international community is also our national interest.

This requires a gearshift in the way we regard the relationship of our country to the rest of the world. It is in our own interest to develop a strong international community that provides an ordered structure for fair trade and the discipline to address common problems such as global warming. Membership of such a community necessarily brings with it, in the New Labour mantra, both rights and responsibilities. It would be a mockery of the very concept of a community if we were to tolerate within it the poverty, hunger and illiteracy that exists only a few flying hours from our own affluent and obese societies. Accelerating technological innovation widens the gulf that divides the world by its life experiences. There are now more telephones in Manhattan than in the whole of sub-Saharan Africa, and while we talk of living in the era of information technology, most of humanity has never received or made a telephone call.

The current rules of trade both reinforce that divide and expose the double standards of the West. We insist that poorer countries permit free trade in their markets for our industrialised goods but simultaneously insist that we retain protection of our markets against their agricultural products. Even worse, North America and Europe spend more on subsidising the farmers of their prosperous continents than their entire development budgets for all the poor countries on the face of the globe. The rebellion of the rest of the world at Cancun demonstrated the impossibility of building agreement on such gross injustice.

The key to a strong international community is a United Nations of authority and legitimacy. But the Security Council cannot continue to command legitimacy if its permanent members reflect the world as it was in the mid-twentieth century, not the world as it is in the twenty-first century. For half a dozen years haggling has continued over the proposal that new permanent members should be recruited from the unrepresented continents of Latin America, Asia and Africa. A more representative Security Council which included as permanent members Brazil, South Africa and India, would be harder for Washington to brush aside. The authority of the United Nations would also be enhanced if the Secretary General was authorised to submit an annual review of outstanding Security Council Resolutions. This would go some way to answering the accusations of double standards that resolutions on the Middle East and Kashmir are ignored for decades, while resolutions to which the West is committed, such as Iraq, receive a higher priority.

For Britain the most immediate test of internationalism is whether we can make a success of our relations with our neighbours with whom we share our continent of Europe. If we cannot form a healthy working relationship with our nearest neighbours we are unlikely to achieve it with peoples on the far side of the globe. And the combined strength of an entire continent acting together gives us much greater leverage in global negotiations, such as on trade and environment, than we could hope to exert on our own. The central fallacy of the Eurosceptics is to rail at the limitations on national sovereignty from agreements in Europe. The real limitations on national sovereignty arise from the new realities of the modern world – transnational economic production, the importance of trade as an engine of growth, global threats to our security and environment. The European Union did not create these new challenges but is a logical response to them.

What depresses me about the British debate on Europe is its pitiable lack of confidence. It is always so desperately defeatist. We are perpetually on our guard against being tricked by one of our partners, and live in constant fear of all fourteen of them ganging up to ambush us and to insist that we do something terribly non-British, like eat straight bananas or drink our gin from round bottles. The great irony is that those who are most suspicious of Europe are the most romantic about Britain's imperial past. In reality nothing could be further from the optimism and self-belief of those who mapped and settled the far corners of the globe than the timidity of those who shrink from the other side of the Channel as a dark, hostile Continent hung about with traps.

The big European test for the government is how it puts some momentum back into the campaign to persuade the British people that it is in their interests to share the same currency as the customers to whom they sell the bulk of their exports. At one of the last Cabinet meetings I attended I expressed concern that an attack on Iraq which put us at odds with our major European partners would rule out a successful referendum for the rest of this Parliament. Gordon Brown, who sat next to me at every meeting, asked me after I had finished, 'Do you really think it is as bad as that?' If anything, it is worse than

I feared. Tony Blair has taken such a battering over the vanishing weapons of mass destruction and the Hutton inquiry into the suicide of David Kelly that he is in no position to appeal to the British public to trust his judgement on the euro. He has exhausted his stock of credibility and trust in delivering Bush's strategic designs on Iraq, and has none left to secure Britain's interest in membership of the euro. Nothing has been heard of the joint roadshow which he and Gordon Brown promised from the same platform the day after the Treasury assessment was unveiled, and the media has been briefed that nothing more will be heard of it.

Yet the rendezvous with destiny cannot be postponed indefinitely. After all, Gordon Brown's statement included a commitment to revisit the assessment in his Budget next spring. At the time this was claimed as a victory for Number 10 in its negotiations with the Treasury to keep alive the possibility of a referendum next year, but probably now appears in Number 10 as a ghastly embarrassment. There is, though, a simple solution: it is for Gordon Brown to announce a target date, such as January 2008, and to commit Britain to be ready for membership by then. This would pave the way for a referendum after the next election, but more immediately it would free government ministers to start speaking up for the euro without the disabling equivocation of our present stance.

The successful societies of this century will not confine cosmopolitanism to their relationships abroad. They will also practise it at home. Those countries who will adapt best to the internationalism of the modern age will be those who have already built diverse multicultural societies.

This should come easily to the British whose history is one of successive waves of different ethnic immigration and new cultural contacts. London was first established as a capital city by the Romans, who were in turn driven out by Saxons and Angles from Germany. The great cathedrals of England were mostly built by Norman Bishops from France and the religion practised in them was secured by a Dutch prince. The Victorians chose Richard the Lionheart to sit defiantly astride his steed outside Parliament, as a permanent symbol of British courage, but in real life he spoke French and might have failed our new English tests for citizenship. It is not purity that has given Britain its character but diversity.

In modern times the cosmopolitan character of Britain has been enhanced by increased migration and the pathways opened up for it by our historic ties around the globe. London is a microcosm of the global village. It is home to over thirty ethnic communities of at least ten thousand residents each. Every evening over a hundred languages are spoken over dinner by residents of our capital city. Such ethnic diversity is an inevitable consequence of globalisation and the population movements that accompany it. The states that will best retain their cohesion through this century will be those that welcome new communities as strengthening their economy and enriching their culture. Those states that will experience the greatest tension in coming to terms with the modern world will be those who struggle to preserve an ethnic or religious monoculture.

For Britain the new migration is essential compensation for the declining workforce from the indigenous population among whom the birthrate has now fallen below the replacement rate. Last year the Treasury released a parliamentary answer which estimated that the economic activity of first-generation migrants alone contributes an additional 10 per cent to GDP – double the contribution of North Sea oil. But a strong multicultural society at home is also a major asset to Britain as it seeks commercial and cultural networks in a multipolar world. Cosmopolitanism on the domestic scene is the best foundation for a cosmopolitan approach to the wider world.

I have set out a prospectus for a cohesive, pluralist society pursuing partnership in its economy and in its dealings with other countries. Not everyone will agree with this depiction of the essential virtues of the good society. That is fine. It does not pretend to be an authoritative, far less a comprehensive, description. It is an unashamedly personal statement of the priorities. I cannot argue for pluralism and object if others do not entirely agree with me. The vital issue is that we restore values, vision and ideology to the centre stage of political debate.

EPILOGUE

The year since I resigned has been personally more fulfilling. I read books rather than Executive summaries. I take our dogs for long country tramps rather than quick marches round the block. I have my coffee after dinner with Gaynor rather than with a red box.

Leftist analysis by tradition tends to the gloomy rather than the uplifting end of the spectrum. It catalogues the wickedness of the world and is cynical about attempts to ameliorate it. Perhaps because I am relieved to have got back a life of my own, I am optimistic about the future, including the prospects for the centre-left. We have a Labour government in power that after seven years in office remains ahead of its rivals as the most popular party on nearly every domestic policy area. This is a position with which most previous governments, and all previous Labour governments, would willingly have traded places.

What Labour needs is more confidence to assert our own values and more ambition in the policies we build on them.

What still troubles me about Iraq is not just that the war was a spectacular mistake, but that the Labour government persists in refusing to accept that it was a mistake at all. Neither Tony Blair nor Britain will be able to put the war on Iraq into the history books unless we recognise that mistakes were made. This is not simply a matter of putting the record straight. The reason why it is important to face up to mistakes is that only then is it possible to learn lessons from them. In the case of Iraq it is essential we learn the lessons that will prevent Britain ever again committing troops to military action on the basis of a false prospectus written in Washington.

APPENDIX

RESIGNATION SPEECH,
17 MARCH 2003

This is the first time for 20 years that I have addressed the House from the back benches. I must confess that I had forgotten how much better the view is from here.

None of those twenty years were more enjoyable or more rewarding than the past two, in which I have had the immense privilege of serving this House as Leader of the House, which were made all the more enjoyable, Mr Speaker, by the opportunity of working closely with you.

It was frequently the necessity for me as Leader of the House to talk my way out of accusations that a statement had been preceded by a press interview. On this occasion I can say with complete confidence that no press interview has been given before this statement.

I have chosen to address the House first on why I cannot support a war without international agreement or domestic support.

The present Prime Minister is the most successful leader of the Labour party in my lifetime. I hope that he will continue to be the leader of our party, and I hope that he will continue to be successful. I have no sympathy with, and I will give no comfort to, those who want to use this crisis to displace him. I applaud the heroic efforts that the Prime Minister has made in trying to secure a second resolution. I do not think that anybody could have done better than the Foreign

Secretary in working to get support for a second resolution within the Security Council. But the very intensity of those attempts underlines how important it was to succeed. Now that those attempts have failed, we cannot pretend that getting a second resolution was of no importance.

France has been at the receiving end of bucket loads of commentary in recent days. It is not France alone that wants more time for inspections. Germany wants more time for inspections; Russia wants more time for inspections; indeed, at no time have we signed up even the minimum necessary to carry a second resolution. We delude ourselves if we think that the degree of international hostility is all the result of President Chirac. The reality is that Britain is being asked to embark on a war without agreement in any of the international bodies of which we are a leading partner – not NATO, not the European Union and, now, not the Security Council. To end up in such diplomatic weakness is a serious reverse. Only a year ago, we and the United States were part of a coalition against terrorism that was wider and more diverse than I would ever have imagined possible.

History will be astonished at the diplomatic miscalculations that led so quickly to the disintegration of that powerful coalition. The US can afford to go it alone, but Britain is not a superpower. Our interests are best protected not by unilateral action but by multilateral agreement and a world order governed by rules. Yet tonight the international partnerships most important to us are weakened: the European Union is divided; the Security Council is in stalemate. Those are heavy casualties of a war in which a shot has yet to be fired.

I have heard some parallels between military action in these circumstances and the military action that we took in Kosovo. There was no doubt about the multilateral support that we had for the action that we took in Kosovo. It was supported by NATO; it was supported by the European Union; it was supported by every single one of the seven neighbours in the region. France and Germany were our active allies. It is precisely because we have none of that support in this case that it was all the more important to get agreement in the Security Council as the last hope of demonstrating international agreement. The legal basis for our action in Kosovo was the need to respond to an urgent and compelling humanitarian crisis. Our difficulty in getting support this time is that neither the international community nor the British public is persuaded that there is an urgent and compelling reason for this military action in Iraq.

The threshold for war should always be high. None of us can predict the death toll of civilians from the forthcoming bombardment of Iraq, but the US warning of a bombing campaign that will 'shock and awe' makes it likely that casualties will be numbered at least in the thousands. I am confident that British servicemen and women will acquit themselves with professionalism and with courage. I hope that they all come back. I hope that Saddam, even now, will quit Baghdad and avert war, but it is false to argue that only those who support war support our troops. It is entirely legitimate to support our troops while seeking an alternative to the conflict that will put those troops at risk. Nor is it fair to accuse those of us who want longer for inspections of not having an alternative strategy. For four years as Foreign Secretary I was partly responsible for the Western strategy of containment. Over the past decade that strategy destroyed more weapons than in the Gulf war, dismantled Iraq's nuclear weapons programme and halted Saddam's medium and long-range missiles programmes. Iraq's military strength is now less than half its size than at the time of the last Gulf war.

Ironically, it is only because Iraq's military forces are so weak that we can even contemplate its invasion. Some advocates of conflict claim that Saddam's forces are so weak, so demoralised and so badly equipped that the war will be over in a few days. We cannot base our military strategy on the assumption that Saddam is weak and at the same time justify pre-emptive action on the claim that he is a threat. Iraq probably has no weapons of mass destruction in the commonly understood sense of the term − namely a credible device capable of being delivered against a strategic city target. It probably still has biological toxins and battlefield chemical munitions, but it has had them since the 1980s when US companies sold Saddam anthrax agents and the then British government approved chemical and munitions factories. Why is it now so urgent that we should take military action to disarm a military capacity that has been there for twenty years, and which we helped to create? Why is it necessary to resort to war this week, while Saddam's ambition to complete his weapons programme is blocked by the presence of UN inspectors?

Only a couple of weeks ago, Hans Blix told the Security Council that the key remaining disarmament tasks could be completed within months. I have heard it said that Iraq has had not months but twelve years in which to complete disarmament, and that our patience is exhausted. Yet it is more than thirty years since resolution 242 called on Israel to withdraw from the occupied territories. We do not express the same impatience with the persistent refusal of Israel to comply.

I welcome the strong personal commitment that the Prime Minister has given to Middle East peace, but Britain's positive role in the Middle East does not redress the strong sense of injustice throughout the Muslim world at what it sees as one rule for the allies of the US and another rule for the rest. Nor is our credibility helped by the appearance that our partners in Washington are less interested in disarmament than they are in regime change in Iraq. That explains why any evidence that inspections may be showing progress is greeted in Washington not with satisfaction but with consternation: it reduces the case for war.

What has come to trouble me most over past weeks is the suspicion that if the hanging chads in Florida had gone the other way and Al Gore had been elected, we would not now be about to commit British troops. The longer that I have served in this place, the greater the respect I have for the good sense and collective wisdom of the British people. On Iraq, I believe that the prevailing mood of the British people is sound. They do not doubt that Saddam is a brutal dictator, but they are not persuaded that he is a clear and present danger to Britain. They want inspections to be given a chance, and they suspect that they are being pushed too quickly into conflict by a US Administration with an agenda of its own. Above all, they are uneasy at Britain going out on a limb on a military adventure without a broader international coalition and against the hostility of many of our traditional allies.

From the start of the present crisis, I have insisted, as Leader of the House, on the right of this place to vote on whether Britain should go to war. It has been a favourite theme of commentators that this House no longer occupies a central role in British politics. Nothing could better demonstrate that they are wrong than for this House to stop the commitment of troops in a war that has neither international agreement nor domestic support.

I intend to join those tomorrow night who will vote against military action now. It is for that reason, and for that reason alone, and with a heavy heart, that I resign from the government.

ACKNOWLEDGEMENTS

This book was possible because of the support of many people. Maggie Pearlstine from start to finish has given me a solidarity in the finest traditions of Labour and guided me through the details of a process in which otherwise I would have been lost. I am indebted to my publishers, Simon & Schuster, for their touching faith that I would finish it in time, in particular Ian Chapman, Suzanne Baboneau and Tim Binding for their experience and encouragement. David Clark, who has worked with me for a decade, corrected my facts and did his best to correct my analysis. Joyce Matheson, Amaleena Damle and Mary Warner all contributed to the typescript and bore with amused tolerance my quaint habit of writing in longhand. As always I have found the staff of the House of Commons library unfailingly patient, courteous and authoritative: it is reassuring to know that at least one part of Parliament does not stand in need of further modernisation.

The Point of Departure records the highs and lows of two full years which were only manageable because of the loyal support of many people. I was fortunate to be served well by an efficient, and happy, private office, who confirmed my view that Britain is fortunate in the dedication of its public servants. My special advisers, Greg Power and Meg Russell, were more than a resource of special expertise, but of wider political wisdom, and bore without complaint their redundancy that came with my resignation. My Parliamentary Private Secretaries, Ken Purchase and Lorna Fitzsimons, were unfailing in their efforts to keep my feet on the ground, and it is not their fault if they did not always succeed. And Jim Devine and John Duncan were as reliable as ever in maintaining my constituency roots throughout my time on the frontbench.

But most of all I am grateful to Gaynor, who lived these events with me and from whom I have learnt so much.

INDEX